Praise for *Meeting the Moment*

"We Americans always have more to learn about the inspiring history of our country and our leaders. In *Meeting the Moment*, Bill Haldeman draws on his own leadership skills and shows us, in vivid prose, how American presidents provided inspirational leadership in perilous times."

— Michael Barone, senior political analyst, *Washington Examiner*, and founding coauthor, *The Almanac of American Politics*

"Haldeman's book offers enduring lessons in leadership. The book is a stirring treatise from a historian whose career combines scholarship and first-hand experience of executive branch policymaking. Correlating six US presidents with a defining quality: judgment, ingenuity, dedication, courage, confidence, and optimism, Haldeman shows how they each made a wise decision at a critical moment."

— Esther Brimmer, James H. Binger Senior Fellow in Global Governance at the Council on Foreign Relations

"Bill Haldeman captures the essence of presidential leadership, drawing upon the historical examples of our nation's greatest presidents to demonstrate how their crucial leadership attributes transformed America and changed the world. From George Washington's judgment to Ronald Reagan's optimism, this thoroughly researched and engagingly written book shows us how American Presidents—and indeed all leaders—can meet the moment and achieve great things."

— Governor Chris Christie

"*Meeting the Moment* should be of interest to both scholars within multiple disciplines as well as general interest readers. Haldeman brings real-world experience within government, along with his academic training, to provide a fascinating assessment of times of crisis and how six presidents rose to meet them. The inclusion of 'traditional' presidents such a Washington and Lincoln as well as 'modern' presidents such as FDR and Reagan enhances the book's appeal."

— Lori Cox Han, coeditor of *In the Public Domain: Presidents and the Challenges of Public Leadership*

"Words are a president's most powerful tools, and Bill Haldeman's *Meeting the Moment* is an engaging, insightful, and yes, powerful study of moments when our chief executive's landmark addresses revealed the qualities that made them truly great. Judgment; Ingenuity; Dedication; Courage; Confidence; and Optimism. We can only pray our future presidents share the traits Haldeman masterfully describes in this thoroughly enjoyable book."

— Jeffrey A. Engel, Founding Director, Center for
Presidential History, Southern Methodist University

"*Meeting the Moment* is a profoundly insightful and engagingly written study of presidential leadership. William Haldeman scrutinizes six of our most important presidents—Washington, Jefferson, Lincoln, Theodore Roosevelt, Franklin Roosevelt, and Ronald Reagan—and demonstrates that through character and long experience each had acquired and honed a leadership quality essential for effectively meeting the supreme challenge of his time. The essential quality varied from president to president, but each possessed a key attribute that inspired others to follow and enabled the leader to successfully confront national adversity and crisis. This important book is a worthy contribution to the study of presidential greatness."

— John Ferling, author of *Winning Independence:
The Decisive Years of the Revolutionary War, 1778-1781*

"There has never been a more important time for us to understand what it takes to create meaningful leadership or to unpack the circumstances, attributes, or words that yielded the leaders that have made us who we are as a society. Dr. Haldeman both reminds us and inspires us by detailing how these leaders met their moment in ways that allow all of us to learn from history and set our expectations for the future."

— Joan Gabel, Chancellor, University of Pittsburgh

"Taking a leadership approach to the presidency, Haldeman unpacks the deep elements that can lead presidents to become transformational. Grounded in lived experiences translated into aspirational communication, this excellent book provides a roadmap for presidential success."

— Michael A. Genovese, President of the
Global Policy Institute, Loyola Marymount University,
and author of *The Modern Presidency*

"Bill's insightful comparison of Reagan and other great American leaders is a beacon of thoughtful reason in our current climate of division. It's a must read for those of us trying to make sense of today's political environment."

— Kim Guadagno, New Jersey's First Lieutenant Governor

"Haldeman offers a fresh, vibrant, and highly readable perspective on presidential leadership through situational and biographical analyses of key presidential decision points, examining and comparing qualities of presidential character permitting selected presidents to be successful, persuasively arguing that no flawless or indisputable set of characteristics distinguishes presidential greatness but, rather, that singular qualities and circumstances combine to produce history-changing or 'transformative' outcomes."

— James Hilty, Professor Emeritus, Temple University, author of *Robert Kennedy: Brother Protector*

"A fascinating read combining history, politics, and leadership development, *Meeting the Moment* reminds us of the insights history offers to today's leaders. With a sharp focus on leadership characteristics and communication, Haldeman deftly uses stories of some of America's most well-known presidents to offer modern lessons applicable to all who hold leadership positions, aspire to hold such positions, and those about to begin their careers in any sector."

— Garry W. Jenkins, president, Bates College; former dean, University of Minnesota Law School; and former professor and cofounder of the Program on Law and Leadership at The Ohio State University

"In these perilous, highly polarized times, we can benefit from a historically grounded work that offers an informed, impartial analysis of exceptional presidential leadership. Bill Haldeman fills that need with his thoroughly researched, persuasively argued analysis of the inspired leadership exhibited by many of our most esteemed presidents, including George Washington, Thomas Jefferson, Abraham Lincoln, Theodore Roosevelt, Franklin Roosevelt, and Ronald Reagan."

— Allan J. Lichtman, Distinguished Professor of History, American University, and author of *Predicting the Next President: The Keys to the White House*

"Bill Haldeman has a storyteller's gift and a cameraman's eye. In *Meeting the Moment*, he impeccably matches six integral qualities of leadership with six of our highly regarded presidents. Haldeman takes his reader into the hearts and minds of each of them, placing us where the action was, and the lessons they still teach us today. With *Meeting the Moment*, Haldeman establishes himself as one of the best historians of his generation."

— Tim McGrath, historian and author of *James Monroe: A Life*

"Presidential scholars have long known Bill Haldeman to be a deeply informed and thoughtful student of the office. These qualities are on full display in *Meeting the Moment*, in which he marshals evidence from the history of the office and its occupants to demonstrate the importance of judgment, courage, dedication and other personal qualities to successful presidential leadership."

— Michael Nelson, Fulmer Professor of
Political Science, Rhodes College

"Much more than a history of presidents, this lively book is as much about America's future as its past. Six leadership qualities are used as a platform to show that leaders do not come in a single stripe; effectiveness can be achieved in ways that are suitable to the individual and to the times, whether in crisis or in the calm in-between. Witty and well-researched, this book provides new insights about important figures, and about ourselves."

— Harris Pastides, President Emeritus,
University of South Carolina

"In our era of political rancor over 'unitary executive power' and legal rancor about Presidential immunity, Bill Haldeman restores the subject of the American Presidency to its roots. *Meeting the Moment* is essential reading about history, politics and, most fundamentally, leadership."

— Marshall Sonenshine, Chairman of Sonenshine Partners
and Lecturer on Law, Harvard Law School

"Bill Haldeman's book offers engaging stories on how American presidents—at pivotal moments and national crises—put to work some of the best qualities of leadership. Embodying these qualities, their compelling words inspired the people, defined their presidencies, and helped shape the country's future. Today, from the halls of government and academia to boardrooms and C-suites in industry and beyond, our leaders—like those I work with every day—are grappling with the impacts of unprecedented technological change and massive transformation on many fronts. As they strive to meet their own leadership moments during these turbulent times, they can learn much from the lessons offered by these American icons."

— Deborah Wince-Smith, President and CEO,
Council on Competitiveness

Meeting the Moment

SUNY series on the Presidency: Contemporary Issues

Robert P. Watson, editor

Meeting the Moment

Inspiring Presidential Leadership that Transformed America

WILLIAM HALDEMAN

Published by State University of New York Press, Albany

© 2024 State University of New York

All rights reserved

Printed in the United States of America

No part of this book may be used or reproduced in any manner whatsoever without written permission. No part of this book may be stored in a retrieval system or transmitted in any form or by any means including electronic, electrostatic, magnetic tape, mechanical, photocopying, recording, or otherwise without the prior permission in writing of the publisher.

Links to third-party websites are provided as a convenience and for informational purposes only. They do not constitute an endorsement or an approval of any of the products, services, or opinions of the organization, companies, or individuals. SUNY Press bears no responsibility for the accuracy, legality, or content of a URL, the external website, or for that of subsequent websites.

For information, contact State University of New York Press, Albany, NY
www.sunypress.edu

Library of Congress Cataloging-in-Publication Data

Name: Haldeman, William Edward, 1976– author.
Title: Meeting the moment : inspiring presidential leadership that transformed America / William Haldeman.
Other titles: Inspiring presidential leadership that transformed America
Description: Albany : State University of New York Press, [2024] | Series: SUNY series on the presidency : contemporary issues | Includes bibliographical references and index.
Identifiers: LCCN 2024012331 | ISBN 9798855800173 (hardcover : alk. paper) | ISBN 9798855800203 (ebook) | ISBN 9798855800180 (pbk. : alk. paper)
Subjects: LCSH: Presidents—United States—History. | Political leadership—United States—History. | Executive power—United States—History. | United States—Politics and government.
Classification: LCC E176.1 .H175 2024 | DDC 352.23/70973—dc23/eng/20240724
LC record available at https://lccn.loc.gov/2024012331

To Erin and Katharine

Contents

Acknowledgments		ix
Introduction		1
Chapter 1	Judgment	7
Chapter 2	Ingenuity	43
Chapter 3	Dedication	81
Chapter 4	Courage	111
Chapter 5	Confidence	143
Chapter 6	Optimism	177
Epilogue		219
Notes		223
Bibliography		281
Index		295

Acknowledgments

The roots of this book can be traced back to my childhood in the shadow of Independence Mall, Valley Forge, and Washington's Crossing. It was not uncommon for Revolutionary War musket balls to be unearthed from one of our local schoolyards. As far back as I can remember, I have been enthralled with the Founders, the American presidency, and the qualities of leadership that guided and defined them. This passion propelled me through graduate study in the American presidency and on to a career in public service, including at the White House, the seventh floor of the US Department of State, and as a member of a governor's senior staff. Across these and other experiences, I've been fortunate to have a front-row seat to many of the crises of our times. These experiences not only help to color the narrative found in this book, but they also follow in the tradition of historians like Arthur Schlesinger Jr., Richard Neustadt, and Doris Kearns Goodwin, who married their academic credentials with government experience at the highest levels. I believe this perspective is invaluable to writing history, and this manuscript reinvigorates this unique precedent and perspective.

In an endeavor like this, there are countless people to thank. From Jim Hilty, Tim McGrath, Tom Anderson, Marshall Sonenshine, Brian Curtis, and Michael Rinella and SUNY Press, to my parents, siblings, in-laws, and incredible friends, I will forever be grateful. And to Erin and Katharine, of course, for their love and the inspiration.

Introduction

This is a book about leadership—presidential leadership. And these are the stories of a selected group of US presidents and their inspired leadership characteristics that set them apart and transformed America—qualities of judgment and ingenuity, dedication and courage, and confidence and optimism.

Forged through biography, history, leadership development, and political science, this book introduces these leaders during times of national crisis. It highlights how their defining leadership quality to meet their moment was cultivated over a lifetime of lived experience and then cemented for the ages through the power of the presidential word—a speech, a letter, or an address, which collectively represent the most transcendent documents in American history.

Viewed through the lenses of nuance, complication, human emotion, pathos, and drama, this book is not intended to include every regarded president or leadership quality. Instead, it seeks to suggest that it was not one leadership quality that made America stronger and better—it was many. It also sets forth the lives of these selected presidents to help inform our own lives, revealing these leaders not as statues and monuments, but as people with spectacular gifts and virtues, along with great sins and flaws.

Anchored in primary and secondary historical sources, as well as the study of the American presidency, this book also importantly extends from firsthand experience, including the workings of the White House, as well as those of the seventh floor of the US Department of State, a governor's office, and the executive suites of university presidents. These vantage points further amplify how, in key moments of decision, leaders of all stripes lean on a defining quality to meet their respective moments. The pages to follow profile how America's most transformational presidents did the same, all the while producing six of the nation's most consequential documents—George Washington's Farewell Address, Thomas Jefferson's Louisiana Purchase charge, Abraham Lincoln's Gettysburg Address, Theodore Roosevelt's First Annual Address, Franklin Roosevelt's first Fireside Chat, and Ronald Reagan's Berlin Wall speech.

In chapter 1, the quality of judgment is introduced as perhaps the most essential characteristic for a leader to possess. Otherwise, a president with ingenuity but lacking judgment may innovate in the wrong places. Or a president without judgment but brimming with confidence may lead the nation boldly in the wrong direction. Ultimately, this chapter aims to make clear that while George Washington didn't get every leadership decision right, he possessed an innate propensity to make the right call when it mattered most. And no president has embodied judgment to make a more important decision than his to step down after two terms in office. Moreover, Washington's Farewell Address, which announced his retirement decision to the world, offers posterity a composite picture of his judgment, including lessons learned that served as warnings and inspiration to help generations of Americans navigate an uncertain future.

Ingenuity is presented in chapter 2 as a historical driver of America's growth and development. Among US presidents, Thomas Jefferson most exemplified this quality, particularly through the magic of his pen. In the most transformational act of his presidency, he authored an April 18, 1802 letter to Robert Livingston, US minister to France, which set the tone and tenor for the negotiations in Paris that would ultimately lead to the Louisiana Purchase, the largest land transaction in US history. Jefferson's ingenuity also marked some of the most significant contributions to the mainsprings of America, from the "Summary View of the Rights of British America" and the Declaration of Independence, to the "Virginia Statute for Religious Freedom."

In chapter 3, the true measure of dedication to America is surveyed from the sacred grounds of Gettysburg, Pennsylvania, home to the bloodiest single battle of the Civil War in July 1863. Four months after the clash, Abraham Lincoln traveled to the small town to speak at a cemetery dedication. The speech he gave there—the Gettysburg Address—represents the exemplar of his dedication to America, drawing listeners to the intersection of the nation's purpose during the Civil War and the difficult fight, while also encouraging the North to stay the course in the challenging days ahead. By exhibiting steely dedication, as well as the hope of success in the face of doubt and uncertainty, Lincoln's

Gettysburg Address not only represents his defining quality, but a great turning point in the national crisis.

The quality of courage headlines chapter 4.[1] At one time or another, all US presidents, in various ways, have confronted the need for this quality.[2] While some presidents fell short in the moment, others embraced a fearless daring spirit to move America forward. Theodore Roosevelt stands out in this latter category. His First Annual Address to Congress most exemplifies his political courage in taking on the most existential issue of his time—the conservation of natural resources. As he noted: "The "forest and water problems are perhaps the most vital internal questions of the United States."[3] Theodore Roosevelt brought these important efforts to the mainstream of American politics, including the floors and cloakrooms of the US House and Senate.

In chapter 5, the well-established American leadership tradition of confidence is considered. While this quality is generally viewed as a necessity to be president, for a select few, it became a distinguishing leadership quality, called out during America's most crucial moments. The most pivotal example occurred during the depth of America's longest and most devastating economic downturn, the Great Depression. Just over a week into his administration, and after a dizzying array of government activity, from state proclamations to federal regulation, Franklin D. Roosevelt (FDR) took to the nation's radios to explain the collective action his administration was taking to address the banking crisis. In less than fifteen minutes and across 1,792 words, FDR's personal quality of confidence fundamentally elevated the nation's confidence. And much like Lincoln's Gettysburg Address was a turning point in the Civil War, so too was Roosevelt's first Fireside Chat in confronting the Great Depression.

The final chapter demonstrates that the United States has always been grounded in an optimistic idea, and as a matter of course, Americans are inclined to look on the bright side. Observers have long marveled at America's seemingly ceaseless optimism, and no US president has embodied the quality more than Ronald Reagan. At a crucial juncture in the Cold War, Reagan gave a rousing speech at the Brandenburg Gate during Berlin's 750th anniversary, a city divided by an insurmountable wall built in 1961. The most iconic line of the speech and his presidency consisted of four optimistic words: "Mr. Gorbachev, tear down this wall!"[4] Twenty-nine months later, on November 9, 1989, the Berlin Wall fell, and the people of Berlin fulfilled Reagan's call to make the city one again.

Within the scholarly literature, the meaning of presidential leadership is as broad as it is diverse. Where Richard E. Neustadt in *Presidential Power: The Politics of Leadership* argues: "Presidential power is the power to persuade,"[5] George C. Edwards III in Richard J. Ellis's and Michael Nelson's edited work, *Debating the Presidency: Conflicting Perspective on the American Executive*, argues: "There is not a single systemic study that demonstrates that presidents reliably move others to support them."[6] Where James David Barber in *The Presidential Character: Predicting Performance in the White House* argues that character, worldview, and political style are the basis for presidential leadership,[7] Stephen Skowronek in *The Politics That Presidents Make: Leadership from John Adams to Bill Clinton* argues that presidential leadership is less about the qualities a president brings to the office than their place in the political cycle of history. Where David Gergen in *Eyewitness to Power: The Essence of Leadership: Nixon to Clinton* notes that presidential leadership can be narrowed down to having "a good grasp of public affairs and an excellent temperament,"[8] Michael Genovese in *Presidential Leadership in an Age of Change* offers a more aspirational picture of what is needed: "The vision of John Kennedy, the political skills of Lyndon Johnson, the strategic insight of Richard Nixon, the genuineness of Gerald Ford, the character of Jimmy Carter, the charisma of Ronald Reagan, the experience of George H. W. Bush, and the interpersonal skills of Bill Clinton."[9] Where Fred Greenstein, the author of *The Presidential Difference: Leadership Style from FDR to Barack Obama* and *Leadership in the Modern Presidency* highlights presidential leadership and job performance through six qualities—the president's proficiency as a public communicator; organizational capacity; political skill; vision of public policy; cognitive style; and emotional intelligence,[10] Thomas E. Cronin and Michael Genovese in *The Paradoxes of the American Presidency* highlight three—vision; skill; and political timing.[11] And where Marc Landy and Sidney M. Milkis argue in their book *Presidential Greatness* that America's greatest presidents developed from "the opportunity and the capacity to engage the nation in a struggle for its constitutional soul" to stage a "conservative revolution,"[12] Charles O. Jones in *The Presidency in a Separated System* downplays presidential leadership by arguing: "The president is not the presidency. The presidency is not the government. Ours is not a presidential system."[13]

If there is any consensus in the scholarly literature, it's that an overriding criteria for, and definition of, presidential leadership does not exist.[14] As Thomas E. Cronin and Michael A. Genovese point out: "Leadership means many things to many people. For some it has a rich, positive meaning. For others it connotes manipulation, deception, or even oppression."[15] Assuredly, this book leans into the former, and like Woodrow Wilson in 1908, it contends: "The President is at liberty, both in law and conscience, to be as big a man as he can. His capacity will set the limit."[16] This book also seeks to address the gap in the presidential scholarship by leading us toward a definition of presidential leadership. As weaved through the narrative to follow, we see US presidents employing their defining leadership quality with action to meet the moment and advance America. The stories to follow demonstrate that the presidents who navigated this intersection most acutely were those who exemplified the right qualities at the right times; like having the experience and instincts to make the right call when it matters most; the ingenuity to identify opportunity around the bend; the dedication to see through a great cause; the courage to act at the intersection of one's passion and purpose; the confidence to hearten the downtrodden; and the optimism to break through seemingly impenetrable barriers.

By holding ourselves and our leaders to this standard, we remind the next American generation of bellwethers of what we are and can be as a nation. We remind an American polity in an era of partisan gridlock, the twenty-four-hour news cycle, and the proliferation of social media, that if we hold firm to these ideals, any talk of an American decline in standing or world power is simply empty conversation. And we remind the world, as John Winthrop preached to his fellow Puritans in 1630, "that we shall be a city upon a hill. The eyes of all people are upon us."[17]

Chapter 1

Judgment

> I shall not be deprived . . . of a comfort in the worst event if I retain a consciousness of having acted to the best of my judgment.
>
> —George Washington to Burwell Bassett, June 19, 1775

Judgment is perhaps the most crucial personal characteristic for a leader to possess. Euripides defined it as best of seers,[1] and the Founding Fathers viewed it as paramount. As noted in Federalist 57: "The aim of every political Constitution is, or ought to be, first to obtain for rulers, men who possess most wisdom to discern, and most virtue to pursue the common good of the society."[2] In his famous 1961 "The City upon a Hill Speech," President-elect John Kennedy framed it as the perceptive nature "of the future as well as the past—of our own mistakes as well as the mistakes of others—with enough wisdom to know what we did not know, and enough candor to admit it."[3]

Contrary to this historical sentiment, the term has been traditionally difficult to define, causing even the most esoteric to pause at the inquiry. Yet most know good judgment when they see it, as well as when they don't—especially when it fails to line up with the elevated leadership qualities discussed in this book: like when those with great confidence but poor judgment lead their followers down the wrong path; those with dedication and no judgment rise with the sun but do all the wrong things thereafter; or those with great candor but without judgment say the wrong thing at the wrong time.

The weight of history in demonstrating collectively poor judgment is unforgiving, and the roster of presidents who lacked good judgment is lengthy and inglorious—for example, James Buchanan, who failed to prevent the South from seceding; Herbert Hoover, who failed to overcome the Great Depression; Richard Nixon, who obstructed the Watergate investigation and resigned; Jimmy Carter, who failed a "Crisis of Confidence";[4] and Bill Clinton and Donald Trump, who were found by the US House of Representatives to have abused presidential power and were impeached. While these and other lapses have, in some cases, constricted the American Dream for generations, sound judgment has, more broadly, unlocked our national promise and propelled it forward. For US presidents, judgment is what enables a sound choice in the face of uncertainty. It's what broadly defines them as a success or failure in the eyes of history, especially when considered against times when it mattered most. And it's what underlies every quality in this book. In other words, not only was the character of American presidents revealed when the stakes and the uncertainly were the highest, but so too was their judgment. And no one before or since has embodied this quality to make a more important decision than George Washington.

The Time and Place

As our opening story begins in 1796, America was a raw start-up in republican government. A generation removed from declaring independence from Great Britain, the United States was slowly beginning to reap the revolutionary harvest of that great crucible. The epicenter of this emerging American progeny was the city of Philadelphia, which as a result of the Residence Act of 1790, was designated as the nation's temporary capital until 1800. The Act was part of a grand bargain hatched over a private dinner party in New York City with Secretary of State Thomas Jefferson, Secretary of Treasury Alexander Hamilton, and representative from Virginia James Madison, where Madison agreed not to block congressional legislation mandating the assumption of the states' debts by the federal government in exchange for locating the permanent US capital on the banks of the Potomac River in what is now Washington, DC. As historian Joseph Ellis noted: "The Compromise of 1790 would top the list of the most meaningful dinner party in American history."[5]

Philadelphia was also the birthplace of the United States, where the Founding Fathers met, discussed, debated, and formed a new nation in 1776, and gathered again in 1787 to produce the first written constitution of any nation in the history of the world. The city was likewise home to the American presidency and its tumultuous Convention debates, which were undertaken under strict privacy in the Pennsylvania State House, or Independence Hall, as it is now called. The doors to the building were locked and guarded by armed sentinels both inside and out, and the windows were sealed, and the curtains drawn.

The delegates to the Convention were a disparate group of colonists—lawyers, doctors, planters, and artisans generally divided between two factions: the "Federalists," who believed like Alexander Hamilton "in the necessity of an energetic Executive,"[6] and the "Anti-Federalists," who believed like Thomas Jefferson in an executive with limited authority. Across the summer of 1787, the Convention's president, George Washington, stressed the importance of continuing to hear all viewpoints. "No doubt there will be a diversity of sentiments on this important subject,"[7] Washington noted on July 1, "and to inform the judgment, it is necessary to hear all arguments that can be advanced. To please all is impossible, and to attempt it would be vain."[8]

These leaders vacillated between positions for weeks before finally reaching a compromise only days before the Convention adjourned. An important point of debate included how the president should be elected, ranging from national and state legislatures to popular election. Some delegates simply did not trust the judgment of the common citizen, while others thought it was simply impractical to track votes across such a large nation. Virginia delegate George Mason echoed this school of thought: "It would be as unnatural to refer the choice of a proper character for Chief Magistrate to the people, as it would be to refer a trial of colours to a blind man."[9] Delegates would vote more than sixty times before resolving the debate with the establishment of the Electoral College.

Two additional issues provoked intense deliberation among the delegates: how long should a presidential term be, and how many terms could a president serve? The general consensus was that the presidency should have a longer term to guarantee continuity and stability, while balancing the suspicion of monarchy and executive power, particularly after having just fought a war against British tyranny.

At the onset of deliberation, three- and seven-year terms were considered, both without the opportunity for reelection. Soon after, a seven-year term, without a provision for reelection was considered. With the matter far from settled, the discussion was referred to the Committee on Postponed Matters, also known as the Committee of Eleven. The Committee's ensuing report called for a four-year term with no term limits.[10] These measures were ultimately ratified with the Constitution on September 17, 1787 with the now-familiar wording: "The executive Power shall be vested in a President of the United States of America. He shall hold his Office during the Term of four Years, and, together with the Vice President, chosen for the same Term, be elected as follows. . . ."[11]

George Washington reported the Convention's success to the Marquis de Lafayette, a French aristocrat and military officer who had fought in the Revolutionary War: "We are not to expect perfection in this world; but mankind, in modern times, have apparently made some progress in the science of Government."[12] While not expecting perfection, Washington nonetheless achieved it with the unanimous support he received from the Electoral College in 1789, a feat no subsequent president has duplicated, and which exemplified the inherent faith Americans had in his judgment to define the role. In a December 6, 1788 letter to him, Gouverneur Morris of Pennsylvania highlighted this sentiment: "I have ever thought, and said that you must be the President. No other Man can fill that Office. No other Man can draw forth the Abilities of our Country into the various Departments of civil life. You alone can awe the Insolence of opposing Factions, & the greater Insolence of assuming Adherents. . . . I form my Conclusions from those Talents and Virtues which the World believes and which your Friends know you possess."[13]

While the Founders recognized the "Talents and Virtues" that Washington possessed, they likewise understood the potential for successors with less desirable attributes, with many fearing the nation could eventually fall back into its monarchical past. In a letter to French scientist Jean-Baptiste Le Roy, Benjamin Franklin echoed this uncertainty: "Our new Constitution is now established, everything seems to promise it will be durable; but, in this world, nothing is certain except death and taxes."[14]

As the first president, Washington was keenly aware that whatever decisions he made or actions he partook would become precedent for the future. "I walk on untrodden ground,"[15] he was noted to say in the days leading up to his first inauguration. In particular, he recognized that the cornerstones he set must make the presidency powerful enough to function effectively in the federal government, but at the same time, not show any tendency toward monarchy or autocracy. Washington further understood that as his success went, so too did the success of America, especially as he sought to create the presidency in a world full of kings. In this endeavor, he had the unenviable task of leading a nascent country through its formative, and perhaps most difficult and divisive years, while remaining faithful to the principles on which it was founded. Indeed, Washington carried the burden for the future of the nation. "We are a young Nation and have a character to establish," he noted. "It behooves us therefore to set out right for first impressions will be lasting."[16] Central to this for Washington was the Constitution, which he avowed "is the guide which I can never abandon."[17]

Anchored to the spirit of that document, Washington's presidency helped to create a living, functioning government, while setting the standard for his successors to follow. First and foremost, he established that the power of the presidency is vested in the office, not the person. In international relations, he instituted a policy of neutrality pertaining to foreign wars that was followed until World War I. He established relations with Great Britain through the Jay Treaty, and despite the War of 1812, the British government remains one of our closest and strongest allies.

Domestically, Washington personally led troops into the field to stop the Whiskey Rebellion, which threatened the stability of America and challenged the authority of the federal government. He supported innovative economic concepts such as national debt and a Bank of America, which would later be adopted. He established social norms, from late afternoon meetings with the public and dinner parties with invited guests, to issuing a proclamation designating November 26 as a national day of Thanksgiving. He welcomed Rhode Island, Vermont, Kentucky, and Tennessee as the thirteenth, fourteenth, fifteenth, and sixteenth states in the nation, respectively, as well as the US Constitution's first eleven amendments.

Administratively, he defined the creation of executive departments, which included arguably the strongest cabinet in American history, and how those roles would function and interact with the president. He sought the advice and consent of the US Senate in making appointments to office and in executing treaties with foreign governments, as constitutionally required. He also advanced the idea that the best qualified people should be selected for office, and with Alexander Hamilton and Thomas Jefferson as key members of his administration, he proved to be a good judge of talent.

Last, despite detesting partisanship, Washington navigated the rise of the two-party system, as politics came to the American presidency. Notwithstanding his advocacy for the virtues of nonpartisan government, he was, in many respects, the nation's first Federalist president based on his preference for a strong executive and his nationalist leaning. This inclined him to favor Hamilton's views over Jefferson's, who diverged on almost every measure, particularly around the establishment of a national bank. As a result, partisan feelings and impulses ran very high.

In fact, the 1790s was one of the most passionate and divisive decades in American history, yet, interestingly, this period is not as far removed from current times as one would imagine. In addition to the deepening division between political parties, France, a leading foreign power at the time, attempted to interfere in a presidential election on behalf of the Republicans, and there were new forms of partisan press and, with them, cries of "fake news."

By 1796, the American presidency was taking shape in ways the Framers of the Constitution could not have envisioned in less than a decade. Every critical judgment that Washington made and every step of consequence that he undertook defined the future of America. And, in this important time of change and division, one decision was more consequential than any other.

The Scene

Sitting off alone, immersed in deep thought, George Washington waited patiently for his requested guest to arrive at the President's House in Philadelphia. Located at the corner of Sixth and Market Streets, in the shadow of Independence Hall, this three-story, red-brick building was the largest home in then the most populated city in the nation. At the suggestion of Alexander Hamilton, Colonel Tobias Lear, Washington's private secretary, arranged a September 15, 1796 meeting between President Washington and David C. Claypoole, proprietor and editor of *Claypoole's American Daily Advertiser*, a leading daily newspaper in Philadelphia.[18] Claypoole's background likely appealed to Washington's sensibilities, having joined the revolutionary cause as a private in 1775, and later accompanying the president in 1793 to suppress the Whiskey Rebellion. Moreover, Claypoole was the first to print two of America's most historic documents, the Declaration of Independence and the US Constitution.

Upon arrival, and after some short pleasantries, Washington motioned Claypoole to a seat near him. Sitting upright in his chair, the president informed Claypoole "that he had for some time past contemplated retiring from public life, and had at length concluded to do so."[19] Further, Washington indicated that he "had some thoughts and reflections on the occasion, which he deemed proper to communicate to the people of the United States, in the form of an address, and which he wished to appear in the Daily Advertiser."[20] As the president paused, Claypoole, while thanking him for having preferred his "paper as a channel of his communication with the people,"[21] must have been quietly astonished by what he was hearing. Was the Father of the Country, the man who dedicated his life to the success of America, the man who would be remembered by the US Congress as "first in war, first in peace, and first in the hearts of his countrymen,"[22] retiring? Silently assenting, according to Claypoole, Washington then "asked when the publication could be made,"[23] and proceeded to hand Claypoole the thirty-two-page manuscript, which was sewed together as a book and written in his own hand. In a pleasing manner, Claypoole reported to the president that "the time should be made perfectly convenient to himself,"[24] and the two agreed that Monday, September 19 would be the day Washington would issue his "Farewell Address" to the nation.

Over the course of the next few days, two revised versions of the Farewell Address were personally reviewed by Washington, with the final set made by candlelight. According to Claypoole, Washington "made but a few alterations from the original, except in the punctuation, in which he was very minute."[25] The president also shared specific instructions on how the message should be displayed in the newspaper, including the headline: "TO THE PEOPLE OF THE UNITED STATES. FRIENDS AND FELLOW CITIZENS," and the layout, which was to be spread out across page two and most of page three in Claypoole's daily (as page one was traditionally reserved for advertisements).

The morning of publication, Claypoole, while returning the final handwritten copy in person to Washington, expressed interest "in the most respectful manner that he should consider it as an inestimable favor if he would allow him to keep it."[26] According to Claypoole, the president responded that "if it would be any satisfaction to him, he was welcome to it—and they then parted."[27]

As Washington's Farewell Address started to make its way through Philadelphia's rain-soaked streets and bustling taverns on Monday, September 19, 1796, the nation's first president departed south to Mount Vernon with his wife, Martha. As he noted in his diary: "Address to the people of the United States was this day published by Claypoole's paper notifying my intention of declining being considered a candidate for the Presidency of the United States of America . . . Left the city on this morning on my way to Mount Vernon."[28]

The Makings of George Washington's Judgment

When Patrick Henry was asked in 1774, who he thought was the greatest man in the Continental Congress, he replied: "If you speak of eloquence, Mr. Rutledge, of South Carolina, is by far the greatest orator; but if you speak of solid information and sound judgment, Colonel Washington is unquestionably the greatest man on that floor."[29] George Washington was born on February 22, 1732 at approximately 10 a.m., at his family's farm on Pope's Creek in Westmoreland County, Virginia, near the banks of the Potomac River. A fourth-generation Virginian, Washington was very much a product of his native state and his lineage—an atavistic prototype of a bloodline known for its physical strength, yet a penchant for early mortality. After the passing of his forty-nine-year-old father Augustine, George poignantly noted: "Tho' I was blessed with a good constitution, I was of a short-lived family."[30] And in one of those strange twists of fate occurring over a half-a-century apart, both father and son met their respective demises by riding horses out into a storm, becoming sick and quickly passing.

Coming to stand over six-feet-tall and weighing over 200 pounds, George possessed the physical attributes necessary of a quintessential American hero: muscular and broad-shouldered, with long arms and legs and steely blue-gray eyes. One of Washington's biographers noted: "His body did not occupy space; it seemed to organize the space around it. He dominated a room not just with his size, but with an almost electric presence."[31] A French diplomat witnessing Washington's first inauguration noted in marvel of the man: "He has the soul, look and figure of a hero united in him."[32] Washington's physical stature set the standard, leaving an indelible mark on the fabric of America.

From his father, George also inherited Ferry Farm, a 260-acre property on the Rappahannock River, not far from Fredericksburg, Virginia. With that responsibility, he was forced to shoulder a heavy familial burden starting at the age of eleven, as George's thirty-five-year-old headstrong widowed mother, Mary Ball Washington, came to rely on her oldest son to support their family, including his younger siblings, Betty, Samuel, John Augustine, and Charles. And while George received from his impactful mother a wide range of qualities, from an unrivaled willpower and stubborn self-reliance, to the ability to resist conceding to social conventions and to rise with the sun, there would forever be a chill in their relationship stemming from her treatment of him during this period. However, if there was a silver lining to his father's sudden death, it was that George's half-brother Lawrence, fourteen years his senior, would play a larger mentorship role in his life, exposing him to things that would later define him, from war to Mount Vernon, while also helping him to navigate his future as if he had drafted the script. But even prior to his father's untimely death, young George's rearing in Tidewater Virginia was largely unsettled. His first home burned to the ground. At age two, he lost his older half-sister Jane, and thereafter the family moved to Little Hunting Creek, a 2,500-acre tract on the Potomac River, which later became known as Mount Vernon. After traversing to Ferry Farm several years later, further loss would ensue; when he was eight and eleven, his baby sister Mildred, and his father Augustine, passed away, respectively.

As schoolchildren we remember the tales of the "man who could not tell a lie." How George Washington chopped down the cherry tree or how he threw a rock across the Rappahannock River—a feat no contemporary had the strength to duplicate. Of course, the most recognizable of these tall tales was how as a six-year-old, Washington had received a hatchet as a gift. The future president proceeded to chop down everything in sight, including his father's favorite cherry tree. When the elder Washington discovered the mischief, he questioned his son, leading young George to ardently admit to the crime: "I can't tell a lie, Pa."[33] Earning praise rather than punishment for his actions, George's father, Augustine, called for his son: "Run to my arms, you dearest boy. . . . Such an act of heroism in my son is worth more than a thousand trees."[34]

Despite his almost mythological reputation and standing, including Nathaniel Hawthorne's assertion that the future first president "was born with his clothes on and his hair powdered and made a stately bow on his first appearance in the world,"[35] Washington's countenance wasn't overtly flashy, but rather simple and proud. If pressed to match some of the executive qualities that have come to define the modern presidency, Washington would be hard-pressed; he lacked the smoothness and charm of a John Kennedy or Barack Obama; the cerebral brilliance of a Richard Nixon or Bill Clinton; or the communication and oratory skills of a Franklin Roosevelt or Ronald Reagan. In fact, Washington was not particularly eloquent in his command and use of vocabulary. According to John Adams: "That he was too illiterate, unlearned, unread for his station and reputation is equally past dispute."[36] Even Thomas Jefferson, who was often generous in his take on friends, said that Washington's "colloquial talents were not above mediocrity," and that he had "neither copiousness of ideas nor fluency of words."[37]

While his contemporaries, such as Adams and Jefferson, were exposed to classical curriculum and were trained at the finest colleges in the colonies, Washington received a modern-day, grade-school education. Rather, combat was his classroom, as he learned from his vast undertakings and the people around him. His judgment was therefore defined by his life experience and whether he deemed something virtuous. As such, he seemed to embody the view of the great philosopher Aristotle: "For the things we have to learn before we can do them, we learn by doing them."[38] Washington leaned into his learned capacities of judgment, and although extremely reliable, they did not always guide him from error. For instance, he was prone to exercise a considerable temper, capable at a whim of creating scenes or tableaux within cabinet or meeting rooms. He also accepted and depended on slave labor at Mount Vernon and the President's House in Philadelphia, and while his thinking started to change on slavery after the Revolutionary War, he did not take on the issue publicly, believing it was a tinderbox that could easily set the fragile nation ablaze. Only through his final will did he order his slaves free, and even then, at the time of his wife Martha's death.

Moreover, as the commanding general during the Revolution, Washington's cognition of strategy and tactics was not overly refined and his actual training was minimal. He was not, by any measure, a military savant. He lost more battles than he won. So, while he may not be labeled a military genius or a political savant, or possess the gift of brilliant oratory or the prowess for wonky policy debates, rather, Washington's true leadership essence is found in his ability to make the right call when it mattered most. It was here that he leveraged this great quality during the War for Independence, learning from his experiences to fashion a strategy to win.[39] It was his "Prudence and Abilities" that led Congress to "confide fully"[40] in him according to John Jay, with President Calvin Coolidge adding that it was because of Washington's judgment and experience that "he was able to assume the leadership of an almost impossible cause, carry it on through a long period of discouragement and defeat, and bring it to a successful conclusion."[41]

Believing that true wisdom rested in a composite judgment, Washington deployed a hub-and-spoke approach, which made it a common occurrence for him to invoke the advice of others. John Adams said of Washington: "He seeks information from all quarters and judges more independently than any man I ever knew."[42] Similarly, Thomas Jefferson noted: "Perhaps the strongest feature in his character was prudence, never acting until every circumstance, every consideration, was maturely weighed."⁴³ Defining his senior leader military meetings, and later, his cabinet meetings as president, Washington was willing to take every moment needed, especially when matters of life and death and the fate of a fledgling nation were at stake. However, while very discerning in decision making, he always reserved the final decision for himself, and when he decided to act, he did so decidedly, with no second-guessing. As Chief Justice John Marshall noted, Washington's "judgment was suspended until it became necessary to determine; and his decisions, thus maturely made, were seldom, if ever, to be shaken."⁴⁴

Take account of his famous crossing of the Delaware River on Christmas night 1776. The year prior had been a series of setbacks for the Revolutionary Army. They came to the river's edge reeling—tired, hungry, and ill-clothed. Washington, after planning the operation seemingly himself, took his troops, which included future US President James Monroe, across the ice-choked river on the cold winter's night. He sought a surprise attack at Trenton in the hopes that a quick victory would bolster sagging morale in his army and encourage more men to join the cause in the new year. The scene painted by German artist Emanuel Leutze in the 1851 work, *Washington Crossing the Delaware*, is etched in America's national psyche, and illustrates a strong, determined Washington navigating the frozen river with his compatriots on their way to victory at Trenton. This image is as important a picture as the signing of the Declaration of Independence earlier that year, or the great gathering of delegates during the Constitutional Convention of 1787.

Crucial moments like Trenton were part of Washington's perpetual aspiration to execute a brilliant move or grand gesture. As his biographer John Ferling noted: "To imagine George Washington thinking any other way is not only to fail to understand the man but to fail to comprehend that it was his inescapable quest for esteem that governed and dictated the life-and-death choices he made."⁴⁵ In this spirit, seven years later, Washington made a decision that would help to define his character and judgment for history. Following the British recognition of American Independence, on December 23, 1783, Washington walked into the Assembly Chamber of the Maryland State House in Annapolis at high noon and took a seat opposite the president of the Congress, Thomas Mifflin, his former aide-de-camp. As those assembled settled into their seats, Mifflin addressed Washington: "Sir, the U.S. in Congress Assembled are prepared to receive your Communications."⁴⁶ With that, Washington rose, pulled his written remarks from his coat pocket, and with his hands visibly trembling and his voice faltering with emotion, he began: "The great events on which my resignation depended, having at length taken place; I have now the honor of offering my sincere Congratulations to Congress and of presenting myself before them to surrender into their hands and trust committed to me, and to claim the indulgence of retiring from the Service of my Country."[47] Needing both hands to steady the page, he informed the US Congress that he was resigning "with satisfaction" as Commander of the Continental Army, the appointment he had "accepted with diffidence."[48] Calling this "the last solemn act of my Official life," he closed his remarks: "Having now finished the work assigned me, I retire from the great theatre of Action—and bidding an Affectionate farewell to this August body under whose orders I have so long acted, I here offer my Commission, and take my leave of all the employments of public life."[49]

After his mere 329 words, there wasn't a dry eye to be found. According to James McHenry: "The spectators all wept, and there was hardly a member of Congress who did not drop tears."[50] Mifflin followed by reading the words of the United States Congress, which were prepared by Thomas Jefferson: "You have conducted the great military contest with wisdom and fortitude. . . . But the glory of your virtues will not terminate with your military command: it will continue to animate remotest ages."[51]

Washington further marked the occasion by offering a "Farewell Address," which he asked to be read aloud at the next session of each state's legislature. The address encompassed his parting thoughts in establishing an independent nation of thirteen colonies, as well as many of the "sentiments" that would help him navigate the presidency and would later define his final "Farewell Address." In particular, he amplified the gravity of America's next steps: "This is the moment when the eyes of the whole World are turned upon them, this is the moment to establish or ruin their national character forever. . . . It is yet to be decided, whether the Revolution must ultimately be considered as a blessing or a curse: a blessing or a curse, not to the present age alone, for with our fate will the destiny of unborn Millions be involved."[52] While the words he expressed in laying down his sword were important, they were less important than what he did. Deemed "extraordinary"[53] from a firsthand account that was printed in newspapers across the country, Washington's profound act not only resonated in America but across the Western world, as he could have become a king or dictator as a result of the Revolutionary War, in the tradition of a Julius Caesar or a later Napoleon Bonaparte or Mao

Zedong. In fact, such intrigue was a distinct possibility among some of Washington's victorious officers and soldiers who were upset over the US Congress's failure to provide back pay and pensions for their service during the Revolution.

In a meeting on March 15, 1783, on the banks of the Hudson River in Newburgh, New York, the scheming troops discussed a plot to march on Congress and commandeer Western lands with Washington as their leader. Catching wind of this murky plan, Washington personally addressed the conspirators with a nine-page speech that, while sympathizing with their grievances, denounced their machinations as treason to the cause for which they had fought. Ever the performer, General Washington proceeded to pull glasses from his pocket as he began his remarks, astounding all but just a select few who had ever seen him this way. He proceeded: "Gentlemen, you will permit me to put on my spectacles, for I have not only grown gray but almost blind in service to my country."[54] Washington's clever act of theater changed the mood among the soldiers, leaving even the most hardened by the depths of war to weep openly. Importantly, it also put an end to "the threat of a dictatorial standing army."[55]

Washington was sincere in his decision to step down after eight years of leading the Continental Army: "To return to our Private Stations in the bosom of a free, peaceful and happy Country."[56] Legend has it that King George III supposedly predicted that if Washington retired from public life and returned to his farm in 1783, "He will be the greatest man on earth."[57] Taken with Washington's virtue and restraint, First Lady Abigail Adams expressed: "If he was not really one of the best intentioned men in the world . . . he might be a very dangerous one."[58] By relinquishing his sword in 1783, Washington was providing America the ultimate recognition of support to this great experiment. Termed "the most important moment in American history"[59] by historian Thomas Fleming, the act was memorialized in one of eight historical paintings adorning the United States Capitol rotunda. Washington's action also made the establishment of an office of the presidency thinkable. He was the only American who possessed the reputation for republican virtue that the untried office of the presidency needed from the outset. Summing up this sentiment when he wrote to Washington from Paris on May 10, 1789, Thomas Jefferson noted: "There was nobody so well qualified as yourself, to put our new machine into a regular course of action; nobody, the authority of whose name could have so effectually crushed opposition at home, and produced respect abroad. I am sensible of the immensity of the sacrifice on your part. Your measure of fame was full to the brim; and, therefore, you have nothing to gain."[60]

The Roadmap

While the roadmap for Washington's decision to step down as president is found in the decision to relinquish his sword in 1783, the spark of action occurred in early 1792, nearly a decade later. After establishing the American presidency and holding the nascent nation together across his first three years as president, Washington wore this sacrifice in the form of physical exhaustion and emotional frustration. To facilitate "his intention of retiring from public life at the expiration of his four years,"[61] Washington sought the advice of James Madison, inviting him to meet at the executive mansion in Philadelphia on Sunday morning, February 19, 1792, if the Congressman "could make it convenient to spare half an hour from other matters."[62] What Washington wasn't unaware of was that for more than a year Madison had produced a dozen and a half essays attacking his administration in the *National Gazette*.

The brief meeting provided Washington the opportunity to put his toe in the water, but it wasn't until their follow-up meeting on May 5, 1792 that a broader picture of the president's mind-set was revealed. Washington opened that conversation by expressing "his intention of retiring"[63] and that he "wished to advise . . . on the mode and time most proper for making known that intention."[64] Washington was customarily inclined to keep his thoughts close hold, especially on matters of this magnitude. Ever true to this tradition, he told Madison that he had spoken "with no one yet on those particular points," with the exception of "Mr Jefferson, Col. Hamilton, General Knox . . . and of late to Mr Randolph."[65] The president was now taking his outreach a step further by soliciting Madison's view. For Washington, time was of the essence, and he appealed to Madison for a draft message to review by the "adjournment of congress" or the Congressman's "departure from Philadelphia,"[66] expected sometime in May.

Washington's decision to retire was enough to make this meeting historic by any standard, but it was the insight into the president's psyche that may be even more significant. In a rare moment of self-doubt, Washington offered the why behind his inquiry. Nevertheless, confiding in the double-dealing Virginia congressman, he expressed "that he could not believe or conceive himself anywise necessary to the successful administration of the Government," believing there were others by experience who "would be better able to execute the trust."[67] He confessed doubts about his overall fitness, noting that "he found himself . . . in the decline of life, his health becoming sensibly more infirm, & perhaps his faculties also."[68] He further expressed concern over the "spirit of party in the Government," and was particularly alarmed in how partisanship was dividing Hamilton and Jefferson and was leading to a rise of "discontents among the people . . . more & more."[69] Rather, Washington preferred to "go to his farm, take his spade in hand, and work for his bread, than remain in the present situation."[70]

Despite Madison's duplicity, he had to be altogether shook by what he was hearing. Granted, he was broadly aware of Washington's inklings on retirement, but few intimates, if ever, were privy to the kind of raw honesty Washington shared about himself personally. Not only was Washington letting him see behind the curtain, but rather than asking him if he should retire, he was asking how he should go about doing it.

In no way did any of Madison's calumnies aim at replacing President Washington, but rather, they focused on electing a Republican vice president to replace John Adams, especially out of fear for Alexander Hamilton's aspirations. Forced into action, Madison pushed back on Washington's assertions and humility. While recognizing that the president's current circumstances were trying personally and professionally, he stressed that it could not be doubted that Washington's "judgment must have been as competent in all cases, as that of any one who could have been put in his place, and in many cases, certainly more so."[71] Madison highlighted as well the president's grace under fire, as "it was well known that his services had been in a manner essential," particularly Washington's role in navigating the burgeoning spirit of party in America, which was "an argument for his remaining, rather than retiring."[72] Madison closed on a high note, impressing on Washington the importance of another four years of his leadership to "give such a tone & firmness to the Government as would secure it against danger"[73] from its enemies. In other words, no one could step in and fill Washington's shoes at this critical time, as "no successor would answer all the purposes to be expected from the continuance of the present chief magistrate."[74] And by successor, Madison meant only "a few characters," including "Mr Adams, Mr Jay & Mr Jefferson."[75] He then proceeded to give Washington a list of cons for each, from Jefferson's "extreme repugnance to public life & anxiety," to Adams's and Jay's "monarchical principles."[76] These were the "others" who Washington believed would be better able to execute the trust, and Madison was shooting down each of their candidacies. Yet, despite the representative from Virginia's best efforts, Washington appeared to "not be any wise satisfied" about what he was pitching and quickly "turned the conversation to other topics."[77] Undeterred as they wrapped up, Washington repeated "his request . . . of the points . . . before the adjournment"[78] to which Madison agreed.

Just four days later, after having heard of the president's imminent travel to Mount Vernon, Madison made an evening call on Washington. He used this follow-up opportunity to express his "favor of a direct address of notification to the public in time for its proper effect on the election,"[79] but moreover to ask Washington to reconsider retirement. As he had in their most recent visit, Washington sidestepped the inquiry without "the slightest assent" to the "idea of . . . relinquishing his purpose of retiring."[80]

Doubling down on May 25, Washington met with Madison on the road from Mount Vernon to Philadelphia to advance his intention. Concerned that "circumstances" could prevent him from speaking directly to Madison either by missing each other or by not having the privacy to engage candidly, Washington instead hand delivered a letter to Madison with his "thoughts and requests."[81] He called on Madison to use his "own judgment" to comprehend "*all* that will be proper" to draft a valedictory address to the public, which highlighted Washington's honor to serve as president, his best efforts to organize and administer the government, his inclination for retirement which had become necessary, and to "invoke a continuation of the blessing of Providence"[82] on the Republic. Of particular importance to the president, he asked Madison to invoke "that we are *all* the Children of the same country," and "however diversified in local & smaller matters," our shared interest "is the same in all the great & essential concerns of the Nation."[83] In other words, and in Washington's view, the United States was greater than the sum of its states or parts.

Twenty-six days later, Madison delivered through a letter and draft enclosure written from Montpelier, his home in Orange County, Virginia. Conveying Washington's core themes and wishes across 1,247 words, Madison emphasized the humbleness of Washington's decision to leave the presidency: "I can only say that I have contributed towards the organization and administration of the Government the best exertions of which a very fallible judgment was capable."[84] He also underscored strong national unity undertones: "We may all be considered as the children of one common country. . . . We have all been embarked in one common cause."[85]

With the draft now in hand, Washington turned his attention to publication. Madison advised that there was no better medium than a simple newspaper, particularly in the mid-September 1792 time frame. After all, America in the 1790s was a nation of words. Furthermore, in choosing this path, as opposed to something like a formal address to the US Congress, the collective intent was clear, Washington served all the people.

It didn't take long, however, for the president's lieutenants to pick up where Madison seemed to have fallen short. Sensing the urgency, Washington's closest associates amplified the pressure. In a May 23, 1792 letter to Washington, Thomas Jefferson began: "The confidence of the whole union is centered in you. Your being at the helm will be more than an answer to every argument which can be used to alarm and lead the people in any corner into violence or succession."[86] Advocating directly at the heart of Washington's national unity concerns and appealing to his political sensibilities, Jefferson concluded: "North and South will hang together, if they have you to hang on."[87] Alexander Hamilton followed on July 30 by tying his argument to Washington's reputation, something the president guarded with the highest order: "The impression is uniform—that your declining would be to be deplored as the greatest evil, that could befall the country at the present juncture, and as critically hazardous to your own reputation—that your continuance will be justified in the mind of every friend to his country by the evident necessity for it."[88]

Even as both of Washington's lieutenants applied their requisite savoir-faire to arrive at a similar outcome, at the heart of their shared advocacy was the real threat of disunion. Despite their political differences, and open sparring in the press, they argued rightly, like Madison, that Washington was the glue holding the national fortunes together. Hearing this from such heated rivals and their varied perspectives spoke volumes to the president under the circumstances. His stepping down would be an incredible disaster for the American experiment, as more time was necessary to strengthen the nation's foundation. They knew it and so did Washington.

Washington knew as well, as historian Garry Wills noted, that he "gained power from his readiness to give it up."[89] He need not have looked any further than his decision to resign as Commander of the Continental Army, which only served to elevate his stature on a mantle of prestige and tradition. He was also not above machinations and guile when needed, especially as a means to gain power for what portended to be a challenging second term, or at least to hold on to power.

But following his approach to making significant decisions, he pondered long and consulted wisely about a second term, even asking his aide Tobias Lear during the summer to canvas sentiment among New England states. Lear reported to Washington on July 21, 1792 that people were "mixed with an apprehension" as to the president stepping down, because the government "had not yet been long enough in operation to give satisfactory proof whether they are beneficial or not."[90] In a follow-up letter on August 5, Lear reported from his travels the "necessity" of Washington's "continuance," as no one could have contemplated anyone but Washington for that office.[91] On the same day, Attorney General Edmund Randolph beseeched Washington "to penetrate the consequences of a dereliction of the reins." Stressing the need for public stability, he further implored: "You alone can give them stability." Randolph also echoed a familiar concern of disunion: "Should a civil war arise, you cannot stay home."[92] By October, Washington seemed to be leaning toward a second term, telling Thomas Jefferson that "if his aid was thought necessary to save the cause to which he had devoted his life principally he would make the sacrifice of a longer continuance."[93] But by early November, it seemed he started leaning the other way, telling his close friend Elizabeth Powel of Philadelphia that he must resign. In a follow-up letter to him on November 4, she strongly expressed why he needed to stay in office, noting: "Your Resignation wou'd [sic] elate the Enemies of good Government and cause lasting Regret to the Friends of humanity."[94] She proceeded to cleverly play on Washington's penchant for legacy, noting that if he stepped down, his critics would highlight how "ambition had been the moving spring" of all his actions, and because the nation "had nothing more" to give him, he would "run no farther Risque [sic] for them."[95] Similar to Washington's other top advisers, she leaned into the threats of disunion: "I will venture to assert that, at this Time, you are the only Man in America that dares to do right on all public Occasions."[96] She also touted the "Soundness" of Washington's judgment, which had "been evinced on many and trying Occasions," and she called on God to help him "form a true Judgement" and serve a second term.[97]

Notwithstanding the physical and personal strain the first term took on him, in the end, it was his personal sense of duty that propelled him to continue in his nation's service, which was made official on February 13, 1793, when he was unanimously reelected with 132 votes by the Electoral College. Writing to Henry Lee the month prior, Washington, while pleased by his electoral showing, noted that "to say I feel pleasure from the prospect of *commencing* another tour of duty, would be a departure from the truth."[98]

∽

Second terms of American presidents historically tend to be less successful and more challenging than first terms. This phenomenon is often referred to by scholars as the "second-term curse," a perceived trend that has impacted the over twenty presidents who navigated terms beyond their second inaugural. James Madison watched Washington, DC burn. Abraham Lincoln and William McKinley were assassinated. Woodrow Wilson had a stroke and was defeated in his quest for a League of Nations. Franklin Roosevelt failed in his attempt to pack the Supreme Court.[99] Richard Nixon resigned. Bill Clinton confronted the Lewinsky scandal and impeachment, and George W. Bush faced the financial crisis of 2007 to 2008, and so on.

George Washington established the mainsprings for this challenging trend, as his second term proved to be even more exhausting physically and mentally than his first. The partisan Republican press managed to do in the political battles during his second term what no British musket could achieve in the War for Independence. In particular, the attacks on his personal character increased steadily in shrillness and intensity. It was said at the time that "gambling, reveling, horseracing and horse whipping" had been the essentials of his education.[100] Washington was described as a senile front man for the Federalist's betrayal of America, and even his record during the American Revolution was questioned. Writing to Edmund Pendleton on January 22, 1795, the president expressed that he was now on the advanced side of his "grand climacteric" and that "no man was ever more tired of public life, or more devoutly wished for retirement than I do."[101] A few weeks later, an observer noted of Washington: "He seemed considerably older. The innumerable vexations he had met with his different public capacities have very sensibly impaired the vigor of his constitution and given him an aged appearance."[102]

Arguably, the greatest cause of his troubles, as well as the most significant crisis he confronted among the many he navigated as president, revolved around the Jay Treaty. In 1794, Washington sent US Supreme Court Chief Justice John Jay to London to negotiate a deal that would avoid a war with England at a time when America could ill afford to fight one. Jay returned in 1795, with a treaty that essentially endorsed a pro-England platform of American neutrality. As part of the deal, England retained rights to tariffs on American exports and received favored status on its imports, although, the impressment of US sailors to supplement the British fleet was not curtailed. Moreover, the treaty required Americans to compensate English creditors for outstanding pre-Revolutionary debts, mostly comprised from Virginia planters. In return, England agreed to arbitration over claims submitted by American merchants for confiscated cargoes and agreed to evacuate their troops from posts on the western frontiers, in compliance with the Treaty of Paris ending the Revolutionary War.

Americans like Thomas Jefferson believed Washington was throwing America on the wrong side of history and that the Treaty was "a curse on [Washington's] virtues."[103] Those of a similar ilk as Jefferson believed that the Jay Treaty was nothing short of a repudiation of the Franco-American alliance of 1778, which secured French military assistance to help turn the tide of the American Revolution. Contrary to the Jeffersonian thesis, which has since been debunked by a consensus of historians, the Jay Treaty is viewed today as a shrewd American bargain. With the benefit of hindsight, it allowed the US to bet on England over France as the European power of the future, it amplified the critical economic impact of American trade with England, and by bolstering US security and economic development with support from the British sea power, American shipping added a layer of protection that extended generations into the future. More than anything, however, it delayed an inevitable war with England until the US was more capable of fighting one. Yet, in 1790s America, short-term vision largely trumped the long view, as the pact grew increasingly unpopular everywhere. John Adams recalled that the president's house in Philadelphia particularly bore the brunt of public protest, as it was "surrounded by an innumerable multitude, from day to day buzzing, demanding war against England, cursing Washington, and crying success to the French patriots and virtuous Republicans."[104] When the US House took up the Treaty over the winter and spring of 1796, the opposition was led by James Madison, who joined the chorus in arguing that the pact was a betrayal of the blood and treasure lost during the Revolution. However, in trying to win this debate, Madison may have lost sight of the "cardinal principle of American politics in the 1790's," as historian Joseph Ellis noted: "Whoever went face-to-face against George Washington was destined to lose."[105]

The Jay Treaty was ultimately ratified because Washington, according to Thomas Jefferson, "was the one man who outweighs them all in influence over the people."[106] Normally very careful never to utter any public criticisms of Washington, Jefferson furthered his rebuke in a letter to his Italian friend, Phillip Mazzei: "Were I to name to you the apostates who have gone over to these heresies, men who were Samsons in the field and Solomons in the council, but two have had their heads shorn by the harlot of England."[107] Although making his point without mentioning any names, it was pretty clear to whom he was referring. Vicious attacks and rumors from Monticello would continue. Well aware of Jefferson's machinations, Washington may have been the first president, but certainly not the last, to recognize that exercising judgment often involves incurring the wrath of close associates, colleagues, and friends alike.

In this context, which coincided at the start of 1796, the time seemed right for Washington to revive the idea of retirement and a Farewell Address to the American people. A first step was to dust off Madison's draft that was in safekeeping and to update it with the events from his second term. Madison's earlier effort was also crucial to Washington for another important reason: "By including the draft, he was undermining any claim that he was now being forced out against his will and would be defeated if he ran again."[108] Contrary to the unpopular Jay Treaty, Washington's retirement was voluntary, and he wanted the world to know it. That didn't stop Federalist's like John Jay from lobbying for Washington to "remain with us at least while the Storm lasts and until you can retire like the Sun in a calm, unclouded Evening."[109] But Washington wasn't playing, making clear "that only "imperious circumstances"[110] could postpone retirement to Mount Vernon.

To build on Madison's draft, Washington called on Alexander Hamilton to assist in early 1796, but it wasn't until May 1796 that their collaboration and correspondence really began to heat up. Recalling the president's wish to "*re dress* a certain paper" Washington had prepared, Hamilton asked for the document as soon as possible as "it is important that a thing of this kind should be done with great care and much at leisure touched & retouched."[111] Less than a week later, Washington shared the rough draft, stressing to Hamilton: "Even if you should think it best to throw the *whole* into a different form . . . My wish is, that the whole may appear in a plain stile; and be handed to the public in an honest; unaffected; simple garb."[112] In line with Madison's prior composition, it's clear the American people were Washington's intended audience, as he sought a tone and tenor that would resonate with the "Yeomanry of this Country."[113] Continuing, Washington echoed his intentions for the draft: "My object has been, and must continue to be, to avoid personalities; allusions to particular measures, which may appear pointed; and to expressions which could not fail to draw upon me attacks which I should wish to avoid, and might not find agreeable to repel."[114]

Discretion around Hamilton's efforts was of the highest priority for Washington. He was hypersensitive that the political forces of the day could use the draft against him given that fact that the earlier version "was known also to one or two of those characters who are now stronger, & foremost in the opposition to the Government; and consequently to the person Administering of it contrary to their views."[115] In no uncertain terms, when Washington referred to "one or two of those characters," he meant Jefferson and Madison. He was also acutely concerned that his letters were being opened nefariously. Taking no chances with his correspondence with Hamilton, he instead relied on personal couriers.

To aid in the drafting, Washington asked Hamilton to consult with John Jay, who was then the governor of New York, and along with Hamilton and Madison, one of the three original authors of the Federalist Papers, the eighty-five essays aimed at urging the ratification of the US Constitution. Hamilton and Jay met at the governor's residence on the south end of Manhattan to edit the text together, and their efforts, along with Madison's preceding draft, likely represented the final collaboration among the historic trio.

At the end of July, Hamilton sent a first draft of his edits to Washington, which "he endeavored to make as perfect as my time engagements would permit,"[116] and followed this correspondence on August 10, with a second draft that was more consistent with Madison's influence. However, by this time, his stealth advocacy was already in full effect, as Hamilton's preferred draft had been marinating with Washington for nearly two weeks. He downplayed his strategy: "Whichever you may prefer, if there be any part you wish to transfer from one to another any part to be changed—or if there be any material idea in your own draft which has happened to be omitted and which you wish introduced—in short if there be any thing further in the matter in which I can be of any, I will with great pleasure obey your commands."[117] After "several serious & attentive readings," it was no surprise that Washington approved of Hamilton's first effort, preferring "it greatly to the other draughts, being more copious on material points; more dignified on the whole; and with less egotism."[118]

In the end, Hamilton, like Madison before him, delivered for Washington. On September 5, Hamilton formally returned his final draft to the president, which represented a capstone of their long working relationship, and an effort that was nearly five times longer than Madison's initial draft. However, he did so with apologies that illness prevented him from sending back a clean version: "Had I had *health* enough, it was my intention to have written it over. . . . I seem now to have regularly a period of ill health every summer."[119] Hamilton also impressed on Washington to hold in publishing the address to the very "last moment," especially if a national or international crisis could force him to consider a third term. As Hamilton explained: "If a storm gathers, how can you retreat?"[120] Interestingly, the far from modest Hamilton never took public credit for assisting Washington with the draft, with only just a few intimates knowing of his work, such as John Jay and his wife Eliza. In particular, she recalled a treasured memory of walking down Broadway in New York City with her husband when an old veteran tried to sell them a copy of the Farewell Address. Alexander humorously quipped to her: "That Man does not Know he has asked me to purchase my own work."[121]

The Farewell Address

Constructed as an open letter to the American people, the Farewell Address represents one of the great amalgamations of political thought in American history. The aggregate of four years and various drafts largely etched in Madison and Hamilton's prose, the Address ultimately coalesced as solely Washington's and his "firm beliefs, clear ideas, and . . . strong personality."[122] Throughout the speech, Washington sought to convey the feeling of "an old and affectionate" parting friend, "who can possibly have no personal motive to bias his counsel."[123] He also expressed his desire to not retire before offering a "solemn contemplation and some sentiments which are the result of much reflection . . . and which appear to me all-important to the permanency of your felicity as a people."[124] Washington would be remiss if he stepped away without "acknowledging" the "debt of gratitude" he owed to his "beloved country" for the many honors it had conferred on him, especially the "steadfast confidence"[125] by which it supported him, and the subsequent service opportunities it entrusted to him. It was this unparalleled support that helped to carry him through the darkest days of the Revolution and over the course of the American experiment. It's also what filled him with love and gratitude for the United States and his inherent belief that the nation's best days were ahead.

In presenting his narrative, Washington didn't waste any time getting right to the point—he would not be seeking a third term: "The period for a new election of a citizen to administer the executive government of the United States being not far distant . . . I should now apprise you of the resolution I have formed, to decline being considered among the number of those out of whom a choice is to be made."[126] It wasn't a decision he made lightly, and he wanted the American people to know it. As a "dutiful citizen to his country," he undertook "strict regard to all the considerations,"[127] including the weight of leaving the young nation in the hands of new leadership, his sense of duty, the kindnesses shown to him by Americans, and the fervent "zeal" for the nation's "future interest,"[128] among others. He further sought to ensure for posterity, in no uncertain terms, that he was not being pushed out and just four years earlier it was an inherent sense of duty that called him to serve a second term despite an "inclination" to retire, which led to "the preparation"[129] of an initial Farewell Address. Rather, he decided to serve another term in 1792, based on the "critical posture of our affairs with foreign nations and the unanimous advice of persons entitled to my confidence."[130] In other words, he was talked out of retirement by America's brain trust—leaders like Jefferson, Madison and Hamilton, among others—and because British and French intrigue had the real propensity to unwind a generational struggle for liberty with one misplaced musket shot.

Washington then pivoted into the core themes within his instructive and inspirational 6,088-word final statement of collective judgment. Amplifying a distinguished forty-five-year record of service, he hoped the lessons he was sharing "may be productive of some partial benefit . . . that they may now and then recur to moderate the fury of party spirit, to warn against the mischiefs of foreign intrigue, to guard against the impostures of pretended patriotism."[131]

Washington's first lesson, interconnected to the rising fury of party spirit, was a deep and real challenge in the early days of the United States. Dismayed by the rise of partisanship, Washington advised against the kind of division that "agitates the community with ill-founded jealousies and false alarms; kindles the animosity of one party against another; foments occasionally riot and insurrection" and "opens the door to foreign influence and corruption."[132] He warned that one "can not shield . . . too much against the jealousies and heartburnings" that come from "expedients of party" seeking to acquire influence within particular districts by misrepresenting the "opinions and aims of other districts."[133] He especially feared this kind of division would lead citizens to seek certainty "in the absolute power of an individual" who takes the reins of control and "ruins . . . public liberty."[134] To prevent such an occurrence, he called on the interests, duty, and "uniform vigilance" of "wise people" to "discourage and restrain" these divisions before their baneful effects went "bursting into a flame."[135]

Although expressing his concerns over the rise of political parties, Washington conjointly believed that if properly engaged in free countries like America, they could serve as "useful checks upon the administration of government and serve to keep alive the spirt of liberty."[136] In this endeavor, according to Washington, religion and morality were indispensable supports in counteracting the rise of partisanship, and thus needed to be cherished equally by both the politician and the pious.

Even more critically important to these matters for Washington was the need for "Unity of Government."[137] Four years earlier, Madison's draft was consumed by the idea, and Washington agreed to serve another term in part for national unity and to avoid the risk of civil war. No sooner than three generations later, a lack of unity in government led Americans to take arms against each other in the American Civil War.

So important was this concept to Washington that he spread out his thoughts on the matter over twelve paragraphs of the Farewell Address. For him, unity represented "a main pillar" of real independence, of tranquility at home, of peace abroad, of safety, of prosperity, and "of that very liberty which you so highly prize."[138] Because this lofty pillar was so crucial to America's future, Washington elevated his concerns over the "internal or external enemies" who would go to great pains to weaken the "conviction of this truth."[139] With the rising fury of party spirit already chipping away at this pillar, other challenges such as "obstruction to the execution of the laws," organized factions, or "combinations or associations"[140] of these types of actions offered the real potential for intrigue. Moreover, Washington was concerned that over the course of time these potential actions could intersect with the grave dangers of demagogues in a democracy and become "potent engines by which cunning, ambitious, and unprincipled men"[141] are enabled by the "love of power, and proneness to abuse it, which predominates in the human heart."[142] It was a potentiality that kept the Framers of the Constitution up a night and continues to strike at the heart of today's political discourse. Washington therefore implored his fellow Americans never to take their unity for granted and never to discount the "immense value of your national Union to your collective and individual happiness."[143] To the president, the continuance of the Union must be the highest aspiration of an American citizen, as no bond was more important, certainly not "any appellation derived from local discriminations."[144] Granted, there may be "slight shades of difference" between the "unrestrained intercourse" among North and South, the East and West, but ultimately, these interdependent regions shared "the same religion, manners, habits, and political principles."[145] And theirs were long-standing bonds earned through shared "efforts . . . dangers, sufferings, and successes," especially in the triumph of American independence and liberty, and in the creation of a government that was an "offspring of our own choice."[146] These collective efforts, according to Washington, created "an indissoluble community of interest as one nation,"[147] and taken together, serve as a reminder that although we have distinct differences, we are stronger together than we ever are apart.

The unity of government to which Washington aspired required a strong federal government with "powers properly distributed and adjusted."[148] Aligned as such, it could serve as an ally of unity, the surest guardian of liberty, and a core representation of the national interest, particularly through the enforcement of laws and the collection of taxes. However, despite his efforts in setting up the government, Washington knew that his departure from the scene would require an even more robust commitment to federal authority in fulfilling the broad role he played. Thus, he proposed action that included, among others, the creation of a national university and national military academy, as well as a call for increasing federal salaries and expanding the navy. His progressive approach represented the most robust effort to enlarge federal power until John Quincy Adams's administration three decades later. And because of his visionary work, he gave America the runway to become the continental nation it is today.

Although, in making his argument in favor of national unity, he was noticeably quiet on the issue of slavery, which above all challenges of the time, had the greatest potential to tear the fabric of the nation apart. Washington saw keeping the Union together as his primary responsibility, even though he believed the peculiar institution was a parasite eating away at the republic. Concurrently, he was making arrangements for his slaves to be freed upon the death of his wife, and to ensure that as pieces of Mount Vernon were sold off, a portion of the proceeds would be used to support his freed slaves and their children for the foreseeable future. In this way, his actions spoke louder than the silence encapsulated in the Farewell Address. And as Joseph Ellis pointed out, Washington's final position on slavery proved to be a "capstone to a career devoted to getting the big things right . . . as if he had known where history was headed; or, perhaps, as if the future had felt compelled to align itself with his choices. . . . His genius was his judgement."[149]

Washington's second lesson, related to the mischief of foreign intrigue, was what he referred to as "one of the most baneful foes of Republican Government."[150] From his experience: "It is folly in one nation to look for disinterested favors from another."[151] For Washington, that price was extremely high, likely a "portion of its independence."[152] The French openly engaged in this intrigue, actively seeking to undermine the off-year congressional elections in 1794, in the hope of influencing policy in their favor. As a result, Washington demanded the recall of French Ambassador Edmond Charles Genêt, and as he presciently anticipated, this challenge has only persisted across American history, most recently with the undercurrent of Russian interference during the 2016 US presidential election.

To counter this intrigue, Washington sought "to have with them as little political connexion as possible,"[153] believing that "Our detached and distant situation invites and enables us to pursue a different course."[154] For Washington, this meant a sense of strength and unity at home and a policy of independence or neutrality abroad; a commitment to "steer clear of permanent alliances with any portion of the foreign world."[155] More formally, Washington's policy emanated from his April 1793 Proclamation of Neutrality, which declared American impartiality to conflicts occurring across Europe, and for which he noted in the Farewell Address: "I was well satisfied that our country, under all the circumstances of the case, had a right to take, and was bound in duty and interest to take, a neutral position."[156] Ever the realist, Washington knew America needed more time "to settle and mature its yet recent institutions" and to gain strength to "command . . . its own fortunes."[157] A May 1, 1796 letter to Charles Carroll, who would become the last surviving signer of the Declaration of Independence, summed up Washington's foreign policy theory: "Every true friend to this Country must *see*, and *feel*, that the policy of it is not to embroil ourselves with any Nation whatsoever; but to avoid their disputes & their politics; and if they will harass one another, to avail ourselves of the Neutral conduct we have adopted."[158]

As practice, the president "continually governed" by the spirit of the neutrality policy, "uninfluenced by attempts to deter or avert"[159] him from it. With a keen eye for the global chessboard, Washington clearly understood Europe's "primary interests" were in "very remote relation" to the United States, and that it would be "unwise to implicate ourselves by artificial ties" in Europe's "frequent controversies."[160] Which elevated Washington's poignant question: "Why, by interweaving our destiny with that of any part of Europe, entangle our peace and prosperity in the toils of European ambition, rivalship, interest, humor, or caprice?"[161] Rather, by pursuing a "different course," the period was not far off, as Washington argued, where "we may defy material injury from external annoyance" and our neutrality will be "scrupulously respected."[162] Washington's policy, with the exception of the War of 1812, would be implemented by his successors well into the twentieth century.

Washington's third lesson was aimed at "the impostures of pretended patriotism."[163] Believing that America should "Observe good faith and justice towards all Nations . . . cultivate peace and harmony with all,"[164] the president deplored the idea of those who seemed to hold "passionate attachments" for, and "permanent, inveterate antipathies" against, a foreign country above their own.[165] Declaring any nation "that indulges toward another a habitual hatred, or a habitual fondness, is in some degree a slave,"[166] Washington was taking a veiled shot at Jefferson and his followers. In particular, he warned that "ambitious, corrupted, or deluded citizens (who devote themselves to the favorite nation)" are prone to "betray or sacrifice the interests of their own country," sometimes with a "virtuous sense of obligation . . . or foolish compliances of ambition, corruption, or infatuation."[167] In these situations, according to Washington, there can be the illusion of shared interests where they don't occur, concessions of privileges to a favored nation, which would be "denied to others," or conversely, the perception of "enmities" that lead nations to quarrel or declare war "without inducement or justification."[168] But far too often, it was this "antipathy in one nation against another" that led to "insult and injury" and to war "contrary to the best calculations of policy," as passion trumps what "reason would reject" to "produce a variety of evils."[169]

To Washington, such attachments should be particularly alarming to the "truly enlightened and independent patriot," especially as they allow "impostures of pretended patriotism" opportunities to "tamper with domestic factions, to practice the arts of seduction, to mislead public opinion, to influence or awe public councils!"[170] Ultimately, as he concluded: "Such an attachment of a small or weak towards a great and powerful nation dooms the former to be the satellite of the latter."[171] Rather, for

Washington, a great nation like America, and its people, should always be guided "by an exalted justice and independence."[172]

In addition to these three core lessons, Washington threaded in other important insight. He advocated strongly for the rule of law, noting: "Respect for its authority, compliance with its laws, acquiescence in its measures, are duties enjoined by the fundamental maxims of true Liberty."[173] He stressed the value of education and morality. According to Washington: "Of all the dispositions and habits, which lead to political prosperity, Religion and Morality are indispensable supports."[174] He called to "Promote, then, as an object of primary importance, institutions for the general diffusion of knowledge" for "it is essential that public opinion should be enlightened."[175] And he asserted that "honesty is always the best policy" in both public and private affairs.

Last, he gave instructions to cherish public credit and its "very important source of strength and security."[176] In other words, while advocating for public credit here, he was inclined to "use it as sparingly as possible," and expressed concern in "avoiding . . . the accumulation of debt,"[177] which is informative for the challenges he had with it across his life. Washington, himself, was land rich, but cash poor, due in part to his decision to marry Martha Dandridge Curtis, which included her large dowry, catapulting him into the top tier of Virginia's planter class.[178]

Closing the Farewell Address in much the same spirit of humble virtue with which it began, Washington called out his "inferiority" of qualifications and experience in his own view and in the "eyes of others," and the "increasing weight of years," which altogether made the "shade of retirement . . . as necessary to me as it will be welcome."[179] A distinctive holdover from the Madison draft, Washington noted that he only acted "with good intentions" and "best exertions"[180] in organizing and administering the government and in discharging the people's trust. And although he was "unconscious of intentional error," he was nevertheless too sensible of "his defects not to think it probable that I may have committed many errors."[181] To this end, and ever a humble servant leader, he believed that those with authority must take responsibility for their actions. He may have "committed errors,"[182] but he was never afraid to admit them, and he never tried to hide from them. Instead, he routinely called on a higher power to ameliorate the transgressions caused by them. In this light, he hoped that after forty-five years of a life dedicated to service and "guided by . . . principles," "the faults of incompetent abilities will be consigned to oblivion."[183]

Impact and Legacy

As newspapers started hitting the streets of Philadelphia on September 19, 1796, reactions to Washington's decision started to roll in. The overwhelming consensus offered expressions of regret for his retirement and homages for his service to the nation.[184] James McHenry, secretary of war, who remained in Philadelphia after Washington's departure noted to the president on September 25: "Your address on the first day of its publication, drew from friends of government, through every part of the City, the strongest expressions of sensibility. I am well assured, that many tears were shed on the occasion, and proposition made in various companies for soliciting your concert to serve another term. . . . I sincerely believe that no nation ever felt a more ardent attachment to its chief; and 'tis certain, that history cannot furnish an example such as you have given."[185]

The legislature of the State of Vermont added: "We shall recollect you with filial affection—your advice as an inestimable legacy; and shall pride ourselves, in teaching our children the importance of that advice, and a humble imitation of your example."[186] The New Jersey House of Assembly followed with a resolution: "Resolved unanimously, That the wisdom, firmness and patriotism of the President of the United States, during his administration, and his faithful and highly important services rendered to the Government of the Union, at the most critical and interesting periods of its existence have a just claim to the thanks of this house."[187]

Despite the broad and positive response to Washington's Farewell Address, it didn't stop the Republican press from jumping on its message. Challenging his partisanship warnings and foreign policy posture, the speech was denounced by his critics as "the loathings of a sick mind."[188]

Over time, though, the legacy and impact of the Farewell Address has only grown in stature. Washington's biographer Douglas Freeman noted: "There is wisdom in every line of Washington's farewell address."[189] But that wisdom has come to mean different things to different generations, with a consistent refrain of seeking meaning in Washington's words to support one's own position. Generations of historians and scholars have considered its long-standing implications and have provided varying interpretations, especially giving great attention to the principles that Washington espoused. As historians Stanley Elkins and Eric McKitrick concluded: "The aggregate of ideas contained in the Address shows a sufficient complexity of intent that there is still no telling when or where the commentary ought to stop."[190]

Volleying the most robust historical and political discourse over time is Washington's simple construct around foreign alliances. Isolationists from the nineteenth century to current times have pointed to Washington to undergird their cause. In particular, during America's emergence as a global power during the twentieth century, some, such as President Harry Truman, viewed Washington's policy as a sacred text for isolationists. Others point out that Washington never sought strict isolation, while some highlight Washington's prophetic "twenty year" peace reference,[191] which foretold the outbreak of the War of 1812.

Across this debate, the term *entangling alliances* is often attributed to Washington, but the words were actually constructed by Thomas Jefferson in his 1801 inaugural address, in which he called for "honest friendship with all nations, entangling alliance with none."[192] However, the phrasing could have easily been trademarked by Washington, along with a commitment to self-sufficiency, particularly his preference in reducing "dependence on imports" and in taking "advantage of vast resources so that America would not be subject to British whims."[193] Washington believed self-sufficiency was the key to freedom, and this continues to play out globally in modern times, such as in America's pursuit of energy independence and in the "America First" agenda advocated by pre–World War II isolationists and more recently by President Donald Trump, among others.

In fairness to Washington, there was no way, despite his consistent focus on the future, that he could know or influence the varying interpretations the "unborn millions"[194] would reveal from his words. It's also noteworthy that Washington feared the Farewell Address would be forgotten by future generations. Far from the case, and in addition to the extensive and continued commentary, his successors have carried on the important act of stewardship, creating a platform for each new generation of presidential leadership to provide words of warning and inspiration for Americans to draw on and navigate challenging times.

Andrew Jackson was the first president to follow Washington in writing a Farewell Address. Writing over forty years later, he devoted the core of his March 4, 1837 effort to banking policies, but also advised that "the lessons contained in this invaluable legacy of Washington to his countrymen should be cherished in the heart of every citizen to the latest generation."[195] Like the many before and the many that followed, Jackson looked to Washington's "paternal counsels . . . to be not merely the offspring of wisdom and foresight, but the voice of prophecy, foretelling events and warning us of evil to come."[196] In fact, Jackson believed that in the context of the times, including threats to succession, "perhaps at no period of time could they be more usefully remembered than at the present moment."[197]

President Dwight Eisenhower's Farewell Address, delivered on January 17, 1961, just three days before he exited the White House, is famous for echoing Washington's warning against "those overgrown military establishments which, under any form of government, are inauspicious to liberty, and which are to be regarded as particularly hostile to republican liberty."[198] Eisenhower idolized Washington, calling him, "my hero,"[199] and not surprisingly, jumped at the opportunity to rekindle his idol's Farewell Address tradition, molding Washington's message for the modern atomic age to coin the phrase: "military-industrial complex."[200]

Like Washington, President Ronald Reagan's Farewell Address famously shared a love for and pride in America. In particular, he offered a description of the "shining city upon a hill,"[201] a phrase that came from John Winthrop in 1630, before he and his fellow settlers reached New England. Reagan routinely borrowed the phrasing throughout his political career and took this historic opportunity to finally put into words its meaning to him: "A tall, proud city built on rock stronger than oceans, windswept, God-blessed, and teeming with people of all kinds living in harmony and peace, a city with free ports that hummed with commerce and creativity. And if there had to be city walls, the walls had doors and the doors were open to anyone with the will and the heart to get there."[202] President Barack Obama also invoked Washington in his January 10, 2017 Farewell Address by noting the importance of self-government in maintaining America's democracy. He channeled Washington's theme of national unity: "That we should reject 'the first dawning of every attempt to alienate any portion of our country from the rest or to enfeeble the sacred ties' that make us one."[203] Further, he echoed Washington by expressing the dangers of "political dialogue to become so corrosive that people of good character aren't even willing to enter into public service."[204]

In the midst of the Civil War, on February 12, 1862, another of Washington's successors, President Abraham Lincoln, issued a proclamation calling on Americans to mark Washington's birthday. Lincoln "recommended to the people of the United States that they assemble in their customary places of meeting for the public solemnities on the 22d day of February"[205] to "celebrate the anniversary of the birth of the Father of the Country by causing to be read to them his immortal Farewell Address."[206] Ten days later, the US Senate called on the Address to boost morale, reading it at a Joint Session of Congress. On the occasion, then Tennessee senator and future US president, Andrew Johnson, said: "In view of the perilous condition of the country, I think the time has arrived when we should recur back to the days, the times, and the doings of Washington and the patriots of the Revolution, who founded the government under which we live."[207]

In the history of the US Senate, there has been no tradition more faithfully sustained than the annual reading of the Farewell Address. Every year since 1896, the US Senate has observed Washington's birthday by selecting one of its members, alternating parties, to read the Farewell Address in session. At the end of the reading, the chosen senator signs and writes their thoughts on the significance of the Address in the pages of a leather-bound book that is preserved by the secretary of the US Senate. In 1956, Minnesota Senator Hubert Humphrey wrote that every American should study the instructive message: "It gives one a renewed sense of pride in our republic. . . . It arouses the wholesome and creative emotions of patriotism and love of country."[208] In 2021, Ohio Senator Rob Portman gave the address, calling Washington's words "timeless" but also "timely because . . . we are in a period of our country's history when we just came through a contentious election and impeachment and in the middle of a crisis, and people are really divided."[209] A year later, Vermont Senator Patrick Leahy carried on the Senate tradition, reminding his fellow senators, "Don't forget the parts of our history that give us our principles."[210]

In 2015, the Farewell Address found a renaissance in pop culture when the critically acclaimed musical *Hamilton* debuted on Broadway, which put the president's prose to music through the song "One Last Time." In the song, Washington instructs Hamilton: "Pick up a pen, start writing, / I wanna talk about what I've learned / The hard-won wisdom I have earned / . . . If I say goodbye, the nation learns to move on, / it outlives me when I'm gone."[211]

Through written or spoken word, quiet reflection, or song, the Farewell Address continues to resonate in how it speaks to the challenges and aspirations we face as a nation; to the "sure," "sound," and "unerring"[212] judgment Washington honed across a lifetime of service and which he sought to pass on to his "unborn millions"; and to his symbolic act as the first leader in two millenniums to relinquish power once in his grasp. This act was the most important he would make as president and was arguably the most critical of his career. It could be easily overlooked, but taken in context with the place and time, it represented a defining moment in American history, with as deep significance today as on the contemporaries of his time, including Thomas Jefferson, who was the first president to confront Washington's two-term legacy. Jefferson addressed the issue directly in a December 10, 1807 letter to the Vermont legislature, declining their request to be "the first example of prolongation beyond the second term in office."[213] In doing so, he confirmed his intention not to disregard "the sound precedent set by an illustrious predecessor,"[214] keenly aware from history "how easily that degenerates into an inheritance."[215]

Washington's precedent would not be broken until Franklin Roosevelt secured a third term in 1940, and so ingrained in the American fabric was his act that it was written into the Constitution as the Twenty-Second Amendment in 1951. Washington's precedent also paved the way for the peaceful transfer of power, which has defined America's system of government for over two centuries. That seemingly certain standard was tested on January 6, 2021, during a violent insurrection at the US Capitol, which sought to disrupt a Joint Session of Congress assembled to certify the 2020 presidential election results. The same building that Washington laid the cornerstone for 228 years prior, was turned into a police state, a reminder of the fragility of American democracy, the vulnerability to demagoguery, and the grave dangers of partisanship to undermine national unity—all concerns Washington elevated in his Farewell Address. The events of January 6, 2021 also serve as a reminder that this guiding doctrine of republican ideals, which sits squarely beside the Declaration of Independence and the Gettysburg Address, can be deployed, along with the judgment defined in Washington's transformational act, to serve as a light for a new generation of Americans, as well as to help navigate the significant challenges of our times—issues of foreign influence and of national unity and character.

As will be highlighted across the pages that follow, the quality of judgment Washington exercised underlies the core presidential qualities that have shaped America as a nation and which define this book. Otherwise, a president with ingenuity but lacking judgment may innovate in the wrong places or a president without judgment but with ample confidence may lead the nation boldly in the wrong direction. As such, America is the nation it is today in large measure due to George Washington's sound judgment, which intimates described as always making "him appear a man of a different cast in the eyes of the world."[216] It was this same judgment that amplified his innate propensity to make the right call when it mattered most—to make the inconceivable inevitable. It was also the same judgment that led him to demonstrate that no one individual has the right to the presidency—that it belongs to the people. And across American history, no other president has made such an important judgment or left such an important legacy.

Chapter 2

Ingenuity

> There is no act, however virtuous, for which ingenuity may not find some bad motive.
>
> —Thomas Jefferson to Edward Dowse, April 19, 1803

America is a great experiment in ingenuity. A start-up in modern terms, the nation's founding ideals and documents are the epitome of creative experimentation. The Framers designed a system of government that championed a spirit of individual initiative and collective ingenuity that has fundamentally shaped American life. The first patent law was passed in 1790, and, in less than a century, the United States went from a rural agricultural economy to the leader of the Industrial Revolution. American ingenuity has defined innovators from Edison, Einstein, Carver, and Jobs, and innovations from the telephone and telegraph, to automobiles and airplanes, to computers, smartphones, e-commerce, and artificial intelligence.

For over two centuries, American ingenuity has also defined the work of US presidents, who have catalyzed a proclivity to innovate and to explore the limits of possibility and frontiers yet foreseen. As a nation, America is at its best when aligned in common cause, and the top performers in the Office have shaped and sharpened this focus, often by providing unique, outside-the-box perspectives and advancements. These bellwethers could teach the course in the art of ingenuity and in seizing the moment. They were critical thinkers who looked around the corner to ask the right questions, leaders with vision and a penchant for bringing new solutions and ideas to the table, along with a firm understanding that history favors the bold. They were versatile in action, agile in thought, and most capable of rising to the challenge, often without a proven roadmap.

One such leader was President John Kennedy. In the midst of Cold War tensions, and on the heels of the Soviet Union's Yuri Gagarin becoming the first human in space, he charged his vice president, Lyndon Johnson, "to make an overall survey of where we stand in space."[1] More specifically, he inquired in an April 20, 1961 memo as to whether "we have a chance of beating the Soviets . . . by a rocket to go to the moon and back with a man."[2] Kennedy asked penetrating questions about cost, whether we were working "24 hours a day on existing programs" and "if not, why not?"[3] Just over a month later, in a message to a Joint Session of the US Congress, Kennedy declared: "I believe that this nation should commit itself to achieving the goal, before this decade is out, of landing a man on the Moon and returning him safely to the Earth."[4] Recognizing this stretch goal, he further explained on September 12, 1962: "We choose to go to the moon in this decade . . . because that goal will serve to organize and measure the best of our energies and skills, because that challenge is one that we are willing to accept, one we are unwilling to postpone, and one which we intend to win."[5]

After his announcement, nearly all of the National Aeronautics and Space Administration's efforts turned toward the common purpose of a lunar landing, which fed into the Apollo Program. His goal was posthumously achieved on July 20, 1969, when Apollo 11 commander Neil Armstrong, watched by some 600 million people across the globe, stepped foot on the Moon's surface and announced: "That's one small step for man, one giant leap for mankind."[6] Four days later, the Apollo 11 crew splashed down safely in the Pacific Ocean, representing the tremendous "win" over the Soviet Union that Kennedy sought, and which honored his vow not to see "the moon and . . . beyond . . . governed by a hostile flag of conquests, but by a banner of freedom and peace."[7] Prior to this impossible mission, which was made possible through an all-inspiring effort of American ingenuity, the idea of landing on the moon was often referred to as a phrase for things that couldn't be achieved. This stunning milestone in human achievement assured that with enough ingenuity and grit, any frontier or achievement was within reach. Thus, the expression *moonshot* became part of the American DNA.

Over a half century later, President Barack Obama echoed John Kennedy's vision during a 2014 commencement speech in which he challenged the graduates on the need for climate action: "When President Kennedy set us on a course for the moon, there were a number of people who made a serious case that it wouldn't be worth it; it was going to be too expensive, it was going to be too hard, it would take too long. But nobody ignored the science. I don't remember anybody saying that the moon wasn't there or that it was made of cheese."[8] In Obama's view: "All it takes are the policies to tap that potential—to ignite that spark of creativity and ingenuity—which has always been at the heart of who we are and how we succeed."[9] President Donald Trump advanced that legacy during the COVID-19 worldwide pandemic in 2020. It what would traditionally take years to accomplish, Trump leveraged the full weight of his administration and the ingenuity of American scientists to develop "a safe and effective vaccine at breakneck speed."[10] The unparalleled timeline took only nine months to achieve, leaving Trump to call the initiative: "The gold standard vaccine."[11]

On the eve of America's entry into World War II, President Franklin D. Roosevelt's ingenuity was also invaluable in uplifting the allied war effort against the Axis Powers. In December 1940, British leaders informed American officials that they were nearly bankrupt and no longer would be able to pay cash for arms as US law required. FDR's solution was the innovative Lend-Lease program, which he likened to lending a garden hose to a neighbor so that the neighbor could put out a house fire. Then the neighbor would then return the hose, but if it got "smashed up—holes in it—during the fire,"[12] they would replace it with a new one. Roosevelt's ingenuity also laid the foundation for the international system after World War II, via the United Nations and Bretton Woods institutions.

In this spirit, as British Prime Minister Margaret Thatcher explained, the most difficult of all political tasks is "changing attitudes and perceptions about what is possible."[13] As leaders like Kennedy, Obama, Trump, FDR, and others have proven, this same reach for the possible has fundamentally defined the course of more than two centuries of American leadership. We've further seen it in the physical development of the United States, from President John Quincy Adams's support for the creation of canals and roads to help connect a growing nation, to President James Polk's expansion of the country's borders to the Pacific Ocean, to President Dwight Eisenhower's push for a national highway system to enhance national security.

We've seen it in efforts to make the world more peaceful, sustainable, and just, from President Woodrow Wilson's vision for a League of Nations, to Lyndon Johnson's Great Society, to George W. Bush's commitment to address global AIDS through the President's Emergency Plan for AIDS Relief (PEPFAR). We've seen it in our ability to lift others, from President Harry Truman's vision through the Marshall Plan, which rebuilt Europe after World War II, to President Dwight Eisenhower's signing of the Agricultural Trade Development and Assistance Act, which created the US Food for Peace program, to President Herbert Hoover's pre-presidential work to feed war-torn Europe during and after World War I, which earned him the nickname, "The Great Humanitarian."[14] We've seen it in our efforts to expand our reach, while defining it for others, from President Bill Clinton's investments in the growth of the internet, to President Richard Nixon's opening of China, to President James Monroe's work to establish the Monroe Doctrine, which became a major tenet of US foreign policy in the Western Hemisphere. And we've seen it exemplified even in our darkest hours, from the improvised and first-of-its-kind air conditioner devised by US Navy engineers to cool James Garfield's room after an assassin's bullet struck him in summer of 1881, to Abraham Lincoln's inspirational leadership during the Civil War, which included the Emancipation Proclamation, leaving as his legacy a nation that was both whole and free. Interestingly, and much similar to Herbert Hoover, arguably Lincoln's most ingenious effort may have happened before he became president. "The Great Emancipator,"[15] who had a long fascination with how things worked, invented a flotation system for lifting riverboats stuck on sandbars. Though his idea was never manufactured, he remains the only US president to have a patent in his name.

Unfortunately, American history is also framed by occasions when we have fallen short in solving challenges, mitigating conflict, or taking necessary steps as a nation. These moments routinely point back to a lack of presidential ingenuity. Presidents Millard Fillmore, Franklin Pierce, and James Buchanan were unable to forge solutions to the tumultuous events of their times, particularly the disputes over slavery, which overwhelmed them and many of their predecessors, accelerating the course toward Civil War. In particular, Millard Fillmore backed the 1850 Compromise that delayed the South's succession by allowing slavery to spread, and Franklin Pierce signed the Kansas-Nebraska Act into law, which allowed the citizens of the Kansas and Nebraska Territories to decide to permit or prohibit slavery within their borders. This Act, more specifically, served to fan the flames of national division, including a period of political chaos and bloodshed that was termed, "Bleeding Kansas."[16]

During the post–Civil War period, President Andrew Johnson demonstrated a lack of ingenuity in attempting to navigate the times. He did far more to extend the period of national strife by opposing policies seeking greater equality and racial justice, including the Fourteenth Amendment, which addresses many aspects of citizenship and the rights of citizens, than in offering constructive solutions to advance the country forward.

Prior to the Great Depression, Calvin Coolidge is recognized for producing seven years of peace and prosperity, and for capturing the prevailing sentiment of the time: "The chief business of the American people is business."[17] However, his tenure in Office is viewed by many historians as one of inaction and complacency in the face of a looming disaster. And his successor, Herbert Hoover, ultimately missed the mark on the requisite solutions needed to address the crisis.

Similarly, Jimmy Carter's administration is remembered most for the challenges that he faced and the lack of ingenuity he advanced in meeting them—from inflation, to an energy crisis, to the Iran hostage situation. Yet Carter demonstrated ingenuity in helping to produce the Camp David Accords, and in his commitment to the protection of human rights around the world, which stretched into important initiatives over ensuing decades.

In the aggregate, each president's collective ingenuity varies considerably, as well as how they measure against peers. While some leaned into more traditional and established methods, the best cultivated creativity and vision to solve important problems and advance the nation. And no president set the standard for American ingenuity more than Thomas Jefferson.

The Scene

The month of April, English playwright William Shakespeare noted, "Hath put a spirit of youth in everything."[18] President Franklin Roosevelt described the month as the "full beauty of glorious springtime,"[19] and April of 1802, in Washington, DC, shared a similar spirit, albeit sans the cherry blossoms that would later be planted as a gift of the Japanese in 1912.

The nation's new national capital was a growing rural village: "romantic but . . . wild," as described by First Lady Abigail Adams.[20] Far from the great city it is today, Washington, DC was still several weeks away from formal incorporation. A cornerstone of the city's planning was the "President's House," as the White House was called then, and which Thomas Jefferson had a significant hand in establishing through the Compromise of 1790. Two years later, in 1792, and despite writing the advertisement for the work as US secretary of State, it is believed that Jefferson secretly entered the competition to design the executive mansion under the pseudonym, A.Z., which was later awarded to Irish architect, James Hoban.

Upon sight of the finished mansion, Jefferson observed that it was "really a pleasant country residence . . . in the style of a good country neighborhood."[21] Only the second resident of the President's House, his lifestyle sought to strike the balance between solitude and engagement. On the one hand, as a widower, he confronted the loneliness of long nights in the mansion, highlighted in a January 1803 letter from his daughter Polly: "My dear papa . . . how much it pains me to think of the unsafe and solitary manner in which you sleep upstairs."[22] On the other hand, Jefferson enjoyed a penchant for entertaining, routinely welcoming dinner guests between three thirty and four o'clock in the afternoon, and where the conversation flowed as freely as the wine. And among his many contributions to the home, from adding north and south terrace-pavilions and drafting up landscaping plans, to furnishing the interior in Federal style, Jefferson kept with his fervent republicanism, opening the house every morning for public visitation, a tradition that has continued largely uninterrupted by his successors, except during pandemic and war.

At the home office, the president's general work attire and vibe was casual and humble by any account. One such guest, British diplomat Augustus Foster, recalled his introduction to Jefferson: "He is dressed and looks extremely like a very plain farmer, and wears his slippers down at his heels."[23] The third American president's aim was to eliminate class distinction at the mansion, despite the fact that three of his own slaves worked on the property.

The hub of the President's House for Jefferson was his private office located in the southwest corner of the residence, in what is today's State Dining Room. It was here he would routinely work "from 10 to 12 and 13 hours a day" at his writing table, giving himself "an interval of 4 hours for riding, dining and a little unbending."[24] A vivid 2008 painting by Peter Waddell, commissioned by the White House Historical Association, depicts Jefferson at work in this space with his private secretary, Meriwether Lewis, a US Army lieutenant who would later lead the Lewis and Clark Expedition. A favorite pastime of the two Albemarle County, Virginians, was to pore over arguably the most significant geographic map collection in North America.

As one of the few finished rooms in the mansion, Jefferson's office was adorned with fireplaces on the east and west ends, along with large south and west windows that brightened the space with natural light. Exemplifying the openness of the city, Jefferson could peer out from the south windows and across the vista to the Potomac River and Alexandria, Virginia. It was in this space where Jefferson cultivated his intellectual pursuits across varied endeavors, and even kept a mockingbird as a pet. Over a century and a half later, it was here where President Kennedy hosted a dinner honoring Nobel Prize Winners of the Western Hemisphere and famously quipped: "I think this is the most extraordinary collection of talent, of human knowledge, that has ever been gathered together at the White House, with the possible exception of when Thomas Jefferson dined alone."[25] And it was here, from his writing table, on Sunday, April 18, 1802, that Jefferson sat down, picked up his pen, and began writing one of the most important letters in the history of the nation, as well as one of his most famous clauses. To Robert Livingston, his fellow Founding Father and US minister to France, Jefferson began: "The cession of Louisiana & the Floridas by Spain to France works most sorely on the US. . . . It compleatly [sic] reverses all the political relations of the US and will form a new epoch in our political course. . . . There is on the globe one single spot, the possessor of which is our natural & habitual enemy. It is New Orleans . . . France placing herself in that door assumes to us the attitude of defiance."[26]

The Time and Place

As our next story begins in 1802, America was oscillating in a whirlwind of transformational change. Half a dozen years from Washington's Farewell, the torrents of the age, according to historian Henry Adams, produced the essence of an American: "Stripped for the hardest work, every muscle firm and elastic, every ounce of brain ready for use, and not a trace of superfluous flesh on his nervous and supple body, the American stood in the world a new order of man."[27] The age also produced a sustained, undeclared war at sea with France that consumed John Adams's presidency, cost millions of dollars in ship and cargo losses, and brought George Washington out of retirement to head the army for fear of a French invasion.

The age further saw two of the most consequential presidential elections in US history, those of 1796 and 1800—the last in a series of elections where each party nominated two candidates. The awkwardness of this short-lived tradition revealed itself in 1796, when Federalist John Adams won the presidency and his rival Democratic-Republican Thomas Jefferson, earning the second most electoral votes, served as vice president. The rematch in 1800 proved to be even more dysfunctional as Jefferson and his running mate Aaron Burr tied for the most electoral votes, with Adams and his running mate Charles Pinckney trailing, thus throwing the election to the US House of Representatives to break the stalemate. After nearly three dozen votes, and among calls for civil war, the "Revolution of 1800" was awarded to Jefferson, representing America's first peaceful exchange of power among *opposing* parties.

In the aftermath of the election and his presidential inauguration, Thomas Jefferson noted to Bay Stater Samuel Adams: "The storm is over, and we are in the port."[28] Yet despite the president's optimistic overtone, within weeks, another storm was emerging on the horizon. It involved another port of import, New Orleans, which was nothing less than the lynchpin of the "Louisiana Territory," a broad landscape stretching the heart of the American continent, from the Canadian border to the mouth of the Mississippi River and its western banks, to the Rocky Mountains.

The territory long held an intense interest of the Old World, first marked in 1581, when Spanish explorer Hernando de Soto engaged the Mississippi River, near what is now Memphis, Tennessee. A century later, in 1682, French explorer Robert Cavelier, Sieur de La Salle, set another marker at the mouth of the Mississippi basin, declaring the land "Louisiana" in honor of Louis XIV.[29]

As a nation looking westward, access to the port of New Orleans and navigation of the Mississippi River was essential to the future of US commerce and expansion. These American staples were formalized with the signing of the Treaty of Paris in 1783, ending the Revolutionary War, which set the Mississippi River as the US western boundary. A year later, in 1784, however, tensions mounted over the western and southern US borders, as Spain, who was ceded the Territory by France's Louis XV in 1763, closed the river to American shipping in an attempt to quell US trade and settlement across the greater frontier.

Spanish diplomat, Don Diego de Gardoqui arrived in Philadelphia in 1785, to negotiate with Secretary of Foreign Affairs John Jay, with instructions not to surrender Spain's claim to exclusive navigation of the river. Diplomatic discussions stalled leading Jay, in August 1786, to ask Congress to abandon navigation rights to the river for twenty or thirty-five years in exchange for the immediate benefits of a commercial treaty with Spain. The varied response to Jay's inquiry revealed a wide fissure among America's geographical regions, which endangered the stability of the nation. Virginian Patrick Henry represented the Southern viewpoint by reporting that he would rather "part with the confederation than to relinquish the navigation of the Mississippi."[30] Bellicose Westerners threatened to take arms to drive the Spanish from the territory, and the North contemplated its own confederacy. These converging passions spilled over into the Constitutional Convention of 1787, leading Southern delegates to seek a two-thirds vote of the Senate to ratify any treaty, especially any which attempted to cede navigation of the Mississippi River.

Over time, Spanish interest in the Louisiana Territory waned as a result of sustained warring in Europe, including from impacts over the French Revolution. Spanish King Charles IV also delegated political affairs to his prime minister, Manuel de Godoy, who was focused on restoring peace with France without antagonizing the British. Thus, a window opened for the US and Spain to come back to the negotiating table. President George Washington seized this opportunity and selected South Carolinian Thomas Pinckney, the US minister to Great Britain, to lead swift negotiations in Spain. The resulting Treaty of San Lorenzo, or "Pinckney's Treaty," signed on October 27, 1795, resolved ongoing territorial disputes, granted American ships freedom to navigate the Mississippi River and duty-free transport through the port of New Orleans, and served to advance western expansion, making the frontier more attractive and profitable. However, the treaty proved to be an ephemeral diplomatic success. In 1800, French leader Napoleon Bonaparte negotiated the secretive Treaty of San Ildefonso with Spain, ceding control of the Louisiana Territory. With that positioning, he intended to dominate the Caribbean and Gulf of Mexico with his naval power and control of the coastlines of present-day Florida, Louisiana, and parts of Mississippi.

Just three weeks into his presidential term, Thomas Jefferson received initial rumblings about the Treaty of San Ildefonso. If the reports were true, Jefferson remarked: "It works most sorely on the U.S."[31] As an ardent supporter of the French Revolution, viewing France as a *"natural friend,"*[32] Jefferson expressed to American philosopher Thomas Cooper: "I am willing to hope as long as any body will hope with me."[33] The president's half-glass full disposition was tested when the secret rumors were confirmed in February 1802, through a copy of the treaty sent to Washington by Rufus King, the chief US diplomat in Great Britain.[34] To makes matters worse, Robert Livingston warned US secretary of State James Madison in a March 14, 1802 letter, that the French viewed Louisiana as "one of the most fertile and important countries in the World" and that Napoleon envisioned the lands as "a mean to gratify his friends and to dispose his Armies."[35] As such, France's First Consul was prepared to imminently send upward of 7,000 troops from its Caribbean colony in Santo Domingo to occupy New Orleans, a port town representing only 8,000 inhabitants.

The Makings of Thomas Jefferson's Ingenuity

Born on April 13, 1743, in a plain wooden house on a central Virginia plantation named "Shadwell," Thomas Jefferson came of age at the foothills of the Blue Ridge Mountains. According to his biographer Dumas Malone: "No influence upon him was more abiding than that of Nature, and throughout life he deeply loved this region of wooded hills and lavender-tinted mountains."[36]

Another important influence on Jefferson was his father Peter, a successful farmer and surveyor who derived his American lineage to the Virginia Company in 1619. Peter Jefferson, like his son, stood apart from his peers as a man of great vigor and strength. A young Thomas owed much to him—from the opportunity and encouragement of an elite education, to the example of hard work and action, to the peace of mind of financial security, including a 5,000-acre inheritance upon his father's passing. He also inherited from his father the ability to wield power, the expectation to lead, and an understanding of how to shape and control the destiny of others, including those in bondage. And despite referring to slavery as a "moral and political depravity,"[37] the younger Jefferson would enslave more than 600 people over the course of his lifetime. His earliest memory was as a late toddler, being carried on a pillow by an enslaved person during his family's move from Shadwell to Tuckahoe. His untoward relationship with the institution has received significant attention by historians, including peeling back layers about the nature of his relationship with Sally Hemings, their children, and the damning dynamics of bondage and bloodlines.

The loss of his father at age fourteen left a huge void in young Thomas's life, especially for counsel, which he would seek through various forms of mentorship. From his mother Jane Randolph, he received a rich Virginia ancestry, an acute attention to detail, and the example of bravery in the face of tragedy, as she experienced not only the loss of a spouse, but of her own children. Overall, however, his maternal recollections are scant and uninspiring, with little mention in his written record, coupled with a 1770 fire at Shadwell that destroyed their shared correspondence. Collectively, from both his parents, he cultivated an affinity for nice things, which later translated into suffocating debt that outlived him.

Much like George Washington, Thomas was tall, measuring over six feet, two inches in height, which was a full six inches above average for the time. He possessed reddish hair and freckles, large hands and feet, was raw-boned, and could be gangly in movement. Yet he had great physical endurance and believed in regular exercise: "Not less than two hours a day,"[38] and according to an account from his grandson, he once swam laps in a millpond equating to over three miles.[39] Thomas also believed that his over a half-a-century daily morning habit of cold-water feet-bathing freed him from common colds and fevers. And while Jefferson described Washington as the best horseman of his age, he was certainly no slouch himself.

His countenance could reveal warmth and he was a rather optimistic soul, but particularly lacked in humor and was especially sphinxlike as described by historian Henry Adams: "Jefferson could be painted only touch by touch, with a fine pencil, and the perfection of the likeness depended upon the shifting and uncertain flicker of its semi-transparent shadow."[40] His biographer Merrill Peterson described Jefferson as "impenetrable,"[41] exemplified in the burning of the correspondence he shared with his wife, Martha, an effort to keep those memories private upon her death in 1782.

Jefferson did not suffer fools gladly, and he had a particular taste for women and wine. Consumed by detail and order, his biographer, Dumas Malone, referred to him as "one of the most systematic of men, he was in character as a cataloguer."[42] In a similar vein as George Washington, he made sure all information passed his desk before making a decision.

Jefferson's temperament could be thin-skinned, yet inherently polite, but often reserved, leaving John Adams to remark during the Continental Congress: "Mr. Jefferson had been now about a Year a Member of Congress, but had attended his Duty in the House but a very small part of the time and when there had never spoken in public: and during the whole Time I sat with him in Congress, I never heard him utter three Sentences together."[43] Conversely, in smaller settings, Jefferson was fond of telling stories, as John Quincy Adams recalled: "You never can be an hour in this man's company without something of the marvelous, like these stories."[44] His varied interests made him intrinsically interesting, earning deep affection and reverence from friends. But he also had the propensity to elicit deep enmity from his foes, such as Alexander Hamilton, and often kept things light to avoid interpersonal conflict.

Jefferson's discipline was extraordinary and self-imposed, and it shaped his unyielding study habits and educational pursuits. He was known to study fifteen hours a day during college and his ability to retain detailed information was otherworldly.[45] According to historian Gordon Wood: Jefferson "had the most spacious and encyclopedic mind of any of his fellow Americans, including Benjamin Franklin."[46] Even during respites from school, the majority of his time was spent reading books, and he relished in asking questions. He would later advise his children and grandchildren through his "Canons of Conduct" about his disdain for indolence, putting at the top of the list: "Never put off to tomorrow what you can do to-day."[47] Further, he once advised his daughter Patsy: "It is wonderful how much may be done, if you are always doing."[48]

It was this spirit that defined Thomas Jefferson's life and his pursuit of knowledge. At age five, his father placed Thomas at an English school with private tutors and in a Latin School at age nine, where he learned Greek, Latin, and French. Beginning at age fourteen, he learned from a classical scholar for two years, and cultivated a love for science "and the system of things for which we are placed."[49] He then turned his study to the law, which later placed him at the bar of the General Court and as a member of the Virginia legislature. He would additionally nourish a passion for history across his lifetime, especially in how it provided lessons to help shape future decisions.

Two of his sisters, Jane and Martha, encouraged his educational ambitions, especially his reading, as well as his love for music, which he would declare as his "favorite passion of the soul."[50] Yet, the greatest return on his learned investment was the incredible ingenuity he engendered to inspire a long trail of unrivaled accomplishments.

Jefferson's architectural prowess led to the design and building of his home Monticello, or "Little Mountain," at the summit of a hill he explored as a child. Describing the home as "my essay in Architecture,"[51] his ingenuity is weaved throughout, including disappearing beds, folding doors, and a clock that continued to run by a series of pulleys and weights, among other things. He was recognized in 1772, when Virginia governor, Lord Dunmore, asked him to design an addition to "the College," currently the "Wren Building" at his alma mater, William & Mary.[52] This work later inspired Jefferson in the design of buildings and grounds for the University of Virginia, which he founded in 1819.

As an inventor, he developed a Moldboard Plow to move through the soil as efficiently as possible, and for which he espoused that his ag-tech design was "mathematically demonstrated to be perfect."[53] As George Washington's secretary of state, he created a wheel cipher aimed as a secure method to encode and decode diplomatic messages to avoid European postmasters from opening and reading sensitive correspondence. He further sought to improve items already in existence, like the copying machine for correspondence, and he relished in the discoveries of others, incorporating these innovations into his daily routine. In particular, he described Eli Whitney, the inventor of the cotton gin as "a mechanic of the first order of ingenuity."[54]

As a scientist, Jefferson explored fields from agronomy and archeology, to meteorology and botany. He delighted in tracking weather patterns and daily temperatures to better understand Virginia's climate, developing standards for handling archeological sites, and in growing plants he procured from travels abroad. As an influencer, he popularized staples of modern American fare, from ice cream and macaroni and cheese, to "pommes de terre frites à cru en petites tranches," or French fries, a recipe he brought back from France.

Leaning into his philosopher roots, he joined the American Philosophical Society in 1780, and would later serve as its president for nearly two decades, calling the invitation to serve the most "flattering incident of his life."[55] His philosophical battles with Alexander Hamilton influenced the creation of the American two-party system and the launch of competing visions for the nation that continue to drive US politics today. When he ran for president in 1796, it was said that he was better qualified to be a college professor than president of the United States. Rather, his biographer Jon Meacham argued that his genius was an "Art of Power," which combined how "philosophers think" and how "politicians maneuver . . . often simultaneously."[56] Accordingly, Jefferson was appreciably taken by the Enlightenment and its best-days-lie-ahead school of thought that dated a century and had ties to Sir Isaac Newton. All said, with the possible exception of Benjamin Franklin, another Enlightenment practitioner, no American Founding Father had such a remarkable footprint across so many fields of thought. Exemplified by his biographer James Parton: Jefferson "could calculate an eclipse, survey an estate, tie an artery, plan an edifice, try a cause, break a horse, dance a minuet, and play the violin."[57]

A Renaissance man by any measure, Jefferson "knew more about more things than any other American,"[58] believing: "Variety relieves the mind, as well as the eye, palled with too long attention to a single subject."[59] This ideal of the Enlightenment and its inherent ingenuity served as the essence of his exceptionality and his penchant to tinker and improve all he touched. However, in particular, it was the ingenuity of his pen that defined his early career and gave posterity some of the most significant contributions to the dawning of America. In 1774, we see it in his clever work, "Summary View of the Rights of British America," where he reminded King George III that "he is no more than the chief officer of the people, appointed by the laws, and circumscribed with definite powers, to assist in working the great machine of government."[60] We see it two years later as a member of the Second Continental Congress, when chosen to draft the Declaration of Independence. With the poetry and potency of his pen from a Philadelphia boarding room, he offered an imperfect but enduring "expression of the American mind,"[61] laying out the colonies' case for American independence and liberty:

> When in the Course of human events, it becomes necessary for one people to dissolve the political bands which have connected them with another, and to assume among the powers of the earth, the separate and equal station to which the Laws of Nature and of Nature's God entitle them, a decent respect to the opinions of mankind requires that they should declare the causes which impel them to the separation. We hold these truths to be self-evident, that all men are created equal, that they are endowed by their Creator with certain unalienable Rights, that among these are Life, Liberty and the pursuit of Happiness.[62]

Later that same year, when serving in the Virginia legislature, he took the lead in drafting the "Virginia Statute for Religious Freedom," a treatise about the separation of church and state. Although a decade of legislative battles would pass before the law was enacted, it would go on to serve as a forerunner in the development of American religious freedom and its protections in the First Amendment of the US Constitution. Of the three inscribed on his epitaph, these latter two accomplishments were "as testimonials that I have lived, I wish most to be remembered."[63]

> Here was buried
> Thomas Jefferson
> Author of the Declaration of American Independence
> of the Statute of Virginia for religious freedom
> & Father of the University of Virginia[64]

Of note, Jefferson did not highlight his service as governor of Virginia, nor the book he authored, *Notes on the State of Virginia*. He did not note his international experience as a trade commissioner and then US minister to France, or as the first US secretary of State. Nor did he note the two highest offices in the land for which he served, US vice president and US president. Rather, those he elevated, including the founding of the University of Virginia, speak to the great causes of his life and his great love of liberty, faith, and the future. Still, despite his effort to define how history remembered him, there is one particularly glaring omission to his list, representing another transformational act of his pen, which forever changed the trajectory of America.

The Roadmap

"There is on the globe one single spot, the possessor of which is our natural & habitual enemy,"[65] noted Jefferson in his cornerstone April 18, 1802 letter to Robert Livingston. The port of New Orleans served as the epicenter of America's territorial crisis with France, and despite his long-standing esteem for the French, Jefferson was firm in his view that "The Big Easy" could never be in the hands of France: "The impetuosity of her temper, the energy & restlessness of her character, placed in a point of eternal friction with us. . . . These circumstances render it impossible that France and the US can continue long friends when they meet in so irritable a position."[66]

Spain, in its "feeble state"[67] was one thing in America's backyard, and, as such, Jefferson felt little pressure to assert sovereignty. But an emboldened and revolutionary France was another: "It completely reverses all the political relations of the U.S. and will form a new epoch in our political course."[68] The president was clear-eyed about the potential military danger the French posed in controlling navigation of the Mississippi River, and about the score, with three-eighths of the Louisiana Territory's produce passing into market through the port of New Orleans: "From its fertility it will ere long yield more than half of our whole produce and contain more than half our inhabitants."[69] He also recognized that the river didn't serve to divide the continent, but rather, brought it together, and that for many Americans the Mississippi was everything.

In a November 27, 1802 letter to US Minister to Spain Charles Pinckney, US Secretary of State James Madison explained the anchor river's significance: "It is the Hudson, the Delaware, the Potomac, and all the navigable rivers of the Atlantic States, formed into one stream."[70] In fact, Madison had been advocating for freedom to navigate the Mississippi River going back as early as 1780, before American independence was realized. In a October 17, 1780 congressional letter to America's Minister to Madrid John Jay, Madison insisted "on the navigation of the Mississippi for the Citizens of the United States" as it tended to the "prosperity and advantage" of America, and that "Spain being in possession of the banks of both sides" nearest New Orleans "cannot be deemed a natural or equitable bar to the free use of the river."[71] And taking the lead from his boss, it was Madison's first order of business as US secretary of state. As President Jefferson noted, it would be "improvident"[72] if the American administration did not shift the paradigm and make arrangements to confront this uncertain future.

The stakes for Jefferson and his administration could not have been any higher. The existential threat posed by France elevated to heights unseen in America since the Revolution, especially with a strident US Congress and free press calling for militaristic action. Projecting confidence about a potential showdown with France, Jefferson expressed to Livingston: "For however greater her force is than ours compared in the abstract, it is nothing in comparison of ours when to be exerted on our soil."[73] Jefferson fully believed that the French would encounter similar difficulties as the British during the Revolutionary War, particularly related to substantial geographic coverage. And, in the event this didn't give the French pause, there was always the possibility of rekindling an old alliance. As Jefferson conveyed to Livingston: "The Day that France takes possession of N. Orleans . . . we must marry ourselves to the British fleet & nation,"[74] and "We must turn all our attentions to a maritime force, for which our resources place us on very high ground."[75] Shifting allegiance from Paris to London was no small diplomatic leap for Jefferson. A longtime Francophile, Jefferson had returned twelve years earlier after serving a five-year tour as the US minister to France. This was also the same Jefferson that, joined by his followers, bludgeoned George Washington in the partisan press over the Jay Treaty's pro-British leaning. In the case of Louisiana, and the fact that as president "the buck stops here,"[76] as Harry Truman noted, Jefferson's ability to adapt (and maybe to bluff) to determine what was needed to maximize his negotiating power demonstrated realpolitik, including his ability to be pragmatic when required.

Becoming in many ways his own secretary of state, Jefferson encouraged Livingston to see what could be done about "ceding to us the island of New Orleans and the Floridas," as "this would certainly in a great degree remove the causes of jarring & irritation between us."[77] The president was prepared to offer $6 million to close the deal, along with the considerable concession that the French would possess the Louisiana Territory west of the Mississippi. In addition to his pivotal instructions to Livingston, Jefferson also posited a back-channel diplomatic strategy, eliciting the help of his longtime friend, French aristocrat Samuel Du Pont de Nemours, who the president had "unlimited confidence in."[78] It was Du Pont who informally advised Jefferson of the cardinal rule for negotiating with Napoleon—neither offend nor threaten him—while also advising him that the thought of purchasing Louisiana is a "salutary and acceptable thought."[79] And it was Du Pont who would hand-deliver the consequential April 18 letter across the ocean to Livingston, with his own added charge to work discretely to "impress on the government of France the inevitable consequences of their taking possession of Louisiana."[80]

In his May 25 correspondence to Du Pont, Jefferson further impressed on the Frenchmen: "This little event, of France possessing herself of Louisiana . . . which now appears as an invisible point in the horizon, is the embryo of a tornado which will burst on the countries on both shores of the Atlantic and involve in its effects their highest destinies. That it may yet be avoided is my sincere prayer, and if you can be the means of informing the wisdom of Buonaparte of all its consequences, you will have deserved well of both countries."[81]

Never one to sit still, the months that passed had to be tortuous for Jefferson as he waited patiently for progress. Livingston didn't confirm receipt of Jefferson's charge until writing to Madison on July 30, where the US minister noted his efforts to prepare "a lengthy memoir on the subject . . . relative to Louisiana," in which he "hoped" to convince France of how disadvantageous it would be for them to possess the land from a commercial and political perspective.[82] He believed "all that can be done" would be "to endeavor to obtain a cession of New Orleans either by purchase or by offering to make it a port of entry to France on such terms as shall promise advantages to her commerce."[83]

In early August, Livingston held "several conferences on the subject of Louisiana" but could not get anything more from the French than what he had "already communicated."[84] On August 31, he approached French Minister of Foreign Affairs Charles Maurice de Talleyrand-Perigord and "made several propositions,"[85] but Talleyrand informed him "that every offer was premature" because the "French Government had determined to take possession first—so that you must consider the business as absolutely determined on."[86] Jefferson begrudgingly echoed Tallyrand's sentiment in a letter to Albert Gallatin: "That Louisiana is to be possessed by France is probable."[87]

After of month of essentially banging his head against the wall, Livingston expressed his frustration to Madison on September 1: "There never was a government in which less could be done by negotiation than here. . . . There is no people, no legislature, no counselors . . . one man is everything."[88] "There is but one will and that will governed by no object but personal security and personal ambition."[89] Everything in Paris went through Napoleon, and according to Livingston, the First Consul seldom asked for advice and never heard it unasked. In the case of Louisiana, Napoleon's advisers conveyed that they were against the French expedition, according to Livingston, but "no one dares to tell him so."[90] "You can hardly conceive anything more timid than all about him are. . . . They dare not be known to have a sentiment of their own or to have expressed on to anybody."[91]

A silver lining in Livingston's sustained engagement was his congealed view that "it will not be long" before there was a serious conflict between Britain and France. "Good may arise out of this evil if it shd. happen,"[92] Livingston expressed to Madison. And while that would soon prove important, that didn't stop Jefferson from beginning to privately question Livingston's strategy to Madison: "I am not satisfied that the ground taken by Chancellor Livingston is advantageous."[93] It probably didn't help that Jefferson's backchannel to Du Pont revealed the week prior: "Our negotiations have not been as successful as I would have wished. However, I am far from believing them in as bad a place as Chancellor

Livingston appears to think, who is irritated at not receiving positive replies in writing, since the verbal ones are good."[94]

Undeterred, Livingston continued to press the French on Louisiana, noting in a letter to Jefferson on October 28 that he had met with Napoleon's brother, Joseph Bonaparte, and expressed America's security interest in the Mississippi, and "not the extention of territory."[95] In the midst of a seemingly fruitless fall, on top of an ineffectual summer, Livingston reported to Madison on November 2: "Nothing very important relative to our affairs having intervened for Some time past I have not thought necessary to trouble you."[96]

However, contrary to what he conveyed to Madison, and despite both his and Du Pont's best efforts across the summer and fall of 1802, something important had changed. America's relationship with France became even more strained. As Jefferson wrote to Livingston on October 10: "It appears evident that an unfriendly spirit prevails in the most important individuals of the government towards us."[97] In relation to the Anglo-French conflict, the president instructed Livingston to remain "disengaged till necessity compels us," and to be "independent . . . ask not favors," ensure "peace . . . the most important of all things to us," and "expect preserving an erect & independent attitude."[98] Despite these measures, Livingston noted to Madison on November 10: "France has cut the knot," as orders had been given to send "two demi brigades" of French troops from Holland to Louisiana. "No prudence will I fear prevent hostilities," according to Livingston, and thus implored on Madison the "necessity of strengthening ourselves as soon as possible both by forces and ships at home and by alliance abroad."[99] Livingston also raised concern over France's "solicitude to acquire wealth," citing the "tyranny of St. Domingo."[100] And even if he had "small hopes" from his earlier Joseph Bonaparte demarche, at this stage Livingston believed "they are of no avail now that the exhibition is determined on."[101]

To make matters worse, in January 1803, Jefferson received word that America was again denied freedom to ship goods originating in US ports through the mouth of the Mississippi duty free and with the right of deposit. This action came despite assurances by Napoleon weeks earlier that America's treaties with Spain should be "Strictly observed," and his "intention to cultivate our friendship & by no means to do anything that would endanger it."[102] The new year also did nothing to change the negotiating dynamic on Louisiana, with Livingston reporting on January

24 that Napoleon was still "immovable."[103] This "attitude of defiance"[104] and infringement on American access of New Orleans by Spain was a clear red line for Jefferson, which harkened back to their 1784 hostile action. The president aptly confirmed the American reaction to Livingston on February 3: "A late suspension by the Intendant of N. Orleans . . . has thrown this country into such a flame of hostile disposition as can scarcely be described."[105]

Hawkish protests ensued on the American home front, inflamed by what was perceived to be Jefferson's measured approach to the broader Louisiana crisis. Taking matters into their own hands, the Kentucky legislature passed a memorial addressed to Jefferson and the US Congress, which was presented to the House of Representatives on January 28, pledging their support "at the expense of our lives and fortunes, such measures of honor, and interest of the United States may require."[106] This fervor would only amplify, as Madison noted to Livingston: "There is now or in two years will be, not less than 200,000 Militia on the waters of the Mississpi, every man of whom would march at a Minutes warning to remove obstructions from that outlet to the Sea, every man of whom regards the free use of that river as a natural & indefeasible right, and is conscious of the physical force that can at any time give effect to it."[107] Madison also made clear that these American passions "ought not be overlooked by France."[108]

With demands for militia call-ups and pressure to take New Orleans by force, time was of the essence for Jefferson. Channeling firsthand lessons in declaring American independence, as well as his extensive and unrivaled experience as US minister to France and US secretary of State, Jefferson knew he needed to balance the diplomatic narrative abroad while influencing public opinion at home. Shifting the dynamic to get at the core of the central issue, Jefferson posited: how best to amicably persuade France to sell the Louisiana Territory? As much as he wanted to, he couldn't travel to France. Rather, he reached into his playbook for the next best thing. After consulting with Madison, he called on fellow Virginian, and protégé, James Monroe, the Governor of "The Old Dominion" state, and former US ambassador to France, to serve as his presidential envoy. In a hastily written offer letter to Monroe on January 10, 1803, Jefferson noted: "The Western mind is thrown by the affair at N. Orleans. . . . In this situation we are obliged to call on you for a temporary sacrifice of yourself, to prevent the greatest of evils in the present prosperous tide of our affairs. I shall nominate you to the Senate for an extraordinary mission to France, & the circumstances are such as to render it impossible to decline; because the whole public hope will be rested on you."[109]

Monroe didn't bite at first, but catching wind of his hesitancy, Jefferson essentially ordered Monroe to take on the assignment. Two days later, on January 12, the president continued to push ahead, establishing a Commission for Monroe and Livingston: "With full power and authority" to negotiate a treaty with France "concerning the enlargement and more effectual security of the rights and interests of the United States in the River Mississippi and in the Territories Eastward thereof."[110] Following up with Monroe on January 13, Jefferson explained the diplomatic landscape and the assignment in more detail: "The agitation of the public mind on occasion of the late suspension of our right of deposit at N. Orleans is extreme."[111] Therefore, according to Jefferson: "It was essential to send a Minister extraordinary . . . and were you to refuse to go, no other man can be found who does this . . . for on the event of this mission depends the future destinies of this republic."[112] As "the moment in France is critical," Jefferson implored Monroe to depart as soon as possible and to arrange his "affairs for an absence of a year at least."[113]

Madison shared the news with Livingston, noting "the importance of the crisis" to President Jefferson and the "weight he attached to such a measure."[114] He affirmed that Monroe would "be the bearer of the instructions by which they would negotiate in Paris: "to procure a cession of New Orleans and the Floridas," establish "the Mississippi as the boundary between the United States and Louisiana,"[115] and enlarge "our rights and our security in the Southwestern neighborhood of the United States."[116] And he made clear that the sum of any agreement, which the president was describing in consultation with Congress at the time as anywhere between ten and thirty million livres, would be set before Monroe sailed in two weeks, and that the "ultimatum" would be communicated by Monroe.[117]

To his credit, Livingston conveyed positivity in his reply back to Madison: "I Shall do every thing in my power to pave the way for him, & Sincerely wish his mission may be attended with the desired effect."[118] But he was only human, revealing to Madison that he wished his fellow citizens should not be led to believe from Monroe's appointment that he "had been negligent of their interests, or too delicate on any of the great points"[119] entrusted to his care. At his core, Livingston believed his efforts and communications revealed that he had gone "as far as it was possible" for him to go and "perhaps farther" than his "instructions would justify."[120] He made clear to Madison that he had "been indefatigable"[121] in his efforts to press "the Government on the subject of Louisiana,"[122] including to engage with "every body that will probably be consulted on the Subject"[123] or "with whom the consul should advise friendly to our views."[124] He did so because "our situation was such as to require something decisive,"[125] and all within "a bustle" of not knowing whether there would be "War or Peace."[126] He also conveyed one downside to Monroe's engagement. It would take Monroe "Some time" to inspire the confidences that Livingston had established and "which I must now relinquish."[127] In that light, given the material change in diplomatic direction that would come with Monroe's imminent arrival, along with a lack of tangible progress to date, it's hard not to think that when Livingston spoke of decisive action, he meant it as much for himself as he did for American diplomacy.

On the home front, the president's action to send Monroe to Paris didn't do much to quell the hawks in Congress, but it did tamp down critics calling for Jefferson to take action. It was within this context that Jefferson wrote to Livingston with a heightened sense of urgency on February 3: "We must know at once whether we can acquire N. Orleans or not. We are satisfied nothing else will secure us against a war at no distant period: and we cannot pass this season without beginning those arrangements which will be necessary if war is hereafter to result."[128]

It was not only under the threat of war that Monroe set to depart for France on March 7, but also inclement weather: "We are now detained by a snow storm and contrary wind, but shall sail as soon as it clears up, & the wind shifts."[129] With the short weather delay, Monroe penned a letter to Jefferson anticipating his important work: "I hope the French govt. will have wisdom enough to see that we will never suffer France or any other power to tamper with our interior; if that is not the object there can be no reason for declining an accommodation to the whole of our demands."[130] With the shifting wind, Monroe's ship departed at 9 a.m. Across the ocean, so too were the fates shifting, as Livingston was on the cusp of a breakthrough in Paris, which he expressed to Jefferson as "gaining ground here for sometime past."[131]

What Livingston didn't report to Washington until May 1803, were his proposals to the French through Napoleon's brother Joseph Bonaparte. Understanding working solely through the French Ministry would limit his options, Livingston sought to open "some other channel of communication with the First Consul than thro the minister."[132] His inspired approach allowed him to get "several unofficial communications"[133] under Napoleon's eye "in an informal way"[134] and "learn his sentiment thereon."[135]

It was also preferable to a "direct address," which was deemed by other French Ministers as "improper," and would "likely offend" Tallyrand, "if not the Consul."[136]

Livingston's preferred approach also presented him the opportunity to meet with Napoleon, but he chose not to for two reasons. First, he didn't have instructions from Washington on "what to offer" and he didn't just want to meet to "talk of [the] justice" and "rights on the Mississippi" as they "would only to Say ingracious truths, & excite prejudices which might may render a future conference more difficult."[137] Second, Livingston understood one of Napoleon's character traits was that he could be immovable: "Once fully avowed a sentiment," he was "not easily [to] change it."[138] Therefore, Livingston took the tact of addressing himself "unofficially to the man who is supposed to have any sort of influence" over Napoleon. Accordingly, he proceeded to put into Joseph Bonaparte's hands "some notes containing very plain truth,"[139] particularly "to Shew how little advantage France is like to make from these Colonies," and "the importance of a friendly intercourse between them & us."[140] Livingston was also not above hinting at "that species of personal attention which I know to be most pleasing here;"[141] or put another way, the French penchant for bribes.

Specific to the Bonaparte backchannel and related Louisiana proposals, Livingston's first overture aimed at giving Napoleon title to New Orleans and the Floridas, and a future home away from Europe in exchange for ten million livres and the United States' right to administer the territory. The second proposal had the United States acquiring New Orleans, West Florida, and all of Louisiana north of the Arkansas River with France retaining lower Louisiana, and both nations sharing navigation of the Mississippi River.[142] Livingston also "hinted at making the Island of New Orleans an independent State under the government of Spain, France, & the United States with a right to depot to each,"[143] especially highlighting the benefits France "would derive . . . as being the only manufacturing Nation of the three."[144]

When Livingston engaged in more traditional diplomacy with Tallyrand, he leaned into American "News paper intelligence,"[145] highlighting growing angst over the right of navigation on the Mississippi River. He impressed on the French minister American resolve on the issue, to never "Suffer our rights on the Mississipi [sic],"[146] and urged France to continue America's right to deposit at New Orleans after taking possession of Louisiana, intimating that it was unpreventable for people in the region to take matters into their own hands.¹⁴⁷ To this end, he implored the inevitable war between France and Native Americans, as well as the "benefits that would result . . . from a friendly connection with us."¹⁴⁸ And because Louisiana was "a very favorite subject" in France, with books "published representing it as a Paradise," Livingston took pains to dispel "the mania."¹⁴⁹ Livingston's collective case "Seemed to make an impression" on Tallyrand, who "promised to represent them Strongly" to Napoleon.¹⁵⁰ And after a "letter & essays" that were "attentively read" by Napoleon, as well as "several informal Notes" to Joseph Bonaparte, Livingston "had reason to think" that they influenced Napoleon, as he was beginning "to waver."¹⁵¹

However, it was the intelligence he received from a drawing room gathering in Paris hosted by Josephine Bonaparte that fundamentally shifted the playing field. As was custom, Josephine entered the room first, followed by Napoleon, with the two initiating conversation with the ladies first and then with the men. "After the first Consul had gone the circuit of one room," Livingston wrote to Jefferson, Napoleon "turned to me & made some of the common enquiries usual on these occasions."¹⁵² Moments later, the French leader approached British diplomat, Lord Withworth with some initial cordiality, and then exclaimed: "I find Milord your nation want war again. . . . *I must either have Malta or war*."¹⁵³ Despite Lord Withworth's wish for peace, Napoleon hastily withdrew to his cabinet, leaving the diplomatic corps in a tizzy. This scene only confirmed Livingston's strong views that "Sentiments of the two nations with respect to each other have totally changed from what they were a year ago"¹⁵⁴ and of "a war not very distant,"¹⁵⁵ "since it is hardly possible that the first Consul would commit himself so publickly unless his determination had been taken."¹⁵⁶ America's top diplomat in Paris initially feared "that this may again throw some impediment in the way of our claims which I believed in so prosperous a train."¹⁵⁷ But sensing the opportunity, he took on a more optimistic footing as the Anglo-French conflict amplified the possibility that France might prefer to downsize its North American footprint and its accompanying expenses and troubles.

Jefferson wasn't privy to Livingston's March 12 intelligence when he wrote to Madison on March 19. Expressing his growing concern with the pace of negotiations, Jefferson told Madison: "I hope the game Mr. Livingston says he is playing is a candid & honourable one. . . . An American contending by stratagem against those exercised in it from their cradle would undoubtedly be outwitted by them."¹⁵⁸ Granted, Livingston was relatively inexperienced as a diplomat compared to Jefferson, but he more than made up for it with an inherent confidence that delivered time-in-and-time-out when it mattered. He served with Jefferson on the committee to draft the Declaration of Independence. As chancellor of New York, he provided the presidential oath of office to George Washington. And what Jefferson and Madison were not privy to were his sustained and deft efforts to close a historic deal that would define America's future for generations.

Yet, as in life in general, serendipitous events played a significant role in supporting Livingston's work. One of particular importance was initiated in June 1801, when Jefferson met at the President's House with Louis Andre Pichon, charge d'affaires of the French Republic. It was not uncommon for Jefferson to take such an appointment, as he believed that providing access to his office was important, and that bridging "the last three feet," as journalist Edward R. Murrow described, was a crucial link in international exchange and policy making.

Seeking to curry and secure Jefferson's friendship, Pichon asked the president about US policy toward Santo Domingo (now part of the Dominican Republic), an area the French sought to restore control over after a slave rebellion led by Toussaint L'Ouverture fueled a revolutionary movement. In a reversal of the John Adams administration, who sent L'Ouverture food and ammo to defeat an invading British army, Jefferson, in an overture to the French replied to Pichon: "Nothing would be easier than to supply everything for your army and navy, and to starve out Toussaint."[159]

The French sprang into action in December 1801. Napoleon, anticipating the operation taking no more than six weeks to complete, believed the French expeditionary force would soon be off to New Orleans, to advance his master plan to fully reestablish the Republic of France's presence in the Western Hemisphere. This potentiality was front of mind for Jefferson for some time. He referenced it in his pivotal letter to Livingston in April 1802, noting France's intention "to proceed to Louisiana after finishing their work in that island."[160] However, Jefferson saw this incursion much differently than Napoleon. He knew it would not be short work for the French to wear down the island, especially with the emergence of L'Ouverture as the leader of some 400 thousand ex-slaves. And he was right. The French expeditionary force lost over sixty thousand troops from the fighting, as well as from the adjoining spread of yellow fever, which took the life of Napoleon's brother-in-law, Charles Leclerc, who led the expedition. Writing to Napoleon shortly before his death,

Leclerc noted: "This colony is lost and you will never regain it. . . . My letter will surprise you but what general could calculate on the mortality of four-fifths of his army."[161]

The bloodletting in Santo Domingo was a game changer and quickly made Napoleon a realist. On Easter Sunday, April 10, 1803, Napoleon, at his Chateau de Saint-Cloud residence, informed his minister of Finance, François de Barbé-Marbois, that he planned to cede the Louisiana Territory to the United States. "I can scarcely say that I cede it to them . . . they only ask of me one town in Louisiana; but I already consider the colony entirely lost."[162]

France was unlikely to maintain a colony on the American continent, especially when it required "a great deal of money for this war [with England]."[163] As a student of geopolitics, Napoleon also understood how a growing United States might serve as a counterweight to England: "I have just given to England a maritime rival that will sooner or later humble her pride,"[164] Napoleon exclaimed. He was also aware of the sentiment in London papers at the time about the British "proposition for 50,000 men to take New Orleans."[165] Rather for Napoleon: "It appears to me that in the hands of this growing Power it will be more useful to the policy, and even to the commerce of France than if I should attempt to keep it."[166]

This was no easy decision. Napoleon made it "with the greatest regret." As Livingston would note in a May 12, 1803, letter to Madison: "Among the most favorite projects of the first Consul was the Colonization of Louisiana." The French leader saw the land as "A new Egypt . . . a Colony that was to counterbalance the Eastern establishments of Britain," and one that included a "provision for his Generals" and importantly, "a pretense for the ostracism of Suspected enemies."[167]

Napoleon closed his April 10 conversation with Marbois by asking him to keep his negotiating redline under the strictest confidence: "I want fifty millions, and for less than that sum I will not treat; I would rather make a desperate attempt to keep these free countries."[168] In follow-up on April 11, Napoleon confirmed to Marbois: "It is not only New Orleans that I cede; it is the whole colony without any reservation. Do not even await the arrival of Mr. Monroe; have an interview this very day with Mr. Livingston."[169]

Interestingly, it would be Talleyrand, as opposed to Marbois, who first approached Livingston on April 11, "pressing the subject, whether we wished to have the whole of Louisiana" and as to "what we would give for the whole."[170] Given Napoleon's wishes, the French were not inclined to concede just New Orleans and the Floridas as Livingston had requested because "the rest would be of little value."[171] Sensing the significance of the moment as he had in so many other important settings across his life, Livingston quickly responded to Talleyrand that if the "policy of France however should dictate to give us the Country above the River Arkansa [sic] in order to place a barrier between them & Canada,"[172] he would be so inclined. To be clear, no one foresaw the scope of Napoleon's action. The fact that the First Consul would be willing to sell all of the Louisiana Territory truly had not even been considered. Thus, the key negotiation question before Livingston was "whether to treat for the whole, or jeopardize, if not abandon the hope of acquiring any part."[173] Playing coy, as to Talleyrand's question concerning price, Livingston responded: "It was a subject I had not thought."[174] Livingston also sought to convince Tallyrand that Louisiana was "worth little."[175] The French minister then pressed his counterpart to "reflect on it and tell him to morrow."[176]

Livingston, however, noted that after twenty-nine days at sea, James Monroe "would be in Town in two days," and as such, would like to "delay my further offer until I had the pleasure of introducing him."[177] But Livingston also was not blind to the moment's magnitude, knowing America needed to act before Napoleon got cold feet. He endeavored "to impress the [US] government that not a moment should be lost,"[178] especially "from every appearance that war was very near at hand" between France and England. He also dabbled in some gamesmanship, informing Tallyrand that he was unaware of what instructions Monroe would deliver, but considering "the little progress" he had made, "his Government" would consider him "as a very indolent negotiator" and would "require a precise & prompt notice" for him, and stronger negotiating terms in relation to France. Although Tallyrand laughed and told Livingston that he would give him a certificate stating that he "was the most importunate he had yet met with,"[179] Monroe's arrival added urgency for the French.

Napoleon's seemingly rash decision did not sit well with those close to him who would not "hear of disposing it [Louisiana] by sale."[180] In particular, his two brothers were despondent and interrupted him soaking in his cologne-scented bath to share their displeasure. Undeterred, Napoleon shot back: "You will have no need to lead the opposition for I repeat there will be no debate, for the reason that the project . . . conceived by me, negotiated by me, shall be ratified and executed by me, alone. Do you comprehend me?"[181]

To advance Napoleon's prerogative, on April 12, Marbois unexpectedly showed up meandering through Livingston's garden during a dinner the US diplomat was throwing in recognition of Monroe's arrival. Two days earlier, Livingston had stopped by Marbois's house but the minister was out of town. The French minister thought Livingston "might have Something particular to Say to him" and had "taken the first opportunity" to call of him."[182] He further asked Livingston to discretely meet him later that evening, a scenario Livingston described to Madison as "Something So extraordinary."[183] After "Mr. Munroe took leave" after dinner, Livingston followed Marbois to the treasury office to "press this matter further."[184]

Marbois started by asking Livingston to repeat what he had said "relative to Mr. Tallyrand requesting a proposition from me as to the purchase of Louisiana."[185] As Livingston recapped this conversation, he also affirmed how the "United States was anxious to preserve peace with France, that for that reason they wished to remove them to the West Side of the Mississipi, that we would be perfectly Satisfied with New Orleans & the Floridas."[186] He also bluffed Marbois by stating, "The consequence of any delay on this Subject . . . would enable Britain to take possession—who would readily relinquish it to us,"[187] as America might decide it was "prudent to throw us into her scale"[188] if war broke out between France and England. One can assume Livingston knew Napoleon, or at the very least, Marbois was keeping up with Britain's proposition about sending troops to New Orleans and was adding another bargaining play to the table. Also, as Livingston told Madison, with Marbois reaching out to him and not Tallyrand, Napoleon "was disposed to sell" and that the First Consul distrusted Tallyrand's intent to bribe and therefore sought to "put the negotiation in the hands of Marbois whose character for integrity is established."[189]

Marbois conveyed Napoleon's ask of "one hundred and twenty-five millions [francs]" or approximately $22 million for the deal—which from a negotiating standpoint, more than doubled Napoleon's confidential redline. Livingston responded that America "would not give any great Sum for the purchase . . . and had no Sort of authority to go up to a Sum that bore any proportion of what he mentioned."[190] However, Livingston noted: "We would be ready to purchase provided the Sum was reduced to reasonable limit."[191] Marbois pushed back, pressing Livingston "to name the Sum."[192]

Livingston then told Marbois that a price that high "would render the present Government unpopular, & have a tendency at the next election to throw the power into the hands of men who were most hostile to a connection with France."[193] In other words, the French-leaning Jefferson administration would be out, giving way to the Federalists, a more British-leaning administration. Marbois countered by asking Livingston to state a "Sum that came near the mark that could be accepted," and on the occasion, he "would communicate it to the First Consul."[194] Marbois also acutely played into Livingston's deep-seated concern with regard to striking while the iron was hot when it came to Napoleon. "You know the temper of a youthful conqueror—everything he does is rapid as lightning,"[195] Marbois noted. Consequently, there were only so many windows to connect with Napoleon in private, as engaging with him in a crowd is of little benefit "when he bears no contradiction."[196]

The negotiations continued until midnight with Livingston taking up his pen at 3 a.m. on the thirteenth to share the fortuitous news: "The field opened to us is infinitely larger than our instructions contemplated,"[197] he wrote to Madison. Yet, he was also concerned about the asking price, conveying to his boss: "We shall do all we can to cheapen the purchase; but my present sentiment is that we shall buy."[198] And with Napoleon leaving for Brussels in a few days, "every moment is precious."[199]

Updating Jefferson the next day, April 14, Livingston expressed a sense of awe: "When I cast my eye upon the Map, and consider the vast and rich Country that lays before us, when I look forward one hundred years & see that Country improved & settled by Millions" who will be "enlisted under our banners as we now decide."[200] He also foreshadowed the legacy of the Jefferson administration as it "will be distinguished, by the acquisition of a territory not less valuable to us than half the United States—That we shall be freed from European controversies, & that we shall rest in the physical impossibility of having an enemy at our doors."[201]

On April 15, Livingston met with Marbois to offer "forty [million francs or approximately $8 million]." Marbois was far from moved by the overture, and rather, proceeded to cast doubt on the deal: "Sorrow that we could not go beyond that Sum because he was sure that it would not be accepted & that perhaps the whole business would be defeated."[202] That same day, Monroe wrote to Madison: "This Government has resolved to offer us by sale the whole of Louisiana."[203]

Reengaging on April 16, Marbois conveyed the First Consul's displeasure that his original proposal (approximately $22 million) was "so greatly lowered."[204] He stressed that he would see Napoleon the next day and that "it was possible that the consul might touch upon the Subject again."[205] However, "if he did it not," Livingston should "consider the Plan as relinquished."[206] Therefore, if he "had any further proposition to make . . . it would be well to State it."[207]

Livingston had previously conferred with "Mr Munroe" and informed Marbois that the US "had resolved to get to the greatest possible length," which was "*fifty millions [francs]*."[208] This was despite the fact that Monroe was only authorized to go as high as $10 million. In making the revised offer, the American diplomats were unaware they had crossed Napoleon's threshold to make a deal. Marbois took the opportunity to try to sweeten it, describing America's new offer as having "very little hopes that anything Short of his propositions would succeed, but that he would make the best use of his arguments."[209] All said, there was nothing left for Livingston to do but resolve "to rest a few days upon our oars."[210]

After two weeks of intermittent negotiations, a $15 million price, or 60 million francs for Louisiana and another 20 million francs to assume American claims against France was agreed to on April 29, in accord with Napoleon's original redline, and what was broadly discussed at the treasury minister's office on April 13. The Treaty was formally signed by Marbois, Livingston, and Monroe on May 2, but was backdated to April 30. As part of the deal, Napoleon would be paid in cash to help infuse his pending war effort, while the US agreed to pay back two European banks at 6 percent interest, increasing the total cost of the deal to over $23 million by the time the loan was fulfilled in 1823.

Upon the signing, Livingston expressed his satisfaction: "We have lived long, but this is the noblest work of our whole lives. . . . From this day the United States takes its place among the powers of the first rank."[211] Livingston would also note that the Louisiana Purchase, "next to the negotiation that Secured our independence" was the most important the United States had "ever entered into."[212]

Writing to Jefferson on May 3, 1803, the day after the signing, Livingston informed the president of the deal, and on May 13, Livingston and Monroe transmitted the Treaty to Madison, noting: "An acquisition of so great an extent was . . . not contemplated by our appointment, but we are persuaded that the Circumstances and Considerations which induced us to make it, will justify us . . . to our Government and Country."[213] Further, the two ebullient diplomats explained that they closed the historic treaty "on the best terms we could obtain for the whole . . . which comprises . . . this great River and all the streams that empty into it, from their sources to the ocean." Their efforts, as they point out, also helped to separate the US "in a great measure from the European World & its concerns, especially its wars & intrigues,"[214] which, in and of itself, proved the deal's financial prudence beyond the $15 million ticket price, as any future war fought as a result of this territory would have cost America more than the amount paid to conclude the Treaty.

Still, Monroe couldn't believe they got "the whole" of Louisiana and was left with "no question or doubt of the advantage of the bargain to the UStates,"[215] as "exclusive jurisdiction of the river with the Island of Orleans is worth twice or three times that sum."[216] Monroe made clear that the deal was not one that was "contemplated" but was "founded on the principles"[217] laid out in his instructions. The only difference being the "favorable occasion presenting itself which indeed was anticipated by the admn. In the measures which led to that event & indeed laid the foundation for it, we have gone further than we were instructed to do."[218] Although not mentioning Livingston explicitly by name, he was crediting him for the groundwork laid in bringing about this agreement. Madison echoed Monroe's take on the haul in his response on June 25: "The dawn of your negotiations has given much pleasure and much expectation. . . . The purchase of the country beyond the Mississippi was not contemplated in your powers because it was not deemd at this time within the pale of probability."[219]

The final word of the "conveyance"[220] of the treaty did not leave Paris until May 26. Because of "the prospect of rupture" between France and England, great care was taken to ensure security, and the documents were sent "by way of England.[221] The monumental news did not reach Washington until July 3. As Jefferson noted in a July 5 letter to his son-in-law, Thomas Mann Randolph Jr.: "On the evening of the 3d . . . we received a letter from mr King (arrived at N. York) covering one from Livingston & Monroe to him in which they informed him that on the 30th. of April they signed a treaty with France, ceding to us the island of N. Orleans and all Louisiana as it had been held by Spain."[222]

Jefferson could hardly contain his excitement, which for all intents and purposes, was the most momentous news he would receive as president. Still processing the scale of the outcome, he touted: "It is something larger than the whole US. probably containing 500 millions of acres, the US. containing 434. millions."[223] The "happily terminated"[224] deal, as Madison referred to it, was by far the best of any outcome, especially considering Jefferson was willing to concede the lands west of the Mississippi in exchange for New Orleans. Now, in one strategic move, Jefferson had doubled the size of the nation and all but eliminated France and Britain's imperial ambitions on the continent. As he expressed to son-in-law: "This removes from us the greatest source of danger to our peace."[225] The deal also had a broader geographic meaning for the young nation as Jefferson explained in a letter to US senator from Kentucky

John Breckinridge: "The future inhabitants of the Atlantic & Mispi [sic] states will be our sons."[226, 227]

Most of the public commentary echoed Jefferson's elation, including Washington DC's *National Intelligencer* on July 4, which noted the "widespread joy of millions at an event which history will record among the most splendid in our annals."[228] However, Federalist Party strongholds were more pointed in their response, including Alexander Hamilton's *New York Evening Post*, which concluded on July 5: "Every man . . . will readily acknowledge that the acquisition has been solely owing to a fortuitous concurrence of unforeseen and unexpected circumstances, and not to any wise or rigorous measures on the part of the American government."[229] Hamilton was clearly taking a shot at his longtime nemeses by arguing that the Louisiana Purchase was the result of luck, rather than anything Jefferson might have done to influence the outcome.

Unmoved by this partisan school of thought, Jefferson formally requested "the favour of Mr. Madison & family to dine with him—at half after three"[230] on July 6. One can only imagine the good wine and cheer that flowed in celebration. However, amid the fever, a key piece of information was missing from the Paris correspondence—the sticker price. Acting very much in the spirit of a child on the eve of Christmas, Jefferson waited "in hourly expectation of the treaty by a special messenger."[231] Soon he was made aware that the unexpected bargain of the Louisiana Territory was to be had at a cost of eight million francs or $15 million, or what amounted to about four cents an acre across states known today as Arkansas, Louisiana, Missouri, Nebraska, North and South Dakota, and Iowa, and parts of Alabama, Colorado, Kansas, Minnesota, Mississippi, Oklahoma, and Wyoming. An incalculable bargain, by any standard, General Horatio Gates largely summed up the public sentiment around the Treaty's incredible haul in a letter to Jefferson on July 18: "Let the land rejoice, for you have bought Louisiana for a Song."[232]

With treaty in hand, Jefferson moved for Madison to inform Livingston and Monroe that the president "expressly" approved of them obtaining Louisiana, and "the sum agreed to be given for it."[233] Jefferson also moved quickly with a letter providing Meriwether Lewis "general credit," written in Jefferson's "own hand" and signed in his name[234] to draw from the full weight of the US government for anything he required in leading an exploring expedition to the Pacific Ocean. In other words, Lewis had carte blanche to get this done, which possibly represents the greatest credit line offered by a president in American history. But that was an easy task for Jefferson—especially since Jefferson and Lewis had been planning this trip in his work study for some time. The more challenging task, however, was convincing the US Congress and the American people of the purchase. To do so, he had until October 30 to close the deal, a date established at Napoleon's insistence.

As a strict constructionist of the Constitution, the president faced an important dilemma when it came to the Louisiana Territory. Because the Constitution did not explicitly give the federal government the right to accept a land purchase, Jefferson believed a constitutional amendment was needed to consummate the deal. On the other hand, he knew the clock was ticking, and as a political realist, he understood how grave an error it would be to time out on the incredible deal before him. Adding to the intrigue, Livingston and Monroe warned him from Paris of growing French discomfort with the deal. In a letter to his Secretary of the Treasury Albert Gallatin on August 23, Jefferson echoed the urgency: "The French government, dissatisfied perhaps with their late bargain with us, will be glad of a pretext to declare it void. It will be necessary therefore that we execute it with punctuality & without delay."[235]

On September 7, Jefferson took to his pen to write US senator from Virginia, Wilson Cary Nicholas: "Whatever Congress shall think it necessary to do, should be done with as little debate as possible; & particularly so far as respects the constitutional difficulty."[236] His greatest challenge was not the timeline, but rather the Federalists, who objected to the treaty for various reasons—from the price, to the fact that they believed the treaty would only benefit the West and the South, to their disapproval of his potential executive action in the absence of constitutional authority.

Despite these headwinds, Jefferson took action, presenting the Louisiana Purchase as a treaty on national security grounds based on the threat France posed to the United States. In his Third Annual Message to Congress he emphasized this point: "We had not been unaware of the danger to which our peace would be perpetually exposed while so important a key to the commerce of the western country remained under a foreign power."[237]

Jefferson's strategic gamble paid off, as two-thirds of the US Senate agreed, by a margin of twenty-four to seven, on October 20, 1803. The seven votes against the measure were cast by Federalists. Yet their criticisms were not without merit. The acquisition of the Louisiana Territory was one of the most, if not the most, significant expansions of executive power and action in our nation's history, and the great irony was that

Jefferson had previously spent his entire public life opposing the thought of this type of presidential maneuver.[238] The president was also spending money the young nation didn't have for more land when, at the time, only a relatively small area of America was inhabited. However, unable to see the forest from the trees, it was in this latter argument that the Federalist's jumped the shark, directly putting themselves on the wrong side of history and as such, on the brink of extinction as a political force in American politics. Conversely, as Jefferson would later explain in his Second Inaugural Address: "The larger our association the less will it be shaken by local passions; and in any view, is it not better that the opposite bank of the Mississippi should be settled by our own brethren and children, than by strangers from another family?"[239]

In addition, and best summing up his prerogative on the legalities of the acquisition, Jefferson wrote to John B. Colvin on September 20, 1810: "A strict observance of the written laws is doubtless *one* of the high duties of a good citizen: but it is not *the highest*. The laws of necessity, of self-preservation, of saving our country when in danger, are of higher obligation. To lose our country by a scrupulous adherence to written law, would be to lose the law itself, with life, liberty, property & all those who are enjoying them with us."[240] In other words, for Jefferson, the Constitution did not say that a president could not purchase additional lands, and as such, the ends of the Louisiana Purchase justified the means.

Impact and Legacy

It was at the intersection of Jefferson's ingenuity, as a man of ideas, and America's spirit of opportunity, that the nation's founding ideals and expansive westward growth were fundamentally shaped—from the Declaration of Independence to the Louisiana Purchase and beyond. And like Washington's decision to retire from the presidency, Jefferson's management of the Louisiana crisis and his unshakable stratagem drew upon a lifetime of lived experience, both victories and defeats. The watershed moment was Jefferson's April 18, 1802 letter to Livingston, and together, with the Treaty it catalyzed, stands next to the Declaration of Independence, the US Constitution, and Washington's Farewell Address, as the core documents that created modern America. It was through Jefferson's letter that the tone and tenor for the negotiations in Paris were set, which included Livingston's demarche and Du Pont's backchannel, making Napoleon fully aware of Jefferson's position on New Orleans, access to the Mississippi River, and the broader Louisiana territory.

In addition to laying out the playbook to acquire New Orleans, Jefferson's letter was a brilliant stroke of diplomacy. If the president had stood before a Joint Session of the US Congress or delivered his pointed message in public, Napoleon would have felt slighted and the cost would have been high. Instead, Jefferson conveyed his interest in controlling the Mississippi River to the French leader without publicly embarrassing him. Although we don't know whether Jefferson's letter was ever read by Napoleon, we do know that his demarche was delivered and packaged with his diplomatic tact and acumen, setting the stage for the consequential negotiation.

Ultimately, in this pivotal moment, Jefferson proved versatile in action and agile in thought, averting the "tornado . . . on both sides of the Atlantic,"[241] albeit with some providence, including the breakout of yellow fever in Santo Domingo and the threat of an Anglo-French war, which both helped to pave the way toward this far from inevitable event. But even then, it was a far cry from the fortuitous perspective Alexander Hamilton intimated about the new treaty in the *New York Evening Post*.

The president was also engaged throughout the process, weaving a web of preparation and action that allowed aspects of luck and fate to take form. His decision to send Monroe to France was especially pivotal in serving as a catalyst for action, inspiring Livingston and the French toward a greater sense of urgency. He further proved prophetic in his April 25, 1802 letter to Du Pont in that "this little event, of France possessing herself of Louisiana, would impact "their highest destinies," which exemplified his "remarkable grasp of political realities."[242] And in rising to the challenge without a proven roadmap, he was responsible for bringing about the largest land transaction in American history; an area larger than Mexico, and on par with the total area of France, Germany, Greece, Italy, Portugal, Spain, and the United Kingdom combined. All or parts of fifteen states would eventually be carved from its nearly 830,000 square miles over the course of a century, from Louisiana as the eighteenth state in 1812, to Oklahoma admitted as the forty-sixth state in 1907. As historian Stephen Ambrose noted: "Since 1803 . . . every American everywhere has benefited from Jefferson's purchase of Louisiana and his setting in motion the Lewis and Clark Expedition."[243]

If Jefferson had played his hand in any other way, from the negotiating table to the interpretation of the Constitution, to his mix of patience and assertiveness, the US might look completely different than it does today. Particularly without his bold action, the possibility of a continental nation would likely have been lost forever and so too the "sea to shining sea" reality that came to fruition in 1869, when in just a week's time an American could travel by train from the Atlantic to the Pacific. Further lost would have been the weight and influence the US came to yield internationally in the twentieth century and beyond. Rather, as a continental nation, America no longer needed to face east toward Europe, but rather west, to align with a rising sun. Although Jefferson would live for over two decades beyond the signing of the Treaty, he would never physically see the fruits of his harvest. Despite his affinity for the west, the farthest he would ever travel in that direction was Hot Springs, Virginia.

In American history, short of the Founding Fathers and the creation of the United States, one would be hard pressed to find a cast of players more noteworthy than those engaged in the crisis of the Louisiana Territory. Leading the way was Jefferson and the most powerful man in the world at the time, Napoleon Bonaparte. Intricately intertwined as well were the succeeding three decades of American presidential leadership, including James Madison, James Monroe, John Quincy Adams, and Andrew Jackson. In particular, Adams, as a freshman US senator, was the sole Federalist to vote in favor of the Treaty, and Jackson, who served as more of a cheerleader, would note on August 7, 1803 to Jefferson: "On the Joyfull event of the cession of Louisiana and New Orleans, every face wears a smile, and every heart leaps with Joy."[244] Of course, it is not possible to speak of this all-star ensemble without referencing the incredible role that Robert Livingston played, and who's unique and routine placement at the center of the arena was so well-deserved.

However, as so often happens in life, with the good of something so complex also comes the bad. The purchase, while allowing for the postponement of succession, eventually moved America closer to Civil War, including by forcing the slavery question out into the open and perpetuating free versus slave states. The acquisition also had the devastating impact of pushing Native American's west of the Mississippi. It was in these two areas where Jefferson could have furthered his ingenuity and leadership, and a lifetime commitment to great causes, but in both word and deed he fell short of delivering justice to the enslaved and the oppressed. Had he considered his own advice to Rev. Charles Clay on January 27, 1790, one can only guess whether by striving to make incremental progress, the history of the Louisiana Purchase would enjoy a more favorable legacy around the issue of slavery and indigenous peoples: "That the ground of liberty is to be gained by inches, that we must be contented to secure what we can get from time to time, and eternally press forward for what is yet to get. It takes time to persuade men to do even what is for their own good."[245] These critical decisions continue to resonate, as does Jefferson himself. In this spirit, and in light of everything the Louisiana Purchase has done transform America, its history could best be summed up by Jefferson in an April 19, 1803 letter to Massachusetts US Congressman Edward Dowse: "There is no act, however virtuous, for which ingenuity may not find some bad motive."[246]

When John Adams spoke his final words: "Thomas Jefferson survives," he may have been mistaken by about five hours, as death linked the two men on July 4, 1826, to a transformational event in their lives, the Declaration of Independence, which was adopted fifty years earlier. Writing over a century later in 1943, historian Carl Becker posed a question that serves a theoretical bridge to Adams's final words: "What is Still Living in the Political Philosophy of Thomas Jefferson?" While Becker surveyed concepts from liberty, to the nature of human rights, religious freedom, and democracy, in the end, the great insight for American leadership in our own times is not so much that Jefferson's political philosophy survives or not, but rather the quality of ingenuity that undergirds it, which "abides with us, as a living force, to clarify our purposes, to strengthen our faith, and to fortify our courage."[247] It is that quality of ingenuity that extends Jefferson's impact further than anyone else in public life. And it's a legacy, as imperfect as Jefferson was, that fundamentally changed America.

Chapter 3

Dedication

> Now we are engaged in a great civil war, testing whether that nation, or any nation so conceived and so dedicated, can long endure.
>
> —Abraham Lincoln

Within the context of this book, the quality of dedication ranks among any other. Commonly referenced as a commitment to a task or purpose, the term traces back to the Latin "dedicare," and is believed to first appear in the fourteenth century, with William Shakespeare as one of its earliest endorsers: "His life I gave him, and did thereto add / . . . My love without retention or restraint / . . . All his dedication. For his sake,"[1] noted his character Antonio in *Twelfth Night*. In today's political vernacular, this same persuasion of dedication may be best described as country over party. And over Revolutionary War, Civil War, World War, and the Cold War, and across the Great Depression, Great Society, and "The Great Communicator,"[2] we've seen this framing most often at checkpoints of great crisis.

We recall the iconic images of George Washington and the Continental Army enduring the difficult 1777–1778 winter in Valley Forge, and Thomas Paine's illustrative words that define the broader Revolutionary struggle: "These are times that try men's souls. The summer soldier and the sunshine patriot will, in this crisis, shrink from the service of their country; but he that stands by it now deserves the love and thanks of man and woman."[3] Washington embodied the utmost dedication to the cause of America across these dark hours and over the course of three fateful decades. In doing so, he cemented his legacy as the "indispensable man,"[4] as defined by his biographer James Flexner.

John Adams shared a similar uncompromising belief in America, and did more than anyone, short of Washington, to ensure the nation's founding. He exemplified this inherent dedication during his presidency by seeking to keep the nascent Republic out of a war with England and France that it could ill afford to fight. His efforts toward a peaceful solution with both nations caused intense friction at home and abroad, and were especially at odds with many in his party who were aligned with Great Britain and its monarchy's efforts to destroy the French revolutionaries. In particular, Adams's path forward eventually translated into the Treaty of Mortefontaine with French leader Napoleon Bonaparte, which released the United States from its Revolutionary War alliance with France and brought an end to the undeclared Quasi-War. However, in the spirit of "no good deed goes unpunished," his act of dedication ultimately proved costly at the ballot box in 1800, preventing the "Colossus of Independence"[5] from winning a second presidential term.

We recall John Quincy Adams echoing his father's legacy of service and dedication to the cause of America through his wish to "never be governed in my public conduct by and consideration other than that of my duty."[6] In navigating two of the worst crises in the twentieth century, the Great Depression and the Second World War, we recall the firmness and reassurance of Franklin Roosevelt during his First Inaugural Address in 1933, when he noted "that the only thing we have to fear is . . . fear itself."[7] In dedication to America as a beacon abroad, we recall Harry Truman's steadfast support to help Europe recover after World War II, through the Marshall Plan. We also recall Gerald Ford's consequential decision to pardon Richard Nixon, which was widely criticized, but is seen in more contemporary circles as the best move for the country at the time. Ford later explained his decision to the House Judiciary Committee: "I was absolutely convinced then as I am now that if we had had this series—an indictment, a trial, a conviction, and anything else that transpired after this that the attention of the President, the Congress and the American people would have been diverted from the problems that we have to solve."[8] Despite his act of dedication to heal the nation, it most likely cost Ford the 1976 presidential election.

Conversely, America has also experienced the antithesis of dedication portrayed in forms ranging from tribalism to a sheer lack of will, including James Buchanan's seeming indifference to the onset of the Civil War and Andrew Johnson's efforts to thwart Reconstruction, including his comments in an 1866 letter to Missouri Governor Thomas C. Fletcher, for which he is quoted by the *Cincinnati Examiner*: "This is a country for white men, and by God, as long as I am President, it shall be a government for white men."⁹ We've also seen the segregationist policies of Woodrow Wilson roll back economic progress for Black Americans, and Donald Trump's rhetoric inspire and propel a mob to challenge the peaceful transfer of power on the floor of the US Capitol.

Across the weight of these and other actions, presidential historians have significantly elevated and diminished the rankings of US presidents. The outliers on each end of the ranking spectrum, in large measure, have been judged on their level of dedication to the highest ideals of America, from family and religion, to service and country. The very best of this Presidential Club distinction, from Washington to FDR to Reagan, also represent the right leaders, with the right profiles, at the most critical times. These leaders, despite any shortcomings, embraced national ideals, and dared to refine them, even at incalculable personal cost, in order for America to become a more perfect Union. Among these exemplars, however, one stands out for his dedication to the cause of America and to the United States' founding principles when it mattered most. That man was Abraham Lincoln, and through his words and example, he changed America and the world.

The Scene

Abraham Lincoln arrived in Gettysburg, Pennsylvania, at sundown on November 18, 1863. Stepping off the director's car at the rear of a four-car train, America's sixteenth president was greeted by an enthusiastic crowd of onlookers, leading one local resident to note: "There was [*sic*] so many people that there was no comfort to be taken. . . . There was [*sic*] 20 thousand people in Town."¹⁰ "All the hotels as well as the private houses were filled to overflowing," the *New York Times* reported. "People from all parts of the country seem to have taken this opportunity to pay a visit to the battle-fields [*sic*] which are hereafter to make the name of Gettysburgh [*sic*] immortal."¹¹

Lincoln couldn't help but feel the warmth of the crowd in that moment, which followed a six-hour train ride "where he put everyone who approached him at ease," regaling his travel companions with "laughable" stories and "others of a character that deeply touched the hearts of his listeners."¹² In particular, at one stop along the way, "a very beautiful little child" extended a bouquet of rosebuds to Lincoln's open window and with a childish lisp said: "Flowerth for the President!" Lincoln stepped to the window, received the rosebuds, and bent down to kiss the child saying: "You're a sweet little rose-bud [sic] yourself. I hope your life will open into perpetual beauty and goodness."[13] Yet, as Lincoln arrived at this little depot on Carlyle Street, he couldn't also escape the solemnness of the occasion, as spread out across the train platform were hundreds of coffins set for reburial, a reminder of the great human cost and sacrifice exhibited in this small community only months earlier.

The Time and Place

As our next story begins in November 1863, America was engaged in a "great civil war,"[14] a national struggle pitting brother against brother, sister against sister, and ultimately, the US and the eleven Southern states that seceded from the Union and formed the Confederate States of America. This "War Between the States" was the result of a growing, decades-long sectional tension over slavery, stretching as far back as the Northwest Ordinance of 1784, which established the first piece of US federal legislation to restrict the "peculiar institutions' "[15] expansion. These pressures accelerated with Thomas Jefferson's acquisition of the Louisiana Territory, as well as the Missouri Compromise of 1820. The latter, in particular, was an effort to preserve the balance of power in the US Congress by admitting Missouri as a slave state and Maine as a free state—and the first of a series of agreements during the prewar period, ranging from the "gag rule" in Congress, to the Crittenden Compromise, over the expansion of slavery into the West.

Undergirding these sectional tensions were distinct differences in the development of the Northern and Southern economies during the period between 1815 and 1861. The North swiftly modernized with extensive investment in transportation systems highlighted by railroads and roads, and steamboats and canals; in robust, inexpensive, and widely available communication platforms, from the telegraph to books and newspapers; and in commercial industries, such as banking and insurance. By 1860, 90 percent of America's manufacturing capacity came from the North, over a quarter of its population lived in its urban centers, and nearly nine in ten foreign immigrants settled there. Lincoln, for his part, helped to fuel this expansion through the Upper Midwest and West, including through the idea of using natural resources to stimulate economic growth and expansion, and the establishment of a transcontinental railroad. By contrast, the Antebellum South's economy was principally agricultural, reliant on crops such as cotton and on slavery as a labor source. In 1815, cotton was the nation's most valuable export, and by 1860, the South was producing three-quarters of the world's share. The financial implications of this trend were astounding, as Southern whites doubled their Northern counterparts in per capita wealth on the eve of the Civil War—not only because cotton had catapulted in value over the previous decade, but also the economic value of slaves exceeded the North's entire investment in banks, factories, and railroads.

Adding to the tension leading up to the war, Northerners became more amplified over the moral repercussions of slavery and the need for the institution's extinction. Southerners, on the other hand, considered any effort to limit the expansion of slavery a firm red line, as well as a direct threat to the institution's survival. These convergent views drove greater polarization, and dramatically reduced the possibility of mitigating the sectional dispute through compromise. The *New York Herald*, the most widely read newspaper at the time, explained: "The people of the North and those of the South are distinct and separate. They think differently; they spring from a different stock; they are different every way; they cannot coalesce; the Puritan and the Cavalier . . . will always fight when they meet. There is nothing in common between them but hate."[16]

With Abraham Lincoln's election in 1860, and despite the Republican Party's stance not to interfere with slavery in the states, the growing sectional tension became untenable, and with it, seven Southern states—South Carolina, Mississippi, Florida, Alabama, Georgia, Louisiana, and Texas—seceded from the Union, fraying the bond that united thirty-four states under a single flag. Shortly thereafter, in the early morning hours of April 12, 1861, Southern rebels opened fire on Fort Sumter at the entrance to the harbor of Charleston, South Carolina. Within weeks, four more Southern states—Virginia, Arkansas, Tennessee, and North Carolina—left the Union to join the Confederacy.

On paper, the eleven Southern states seemed a poor match for the twenty-three states remaining in the Union, particularly given the population split between nine million Confederates and twenty-one million Northerners. Yet, despite these disadvantages, the Confederacy was certainly not predestined to defeat. Over the course of the next two years, the South leveraged their strengths, ranging from control of a long coastline to defy blockade, to their commitment to Southern "institutions," to gain traction and galvanize support. As President Lincoln noted during the summer of 1862, "Things had gone from bad to worse until I felt that we had reached the end of our rope on the plan of operations we had been pursuing; that we had played our last card and must change our tactics."[17]

Lincoln's issuance of the Emancipation Proclamation to start 1863, which declared "that all persons held as slaves" within the rebellious states "are, and henceforward shall be free,"[18] failed to quell the South's growing momentum, as Confederates experienced their greatest military successes across the first half of 1863, while the Union remained stifled, particularly in efforts toward victory at Vicksburg, Mississippi. Like his Army, Lincoln himself was showing wear. His commissioner of Public Buildings, Benjamin Brown French, noted that the president was "growing feeble. . . . His hand trembled as I never saw it before, and he looked worn & haggard."[19]

By summer 1863, with an emboldened Confederacy and the Union's tenuous predicament, the fate of America hung in the balance. Three fateful days at the beginning of July 1863 would dramatically shift the balance of the war and American history forever.

The Confederate Army, led by General Robert E. Lee, was coming off a recent victory at Chancellorsville, Virginia, in early May 1863. Military historians largely view Chancellorsville as not only a tremendous victory for the South, but a master class in tactics, as Lee split his force on two occasions in the face of an opponent twice in size. It's also very likely Lee and his army believed they were invincible as a result of the battle. Marching north into Gettysburg, Pennsylvania, on a high note, the Confederates brought the war directly into the backyard of the Union.

The small market town of Gettysburg was home to approximately 2,400 residents and was situated 110 miles west of Philadelphia, 80 miles north of Washington, DC, 35 miles southwest of Pennsylvania's capital city, Harrisburg, and less than 10 miles north of the Maryland border. With a victory at Gettysburg, Lee could move east to Philadelphia, and onward to Baltimore and Washington, DC, potentially making real one of Lincoln's constant fears, the fall of the border states—Delaware, Maryland, Kentucky, and Missouri—slave states that did not secede from the Union. All the while, negotiations would quicken toward French and British recognition of the Confederacy's independence, all but ending the war.

Union Major General George Meade, on only his fourth day of command of the Army of the Potomac, met the Confederate incursion at Gettysburg. What began as a chance encounter quickly elevated to the bloodiest battle of the war, with over fifty-one thousand killed, wounded, or missing in action. The death rate was simply astonishing and it's even more significant when considered that the population of the US at the time was one-tenth of what it is today. Put in broader perspective, during America's multidecade conflicts in Vietnam and post-9/11, fifty-eight thousand and seven thousand Americans, respectively, lost their lives in military service.

On July 1, the first day of the conflict, nine hours of relentless fighting included the death of Union General John F. Reynolds and closed with a clear victory for the Confederacy. Union troops quickly retreated through the town of Gettysburg to Cemetery Ridge south of town, where General Meade assembled the rest of the army that evening.

On the second day of battle, the North's nearly ninety-four thousand troops took a strong defensive fishhook-shaped posture along the higher ground, running northward from Little Round Top along Cemetery Ridge, and around Culp's Hill. General Lee, countering with more than seventy thousand troops, ordered an attack on Union positions in the late afternoon and evening of July 2, overtaking Wheat Field, Peach Orchard, Devil's Den, and part of Culp's Hill, but falling short on Cemetery Hill and the critical Little Round Top. Over fourteen thousand soldiers would become casualties of war on the second day of fighting, leading Confederate General James Longstreet to remark that it was the "best three hours fighting ever done by any troops on any battlefield."[20]

On the morning of July 3, General Meade quickly drove the Confederates back from their gains on Culp's Hill. Then, in what has been historically coined, "Pickett's Charge," came arguably the greatest infantry charge in American history. General Lee, going against the advice of his advisers, sent fifteen thousand soldiers under the command of General George E. Pickett against the center of the Union's lines on Cemetery Ridge. After intense fighting, only several hundred Confederate soldiers temporarily breached the Union's positioning; the overwhelming majority were pushed back, shot down, or captured. In sum, only 40 percent of those who engaged in the charge survived. With General Meade's failure to counterattack, Lee's Army retreated into Virginia, leading to a largely uneventful fall 1863, and a subsequent winter quartering for both sides.

Given the events leading up to Gettysburg, President Abraham Lincoln believed a Union victory was far from a definitive outcome. While he spent a large portion of his time during the multiday battle at the telegraph office in the War Department, at one critical moment during the battle, as he would describe to one of his generals: "He went into a room at the White House, got down on his knees, and asked God to avert another Fredericksburg or Chancellorsville."[21] His exuberance upon hearing the news of the Gettysburg victory on July 4, therefore, should come as no surprise: "The great success to the cause of the Union . . . that on this day, He, whose will, not ours, should ever be done, be everywhere remembered and reverenced with profoundest gratitude,"[22] the *New York Times* reported the president as saying. All around him revelry filled the Independence Day air in the nation's capital. As one onlooker recalled: "Everybody seemed determined to make it known publickly that secession was at a low ebb in the Federal City," as "the noise of juvenile firecrackers, the exploding of muskets, pistols, and . . . uncommonly noisily explosive firework, commenced & was kept up without cessation till nearly, or quite, midnight."[23]

However, Lincoln was also quick to chide Union General Meade for his failure to go after Lee's Army. Regarding Meade's forward-looking pronouncement to "drive from our soil every vestige of the presence of the invader," Lincoln exclaimed: "Will our Generals never get that idea out of their heads? The whole country is *our* soil."[24] In retrospect, Lee's decisions on July 3 have served as a significant source of debate among historians. In many ways both he and his army channeled invincibility after their masterful victory at Chancellorsville. Overconfidence likely played a role in his momentous decision-making, and the consequences proved decisive. The Confederates lost a number of senior leaders in the fighting, including generals, who could never be replaced. Lee would also never again have the opportunity to bring a full-scale fight to Northern soil, as he would spend the rest of the Civil War on the defensive.

Historical consensus informs us that the Battle of Gettysburg was the high-water mark of the Confederacy. The loss all but ended the South's hope of formal recognition by foreign governments, as well as their cause for independence. Although, at the time, the final result of the war was far from clear, as thousands of lives would be lost in nearly two more years of fighting and suffering.

The streets and fields of Gettysburg were likewise changed forever. During the thunderous battle and the circling warfare across three treacherous days, most residents burrowed in their cellars, and miraculously, only one Gettysburgian lost their life during the fighting—Virginia "Ginnie" Wade, who caught a stray bullet "by one of our own sharpshooters"[25] while baking bread. On the one hand, as noted by Robert G. Harper, editor of the weekly Gettysburg periodical the *Adams Sentinel* on July 7, 1863, the battle was "Glorious in the fruits gathered, the vindication of truth, the triumph of right, the victory achieved for Liberty, Justice, the Union and good Government."[26] On the other hand, the days that followed brought into full view the devastation to the town, as seemingly every garden and field honored the fallen, while homes and public buildings served as makeshift hospitals tending to the injured and dying. Summing up the gruesome scene of the battlefield on July 4, 1863, a soldier from New Jersey recounted:

> Upon the open fields, like sheaves bound by the reaper, in crevices of the rocks, behind fences, trees and buildings; in thickets, where they had crept for safety only to die in agony; by stream or wall or hedge, wherever the battle had raged or their waking steps could carry them, lay the dead. Some with faces bloated and blackened beyond recognition, lay with glassy eyes staring up at the blazing summer sun; others, with faces downward and clenched hands filled with grass or earth, which told of the agony of the last moments.[27]

Four months later, the town, still grieving, extended its hospitality to thousands traveling from across the country to dedicate a new national soldiers' cemetery and hear the words of their president and commander in chief.

The Roadmap

Abraham Lincoln's arrival and participation at Gettysburg was far from a foregone conclusion. The president was the last speaker invited for the cemetery dedication, only seventeen days before the event, and his invitation framed the nature of his participation: "It is the desire that, after the Oration, You as Chief Executive of the Nation formally set apart these grounds to their sacred use by a few appropriate remarks . . . [and] perform this last solemn act to the Soldiers dead on this Battle Field."[28] Previously, Lincoln had turned down various invitations to speak outside of the nation's capital, and on the instances when he did leave town, it was to visit the Army of the Potomac in the field.

In addition, had Lincoln accepted Secretary of War Edward Stanton's itinerary, which called for a 6:00 a.m. departure for the eighty-mile journey and a noon ceremony, he very likely would not have made it on time. Fortunately, Lincoln believed that margin of error must always be built into planning and preferred to get to Gettysburg the night before the dedication, noting: "I do not wish to so go that by the slightest accident we fail entirely, and, at the best, the whole to be a mere breathless running of the gauntlet."[29] His planning and prognostication served him well, as even his trip on November 18 took six hours, with transfers in Baltimore and Hanover Junction.

The significance of Lincoln's presence in Gettysburg is further amplified when considered in light of his wife Mary's fear, and his own, concerning their son Tad's grave, bed-ridden condition. This followed the death of their son Willie from typhoid fever twenty-one months earlier. Upon arrival, Lincoln received a telegram from his Secretary of War Edwin Stanton, who conveyed that "Mrs. Lincoln informed me that your son is better this evening."[30]

That invariably was a huge sigh of relief for the president, and throughout his trip, he would receive telegraph updates from Washington on his son's condition. In a letter the day after the cemetery dedication to esteemed Massachusetts politician and American diplomat, Edward Everett, who also served as the featured orator for the ceremony, Lincoln reported: "Our sick boy . . . we hope is past the worst."[31]

Among the enthusiastic Gettysburg crowd to greet the president was Everett, along with David Wills, a prominent thirty-two-year-old local attorney, and Ward Hill Lamon, a friend of the president and the marshal-in-chief for the dedication. Together, the entourage of dignitaries led Lincoln on the two-block walk through the heart of the town square or the "Diamond," as locals called it, to the Wills residence, where a lengthy dinner awaited. This impressive three-story brick mansion served as hub of activity during and after the fateful battle, with its cellar serving as a refuge during the war, and its living area providing inspiration for the plans to establish a soldier's cemetery to honor the fallen.

As dinner wrapped up, a mass of people gathered in the Diamond eagerly shouted out for Lincoln to appear and make some brief remarks. This was mostly led by Pennsylvania College students, who had been given early dismissal from classes, and from repeated calls and serenades by the Fifth New York Artillery Band.[32] As Lincoln emerged, a loud cheer filled the square, and he began.

> I appear before you, fellow citizens, merely to thank you for this complement. The inference is a very fair one that would hear me, for a little while at least, were I to commence to make a speech. I do not appear before you for the purpose of doing so, and for several substantial reasons. The most substantial of these is that I have no speech to make [Laughter]. In my position it is somewhat important that I should not say foolish things.[33]

Lincoln's hesitation elicited a sneer from a voice in the crowd: "If you can help it." Lincoln's quick reply amused those assembled: "Very often happens that the only way to help it is to say nothing at all." He then closed: "Believing that is my present condition this evening, I must beg of you to excuse me from addressing you further."[34] Lincoln's brief remarks were met with "loud cheers,"[35] and only added to the anticipation for the day ahead.

The president was shown the steep stairs to his bedroom on the second floor, which overlooked the town square, including US Congressman Thaddeus Stevens's old law office.[36] According to David Wills, it was here that Lincoln "wished to consider further the few words he was expected to say the next day."[37] As a writer, Lincoln was careful and methodical, liking to noodle on phrasing while tediously tightening his logic and prose. He shared the same school of thought as author Mark Twain, believing that the difference between the right word and the almost right one is that between lightning and a lightning bug. He preferred to read his words out loud as a form of revision, and as President George W. Bush later noted, Lincoln did so "to persuade, to challenge, and to inspire."[38] On this Gettysburg occasion, as had become his practice, Lincoln liked to make edits in pencil. He also preferred to order his thoughts, and this sequencing and deployment of logic and clarity served him well on important remarks and statements throughout his life, and the lead up to Gettysburg was no different.

Requiring time and concentration to weigh his words, Lincoln would not be one to wait until the evening before a big event to pick up his pencil, or even to leave it to the train ride to Gettysburg, which he knew would be filled with inherent distractions, including the endless greeting and engaging of dignitaries. Rather, as reported by Ward Hill Lamon: "A day or two" before the dedication, Lincoln pulled "a memoranda of his intended address" from his hat, which he often reserved as "the usual receptacle for his private notes and memoranda."[39] Although the president "was extremely busy, and had not time for preparation," what he shared with Lamon "proved to be in substance, if not the exact words, what was afterward printed as his famous Gettysburg Address."[40]

The substance of his remarks at Gettysburg, however, were years in the making, a culmination of his lived experience and inherent dedication, including his affinity for the principles of the nation's founding. As historian Garry Wills aptly noted: "Without Lincoln knowing it himself, all his prior literary, intellectual and political labors had prepared him for the intellectual revolution contained in those fateful 272 words."[41] And it was those words that adorned a two-page draft, written on white, blue-lined White House stationary, that Lincoln tucked away safely in his hat for the train ride to Gettysburg.

The Makings of Abraham Lincoln's Dedication

President Abraham Lincoln came of age at the same time his nation did. Born on February 12, 1809, in a small log cabin in Hardin County, Kentucky, Lincoln's beginnings exemplified the rawness of the frontier and Thomas Jefferson's agrarian vision of America. The one-room dwelling rested on a little knoll near a spring, and its sixteen-by-eighteen-foot foundation was made of logs and clay, with a dirt floor and stone fireplace representing the standard amenities of the day.

Lincoln was known to reflect on his meager mainsprings, particularly at formative moments in his life. During his first campaign speech during a run for the Illinois state legislature at age twenty-three, the emerging politician said: "I was born, and have ever remained, in the most humble walks of life."[42] In the 1840s, when revisiting his old neighborhood in Indiana, he summed up a similar retrospection in verse.

> My childhood's home I see again,
> And sadden with the view;
> And still, as mem'ries crowd my brain,
> There's pleasure in there too.
> . . .
> I range the fields with pensive tread,
> And pace the hollow rooms,
> And feel (companion of the dead)
> I'm living in the tombs.[43]

Moreover, on the cusp of his presidency in 1860, Lincoln told John Locke Scripps of the *Chicago Tribune*: "It is a great piece of folly to attempt to make anything out of my early life. It can all be condensed into a single sentence, and that sentence you will find in Gray's Elegy."[44] Lincoln was referring to the phrase "the short and simple annals of the poor,"[45] in eighteenth-century English poet Thomas Gray's work, "Elegy Written in a Country Churchyard."

When the future president was two, his family moved from Sinking Spring Farm at the south fork of Nolin Creek to a smaller and more fertile farm approximately ten miles away on Knob Creek. At age seven, they crossed the Ohio River into Indiana, and two years later, he tragically lost his mother, Nancy Hanks, a result of tainted milk from a grazing cow that ingested a poisonous snakeroot plant. This loss was an especially formative event in young Abraham's life, and years later he would express the great appreciation he had for his mother in the often-cited tribute: "All that I am or ever hope to be I owe to her."[46] As Lincoln would later confide to his law partner William Herndon, Nancy Hanks was "highly intellectual by nature, had a strong memory, acute judgment and was cool and heroic."[47] She was also born out of wedlock, and beyond the lineage of a well-bred Virginia ancestry; Lincoln likewise inherited his maternal grandfather's "power of analysis, his logic, his mental activity, his ambition, and all the qualities that distinguished him from the other members of the Hanks family."[48] And although Lincoln would portray himself as a self-made man, he would leverage this noble distinction to help explain to himself why he was so different from the rest of his clan.

Lincoln's adoration for his "angel mother" and for his older sister, Sarah, who tragically passed during childbirth when Abe was eighteen, only serve to amplify the absence of affirmation for his father Thomas in any of his published writings. Beyond inheriting his father's virtuous nature and lineage as an eighth-generation American, his paternal connection was challenged to inch much further. Yet a young Abraham was particularly taken by his father's recollection of his grandfather and namesake's striking death. At age forty-two, on the fringes of the Kentucky frontier, the elder Abraham was shot and killed by a Native American from the cover of woods. While the middle son, Josiah ran for help, and the eldest, fifteen-year-old, Mordecai, sought a weapon, as the assailant ran at Thomas Lincoln, who was sitting next to his father's body in a field. With no time to waste, Mordecai shot and killed the aggressor before the youngest son could be harmed. Had the situation gone the other way, the lineage between the elder and future Abraham Lincoln would have been lost forever.

Physically, Lincoln was unique, and it set him apart from his contemporaries and among his presidential peers. He was tall, lanky, and raw boned, with a wild shock of black hair. According to the great American poet Walt Whitman, his facial qualities were "so awful ugly it becomes beautiful, with its strange mouth, its deep cut, crisscross lines, and its doughnut complexion."[49] Lincoln understood his physical uniqueness and often disarmed it with humor, such as when Stephen A. Douglas called Lincoln two-faced during one of their famous debates for the US Senate seat from Illinois in 1858. Lincoln wryly responded: "I leave it to my audience. If I had another face, why would I be wearing this one?"[50]

Despite his wiry frame, Lincoln possessed great strength and power and was widely known for his skill in wielding an axe. His endurance was inexhaustible, and even as president, he would bound up staircases two or three steps at a time. He also possessed a powerful emotional intelligence, including an innate sense for passing along a timely complement. And despite his rather high, shrill tone, his oratory skills far exceeded his contemporaries. When Lincoln spoke, his voice carried, and people listened.

His personality could be rather winsome and he loved to laugh, especially at himself. His penchant for William Shakespeare and the English playwright's inclination to an amalgam of humor and tragedy, served as a needed distraction during the darkest hours of the Civil War. He also had a streak of melancholy and was prone to anger, which he would often release by penning "hot letters" to critics or colleagues that he would never sign or send but rather tucked away in his desk drawer.[51]

Through all seasons, young people gravitated to him, exemplified by a letter he received a few weeks before his election from Grace Bedell, an eleven-year-old girl from Westfield, New York, who urged him to grow a beard to help him get elected. While his response gave no promises, he did grow his beard out, and during his inaugural journey by train to Washington, he stopped in Westfield and from just off his train car gave the girl "several hearty kisses . . . amid yells of delight from the excited crowd."[52]

Lincoln gained energy from challenging questions and cultivating innovative solutions. Following the tradition of Washington and Jefferson, he sought all sides of an issue, even those contrary to his own before making a decision. He welcomed arguments among his team but left no room for mean-spirited behavior, for grudges or personal resentments. Leading by example, he was merciful and magnanimous toward others, as well as for his own errors. For instance, he wrote Union General Ulysses S. Grant after his important victory at Vicksburg: "I write this now as grateful acknowledgement for the almost inestimable service you have done the country. I wish to say a word further. . . . When you got below, and took Fort-Gibson, Grand Gulf, and vicinity, I thought you should go down the river and join General Banks; and when you turned Northward East of Big Black, I feared a mistake. I now wish to make the personal acknowledgment that you were right and I was wrong."[53] The standards of decorum he demanded were based on an understanding that all were involved in a challenge "too vast for malicious dealing."[54] This sense of common purpose guided the formation of his presidential cabinet, which historian Doris Kearns Goodwin described as Lincoln's "Team of Rivals,"[55] a group of ambitious and gifted competitors for the 1860 Republican nomination who also represented the leading geographical, political, and ideological factions of the Union.

Across his endeavors, Lincoln was comfortable with uncertainty, mediating disputes, and navigating the tension between his ambition and conservative temperament. He was adept at shaping public opinion and would have likely been considered a social media influencer in modern terms, noting: "With public sentiment, nothing can fail; without it, nothing can succeed."[56]

His formal education was limited and "defective,"[57] which he noted "did not amount to one year."[58] Yet, he was a voracious reader, and would travel miles to borrow a book. He possessed an innate story-telling ability, which was aided by a great intellectual curiosity, and his stepmother Sarah's love and encouragement. His classmates thought "he was clearly exceptional,"[59] as his biographer David Herbert Donald pointed out. "He carried away from his brief schooling the self-confidence of a man who has never met his intellectual equal."[60] Yet in many ways Lincoln was similar to George Washington, in that what he had in the way of education, "he picked up."

He was enthralled by history and the nation's Founders, to which historian Richard Brookhiser concluded: "He wanted to wrap himself in their aura . . . and drew on them for rhetoric and inspiration."[61] Some of Lincoln's most vivid memories as a young boy were escapades from the Revolutionary War that were found in Parson Weem's *Life of George Washington*, including General Washington's crossing of the Delaware River on Christmas Night 1776, and his subsequent victories at Trenton and Princeton. As he would tell members of the New Jersey State Senate on the eve of his presidency: "There must have been something more than common that those men struggled for; that something even more than National Independence; that something that held out a great promise to all the people of the world to all time to come."[62]

It was this sense of higher purpose that guided and propelled Lincoln, first as a child, and on through even the darkest hours of the Civil War. It likewise helped to form the core root of dedication from which all aspects of his life took shape—from knowledge, to the Bible, to the soil, to the memory of his mother, to America; and which would grow and find strength in the many trials he fought throughout his life.

In this way, Lincoln could easily represent the prototype for the famous definition of dedication John Kennedy delivered in a speech just days before his 1961 presidential inauguration. Describing the quality as one of the four most important any leader could possess, Kennedy declared that the high court of history would judge him and fellow office holders by whether they were "truly men of dedication—with an honor mortgaged to no single individual or group, and compromised by no private obligation or aim, but devoted solely to serving the public good and the national interest."[63]

This definition can be seen in Lincoln's firm belief that the role of each generation is to reenergize the principles of the Declaration of Independence to meet the challenges of the time. It can be seen in his work ethic and how he would toil from sunup to sundown. It can be seen in his late teens, when despite having challenges with his father, and an itch to go out on his own, he met his obligation to Thomas Lincoln for another year of lawful labor, helping to move his family from Indiana to Illinois.

It can be seen in his volunteer service in the Black Hawk War, despite the fact that the fighting consisted more of a "good many bloody struggles with the mosquitos [sic]."[64] It can be seen when his general store in New Salem, Illinois, "winked out,"[65] and instead of cutting and running from significant debt, which was commonplace in frontier America, he honored what he called his "National Debt."[66] To this end, the dedicated and conscientious manner for which he engaged with people and handled his affairs during this experience, earned him the nickname "Honest Abe."

It can be seen in the dedication he had to finding his purpose, in work ranging from carpentry, to river boating, to blacksmithing, and finally to lawyering, and elected office, the latter two of which he viewed as public service and relished their practice as a craft. And even then, his dedication was routinely tested, as he lost his first race for the Illinois state legislature, and after finally gaining election, he twice ran unsuccessfully for speaker of the Illinois House. He also failed to win his party's vice presidential nomination in 1856, and in 1858, he was defeated in his run for the US Senate in Illinois. Yet he ignored defeat and persevered. As historian W. E. B. Du Bois said of Lincoln: "I love him not because he was perfect but because he was not and yet triumphed."[67]

It can be seen in his dedication to improve the lives of his constituents and beyond when in office, including through the advancement of transportation infrastructure. It can be seen after the passage of the Kansas-Nebraska Act in 1854, and how this legislation shook his conscience to act, eventually leading to the important campaign debates with Stephen A. Douglas in 1858, when he noted: "A house divided against itself cannot stand."[68]

It can be seen in his adherence to what he described in his First Inaugural Address as the "better angels of our nature,"[69] and through his commitment to his family and faith. It can be seen in his conduct of the war and in the face of criticism, including when Lincoln once visited the home Union General George B. McClellan, who decided he did not want to see the president and instead retired to bed. Advisers close to the president asked him why he would allow the general to rebuff him in such a way. Lincoln replied: "All I want out of General McClellan is a victory, and if to hold his horse will bring it, I will gladly hold his horse."[70]

It can be seen in his reputation as the Great Emancipator, and in the singular sentence in the Emancipation Proclamation that fundamentally changed the course of "the world's best hope,"[71] "That on the first day of January, in the year of our Lord one thousand eight hundred and sixty-three, all persons held as slaves within any State or designated part of a State, the people whereof shall then be in rebellion against the United States, shall be then, thenceforward, and forever free."[72] It can be seen in his long-standing belief that "if slavery is not wrong, nothing is wrong," which was echoed by Frederick Douglass in noting Lincoln's "entire freedom from prejudice against the colored race."[73] And, above all others, it can be seen culminated in his timeless 272-word oratory at Gettysburg—the most transcendent act of dedication by a US president in the span of American history.

The Gettysburg Address

In his room at the Wills house, Lincoln all but put the finishing touches on his remarks. Before turning in for the night, sometime after 11 p.m., Lincoln visited his Secretary of State, William Henry Seward, who was lodging next door at the home of Robert Harper, editor of the *Adams Sentinel*. Previously keeping his remarks largely close hold, Lincoln sought Seward's counsel, as he did across various high-profile documents, including his First Inaugural Address.

After an hour,[74] Lincoln returned to his room at Wills's house and spent some more time editing the draft, then turned in around midnight. However, the crowd did not turn in as early as the president: "They sang, & hallooed, and cheered," according to an account from Benjamin Brown French. Ringing out through the town square was the popular refrain: "We are coming Father Abraham, three hundred thousand more."[75]

Rain swept Gettysburg overnight, but moved out swiftly, leaving behind a cloudless sky and an unfettered sunrise. Early that morning, Lincoln was joined by Seward for a carriage ride and tour of the Gettysburg battlefield near Seminary Ridge, the site of intense fighting on July 1, 1863, which also served as the Confederate line of fighting against Union strongholds on July 2 to 3, 1863. Setting out onto the Diamond and then along Chambersburg Street, the two proceeded right into the face of the route Lee's Third Corps travelled into town on the first day of the battle.

The tour couldn't have been a more sobering experience for the president, as it was noted: "The ground in these vicinities is yet strewn with remains and relics of the fearful struggle—ragged and muddy knapsacks, canteens, cups, haversacks, threadbare stockings trodden in the mud, old shoes, pistols, holsters, bayonet sheaths, and here and there fragments of grey and blue jackets," not to mention the "hides and skeletons of horses,"[76] and the seemingly countless grave marking, from mounds of dirt to large burial pits. Lincoln, who was well known for visiting battlefields, additionally toured the location where General John F. Reynolds tragically lost his life. It's hard not to imagine that the president was thinking of how, just days before the battle, he offered Reynolds command of the Army of the Potomac. It's equally easy to imagine Lincoln Monday morning quarterbacking the fate and outcome of the Gettysburg battle had Reynolds accepted his offer.

By midmorning, and carrying the weight of that experience, Lincoln, made a few final edits to his remarks, and then joined those assembled outside of the Wills House, including governors, members of Congress, cabinet and military leaders, and foreign officials at ten o'clock for a large, one-mile procession to the cemetery dedication site. Dressed in a new black suit and coat, with his famous tall silk hat, which recently was adorned with a mourning band in memory of his late son Willie, Lincoln mounted a horse so small that his long legs nearly touched the ground. He also wore a pair of white riding gloves that sharply contrasted with his all-black attire.

Because the parade was delayed twenty minutes, the crowd enthusiastically pressed up to get an up close and personal look at the president. To observers, Lincoln seemed somber and absorbed in thought. Once started, it was noted: "Never was a procession better formed or more orderly,"[77] as "nearly 2,000 troops of all arms"[78] guided participants along the "grand military and civic display,"[79] down Baltimore Street, where American flags, patriotic fervor and "oft-repeated cheers" of "Hurrah for Old Abe" and "We're coming, Father Abraham," as well as one solitary greeting, "God save the President,"[80] filled the air. Yet, even as children sold lemonade and cookies, one could not escape the coarseness of the battlefield and the war, from bullet holes blemishing the home fronts, to the pockmarked trees and charred landscape. "Within a stone's throw of the whitewashed hut occupied as the headquarters of Gen. MEADE . . . no less than ten carcasses of dead horses, lying on the ground where they were struck by the shells of the enemy,"[81] reported the *New York Times*. *The Press of Philadelphia* added: "The grounds in these vicinities is yet strewn with remains and relics of the fearful struggle . . . mournful and appealing mementos of the civil strife."[82]

Led by the Marine Band, the formal procession came to an end in the cemetery after about twenty minutes and directly in front of the speaker's platform, a twelve-by-twenty-foot stand lined with three rows of chairs and buttressed with military personnel. Approximately 250 dignitaries were seated,[83] looking out over the "immense crowd"[84] of fifteen thousand people who gathered for the event and were wedged up close to one another, leaving some participants to note that they had never been so close to so many people before. The bright blue November sky only added to the backdrop.

As Lincoln arrived and dismounted, those assembled went silent, with men removing their hats. As the president took his seat, he was flanked by Seward and Everett. After a short invocation and hymn, and the band's rendition of "Old Hundred," Everett stepped forward to deliver his oration. One of the finest speakers of the time, Everett delivered his well-researched and -memorized address for over two hours and eight minutes, recounting the historic and dramatic battles that occurred across those three fateful July days. Lincoln and the assembled crowd followed his 13,500-word tour de force ever so closely.

Everett closed by emphasizing: "In the glorious annals of our common country, there will be no brighter page than that which relates THE BATTLES OF GETTYSBURG."[85] With that, Lincoln shook Everett's hand with great sincerity, telling the Massachusetts orator: "I am more than gratified, I am grateful to you."[86] Others were less moved, contending Everett's words revealed more of the battle's story than its heart. According to the Philadelphia *Daily Age*: "Seldom had a man talked so long and said so little. He told us nothing about the dead heroes, nothing of their former deeds, nothing of their glories before they fell like conquerors before their greater conqueror, Death. He gave us plenty of words, but no heart."[87]

After a "Consecration Hymn"[88] and the choir singing out: "This holy ground / Let tears abound / A thousand years shall pass away / A nation still shall mourn this day / The soil is blest,"[89] Ward Hill Lamon offered a brief introduction for the gaunt, war-wearied Lincoln before his dedicatory remarks. Just under the speakers stand, directly below Lincoln was fifteen-year-old George Gitt, who recalled how the president stepped slowly to the front of the platform: "The flutter and motion of the crowd ceased the moment the President was on his feet. Such was the quiet that his footfalls, I remember very distinctly . . . the creaking of the boards, it was as if some one were walking through the hallways of an empty house."[90]

As Lincoln looked out on the sea of people assembled, which contrasted with the rows of fresh graves just beyond them, he pulled his prepared remarks out from the left breast pocket of his jacket, adjusted his glasses, shifted the papers from his right hand to his left and began "in a very deliberate manner, with strong emphasis, and with a most business-like air":[91]

> Four score and seven years ago our fathers brought forth on this continent, a new nation, conceived in Liberty, and dedicated to the proposition that all men are created equal.

From the outset, Lincoln was planting a marker in the ground, deliberately linking the Union's purpose to the Declaration of Independence's self-evident truths: "That all Men are created equal, that they are endowed by their Creator with certain unalienable Rights, that among these are Life, Liberty, and the Pursuit of Happiness,"[92] and not to the US Constitution of 1787. He was therefore seeking to redefine America as not solely pledged to constitutional liberty but to human liberty, including a defense of the Emancipation Proclamation that had fundamentally changed the psychology of the war.

An important window into his thinking, representing a quasi-first draft of his words at Gettysburg, occurred during his July 7, 1863 "Response to Serenade," a brief, impromptu speech outside the White House. Unlike today, where the White House is secured by fencing, Secret Service agents, and, at times barricades, the property in Lincoln's day allowed for a more intimate interaction between the presidency and the citizenry. On this occasion, a group of enthusiastic local residents assembled in the White House driveway to serenade the president upon hearing of the newly announced victories at Gettysburg and Vicksburg. After thanking the crowd, Lincoln began: "How long ago is it?—eighty odd years—since on the Fourth of July for the first time in the history of the world a nation by its representatives, assembled and declared as a self-evident truth that 'all men are created equal.' [Cheers.] That was the birthday of the United States of America."[93] The informality of his "eighty odd years"[94] of prose would evolve over the next four months into the more thoughtful and iconic phrasing, "Four score and seven years ago."[95] During these impromptu remarks he also declared his affinity for the Declaration of Independence, as he called Thomas Jefferson and John Adams, "Two of the most distinguished men in the framing and support of the Declaration . . . the one having penned it and the other sustained it the most forcibly in debate."[96] He furthermore defined the essence of the "gigantic Rebellion" as "an effort to overthrow the principle that all men were created equal."[97]

Lincoln's expressed affinity for the Declaration, however, was far from novel. He shared a similar affinity a decade prior to Gettysburg in an 1854 speech on the Kansas-Nebraska Act.

> Let us re-adopt the Declaration of Independence, and, with it, the practices, and policy, which harmonize with it. Let north and south—let all Americas—let all lovers of liberty everywhere—join in the great and good work. If we do this, we shall not only have saved the Union; but we shall have so saved it, as to make, and to keep it, forever worthy of the

> saving. We shall have so saved it, that the succeeding millions of free happy people, the world over, shall rise up, and call us blessed, to the latest generations.[98]

He would also amplify this inherent spirit across the back half of the 1850s, calling the Declaration an "apple of gold,"[99] and advocating that if all men are created equal, they could not be property, and if America was to govern by its own creed, then equality for all could not be denied. Lincoln's biographer, Carl Sandburg aptly summed up the president's view: "To give man this equal chance in life was the aim, the hope, the flair of glory, spoken by the Declaration of Independence."[100]

With this important historical continuity and lineage established, Lincoln quickly pivoted to the current moment, taking stock of a devastating war that persisted and by defining its meaning of service and sacrifice as a test to America's founding ideals and whether they could survive in confronting the greatest moral challenge in the nation's history.

> Now we are engaged in a great civil war, testing whether that nation, or any nation so conceived and so dedicated, can long endure. We are met on a great battlefield of that war. We have come to dedicate a portion of that field, as a final resting place for those who here gave their lives that that nation might live. It is altogether fitting and proper that we should do this. But, in a larger sense, we cannot dedicate—we cannot consecrate—we cannot hallow—this ground. The brave men, living and dead, who struggled here, have consecrated it, far above our poor power to add or detract.

The fifteen thousand souls gathered to hear the president knew the cost. They could see and feel it everywhere around them, from the war-torn fields, to the empty coffins at the railroad depot and the freshly dug graves that awaited the dead. These "were fathers, mothers, brothers, and sisters, who had come from distant parts to look at and weep over the remains of their fallen kindred, or to gather up the honored relics and bear them back to the burial ground of their native homes—in relating what they had suffered and endured, and what their loved ones had borne in the memorable days of July."[101] The president and their loved one's commander and chief was attempting to console the inconsolable. He was attempting to channel their collective grief and what transpired here among the 170 thousand Union and Confederate soldiers who clashed here, and died here, in the largest battle ever engaged in the Western Hemisphere. They knew, as the president knew, this was sacred ground.

Lincoln even consulted with William Saunders, the landscape architect responsible for planning the Gettysburg cemetery, to better learn the topography. Actions like this, along with his message and delivery about the sacrifices made here spoke to the authenticity of the man in this solemn and historic moment. As the *Cincinnati Daily Commercial* reported, Lincoln revealed "A Scotch type of countenance . . . a thoughtful, kindly, care-worn face . . . eyes cast down, the lids thin and firmly set, the cheeks sunken, and the whole indicating weariness, and anything but good health."[102] From his sheer appearance, those assembled could see his utmost dedication to the greater cause of America. They could see how much it meant to him what their loved ones gave up in order to keep that flame alive. And conversely, he could clearly see how much his presence and words meant to them.

Following this similar spirit, Lincoln humbly sought to close the Address by first offering an important distinction: "The world will little note, nor long remember what we say here, but it can never forget what they did here." While the events of Gettysburg are far from forgotten in the annals of American history, and we may not "long remember" what Edward Everett said at the dedication, Lincoln's humble offering that history would forget his words represents the singular fault to lay at his feet as a result of his summit of eloquence. Continuing, the president leaned into our role as the living to imbue the theme of dedication that both defined and gave meaning to his life and his commitment to preserve the Union. He did so by harkening back to his New Jersey State Senate address in February 1861, when he highlighted the source of dedication of the revolutionary generation at the Battle of Trenton: "There must have been something more than common that those men struggled for; that something even more than National Independence; that something that held out a great promise to all the people of the world to all time to come."[103] Lincoln was seeking to bridge the legacy of Washington's historic 1776 victories at Trenton and Princeton undertaken in a defense of Union and the universal truths defined in the Declaration of Independence with that of Gettysburg, as both were "perpetuated in accordance with the original idea for which that struggle was made."[104] "It is for us the living, rather, to be dedicated here to the unfinished work which they who fought here have thus far so nobly advanced. It is rather for us to be here dedicated to the great task remaining before us." Lincoln then attached the same dedication that defined the revolutionary cause and his own to four clauses, each beginning with the word *that*, which draws on Thomas Jefferson's analogous phrasing in the Declaration of Independence. Thus, it can be argued that Jefferson's adoption created an American nation, and Lincoln's application reimagined it.

He too called on Americans to remember those who gave everything in the darkness of war so that the United States could thrive in the light of a new birth of freedom—or more specifically, "A second birth of freedom," the fulfillment of the unfulfilled promise of "our fathers"—in 1776. For Lincoln, an acute reality of the war was that some had to die in order for all to live under the auspices of a new birth of freedom: "that from these honored dead we take increased devotion to that cause for which they gave the last full measure of devotion—that we here highly resolve that these dead shall not have died in vain—that this nation, under God, shall have a new birth of freedom." For his final thought, Lincoln leaned into language from his Special Session Message to the US Congress on July 4, 1861: "A government of the people, by the same people,"[105] which was no doubt inspired by Daniel Webster's overture about American government in 1830, "Made for the people, made by the people, and answerable to the people,"[106] as well as American transcendentalist Theodore Parker's sermon, which defined democracy as "government of all the people, by all the people, for all the people."[107] As such, Lincoln enhanced this construction to famously close the Address: "and that government of the people, by the people, for the people, shall not perish from the earth."[108]

Impact and Legacy

At its core, the Gettysburg Address exemplifies Lincoln's dedication to preserve the Union, drawing his listeners to the intersection of the nation's purpose and the difficult fight, while also encouraging the North to stay the course in the challenging days ahead. By providing his inherent dedication and the hope of success in the face of doubt and uncertainty, the speech represented a great turning point in the national crisis.

As a master communicator, Lincoln knew the power he wielded to define public perception of the war, and thus, how Gettysburg provided him the ideal platform to reframe the narrative, and broaden the war aims from Union—to liberty and Union—a coupled step the Founders had been disinclined to take. And as much as the Civil War was fought on battlefields from Fort Sumter to Bull Run, from Antietam to Vicksburg, Lincoln also knew that the broader fight to secure the nation's shared destiny would be waged with his words at Gettysburg, which required a decisive break from Thomas Jefferson and the America of the Founders.

In a work encompassing 272 words, across ten sentences and four paragraphs, Lincoln took his listeners on a lexical, structural, and biblical-rhythmic voyage of the past, present, and future. Multisyllable words could be described as outliers, as approximately three-quarters of the words in the Address had just one syllable. Of those he did include were terms of great personal meaning and heart such as dedicate or dedicated, which were used six times and described by an associate as Lincoln's "unswerving fidelity to purpose."[109] Importantly, the president weaved the word "nation" through the Address five times.

At no point did he specifically call out the Confederacy by name, instead leaving his audience to contrast "those who here gave their lives that that nation might live," with those across the Gettysburg battlefields who gave their lives so that nation might die. He made no reference to slavery, the Union, Gettysburg, the soldier's cemetery he was dedicating, or the Constitution. Nor did he introduce one first-person singular pronoun. These omissions take on heightened meaning given Lincoln's penchant to labor over every syllable and word choice.

As Lincoln closed his remarks, those assembled "stood motionless and silent," according to George Gitt. "The extreme brevity of the address together with its abrupt close had so astonished the hearers that they stood transfixed. Had not Lincoln turned and moved toward his chair, the audience would very likely have remained voiceless for several moments more."[110] Even the on-site photographer failed to begin before Lincoln concluded his address. Giving pause himself in finishing, Lincoln quickly turned to his friend: "Lamon, that speech won't scour!"[111] However, as Gitt countered: "Finally there came applause. . . . It was as if the Blue Ridge Mountains to the west were echoing Lincoln's concluding and keynote thought."[112] Those on or near the stage like Gitt echoed the magnanimity, including Benjamin Brown French, who helped plan the ceremony: "Anyone who saw & heard as I did, the hurricane of applause . . . would know that he lived in every heart . . . it was a tumultuous outpouring of exultation . . . the spontaneous outburst of heartfelt confidence in *their own* President."[113]

Across the nation and beyond, newspapers reprinted the speech, offering a more mixed review depending on either geographic affinity or political persuasion. Even Lincoln's leading home state newspapers varied. The *Chicago Tribune* reported: "The dedicatory remarks by President Lincoln will live among the annals of man,"[114] while the *Chicago Times* responded: "The cheeks of every American must tingle with shame as he reads the silly, flat, and dishwatery utterances."[115] Similarly, where the *Press* of Philadelphia called it a "brief, but immortal speech"[116] and the *Springfield* (Massachusetts) *Republican* called "his little speech . . . a perfect gem; deep in feeling, compact in thought and expression, and tasteful and elegant in every word and comma,"[117] the *Harrisburg Patriot and Union* passed over "the silly remarks of the President."[118]

The president of Brown University, James Burrill Angell added to the positive response ledger, noting that he was unsure "where to look for a more admirable speech than the brief one which the President made at the close of Mr. Everett's oration. It is often said that the hardest thing in the world is to make a five minute speech. But could the most elaborate and splendid oration be more beautiful, more touching, more inspiring than those few words of the President? They had in my humble judgement the charm and power of the very highest eloquence."[119]

Writing to Lincoln the day after, Edward Everett recalled from his front row seat: "Permit me also to express my great admiration of the thoughts expressed by you, with such eloquent simplicity & appropriateness, at the consecration of the cemetery. I should be glad, if I could flatter myself that I came as near to the central idea of the occasion, in two hours, as you did in two minutes."[120] Accordingly, Lincoln revealed to his soon to be US attorney general, James Speed, that "he had never received a complement he prized more highly."[121] Yet in response to Everett, Lincoln simply conveyed humbleness: "In our respective parts yesterday, you could not have excused to make a short address, nor I a long one. I am pleased to know that, in your judgment, the little I did say was not entirely a failure."[122]

Rather, few moments in American history have been more intensely scrutinized by writers and scholars than what Lincoln said at Gettysburg, and no single effort of inspired prose has had the longevity or commanded the universal reverence. Maybe more than anything, however, the fact that five copies of the Address exist in Lincoln's own handwriting, demonstrates the immediate and significant impact of his words on the nation.

After the ceremony, the route back to town was filled with cheering and adoring crowds. Lincoln proceeded to meet at Wills's House for dinner and a reception for an hour with "all who chose to call on him." To many,

Lincoln looked tired. On top of staying up late, and getting up early, he bore the weight of such an emotional day, along with feeling weak and dizzy, which proved to be the onset of a three-week bout with varioloid, or what is known as a mild case of smallpox.

Of the "thousands who took him by the hand,"[123] one was seventy-year-old John L. Burns, a Gettysburg shoemaker and veteran of the War of 1812 and the Mexican War. Months earlier, dressed in his "Sunday clothes," and in defense of his town, Burns went right into the early July fight, "which he did not leave until he received three wounds."[124] Upon meeting the local hero, Lincoln remarked: "God bless you, old man." Then, "Arm-in-arm with the President and the Secretary of State," Burns was escorted to the town's Presbyterian church. It was reported that the encounter "must ever be inseparable from this occasion . . . which deserves a place in the story of the war as a noble representative fact,"[125] and "in this touching incident, perhaps, more than any other, Gettysburg was truly dedicated." And with that, at 6:30 p.m. the president departed Gettysburg on a special train for Washington, DC. For all those fortunate to partake in the ceremonial events, the *Press* of Philadelphia may have best summed up the feeling: "The memory of the day, and especially the profound impressiveness of the hallowed battle-ground, will never leave them."[126]

Over time, the Gettysburg Address has grown in fame and stature. The president's assassination in April 1865 only advanced this sentiment, highlighted by American writer Ralph Waldo Emerson's funeral oration for Lincoln, in which he noted that the Address "will not easily be surpassed by words on any recorded occasion."[127] By the late 1860s readings of the Address were commonplace in patriotic celebrations across the North, and over time inspired many wide-ranging impacts, from Article 2 of the French Constitution, which states: "The principle of the Republic shall be: government of the people, by the people and for the people," to Martin Luther King's 1963 "I Have a Dream" speech on the steps of the Lincoln Memorial in Washington DC, when he opened: "Five score years today, a great American, in whose symbolic shadow we stand today, signed the Emancipation Proclamation."[128]

Across American history, presidential aspirants and peers have routinely lauded Lincoln's efforts at Gettysburg. In 1896, presidential candidate and arguably the greatest orator of his day, William Jennings Bryan expressed: "His Gettysburg Address is not surpassed, if equaled, in simplicity, force, and appropriateness by any speech of the same length of any language. It is the world's model in eloquence, elegance, and condensation. He might safely rest his reputation as orator on that speech alone."[129] In this light, it's hard not to consider Lincoln the "father of the rhetorical presidency."[130]

Presidents from Franklin Roosevelt and Ronald Reagan to Dwight Eisenhower and Barack Obama and beyond, shared a reverent magnanimity for the Address. In particular, President Barack Obama remarked, as follows:

> One of the great treats of being president is, in the Lincoln Bedroom [at the White House], there's a copy of the Gettysburg Address handwritten by him. . . . And there have been times in the evening when I'd just walk over, because it's right next to my office, my home office, and I just read it. And perspective is exactly what is wanted. At a time when events move so quickly and so much information is transmitted, the ability to slow down and get perspective, along with the ability to get in somebody else's shoes—those two things have been invaluable to me.[131]

Moreover, Dwight Eisenhower, who would often borrow from Lincoln's phrasings, established his first real residence in Gettysburg, just adjacent to the battlefield. Eisenhower said of the sixteenth president: "Abraham Lincoln has always seemed to me to represent all that is best in America, in terms of its opportunity and the readiness of Americans always to raise up and exalt those people who live by truth, whose lives are examples of integrity and dedication to our country."[132]

Similarly, as noted by Lyndon Johnson on the steps of the Lincoln Memorial on February 12, 1967: "There is a singular quality about Abraham Lincoln which sets him apart from all our other Presidents . . . his total dedication to hard responsibility."[133] And it was through his "mystical dedication to this Union,"[134] Johnson continued, "and an unyielding determination to always preserve the integrity of the Republic"[135] that he gave us the Gettysburg Address. And as scholar Kent Gramm noted, it was Lincoln's faith and dedication at Gettysburg that defined the spirit in which young soldiers navigated relentless bullets, steep cliffs, and "concrete defenses at Normandy"[136] in World War II.

Dedication was Lincoln's defining quality. He applied and strengthened it over the course of his life, so when confronted at his most important moment of leadership—defending the cause of America and the nation's founding principles—he was resolved and ready.

Over a century and a half removed from the Gettysburg Address, "Lincoln endures in our public memory," noted historian Jim Hilty. "We still strive to measure his influence on our national character. Rather than fading with the passage of time, he remains a central figure in our public memories and in our collective identity. He is one of us, yet better than any of us. He penetrates our psyche, guides us even today toward the better angels of our nature."[137]

We are the fortunate heirs of that harvest—a bounty that has helped us to understand who we are, where we come from, and what we aspire to be. A bounty that has provided a roadmap to channel Lincoln's legacy in our own time and in the "unfinished work" ahead of us.

In the end, Lincoln's contemporary, Massachusetts Senator Charles Sumner, may have said it best: Lincoln "made speeches that nobody else could have made. . . . Therefore, we honor him, & Fame takes him by the hand."[138] He was indeed "Such a man the times have demanded,"[139] words that could have been said of Lincoln as easily as he stated them in eulogy of his hero, Henry Clay. In being the leader the times demanded and taking his pen to define the struggle for America's founding principles, Lincoln changed the nation and the world. What a powerful example for any leader at every level.

Chapter 4

Courage

No man is worth much anywhere if he does not possess both moral and physical courage.

—Theodore Roosevelt

Courage is boldness. Courage is risk. It's "being scared to death, but saddling up anyway,"[1] according to actor John Wayne. It's "the guard and support of the other virtues,"[2] noted philosopher John Locke, while for Aristotle it represented the mean between cowardice and recklessness.[3] *Merriam-Webster Dictionary* defines it as "mental or moral strength to venture, persevere, and withstand danger, fear, or difficulty."[4] It's also been said that it is "not simply one of the virtues but the form of every virtue at the testing point."[5]

Among American presidents, George Washington set the tone for this tradition when confronting the first substantial challenge to US federal authority in 1794. After US Secretary of the Treasury Alexander Hamilton introduced, and the US Congress approved, a tax "upon spirits distilled within the United States, and for appropriating the same,"[6] Western Pennsylvanian residents refused to pay the tax, believing it was another example of unbalanced policy making by eastern elites at the expense of frontier folk. President Washington initially sought to resolve the "Whiskey Rebellion" peacefully, but protests became violent. The home of the regional tax collection supervisor, John Neville, was set ablaze near Pittsburgh, leading Washington to organize a militia force of nearly thirteen thousand troops. In what would seem unfathomable today, he *personally* led the force into Western Pennsylvania, while warning the locals "Not to abet, aid, or comfort the Insurgents aforesaid, as they will answer the contrary at their peril."[7] His courageous action dispersed the rebellion.

Andrew Jackson, who rose to prominence as the triumphant general at New Orleans during the War of 1812, followed Washington's important tradition. Upon taking office as president in 1829, Jackson encountered elevated sectional rancor resulting from the passage of the Tariff of 1828, or better known as the Tariff of Abominations. The bill aimed to protect US industrial products from competition by increasing taxes on foreign imports, thus increasing their price and giving similar American products a competitive advantage. However, unlike in 1789, when the first protective tariff was passed, the tax rate was approximately 5 percent on most imported goods. Under the 1828 Tariff, the rate neared 50 percent, causing a windfall for northern manufacturers but a burden for southern planters who were concerned about the possibility of retaliatory tariffs and lower international demand for US agricultural exports.

In 1832, the state of South Carolina, led by their native son and former Vice President John C. Calhoun, declared the 1828 tariff unconstitutional, null and void, and openly defied the federal government by taking steps to block tariff collections within its borders. Calhoun threatened to mobilize men and arms and possibly secede. Jackson, as a slave owner and a proponent of state's rights, had strong feelings about nullification, which he highlighted in an official proclamation: "Disunion by armed force is treason."[8]

Like Washington before him, Jackson took firm action to uphold federal authority, expressing to his Secretary of War Lewis Cass: "We must be prepared to act with promptness and crush the monster in its cradle before it matures to manhood. We must be prepared for this crisis."[9] Jackson urged Congress to pass the Force Bill, which gave him authority to enforce the federal tariff via the military. He also sought to defuse the situation by lobbying Congress again for a tariff reduction. In succeeding on both measures, Jackson resolved the immediate crisis and reinforced that the US federal government would not tolerate state nullification.

Other presidents have also exemplified courage to advance the nation's interests, from Harry Truman integrating the US armed forces and the nation's capital through executive order in 1948; to Dwight Eisenhower sending the National Guard into Little Rock, Arkansas in 1957 to enforce federal court orders for integration despite strong Southern opposition; to George H. W. Bush, who championed the cause of the disabled, advocating for federal legislation to uplift and provide protections. Yet, contrary to these and others acts of presidential courage, many chief executives have fallen short. Andrew Jackson encouraged Congress to adopt the Indian Removal Act of 1830, which began the forced relocations of thousands of Native Americas in what became known as the Trail of Tears. James Buchanan missed in efforts to quell the growing tide toward Southern secession from the Union before the American Civil War, leading scholar Fred Greenstein to conclude of the nation's fifteenth president: "When strong national leadership was needed, he lacked the fiber to confront the situation, taking to his bed."[10] Richard Nixon went to lengths to cover up Watergate, initially agreeing to allow his senior aides to instruct the CIA to thwart the FBI investigation, which, among other things, led him to become the only president to resign from office. And Donald Trump was widely criticized, including by his successor Joe Biden, for "lacking the courage to act"[11] during the attack at the US Capitol on January 6, 2021.

All US presidents, at one time or another, and in various ways, have confronted the need for courage, as described by John Kennedy in his Pulitzer Prize–winning book, *Profiles in Courage*. They faced the sacrifices, "the loss" of friends, "fortune . . . contentment, even the esteem" of their fellow men. In each case they decided for themselves "the course"[12] they would follow. While some withered in the moment, others exemplified a fearless daring spirit to move America forward. Among those in the latter company, one stands out. His name was Theodore Roosevelt, and through his courageous action, the landscape of America was fundamentally transformed for all Americans, and their children's children and beyond.

The Roadmap

Article II, Section 3, Clause 1 of the US Constitution requires an American President "from time to time give to the Congress Information of the State of the Union, and recommend to their Consideration such Measures as he shall judge necessary and expedient."[13] The "State of the Union," as it is now known, was established on January 8, 1790. At Federal Hall in New York City, the then temporary seat of government, President George Washington gave his first "Annual Message." Washington's in-person tradition continued through the John Adams administration, but in 1801, Thomas Jefferson broke with his predecessors. Instead, President Jefferson sent his message to Congress in writing, a precedent lasting over a century until President Woodrow Wilson personally addressed Congress on December 2, 1913. Since then, with few exceptions, presidents have appeared annually before Congress to deliver their message, although the timing has since changed from every December to every January or February—the result of the ratification of the Twentieth Amendment on January 23, 1933, which amended the opening of Congress from early March to early January.

Of the more than 200 "Annual Addresses" by American presidents, a select number stand out historically. President James Polk used his 1848 message to launch a massive migration westward with "accounts of the abundance of gold."[14] President Abraham Lincoln eloquently expressed the stakes of the raging Civil War in 1862: "In giving freedom to the slave, we assure freedom to the free."[15] Similarly, President Franklin Roosevelt called out America's World War II aims in 1941, with reference to four freedoms: the freedom of speech and worship, and freedom from want and fear.[16] President Gerald Ford ominously declared in 1975: "The state of the Union is not good,"[17] in the context of a dire economy. President Bill Clinton expressed "the era of big government is over"[18] in 1996, on the heels of the "Republican Revolution," which saw the GOP sweep both houses of Congress in the 1994 off-year elections, and President George W. Bush identified Iraq, Iran, and North Korea as an "axis of evil"[19] in 2002.

While these State of the Union addresses prove impactful for their memorable soundbites, more important is how each effort sought to elevate distinct policies aimed at advancing the American experiment. However, from among two centuries of policy prescribed manuscripts, one strike of the pen has been largely overlooked, representing not only a transformational moment in US history, but also the defining leadership quality that set an American president apart.

The Scene

The third day of December 1901 began rather inauspiciously in the District of Columbia, as a cold and steady rain soaked the nation's capital. On Capitol Hill, the inclement weather did little to dampen a burgeoning buzz murmuring throughout the halls and cloakrooms of the Fifty-Seventh Congress. Gathering unusually early on the second day of the session, senators and congressmen, in their respective wings of the building, bantered about "prospective legislation,"[20] but more so regarding "the personality of the new President,"[21] and what Theodore Roosevelt would say in his first "annual address" to Congress.[22] A similar spirit swept the galleries in the House of Representatives and the Senate, which were awash with "very good attendance."[23]

The scene was a far cry from the one described by Abigail Adams a century earlier, when she called Washington, DC "romantic but . . . wild."[24] Over the nineteenth century, the capital city and its signature national stage was living up to the standard set by George Washington when he noted in a 1792 letter to Thomas Jefferson: The Capitol "ought to be upon a scale far superior to anything in *this* Country."[25]

Fair to say, though, it didn't start that way. After President Washington laid the Capitol's cornerstone in 1793, only gradual progress was made to the building by a series of architects. The House and Senate wings were not completed until 1811. Three years later, British troops torched the building during the War of 1812, and only a serendipitous rainstorm prevented the structure from complete destruction. Although rebuilt by 1826, within a generation, the US Capitol required appropriations necessary to expand and match the nation's growth. But notwithstanding the buildings' varying size and shape, the Capitol retained its place at the center of American national life in the nineteenth century. "The People's House" hosted the most consequential policy debates, including the Louisiana Purchase, slavery and the Civil War, as well as the process to decide the 1876 national election. And it celebrated the presidential inaugurations of Thomas Jefferson and his successors, while also paying solemn tribute to the fallen, including President's Abraham Lincoln, James Garfield, and William McKinley, and congressional leaders such as Massachusetts Senator Charles Sumner, Pennsylvania Representative Thaddeus Stevens, and Kentucky Senator Henry Clay.

On the first Tuesday in December 1901, the US Capitol was on the precipice of another consequential moment, this time in a new century—one that publisher Henry Luce would later describe as "The American Century."[26] As the hands of the clock pointed to twelve noon, David Henderson of Iowa, the first individual from a state west of the Mississippi River to be elected as Speaker of the House, called the lower chamber to order.[27] After some brief housekeeping and a chaplain's blessing,[28] he announced the appointment of the committee on rules, which included himself and House colleagues John Dalzell of Pennsylvania, Charles Grosvenor of Ohio, James Richardson of Tennessee, and Oscar Underwood of Alabama. Joining the committee from the upper body were Senators Eugene Hale of Maine and John Morgan of Alabama. Just prior to the start of the day's session, this bicameral contingent traveled down Pennsylvania Avenue to the White House to inform President Theodore Roosevelt that Congress was in session. They also expressed their readiness "to receive any communication" he might want to share. In other words, these select lawmakers and their colleagues sought the new president's much anticipated first annual address to Congress.

As Roosevelt biographer Edmund Morris noted, Theodore Roosevelt's message "was the worst-kept secret since the Declaration of Independence."[29] In the weeks leading up to this moment, Roosevelt had invited guests to the White House to partake in his energetic readings of favorite verses, and although the text was embargoed by American media outlets, in Europe it had already hit the presses. Nevertheless, and despite some having a sense of what Roosevelt might say, America's legislative body and the public at large were flush with anticipation.

Never one to underdeliver, Roosevelt received the committee's message "with pleasure,"[30] informing the members that "he would at once communicate with the two houses in writing."[31] After a short interlude, Roosevelt tasked thirty-year White House hand and assistant secretary to the president, Octavius L. Pruden, to personally deliver two copies of the address, "one of the House and the other for the Senate."[32] This wasn't the nearly sixty-year-old Pruden's first rodeo. He carried many similar messages from presidents and "was one of the best-known figures in the capital,"[33] entrusted with the duty of "putting down in writing the history of every official transaction in the White House."[34] Appearing at the main door of the House chamber, Pruden, guarded by Secret Service, was immediately recognized. Presented as "a message to the Congress,"[35] Roosevelt's annual address was brought to the Speaker's desk, where the great seal of the United States on the document was broken by Speaker Henderson.

For the first time in American history, the message was presented in printed form as opposed to traditional copperplate-style. And although sharing the same sized paper, Roosevelt likewise broke tradition with his preference for heavy white paper instead of one with a blue tint. Altogether, "Each copy was richly bound in brown morocco, with stiff covers, a simple gold border, and gold lettering."[36]

As Washington, DC's *Evening Star* reported: "Ordinarily presidential messages at the opening of a Congress are listened to in a perfunctory fashion."[37] But on this occasion, as Speaker Henderson announced: "A message from the President of the United States,"[38] the only sound to be heard was that of Roosevelt's prose, "as the noisy hum of conversation which usually pervades the hall even when important legislative business is being transacted was stilled."[39] This was true on both the House and Senate sides where the president's annual message was to be read nearly simultaneously, with the collective membership glued to their seats following along with their printed copies. In the Senate, particularly, it was reported as the "largest and most attentive gathering . . . during the recital of the contents of a document from a Chief Executive."[40]

The forty-six-page document was handed to Michigan native and Chief Clerk,[41] Henry M. Rose, who began reading the message clearly and distinctly: "The Congress assembles this year under the shadow of great calamity . . ."[42]

The Time and Place

Our next story begins in December 1901, when America was at an inflection point. Three months earlier, on September 6, 1901, at the Pan American Exposition in Buffalo, New York, President William McKinley was twice shot point-blank in the chest with a concealed .32 Iver Johnson revolver. Eight days later, he died from the coalescence of gangrene around his bullet wounds. After a speedy trial, and an admission of guilt, his assassin, twenty-eight-year-old Leon Czolgosz, was sentenced to death by electric chair at Auburn Prison in New York on October 29, 1901. The unrepentant anarchist's final utterance: "I killed the president because he was the enemy of the good people—the working people."[43]

Against the backdrop of a nation mourning its fallen president was a roaring American industrialism that went largely unchecked since the Civil War. In the final three decades of the nineteenth century, or the "Gilded Age," the nation experienced extraordinary growth, particularly in the Northern and Western United States. By 1901, America's ever-expanding population crested over seventy-six million, a fifteen-fold increase across the previous century. States in the Union nearly tripled from sixteen to forty-five over the same period. The proliferation of change in work, home life, and the rise of new immigration led more and more people into bustling cities. New York, America's largest city, experienced a fifty-seven-fold increase to over three and a half million,[44] up from a mere sixty thousand residents in 1800.

With rapid population growth came great innovation. Across the nation, urban architecture ushered in the rise of skyscrapers, major cities became electrified, and telephones flourished. Transportation proliferated as the automobile came of age, flight was within reach, and five railroad systems connected nearly 200 thousand miles of transcontinental track. The idea of "rags to riches" and the "American Dream" defined the world's most affluent nation from "sea to shining sea."[45] Yet these advances came at a concomitant cost. In addition to the overcrowded cities, poor working conditions, and economic disparities, life expectancy curtailed at forty-eight years for men and barely crossed fifty for women. Upward of half of all Americans could be defined as poor, and one in three urban dwellers, or approximately ten million people, were close to starvation. A mere 2 percent of the population finished high school, and depending on who was asked, America was either a nation of great wealth or want.

To make matters worse, a seemingly endless supply of natural resources was consumed at a breakneck pace and largely without recourse, creating an existential threat to water and wildlife, forests and the frontier. The frontier, in particular, was challenged by homesteading and the introduction of barbed wire, which helped bring about its demise, and with it, as historian Frederick Jackson Turner described, the close of the "first period of American history."[46]

Furthermore, Native Americans were driven onto reservations. Oilfields crossed the South and Midwest. And mining companies engaged in wasteful and improper practices, while developers and land speculators pilfered vast tracts of forests. In Maine, for example, the state's forests were "at an all time low . . . a growing number of wildlife species were threatened" and "widespread unease over the future of Maine's forests was evident."[47] Similarly, the State of Minnesota was experiencing its heyday in logging, where over twenty thousand lumberjacks, strong, axe-wielding individuals, earned a living chopping down massive trees across all seasons, even during bone-chilling winters. The year 1901, specifically, marked a high point for white pine logging in Minnesota, with over 2.3 billion board feet of lumber cut from the state's forests, equating to over 600 thousand two-story homes or a "boardwalk nine feet wide encircling the earth at the equator."[48]

In the West, access to water and irrigation reached grave proportions as the survival for crops, livestock, and people were teetering in the balance. Intermittent precipitation impeded agricultural growth and failed to adequately meet the needs of farmers on arid lands, while efforts to capture rain and snow runoff fell short of an elixir. As such, no collective water management effort existed, including any system of dams and canals that would eventually cultivate western rivers and water sources making broad settlement possible.

The "gold rush" propelled the eradication of wildlife species for "profit and sport," as laws were essentially nonexistent or unenforceable.[49] Approximately forty million bison were exterminated from the Great Plains, and in Florida, the once deemed abject swampland became a treasure trove for colorful bird feathers adorning hats, capes, gowns, and other clothing accessories of affluent women. The proliferation of fashion magazines only amplified the demand, driving a cottage millings industry to employ over eighty thousand workers, mostly women, to "trim bonnets and make sprays of feathers known as aigrettes."[50] Feeding these urgings, plume hunters crisscrossed the Sunshine State for wading birds and other fantastical feathered prey, many with semiautomatic rifles, resulting in the slaughter of millions of birds each year. A pound of great white heron wings, notably, was worth more than a pound of gold.[51]

The existential threats posed by industrialization, wasteful consumption, and environmental degradation experienced in America's cities and countryside began to enter the public consciousness. A critical footnote for this school of thought came in the form of George Perkins Marsh's eye-opening 1864 work, *Man and Nature*,[52] where he challenged the general view by arguing that humanity could impact the environment in permanently damaging ways. In his focus on the ancient Mediterranean civilizations, Marsh found their self-inflicted decline resulted from environmental abuse, particularly through deforestation and the profligation of waste.

This paradigm shifting thesis instantly proved influential in stoking the energy and advocacy of Americans at the local level, particularly toward solutions, including restrictive seasons for hunting and fishing. Soon Congress passed legislation granting Yosemite Valley to the State of California as a public park, and Marsh's view became particularly instructive to Franklin B. Hough of the American Association for the Advancement of Science, who called on Congress to form a national forestry commission in 1873, which was enacted three years later. A decade thereafter, New York State established the Adirondack Forest Preserve in 1885, a bellwether in conservation legislation, and later as a state park to "be kept forever as wild forest lands."[53] Although the collective grassroots response was far more heterogeneous than unified, the core sentiment of the movement can be found in the words of author and era contemporary, Henry David Thoreau: "In Wildness is the preservation of the world."[54]

Conservation advocates like Thoreau used their words to help stir the public to action. Environmentalist William H. Waddle Jr. railed against the indiscriminate destruction of American wildlife in *Harper's New Monthly Magazine*. Author William E. Smythe published *The Conquest of Arid America* in 1900, which advocated for an irrigated West.[55] And editorials by Robert Underwood Johnson in *Century* magazine aimed to shift the tide of public opinion toward federal forest conservation.

Around the same time in 1890, and at the request of Johnson, John Muir, "Father of the National Parks," published two cornerstone articles on wilderness preservation in *Century* magazine, "The Treasures of Yosemite" and "Features of the Proposed Yosemite National Park," where he advocated for Congress to take action to protect the lands from being "devastated by lumbermen and sheepmen, and . . . made unfit for use as a pleasure ground."[56] Muir and other supporters later founded the Sierra Club in 1892, dedicated to the preservation of the wilderness and "to make the mountains glad."[57]

Similarly, the Boone and Crockett Club was established in 1887 by George Bird Grinnell, editor of the influential *Forest and Stream* magazine, and the future president, Theodore Roosevelt, out of fear that America's large game was being overhunted to the point of extinction. The Club was instrumental in getting the Lacey Act of 1894 enacted, which protected wildlife in Yellowstone National Park. Additionally, in 1896, the American Academy of Sciences established a committee on forests, chaired by Charles Sprague Sargent, with Gifford Pinchot as its youngest member. Two years later, Pinchot was appointed chief of the Division of Forestry at the US Department of Agriculture and would soon exert remarkable influence over American conservation policies and how conservation was defined in the political space. As Pinchot noted: "Conservation means the greatest good to the greatest number for the longest time."[58]

American presidents took steps, albeit limited, to advance conservation and steward America's natural resources over the second half of the nineteenth century. Collectively, they lacked long-term vision, and rather focused on putting out the fire of the moment, from water shortages, to land and wildlife preservation crises. President Abraham Lincoln served as a bellwether for the movement against the backdrop of the Civil War in 1864, when he signed a law setting aside the Mariposa Grove and Yosemite Valley as protected lands, which "is widely considered the initial federal intervention on behalf of wildlife resources."[59] Five years later, President Ulysses S. Grant, while not a vocal advocate for conservation, set aside Alaska's Pribilof Islands as a reserve for northern fur seal, the earliest effort to use federally owned land to protect the nation's wildlife. Two years prior, in 1867, Secretary of State William Seward purchased Alaska for $7 million, or approximately two cents an acre. While ridiculed in Congress and in the media as "Seward's Folly" and a frozen wasteland, the purchase eventually prevented Russia and Japan, as well as an influx of US citizens, from killing American seals from the Bering Seas rookeries. The area also proved rich in natural resources, contributing to America's growth henceforth. Not finished, Grant also established Yellowstone as the nation's first national park in 1872.

In 1879, President Rutherford B. Hayes founded the US Geological Survey as a bureau of the US Interior Department with responsibility for "the classification of the public lands,"[60] and ten years later, President Benjamin Harrison furthered Ulysses S. Grant's work by signing "An Act to provide for the protection of the salmon fisheries of Alaska."[61] Harrison similarly intervened at Sequoia, Yosemite, and General Grant National Park's in California, and in 1891, he signed "An act to repeal timber-culture laws, and for other purposes,"[62] known as the Forest Reserve Act, which empowered American presidents to set aside federal land to create national forests. In addition, later that same year, he issued a presidential proclamation creating the first national forest, known initially as the Yellowstone Park Timberland Reserve, because "some question has arisen as to the boundaries proclaimed being sufficiently definite to cover the forests intended to be reserved."[63]

In 1887, President Grover Cleveland took action to keep the Seal Rocks off Point Lobos near San Francisco "free from encroachment by man."[64] In 1894, he also established "An Act to Protect the Birds and Animals in Yellowstone National Park,"[65] which affirmed that national parks exist to protect wildlife and are not to be used for hunting. Rounding out the era, in 1899, President William McKinley established Mount Rainer National Park in Washington, and signed the Lacey Act, which outlawed the interstate shipment of any wild animals or birds killed in violation of state laws.

The important but modest advances of the Gilded Age gave way to a bourgeoning reformist energy. The "Progressive Era," which launched at the turn of the twentieth century, saw "progressives" seek to remake American society as a better and safer place for all, including calls for greater business and government regulation, electoral access, and working and environmental conditions. Mirroring this reformist energy, a new kind of leader came to the American presidency after the assassination of President McKinley in 1901—a leader who intimately understood modern challenges to both the silence of the plains and the throbbing heartbeat of the cities; who defined the boldness of the moment and a new century; and who would direct the federal government to take on the big challenges that faced the nation, including for the first time, to elevate conservation and the stewardship of America's natural resources to the top of the national political agenda.

The Makings of Theodore Roosevelt's Courage

Halfway between Broadway and Park Avenue, blocks from Madison Square, Gramercy Park, and Union Square, stood a large, five-story brownstone townhouse at 28 East Twentieth Street in New York City. The dwelling was an original wedding present of Cornelius Roosevelt to the youngest of his five sons, Theodore Sr., and his wife Martha Bulloch in 1854. The "charming, open house,"[66] was much in the tradition of a "southern than northern household,"[67] and was "furnished in the canonical taste of high New York society, which George William Curtis described in the 1856 satire, *The Potiphar Papers*."[68] It followed the style and layout of traditional brownstones of the day, with its warm color, and its tall stoop leading to a front door, which opened to a long, narrow second-floor hallway, with a parlor in the front and family dining room in the rear, the bedrooms upstairs, and the kitchen and servant quarters on the ground floor. From the front windows, one could look down on cobblestones and carriages and out onto the vibrant city, while the back of the house gave way to a blockwide vista of gardens, trees, and flowers peregrinated by oriental peacocks. In the master bedroom of this near-palatial setting, on October 27, 1858, an eight-pound, six ounce, Theodore Roosevelt Jr., or "Teedie," and later "Teddy" as he was nicknamed, came into the world with an ease of entrance at 7:45 p.m.—the first future US president born in the world's greatest city.

From first breath, Teedie, was hyperactive and inexhaustible, never one to waste a minute of time. Even his art of hand shaking later as president amplified this propensity, as he would engage in an average of fifty grips per minute.[69] Across all endeavors, he seemed to channel an inhuman amount of energy. Yet, none of this was a certainty, for as high energy as he was, and at times wanted to be, and would later become,

Roosevelt self-described as "a sickly, delicate boy,"[70] who "suffered much from asthma,"[71] as well as other ailments, including headaches, fevers, intestinal pain, and nausea.

Accordingly, Teddie's favorite childhood pastime was sitting in a little red velvet chair in the family's parlor, spending hours reading about the natural world and regaling in stories of history and adventure. He was captivated by the "fearless"[72] heroes in these stories and "had a great desire to be like them."[73] He was particularly taken by those "who could hold their own in the world,"[74] such as the "soldier of Valley Forge and Morgan's rifleman,"[75] in the spirit of George Washington and the American Revolution.

Roosevelt's societal status brought him great access to books, a luxury for the time. As he grew older, he set aside time to read, especially in the evening, and was known to get through at least one book a day as president. Complementing his voracious hunger for books was a near photographic memory, a remarkable attention span and imagination, and like his hero, Abraham Lincoln, a gift for storytelling. His sister, Corinne would recall Teedie's stories "about jungles and bold, mighty and imaginary fights with strange beasts." In these stories "there was always a small boy," she recalled, "who understood the language of animals and would translate their opinions to us."[76]

Despite his later distinction as one of the most intellectually gifted presidents, Roosevelt's formal education was nothing more than a miscellany. As he noted: "I never went to the public schools,"[77] and instead, "Most of the time I had tutors."[78] Even so, as a teenager, a friend remarked that Teddy was "the most studious little brute I ever knew in my life."[79] Besides a brief stint in a Manhattan private school, he was coached up on subjects from English, Latin, French, and German, to the wonders of taxidermy. His family also trekked on two yearlong journeys, first to Europe and second to the Middle East, including the Holy Land, and Africa. Together, they enjoyed extended stays in Rome, Greece, Lebanon, Palestine, Egypt, and Germany, where among other things, Teddy kissed the Pope's hand, climbed the Great Pyramid, traced the footsteps of Jesus, and experienced much of the world's greatest art and architecture. His highly esteemed tutor, Arthur Cutler, who helped him prep for Harvard's challenging entrance exam, remarked of his restless pupil: "[TR] never seemed to know what idleness was. Every leisure moment would find the last novel, some English classic, or some abstruse book on Natural History in his hand."[80] This spirit would have made Thomas Jefferson proud.

Roosevelt's prodigious interest in, and knowledge of, the natural world was also uncommon. He was enthralled by firsthand observation, which was cultivated by childhood summers spent in the country, which he and his three siblings, Anna, Elliott, and Corinne, "loved . . . beyond anything."[81] The Roosevelt brood were "always wildly eager"[82] to get closer to nature "when spring came, and very sad when in the late fall the family moved back to town."[83] For several summers the family stayed at Loantaka, in Madison, New Jersey, where Teddy enjoyed pastimes like running barefoot, picking apples, and hunting frogs, and had "all kinds of pets—cats, dogs, rabbits, a coon, and a sorrel Shetland pony named General Grant."[84] Time was also spent on the Hudson River in Barrytown, New York, the Maine wilderness, and at Oyster Bay, Long Island, where TR later built his home, Sagamore Hill, which looked out "over the bay and the Sound" and where he lived full time, beginning in 1887.[85]

Roosevelt also read about the natural world through all seasons. He put his thoughts to paper through semiregular diaries, and as a boy, wanted to follow the path of ornithology, revealing: "There are no worlds that can tell the hidden spirit of the wilderness, that can reveal its mysteries, its melancholy and its charms."[86] Entranced by stories of Yellowstone and its grizzly bears and elk and time-clock geysers, Teddy vowed to visit the new national park one day. He had a fondness for the "big trees" (Sequoias) of California which "rose . . . like the pillars of a mightier cathedral than ever was conceived even by the fervor of the Middle Ages,"[87] and for adventure novels by Mayne Reid and works by Dr. David Livingston and Roualeyn Gordon-Cumming on African exploration.

Teddy's father, Theodore Roosevelt Sr., or Thee as he was called, was a signature influence on him in this fora, calling on his son to "work"[88] and to make his "own way in the world,"[89] including to give him the important blessing during his freshman year at Harvard to "become a scientific man"[90] if he chose to do so. Teddy "fully intended"[91] to embrace his father's blessing but was soon dismayed that scientific study virtually all took place indoors. Instead, he rather ironically took up the study of politics and history, which eventually led him to Columbia Law School. There he soon realized the law was also not a fit, and never completed his degree, but was posthumously awarded one in 2008.

Nonetheless, despite leaving the trained study of the natural world behind at Harvard, his self-guided study would serve as a lifelong interest. As historian Paul Russell Cutright noted: "Roosevelt began his life as a naturalist, and he ended it a naturalist. Throughout a half century of strenuous activity his interest in wildlife, though subject to ebb and flow, was never abandoned at any time."[92]

Thee Roosevelt's influence on his son stretched far beyond his life's work. Representing a combination of "strength and courage with gentleness, tenderness, and great unselfishness,"[93] the elder Roosevelt was a vibrant and handsome man with an abounding exuberance for life. He could equally be found waltzing at a society ball, riding his horse through Central Park, exercising with the energy of a teenager, or giving "every seventh day of his life" to teaching in mission schools or applying his time to "an immense amount of practical charity work."[94] He was also someone who "excelled at improving every spare half-hour."[95] As such, Teddy believed there was "never anyone who got greater joy out of living than did my father, or anyone who more whole-heartedly performed every duty."[96]

Describing his father as "the best man he ever knew"[97] and "the only man" he was ever really afraid of,"[98] Thee's Renaissance spirit came to define his son, as well as his penchant for risk taking and courageous maneuvering, as the elder Roosevelt "liked to take chances . . . and was even better at getting out of a scrape than into it."[99] It was likewise Thee who pushed Teddy past his asthma and poor physical condition as a child, telling him: "Theodore, you have the mind, but you have not the body, and without the help of the body the mind cannot go as far as it should."[100] He further implored: "You must make your body. It is hard drudgery to make one's body, but I know you will do it."[101] To which Teddy replied, committing to his father: "I'll make my body."[102] And he did.

After Thee fitted a workout room in their home, Teddy's physical transformation proved dramatic: "Having been a rather sickly and awkward boy . . . I had to train myself painfully and laboriously not merely as regards my body but as regards my soul and spirit."[103] This followed Teddy's worldview that an individual's strong and clean character was better than either a sound body or sound mind.

Through this metamorphosis, Roosevelt taught himself to be brave: "By acting as if I was not afraid, I gradually ceased to be afraid."[104] He was particularly "impressed"[105] by a passage "in one of Marryat's books"[106] where "the captain of some small British man-of-war is explaining to the hero how to acquire the quality of fearlessness."[107] At the outset, Teddy noted, almost every man is frightened when going into action, but that the key was to keep "a grip on himself that he can act just as if he was not frightened."[108] This resonated with him, as there were "all kinds of things"[109] he was afraid of at first, "ranging from grizzly bears to 'mean' horses and gunfighters;" but by acting as if he was not afraid, he "gradually ceased to be afraid."[110] Roosevelt concluded that "Most men can have the same experience if they choose,"[111] and as the habit grows, they will "behave well"[112] under pressure.

Etched into him was this courage in action as well as hundreds upon hundreds of hours of strength training. He took up boxing after an incident with some "mischievous"[113] boys at Moosehead Lake in Maine who "proceeded to make life miserable"[114] for him. After a bit of a scrum, he made up his mind to never again "be put in such a helpless position."[115] Heeding a theory that "One learns fast in a fight,"[116] and after some slow progress, Teddy worked himself up to winning a lightweight boxing contest, and a pewter mug he received became one of his "most prized possessions."[117] A heavyweight sparring partner would later remark of him: "Theodore Roosevelt is a strong, tough man; hard to hurt and harder to stop."[118]

Topping out at 125 pounds at Harvard, he would eventually develop into a five-feet, nine-inches, 200-pound force of a man, possessing blue eyes, a sprawling mustache, and a million-dollar smile and laugh. His physical journey continued as president, as he "tried to get a couple of hours' exercise in the afternoons,"[119] from tennis and swimming naked in the Potomac River, to wading into the frozen stream at Rock Creek Park "when the ice was floating thick upon it,"[120] followed by shivering members of his cabinet.[121]

Always the center of attention, Roosevelt's oldest daughter Alice humorously noted of her father: he was "the bride at every wedding, and the corpse at every funeral."[122] TR possessed great warmth and charm, a positive countenance, unflagging self-confidence, and exquisite manners. "To know him was to love him," American naturalist John Burroughs said of Roosevelt."[123]

One of Teddy's favorite expressions was "dee-lighted," which complemented his youthful spirit, especially when he was around children, leaving the best man at his second wedding, British Ambassador Cecil Spring Rice, to remark: "You must always remember that the President is about six."[124] Similarly, another Roosevelt friend, Massachusetts Senator Henry Cabot Lodge noted: "Theodore is one of the most lovable as well as one of the cleverest and most daring men I have ever known."[125] His classmates at Harvard found him absolutely fascinating and it was said that he navigated the college campus like a man with the morning on his face.

The future US president "Thoroughly enjoyed Harvard,"[126] believing that it did him good, but it was also during his time there that he lost his father to a monthlong battle with a gastrointestinal tumor. Initially Thee's struggles were kept from his son, but when he was finally informed, Teddy swiftly took the train from Cambridge to New York City. He would miss his father's death at the age of forty-six by a few hours, expressing in his diary: "I felt as if I had been stunned, or as if part of my life had been taken away. . . . He was everything to me, my father, companion, friend."[127] Further exemplifying his father's profound impact on his life, TR added: "How I wish I could ever do something to keep up his name."[128]

The Roosevelt name dated back to "about 1644,"[129] when the patriarch Klaes Martensen van Roosevelt, became one of the early settlers of New Amsterdam. From that day forward and over the next two centuries, every generation of Roosevelt's was born on Manhattan Island, including Teddy, who represented the seventh generation, as the industrious family quickly rose in society as bankers, engineers, and merchants, including one descendent who helped ratify the US Constitution alongside Alexander Hamilton.[130] The maternal line of the Roosevelt side of the family tree was also especially significant, tracing roots back to the ship that brought William Penn to America and the subsequent founding of Pennsylvania.[131]

On TR's mother's side were the Bulloch's, who traced their lineage in America to 1729, when the family patriarch, James, emigrated from Glasgow, Scotland, to Charleston, South Carolina. The family eventually made its way Georgia, where Teddy's great-great-grandfather, Archibald Bulloch, would serve as the state's first Revolutionary president,[132] establishing a string of family politicians with a natural propensity for power. His mother Martha, or Mittie as she was called, was the epitome of "a sweet, gracious, beautiful Southern woman,"[133] with blue eyes, black hair, and radiant skin, along with a sharp mind and "a strong sense of humor."[134] Regarded as "a delightful companion,"[135] she surrounded herself with beautiful things, from violets to works of art, and was an enthusiast for taking two daily baths, "one for cleaning, one for rinsing"[136] as "No dirt . . . ever stopped near her."[137] According to Teddy, his "devoted" mother was entirely "unreconstructed"[138] to the day of her death, and it is believed the character, Scarlett O'Hara, in Margaret Mitchell's novel *Gone with the Wind* is partly based on her.

Joining Mittie at the East Twentieth brownstone was her mother, Martha, and sister Anna, who shared with young Teddy tales from Bulloch

Hall, the white-columned antebellum plantation mansion in Roswell, Georgia, where their family needs were met by dozens of slaves. From his mother and his Bulloch forebearers, Teddy inherited a sense of power, southern refinement, and the responsibilities of charity. Moreover, Mittie, in accord with Thee, "warmly"[139] encouraged TR's enthusiasm for natural history, including a fascination for birds.

Roosevelt was particularly grateful to his parents for "the happiest home life of any man,"[140] and because he "literally never spent an unhappy day, unless by my own fault!"[141] He further remarked that he hardly knew a "boy who is on as intimate and affectionate terms"[142] with his family as he was.

Tragically, Mittie met a premature death like Thee, passing away from typhoid fever on Valentine's Day 1884, at the age of forty-eight. However, unlike with his father, Teddy was at his mother's bedside when she took her last breath at 3 a.m. Making the lowest point of his life even worse, less than twelve hours later, he watched his wife Alice, who he described as "so radiantly pure and good and beautiful,"[143] die in his arms on the fourth anniversary of their wedding engagement from complications of childbirth and Bright's disease. In his diary that night, Teddy placed a large X, along with the simple words: "The light had gone out of my life."[144]

Distraught, Roosevelt took refuge on the western frontier, far away from bustling New York City or his role in the state legislature in Albany, to a place where mighty rivers and open terrain represented the major markings on the map. Arriving at a train depot near the Little Missouri River near Medora, North Dakota, the vastness of the rugged landscape was inescapable. In the open frontier's last days, it was here he became another man, building his own cabin, hunting and fishing, laboring, exploring, and cowboying. It was here he healed from tragedy and became close to whole again within the solitude of the wilderness.

TR called his time away in the Badlands "the most important educational asset"[145] of his entire life, feeling "absolutely free as a man can feel," and affirming: "I would not have been president had it not been for my experience in North Dakota."[146] He would likewise escape to the wilderness at other important moments of decision in his personal and political life, but at the end of the day, as historian R. L. Wilson noted about Roosevelt: "His heart belonged to the West, his mind to the East."[147]

For his time away and thereafter, he owed much to his siblings. His older sister Anna or "Bamie" took care of his young baby. His sister

Corinne or "Conie" reintroduced him upon return to New York to their childhood next-door neighbor Edith Kermit Carow, and TR quickly turned their friendship into marriage and five children. And his brother Elliott would become a first-time father to future First Lady, Eleanor Roosevelt, who Teddy would walk down the aisle in marriage to Franklin Roosevelt, after his brother lost his battle with alcoholism.[148]

Back in Manhattan, Roosevelt resumed his political career, running for mayor of New York in 1886. Although he lost the race, he enjoyed the venture, noting: "Anyway, I had a bully time!"[149] He went on to serve as civil service commissioner under two US presidents, New York City police commissioner, assistant secretary of the Navy, colonel of the Rough Riders, governor of New York, and US vice president and president. He also served as an original member of the American Institute of Arts and Letters, a founder of the Boone and Crocket Club and the National Collegiate Athletic Association, and as president of the American Historical Association. Collectively, he wrote over thirty-five books, and over 150,000 letters to an expansive network of friends and colleagues.

Over his life and career, Roosevelt believed there were three qualities needed for success for "which no brilliancy and no genius can atone . . . Courage, Honesty and Common Sense."[150] While he cherished each, it was the quality of courage that most defined not only his own success but his impact on the American experiment. We see this through the words of author Orison Swett Marden, who noted: "Most of our obstacles would melt away if, instead of cowering before them, we should make up our minds to walk boldly through them,"[151] and in how Teddy transformed his body past his asthma and poor physical condition as a child and taught himself to be brave. Or through Roosevelt's worldview that, "Far better is it to dare mightily things, to win glorious triumphs, even though checkered in failure, than to take rank with those poor spirits who neither enjoy nor suffer much, because they live in a gray twilight that know not victory nor defeat."

We see this through the words of L. Frank Baum, author of *The Wonderful Wizard of Oz*: "True courage is in facing danger when you are afraid,"[152] and in how Teddy stood down and killed a charging lion and bull elephant on an African plain, and narrowly escaped death from an American grizzly bear. Or through his actions in leading his volunteer troops, the Rough Riders, in taking San Juan Hill under a hail of bullets. Calling the experience "the great day of my life,"[153] his efforts changed the course of the battle and the Spanish-American War, for which he was posthumously awarded the Medal of Honor by President Bill Clinton.

We see this through the words of French author André Gide: "Man cannot discover new oceans unless he has the courage to lose sight of the shore,"[154] and in Teddy's journey to the Dakota Badlands to rediscover himself after the lowest point of his life. Or, through his actions to mediate the Russo-Japanese War, which earned him distinction as the first American to win the Nobel Peace Prize.

We see this through Ernest Hemingway's definition of courage or "grace under pressure,"[155] and in Roosevelt's election to the New York legislature as the "youngest man"[156] in that body at the age of twenty-three, the same age Abraham Lincoln first ran but lost a bid for the Illinois legislature. Or through Teddy's actions after being shot in the chest by a fanatic at close range outside the Gilpatrick Hotel in Milwaukee, while campaigning for president in 1912. Despite his wound, he went on to deliver his previously scheduled speech with the .32 caliber bullet still in his body. After pulling the bloodstained speech from his breast pocket, he declared: "You see, it takes more than one bullet to kill a Bull Moose."[157] He would speak for eighty-four minutes before being rushed to the hospital.

We see this through the eyes of tech innovator Steve Jobs, who called on Stanford University graduates in 2005 to "have the courage to follow your heart and intuition,"[158] and in Roosevelt's decision to choose a career in public service over science. This career also included time as police commissioner in New York, and a commitment to "administer the police department with entire disregard of partisan politics"[159] and to use his position to help make "the city a better place in which to live and work for those to whom the conditions of life and labor were the hardest."[160] As such, he believed one could not be "neutral between right and wrong, but in finding out the right and upholding it, wherever found, against the wrong."[161]

And we see it through the words of Roman statesman Marcus Tullius Cicero: "A man of courage is also full of faith,"[162] and in Teddy's belief that "we must strive in good faith to play a great part in the world. We cannot avoid meeting great issues. All that we can determine for ourselves is whether we shall meet them well or ill."[163] And through his First Annual Message to Congress, we see him use his political courage and put his full faith into taking on the most existential issue of his time.

The Annual Address

Those assembled "under the shadow of a great calamity,"[164] as described by Roosevelt in his opening prose, sensed something different in the air. At the outset, the new president was striking a different tone from annual messages of the past. It was certainly different from George Washington's opening in his "First Annual Address to Congress" in January 1790, in which he said, "I embrace with great satisfaction the opportunity which now presents itself of congratulating you on the present favorable prospects of our public affairs."[165] And it was a far cry from Abraham Lincoln, who began his first message to Congress forty years to the day earlier in December 1861: "In the midst of unprecedented political troubles we have cause of great gratitude to God for unusual good health and most abundant harvests."[166]

It's not that Washington's or Lincoln's words or platitudes were not meaningful, rather, it was that Roosevelt was bypassing these traditional pleasantries in a business-like fashion. And from the "clear, firm, and distinct tones,"[167] "emphasis and expression,"[168] and without the "usual sing-song monotone"[169] provided by Chief Clerk Henry M. Rose, Roosevelt had the right conduit to amplify his voice and vision.

Getting straight to the heart of the matter, Roosevelt began with an "eloquent funeral oration"[170] of the slain president. He referred to his predecessor, William McKinley, as the "most widely loved man in all the United States . . . wholly free from the bitter animosities incident to public life."[171] Roosevelt's words stirred both the House and the Senate, as many were moved to "bow their heads"[172] in remembrance. As the *Chicago Daily Tribune* reported: "The President's literary art had been expected, but it was hardy supposed he would begin his message with such a rhapsody of affectionate regret."[173]

He then pivoted to the harsh reality. McKinley was "shot by an anarchist,"[174] the third elected president of the last seven to be murdered. Compelled to action, Roosevelt sounded the "grave alarm"[175] for "all loyal American citizens."[176] With a verve solely his own, TR's words thundered across Capitol Hill at the slain president's killer, who he deemed was an "utterly depraved criminal,"[177] opposed to "all governments,"[178] and to "any form of popular liberty."[179] To the new president, this anarchist represented a different brand of killer, a "more dangerous"[180] criminal than any other,"[181] and a contradistinction to those who took the lives of

President's Abraham Lincoln and James Garfield because of the type of government they believed in.

Relentlessly digging in, Roosevelt spent nearly ten minutes reviewing the sins of anarchism, calling the doctrine a "crime against the whole human race,"[182] and making clear that he wasn't going to stand for it. On his watch, America would not "fall into anarchy,"[183] because, as the reading clerk closed this topic with emphasis: "American people are slow to wrath, but when their wrath is once kindled it burns like a consuming flame."[184] With that, the preceding strict "heed and attention" of Congress gave way to roaring applause, as Roosevelt's words "fell with force and effect upon each hearer."[185]

"During the last five years business confidence has been restored,"[186] the reading clerk continued. "The captains of industry who have driven the railway systems across this continent, who have built up our commerce, who have developed our manufactures, have on the whole done great good to our people."[187] As Roosevelt pivoted to big business, the Senate, or "Millionaire's Club" became particularly animated. As Washington's *Evening Star* reported: "Probably no other portion of the message attracted so much attention as that relating to trusts."[188]

Massachusetts Senator Henry Cabot Lodge, Roosevelt's best friend, while lying back in his chair, which was his norm, took to his fountain pen to vigorously underscore select passages. As the reading clerk's voice echoed through the chamber, Lodge was often seen turning to the row behind him to highlight noteworthy phrasings for US Senator Mark Hanna.

Hanna, ever the bowtie enthusiast, in contrast, "seemed to have learned the message by heart beforehand, as he did not refer to his copy, but punctuated paragraphs with solemn nods of his massive head and chin."[189] Across the chamber there was Arkansas US Senator James Kimbrough Jones and Kentucky US Senator Joseph Clay Stiles Blackburn, who rubbed their heads together "page after page"[190] in shared copy of the message. Arguably the most innovative among the ninety US senators was the member from Illinois, Shelby Cullom, who, in order to have easier access to the document, "ripped the cover from his copy, separated the leaves, and read them one at a time."[191]

At the front the chamber, engulfed in rapt stillness, like most of the room, was the seventy-four-year-old Connecticut US Senator Orville Platt. An unyielding advocate of big business, Platt leaned in from his front row position to hear the reading clerk just above him: "There is a widespread conviction in the minds of the American people that the great corporations known as trusts are in certain of their features and tendencies hurtful to the general welfare,"[192] the clerk continued. At the same time, Wisconsin US Senator John Coil Spooner raised from his seat to walk across the room. Spooner, like Platt, was part of the "Big Four," a group of Republicans who controlled major decisions in the Senate. Rounding out the group was William Allison of Iowa and Nelson Aldrich of Rhode Island, the latter of whom Theodore Roosevelt described as the "King Pin" of the Republican Party.[193] Spooner, in particular, had a close working relationship with Roosevelt, and would later author the Spooner Act, which gave President Roosevelt the authority to purchase the Panama Canal Zone. Upon his retirement from the Senate in 1907, TR noted warmly of Spooner: "We lose one of the ablest, most efficient, most fearless, and most upright public servants that the nation has."[194]

Spooner was one of no more than a dozen legislators who left their seat before the full message was completed,[195] but it was clear that conservative statesmen like himself and the business-class "approved of his treatment of this important subject."[196] As he made his way back to his seat, the clerk continued to steamroll through Roosevelt's policy prescriptions on trusts, which the *Washington Post* reported as the president having the "courage to speak the truth."[197] These included calls for a "Secretary of Commerce and Industries"[198] to regulate industry and "deal with commerce in its broadest sense;"[199] a potential "constitutional amendment"[200] to regulate interstate commerce; and legislation to promote the "welfare of the wage-workers,"[201] or as the president put it: "If the farmer and the wage-worker are well off, it is absolutely certain that all others will be well off too."[202] The latter to TR also meant that labor must be "protected by the tariff,"[203] as well as from harsh conditions, including those faced by women and children, from night work and unsanitary conditions, to working more than an eight-hour day.

As the reading clerk pivoted to immigration, the hands of the clock stretched well past one in the afternoon. By this time, some members began to cheat through their printed copies to see how much of the message remained. Just over a quarter of the way through, the well-stocked saloon and warm lunch trays of the cloakrooms waited idly by as the president strategically saw to it that important items were interlaced among others less weighty to maintain the fullest attention of the Congress. Moreover, as the *Washington Times* explained: Roosevelt's "warnings and suggestions"[204] in his annual message "were more than mere words."[205] As those assembled could attest: "They seemed clothed with the energy of the hand which had penned them and the brain which had given them birth."²⁰⁶ The "freshness and vigor"²⁰⁷ of the president's style "captivated the members."²⁰⁸ The *Chicago Daily Tribune* reported that there was a "force and fluency to the straightforward Anglo-Saxon sentences of President Roosevelt which forced dozens of members who usually retire to the cloakrooms to listen with close attention, and even to follow the reading with the utmost care in the pamphlet copies."²⁰⁹

Continuing, the reading clerk highlighted TR's view that America's immigration laws were wholly "unsatisfactory,"²¹⁰ and his prescription was to fit "every honest and efficient immigrant to become an American citizen,"²¹¹ while also calling for a "threefold improvement,"²¹² which included a ban of individuals with low mental acuity, low wage requirements, and low moral tendencies or "anarchistic principles."²¹³ Roosevelt further called for reenacting the law "excluding Chinese laborers,"²¹⁴ which drew applause from both sides of the aisle.²¹⁵

He argued for keeping gold as the standard money, and requested a status quo on tariffs, and for reciprocity "without injury to . . . home industries,"²¹⁶ adding: "Nothing could be more unwise than to disturb the business interests of the country by any general tariff change at this time."²¹⁷ He criticized railway rebates and price-fixing, and yet was against any legislation that unnecessarily interfered with the "development and operation"²¹⁸ of America's railways, or as he called them, the "commercial lifeblood"²¹⁹ of the nation.

He called for the continued work of "upbuilding the Navy,"²²⁰ including "additional battleships and heavy armored cruisers,"²²¹ while also advocating to maintain current Army levels and efficiency. He believed that "American goods should be carried by American-built ships"²²² and urged accompanying remedial action by Congress to enhance the merchant marine. He conveyed optimism about America's developing relationships with Puerto Rico and a free Cuba, as well as the future of the Philippines, including efforts to help "the stony and difficult path that leads to self-government,"²²³ and the need for additional legislation to "introduce industrial enterprises."²²⁴ He advocated for "international relations of mutual respect and good will,"²²⁵ expressing heartfelt thanks to Britain and Germany for their "expressions of grief and sympathy"²²⁶ over the death of President McKinley. On the other hand, he described China as the "keenest national concern,"²²⁷ aiming to bring the Asian nation "into peaceful and friendly community of trade with all the peoples of the earth."²²⁸

He affirmed the Monroe Doctrine as the "cardinal feature of the foreign policy,"[229] which also connected his address to President James Monroe's Annual Address "just seventy-eight years"[230] prior. In that same spirit he also called for "the building of a canal across the Isthmus connecting North and South America,"[231] which after a treaty with Great Britain, was ready for Senate ratification. He advocated for the incomparable work of the Library of Congress and Smithsonian Institution, a revised consular service, permanent census bureau and free rural mail delivery. Connecting the dots with Thomas Jefferson, he called on Congress and "all the people"[232] to support the "One Hundredth Anniversary of the Louisiana Purchase,"[233] which he described as "one of the three or four great landmarks in our history"[234] and the decider in America becoming "a great continental republic."[235]

Over an incredible two and a half hours, Theodore Roosevelt's presidential vision was laid out before Congress and the world. His message boldly and courageously took on the most important issues facing the nation, both domestically and internationally. But it was his trailblazing advocacy a third of the way through the address that fundamentally changed the makeup and soul of America, fulfilling Jefferson's promise of America as a "great continental republic."[236]

Roosevelt was known for coining the term "bully pulpit," as he was quoted using it in the *New York Times*: "I suppose my critics will call that preaching, but I have got such a bully pulpit!"[237] It was the president's belief that an office or position provides an incumbent with the platform to speak out on issues. Filling in the last jigsaw pieces of his historical message, he embraced as much the bully pulpit as the preacher's pulpit, with a prescient sermon for the conservation of natural resources, noting: "The "forest and water problems are perhaps the most vital internal questions of the United States."[238]

The section represented over 11 percent of the draft, covering more than his combined McKinley eulogy and strike against anarchy. Even Members of Congress who knew of Roosevelt's propensity for wildlife protection and forest protection as a Boone and Crockett Club enthusiast or as governor of New York were caught off guard by the strength and boldness of his conservationist platform.

And, in such a deeply personal address, which included the impact of McKinley's assassination, his naval advocacy as a former assistant secretary of the Navy, his mindfulness of the wage earner, and his faith in the American citizen, it was this final piece that meant the most to him. It represented who he was at his core. And it was drafted for posterity, representing the culmination of his lived experience.

Shortly after McKinley's assassination, when Roosevelt was staying at his sister Anna's house in Washington, DC, which became an important second White House for him, he received Gifford Pinchot and Frederick Hayes Newell as guests. The two conservation experts pitched the president on "their plans for national irrigation of the arid lands of the West, and for the consolidation of the forest work of the government in the Bureau of Forestry."[239] An advocate for both, Roosevelt asked them to "prepare material on the subject"[240] for him to use in his first message to Congress. In preparation, TR also wrote John Muir to solicit his view on forests, to which he responded by endorsing the creation of a Bureau of Forestry, also supported by Pinchot.

As the reading clerk articulated: "Public opinion throughout the United States has moved steadily toward a just appreciation of the value of forests, whether planted or of natural growth."[241] Demonstrating a deep grasp of the subject from decades of study, Roosevelt explained the role of forests and their relation to the "creation and maintenance of . . . national wealth,"[242] and how now that was more apparent than ever, as almost half of the nation's timber was gone.[243] To Roosevelt, the "reserves were neither well protected [n]or well used."[244]

Providing Congress with their wake-up call, he advocated for "wise forest protection,"[245] not as a means to retract resources from "wood, water, or grass,"[246] but to "increase and sustain the resources of our country and the industries which depend on them."[247] To this end, he advocated for additions to America's forest reserve "whenever practical."[248] His collective advocacy was a business necessity he believed, but also a remedy to the destruction of the forest, which was ultimately a threat to America's well-being. Under his watch, no western states were off limits.

As part of "wise forest protection,"[249] he also called for in "some at least of the forest reserves"[250] federal protection of "native fauna and flora, safe havens of refuge to our rapidly diminishing wild animals of the larger kinds, and free camping grounds for the ever-increasing numbers of men and women who have learned to find rest, health, and recreation in the splendid forests and flower-clad meadows of our mountains."[251] From his own experience, Roosevelt believed the forest reserves "should be set apart forever for the use and benefit of our people as a whole and not sacrificed to the shortsighted greed of a few."[252]

Imperatively, the reading clerk continued: "At present the protection of the forest reserves rests with the General Land Use Office, the mapping and description of their timber with the United States Geological Survey, and the preparation of plans for their conservative use with the Bureau of Forestry, which is also charged with the general advancement of practical forestry in the United States."[253] For Roosevelt, this current arrangement was too siloed and too diffused in terms of responsibility for his liking. He preferred "effective co-operation"[254] and asked that these "various functions"[255] be coalesced within the "hands of the trained . . . Bureau of Forestry,"[256] "to which they properly belong."[257] He also pitched Congress for greater presidential power in transferring lands for use as forest reserves to the US Department of Agriculture. In making his case, he made clear that he already had such authority in the case of lands needed by the Departments of War and the Navy. "The water supply itself depends on the forest,"[258] the reading clerk continued. "In the arid region it is water, not land, which measures production. The western half of the United States would sustain a population greater than that of our whole country to-day if the waters that now run to waste were saved and used for irrigation."[259]

"As an arid-land man at heart,"[260] Roosevelt then began to connect the dots regarding forest conservation as "an essential condition"[261] of water conservation. Describing forests as natural reservoirs, he explained that by "restraining the streams in flood and replenishing them in drought they make possible the use of waters otherwise wasted."[262] But he made clear that the forests alone could not fully regulate and conserve the waters of the arid region. He therefore appealed for the reclamation of arid public lands so that water could be "brought into reach."[263]

Gone were the days when the initial settler chose their homes along streams from which they could themselves "divert the water to reclaim their holdings." Instead, there were vast tracks of public land that could be settled "but only by reservoirs and main-line canals impracticable for private enterprise."[264]

To "aid irrigation in the several States and Territories,"[265] Roosevelt called for a plan so industrious that only the "National Government"[266] could execute it. But he was clear about his measured approach, imploring that was prudent to study the "existing situation"[267] and "avail ourselves"[268] to best practices. "We are dealing with a new and momentous question, in the pregnant years while institutions are forming, and what we do will affect not only the present but future generations,"[269] he noted.

The president's plan amalgamated around the ingenuity of American engineering. Innovations like reservoirs and levees, Roosevelt believed, would serve as a catalyst to drive safe and sustainable interstate solutions, which could be paid for by the land reclaimed. From the policy side, his plan aimed to champion policies elevating the "broadest public interest,"[270] and not "selfish personal or local interests."[271] It further aimed to "improve the condition"[272] of those already living on irrigated lands," and to help local communities help themselves by stimulating needed reforms in state laws and regulations governing irrigation, including to help make their "irrigation system equal in justice and effectiveness"[273] to any other in the world. But he firmly warned those localities who attempted to play on the fringes: "Nothing could be more unwise than for isolated communities to continue to learn everything experimentally, instead of profiting by what is already known elsewhere."[274] Roosevelt was likewise concerned about recent reports of private speculators nefariously attempting to control water flow, leading the president to note: "The doctrine of private ownership of water apart from land cannot prevail without causing enduring wrong."[275]

If all went to plan, what did Roosevelt believe would be the outcome? As the reading clerk echoed across the chamber: "Our aim should be not simply to reclaim the largest area of land and provide homes for the largest number of people, but to create for this new industry the best possible social and industrial conditions."[276] He continued: "The reclamation and settlement of the arid lands will enrich every portion of our country, just as the settlement of the Ohio and Mississippi valleys brought prosperity to the Atlantic States."[277] In sum, the reclamation of arid public lands was a rising tide to lift all boats, upbuilding and uplifting an entire nation.

Impact and Legacy

After nearly twenty thousand words and over two hours, the reading was concluded at 2:25 p.m. in the House and Senate, eliciting applause from the spellbound statesmen and spectators of both chambers as the clerk finished.[278] Minnesota Congressman and Republican Whip James Tawney remarked: "Probably the best message ever sent to Congress."[279] Massachusetts. Representative William Moody stated: "The voice of a new generation,"[280] and Illinois Representative George Washington Prince said the message met the issues of the day in a "fearless manner."[281]

The response outside of Congress was similarly positive. The *Topeka Capital* called it as "one of the strongest messages ever sent to Congress by any President, and by far the most unique."²⁸² The *Washington Post* likewise found the message "Strikingly unlike any similar paper" in that it was "interesting from the first word to the last,"²⁸³ and altogether marked by "courageous frankness,"²⁸⁴ for Roosevelt was taking on issues that the "mere politician is apt to skip lightly."²⁸⁵

City after city, paper after paper, the commentary connected the message to the man. The *Boston Globe* and *Detroit Free Press* described the annual address as "vigorous"²⁸⁶ and "virile,"²⁸⁷ respectively, while the *Cincinnati Press* called it "thoroughly Rooseveltian."²⁸⁸ In like manner, the *Chicago Tribune* noted the message's "uncommon fullness of thought,"²⁸⁹ and the *Indianapolis News* described Roosevelt himself as "wise as well as brave."²⁹⁰

As would be expected, Roosevelt's message resonated in the West. George H. Maxwell, executive chairman of the National Irrigation Association, could barely control himself, noting that Roosevelt's recommendation on reclamation would "Electrify the West," and practically double "the wealth resources and population of the United States within a generation."²⁹¹ Internationally, the London *Telegraph* viewed it "as the opening of an epoch of heroic legislation," while other London daily papers regarded it as one of the most remarkable messages ever sent to Congress.²⁹² In Germany, it was received "with uncommon interest,"²⁹³ as well as across the globe from the *Times of India*²⁹⁴ to the *Figaro* in Paris.²⁹⁵

In sum, according to TR biographer Edmund Morris: "Only 12 percent" of editorial comments were critical of Roosevelt and "a mere half of one percent" was condemnatory. Possibly one of the harshest criticisms was offered by the *New York Post*, which called the message "much too long."²⁹⁶ If there were criticisms, as the *St. Louis Republic* keenly noted, they were largely on policy and not prose as the "message may be commended even by those who differ politically with the president."²⁹⁷ In retrospect, if there was criticism to be leveled at Roosevelt, it would be his silence on black America in the message, particularly the issue of lynching, which took over 100 known lives in 1901.²⁹⁸

Later that evening, on the heels of a historic day, Roosevelt entertained Republican leadership for dinner at the White House as there was much to celebrate. Not in two generations, or since the earliest days of the Abraham Lincoln administration, had a president's first thoughts received such attention. Roosevelt soaked in the glow of a steady flow of congratulatory telegrams, as the group of about a dozen "remained for some time"[299] past dinner to continue the conversation. All the while, staffers hurriedly drafted a dozen and a half of Roosevelt's proposals into bills.

In many ways, this group of leaders, largely sixty- and seventy-year-old white men used to power and colleagues cut from a similar cloth, were feeling the new president out. Born a generation earlier, many of these men fought in the Civil War and were old enough to be TR's father. Conversely, Roosevelt recently turned forty-three years old and was the youngest man ever to hold the office. On this occasion, he was also the third youngest in the room besides thirty-nine-year-old Indiana US Senator and Roosevelt loyalist, Albert J. Beveridge, and Teddy's second-in-command during the Rough Riders, General Leonard Wood, who was forty-one. It would be hard to escape the feeling that Roosevelt's ascendency was a changing from an old guard to a new one—a change that was happening right before their own eyes.

Writing about this contrast in the *Chicago Record-Herald*, Walter Wellman noted: "It is not so much what he has done as what he may do that fills [them] with anxiety. . . . They have been accustomed to a certain way of playing the game. They know all the rules. . . . Naturally the question arises in many minds: What of the future? What will it all come to? The significance of this great Message, this remarkable piece of writing, is that it has raised up a new intellectual force, a new sort of leader, against whom the older politicians are afraid to break a lance, lest he appeal to the country . . . and take the country with him."[300]

Roosevelt would indeed take America with him. The first significant outcome occurred on June 17, 1902, when Roosevelt signed the Reclamation Act of 1902, allowing the federal government to begin designing and building dams and canals to expand agriculture in the arid West. Although most of the construction took place decades later, the Act paved the legal groundwork for the transformation of the West through the conservation of water in arid environments, making possible the promise of further expansion.

From his time in North Dakota, Roosevelt understood that the West would never be able to grow if it did not have access to water, and without this transformational act, the West could not have been settled. In particular, he believed that these irrigation projects would be of "greater consequence"[301] to the West over the next half century than "any other material movement whatsoever."[302] And he was right. Between 1910 and

2020, the West experienced an eleven-fold population increase, according to the US Census Bureau. No other region in the country compared in percentage growth over the same timeline.[303] This growth, emanating from the Reclamation Act, was in TR's view "a most effective contribution to national life, for it has gone far to transform the social aspect of the West, making for the stability of institutions upon which the welfare of the whole country rests."[304] Theodore Roosevelt's vision for the West had come to life.

Moreover, over seven and a half years in office, Roosevelt would go on to protect 150 national forests, and his relentless advocacy led to the Transfer Act on February 1, 1905, which as he noted: "Transferred the national forests from the care of the Interior Department to the Department of Agriculture, and resulted in the creation of the present United States Forest Service."[305]

From his own estimates, "the area of the nation's forests had increased from 43 to 194 million acres" under his watch and "saved for public use in the National Forests more Government timberland . . . than during all previous and succeeding years put together.[306] These efforts equated to "almost the size of the Atlantic coast states from Maine to Florida,"[307] and the collective 230 million acres Theodore Roosevelt set aside for posterity represented nearly half the landmass of Jefferson's haul in the Louisiana Purchase. These efforts, stemming from the initial advocacy in his annual message, represent the fulfillment of the Louisiana Purchase a century removed.

In addition to national forest land, Roosevelt would go on to protect four big game preserves in Arizona, Montana, Oklahoma, and Washington; fifty-one bird refuges; five national parks from Crater Lake to Wind Cave; and twenty national monuments, including the Grand Canyon, about which historian Douglas Brinkley observed: "If Roosevelt had done nothing else as president . . . his advocacy on behalf of preserving the canyon might well have put him in the top ranks of American presidents."[308] Roosevelt would also do more to protect US wildlife than in all previous years, short of when Yellowstone Park was created.

In the face of a roaring American industrialism that ran unregulated and unchecked, and where America's natural resources were procured with any cost mentality creating an existential threat to America, Roosevelt elevated conservation and the stewardship of America's natural resources to the top of the national political agenda for the first time. In doing so, his courage followed his conscience, and like Washington, Jefferson, and

Lincoln before him, he never lost sight of the "unborn millions." As noted in his own words: "There can be nothing in the world more beautiful than the Yosemite, the groves of giant sequoias and redwoods, the Canyon of the Colorado, the Canyon in the Yellowstone, the Three Tetons; and our people should see to it that they are preserved for their children and their children's children forever with their majestic beauty unmarred."[309]

As Roosevelt took his first postpresidency steps, the *New York Times* posed the question: "Has Theodore Roosevelt in the Presidency done more good than harm?"[310] Summing up their view in one sentence: "The good he has done will live long after him, the evil will soon be cured."[311] America's good fortune is in the "good he has done." "Sustained by unfailing courage,"[312] his "First Annual Address" to Congress set in motion an arc of momentum that fundamentally and forever changed America. His greatest legacy, the expansion of public lands, is grounded in a lifetime study of the natural world and the nearly 2,200 words etched in the message. It's a legacy reflected in the incredible growth of the West, the rich bounty of national parks, vibrant bird sanctuaries, stocked streams, and game-abundant forests and refuges, as well as the US National Park Service's reference to TR as the "Conservation President."[313]

In the end, it was Theodore Roosevelt's developed virtue of courage, that when called upon, drove him to not do the politically expedient thing—but the right thing. His "First Annual Address" to Congress is a document that has been largely overlooked, but particularly through its calls for reclamation and conservation, represents not only a transformational document and moment in American history, but also the defining leadership quality that sets Theodore Roosevelt apart.

In taking this important step, TR was simply following a personal creed, one that leaders would be wise to emulate in their own times: "Let us therefore boldly face the life of strife . . . resolute to be both honest and brave, to serve high ideals, yet to use practical methods. Above all, let us shrink from no strife, moral or physical . . . for it is only through strife, through hard and dangerous endeavor, that we shall ultimately win the goal of true national greatness."[314]

Because of Theodore Roosevelt's courage, America is one step closer to fulfilling that creed.

Chapter 5

Confidence

> Confidence and courage are the essentials of success in carrying out our plan.
>
> —Franklin D. Roosevelt

Confidence is a longstanding American leadership tradition. Born out of Revolution, with an air of swagger, it is exemplified by John Hancock's authentic, oversized signature on the Declaration of Independence: "So that someone can read my name without spectacles."[1] President Barack Obama called it "a prerequisite"[2] to be president, and, while most, if not all of his predecessors and successors embodied it, for a select few, it became their distinguishing leadership quality, called out during America's most crucial moments.

One of those president's was George W. Bush. On Tuesday, September 11, 2001, he awoke before dawn in his suite at the Colony Beach and Tennis Resort near Sarasota, Florida. During the eight o'clock hour, he visited the Emma E. Booker Elementary School to highlight education reform and congratulate the students for the success they had made in their reading. Upon arrival, Karl Rove, the president's adviser, informed him that an airplane had crashed into the World Trade Center in New York City. President Bush immediately envisioned "a little propeller plane horribly lost."[3] As his team gathered more details, the president joined the second-grade class of Sandra Kay Daniels, who was walking her students through reading drills that focused on the story, "The Pet Goat." Moments later, Andrew Card, the president's chief of staff, entered the classroom, walked to the president, and whispered in his ear: "A second plane hit the second tower. America is under attack."[4]

While the president's initial feeling was one of "outrage,"[5] he knew his physical reaction was critical. "If I stormed out hastily, it would scare the children and send ripples of panic throughout the country,"[6] Bush noted. He remained in the room for another seven minutes before calmly walking to an adjoining holding room. There he first saw the slow-motion footage of United Airlines 175 crashing into the south tower of the World Trade Center. He also saw the gaping, burning hole near the eightieth floor of the north tower which was caused by the impact from American Airlines Flight 11.

President Bush sought to get on TV at the school to confidently reassure the nation that the government was responding. "Today, we've had a national tragedy. Two airplanes have crashed into the World Trade Center in an apparent terrorist attack on our country," Bush said. "Terrorism against our nation will not stand."[7]

On the way back to Air Force One, Bush called National Security Advisor Condoleezza Rice on a secure line and was advised that a third plane had hit the Pentagon. His thoughts clarified: "The first plane could have been an accident. The second plane was definitely an attack. The third was a declaration of war."[8] A fourth plane would soon crash into a Shanksville, Pennsylvania field.

In sum, nineteen militants associated with the Islamic extremist group al Qaeda hijacked four airplanes and carried out suicide attacks against targets in the United States, killing nearly three thousand people. For the first time since the War of 1812, the American capital was attacked, and the shock and magnitude led to immediate comparisons to Pearl Harbor.

Later that evening the president addressed the nation from the Oval Office: "A great people has been moved to defend a great nation. Terrorist attacks can shake the foundations of our biggest buildings, but they cannot touch the foundation of America. These acts shattered steel, but they cannot dent the steel of American resolve. America was targeted for attack because we're the brightest beacon for freedom and opportunity in the world. And no one will keep that light from shining."[9]

Three days later, the president toured the World Trade Center site in New York City. As he walked through the crowd, Andy Card pointed to a mound of metal for the president to make some informal remarks. With a bullhorn in hand, and standing next to Bob Beckwith, an older firefighter who had helped pull him up on the pile, the president began: "Thank you all. I want you to know . . ." A voice in the crowd yelled: "We can't hear you." The president replied: "I can hear you." Cheers erupted. "I can hear you," the president continued. "The rest of the world hears you. And the people who knocked these buildings down will hear all of us soon." The crowd immediately broke out into chants of "USA! USA! USA!"[10]

As President Bush recalled later, the "story of that week is the key to understanding my presidency."[11] His aim, above all else, was to keep Americans safe and to project confidence in American leadership: "I would pour my heart and soul into protecting the country, whatever it took."[12] And he did. And American's believed him, evidenced by his 90 percent approval rating in the weeks after the attack, the highest recorded job-approval rating in US presidential history. On the other hand, and contrary to Bush's initial response to 9/11, American history is littered with presidents whose misdirected confidence in the moment left a chilling effect on America's progress. As Abraham Lincoln said: "If once you forfeit the confidence of your fellow-citizens, you can never regain their respect and esteem."[13]

To this end, we can look to the 1850s presidential cast of Zachary Taylor, Milliard Fillmore, Franklin Pierce, and James Buchanan, who either refused to challenge the spread of slavery, or actually perpetuated it, helping to set the stage for Civil War. In the twentieth century, we can look to Herbert Hoover, who, despite taking action and leaving a potential playbook for his successor, exacerbated the Great Depression with his policy making and public perception, such as signing into law a tariff act that fueled international trade wars, as well as his unshakeable branding as a heartless leader, exemplified with the homeless dubbing their shantytowns Hoovervilles. The great irony is that Hoover was far from heartless, and on paper, was arguably the best equipped to fight the Depression, with a record of mastering detail and solving problems through World War I adversity. He also served as US secretary of Commerce under Presidents Harding and Coolidge, where in 1927, he successfully oversaw relief efforts after devastating Mississippi River flooding left 700,000 homeless. However, the public's lack of confidence in his ability to navigate the Depression cost him reelection.

We can also look to Jimmy Carter who spoke to the nation in July 1979 about a "crisis in confidence," relating to the nation's energy crisis and accompanying recession. Carter believed that the core of the nation's inability to navigate its economic challenges was an "erosion of our confidence in the future,"[14] admitting that part of the problem was a lack of leadership. A year later he was voted out of office. And, in the twenty-first century, we can look to Donald Trump, who would never be personally mistaken for having a crisis of confidence. Based on a narrative that the 2020 presidential election was stolen, Trump's bravado inspired his supporters to sack the Capitol on January 6, 2021, as the certification of the election was taking place, and then he watched the madness unfold on television at the White House. He was impeached a week later by the US House of Representatives, representing the only time in US history that an American president had been impeached twice.

Ultimately, these examples demonstrate that the confidence a president possesses matters, as well as the confidence the American people have in that individual, especially in times of crisis. How and when this quality has been channeled and projected by US presidents has fundamentally transformed the trajectory of America. And from among this presidential pack, one leader stands out. His name was Franklin Roosevelt, and through the aura of his confidence, he saved America from the brink of disaster.

The Scene

After a beer and strategy session over dinner with his longtime adviser Lewis Howe, Franklin Roosevelt entered his personal study in the White House just before 10 p.m. on Sunday, March 12, 1933.[15] Known traditionally as the "Yellow Oval Room," Franklin's study sat centrally on the second-floor residence level with large windows facing south overlooking the Washington monument. Today, a door provides a gateway to the Truman Balcony, which was completed in 1948.

Historically, the room has served as everything from a meeting space to a library to a family parlor. On New Year's Day 1801, the layout accommodated the White House's first presidential reception, and in 1889, the mansion's inaugural Christmas tree. Also referred to as the Treaty Room, Monroe Room, and doubling as Theodore Roosevelt's Cabinet Room, under FDR, it was converted to a study, and decorated with his collection of model ships and naval prints, as well as prominent portraits of his wife and mother, two guideposts in his life. As historian Blanche Wiesen Cook noted: "When seated at his desk, FDR faced a pastel portrait of his wife which hung about the hall door," and "a portrait of his mother was directly behind him." However, when he sat on the long leather couch in the room, "which he frequently did during meetings and in moments of relaxation, he faced his mother and had his wife behind him."[16]

FDR's study was where the president worked, often ate lunch, and relaxed. After 5:30 p.m., the room regularly included staff and guests for "the children's hour" of cocktails and gossip. With an adjoining door directly to his bedroom, it was where he worked late at night and on weekends. White House historian William Seale maintained that the study was "the most important room of Roosevelt's presidency."[17] Of note, it was here that Franklin learned of Japan's December 7, 1941 attack on Pearl Harbor. But on this evening, overrun by hundreds of feet of cable wire and accompanying electrical equipment, the room took on a markedly different look and purpose. Earlier in the day, a memo to the press went out on White House stationary highlighting an "Address of President Roosevelt by Radio, delivered from the President's Study in the White House at 10 p.m. today."[18] The message also included instructions embargoing the president's prepared remarks until after he began the radio address.[19]

For the broadcast, Roosevelt dressed in one of his traditional dark gray suits, accompanied by a white dress shirt and striped tie. He settled into a high-backed chair, facing a dark-wooded desk and a strategically positioned Columbia Broadcasting System (CBS) microphone. Framing the scene were curtains, and to his direct right was the room's fireplace. But no sooner did Franklin arrive when a sense of panic engulfed the space. The talking points prepared for the president's broadcast with his "regular pica type, triple-spaced"[20] preference could not be found. White House staffers scurried around at a heightened pace. Grace Tully, the president's longtime assistant recalled that the only person not panicked was "the Boss himself."[21] Rather, FDR "simply took over one of the mimeographed copies that had been prepared for the press, single-spaced and difficult to follow."[22] A definitive explanation for the disappearance never was affirmed, representing "one of the few addresses of which there is no official record since the reading original never was found."[23]

As the hubbub subsided, FDR took a sip of water, stubbed out a cigarette, and before speaking, took a moment to envision his audience. Broadcasting live from coast to coast, the March 12 radio program was introduced by Robert Trout of CBS who read the script prepared for him by his Washington bureau manager, Harry C. Butcher: "The president wants to come into your home and sit at your fireside for a little fireside chat."[24] With his warm and reassuring Hudson Valley, New York tone and relaxed and informal tenor, FDR began his remarks to the sixty million people listening by their radios with the spontaneous words: "My friends."[25]

The Time and Place

As our next story begins, the United States was mired at the depth of its longest and most devastating economic downturn. By March 1933, the "Great Depression" had touched its fourth year and would ultimately stretch for a decade. Immediately preceding the Depression was the period known as the "roaring twenties," an era in which America greatly expanded its economic growth and prosperity, including to double national wealth. Calvin Coolidge, US president from 1923 to 1929, best summed up the period with his motto: "The chief business of the American people is business."[26]

For most at the time, business was indeed good. Jobs abounded, unemployment was low, and a seemingly unlimited set of resources, labor, and industry defined the era. For the first time more Americans lived in large cities than in rural communities. It was during this period that America became a consumer economy, as movie theaters became a popular weekly pastime, and home appliances, radios, cars, and the like raced off assembly lines into everyday lives.

Wall Street served as a beacon for this entrepreneurial spirit. Across the 1920s, Americans increasingly viewed the securities market as a quick and easy way to make a buck. Experienced investors and amateurs alike invested their disposable income and even mortgaged their homes to buy stocks. Hundreds of millions of shares were carried on margin, financed by interest loans predicated on the expectation of profits generated from increasing share prices. This hyperinterest led the market to grow more than fourfold, as securities speculation ran rampant. But something had to give. In response, the Federal Reserve raised interest rates in 1928 and 1929. And while economists and historians differ as to the exact cause of the Depression, at the core was the action taken by the Fed. In a speech nearly three-quarters of a century later, Ben Bernanke, then a member of the Federal Reserve Board of Governors, who later served as Board Chairman, noted that the mistakes made by the Fed contributed to the "worst economic disaster in American history."[27]

Granted, the Fed's decision did serve to cap the rise of stock prices, but the collateral damage was far from anticipated. Coupled with the chilling effect the directives had on interest-driven spending in areas such as automobiles and home building, and thus, production, these outputs converged in a perfect storm. On October 24, 1929, or "Black Thursday," panicked Wall Street selling led millions of overextended investors rushing to liquidate their holdings. After the dust had settled, the stock market declined 33 percent. Billions of dollars were lost, and thousands of investors were ruined.

The Great Crash of 1929 soon gave way to a series of extended banking panics between 1930 and 1933. Fearful of their hometown banks' solvency, hordes of customers rushed to withdraw their cash holdings. For these anxious patrons, stuffing their money and treasures away under a mattress, in a sock, or under the floorboard of an automobile were safer options. As a result, one in five banks shuttered, with almost half occurring in 1933. Gone were the savings, investments, and retirements of thousands of Americans. As Roosevelt's incoming Interior Secretary Harold Ickes noted: "Panic was in the air."[28] The swift contagion spread further across the financial system. Stocks continued to plummet. Businesses folded. Industrial production was nearly cut in half, as gross domestic product (GDP) declined by 30 percent (conversely, GDP declined by 4.3 percent during the Great Recession of 2007 to 2009). Bank failures wiped out seven billion dollars in account deposits. Unemployment spiked. Less than half of the country's labor force was working full-time and one out of every four workers was completely out of work. The times were so dire that nearly thirteen million Americans gave up completely in their search for employment, while hundreds of thousands roamed the country on foot or by boxcar in a hopeless pursuit of income. Some desperate men, women, and children engaged in hourly labor for literally pennies. With soup kitchens running out of food, families searched city dumpsters for something to eat. Without jobs and the safety net of savings, mortgage rate delinquency[29] and foreclosures swelled, with 273 thousand Americans losing their homes in 1932.

The once great pulse of the nation's city streets gave way to an eerie stillness. On their fringes, the poor and downtrodden stood up makeshift shacks in so-called Hoovervilles. The uncertain future led suicides to triple and the birth rate to decline 15 percent. Echoing the hopelessness experienced by so many at the turn of 1933, former President Calvin Coolidge noted: "In other periods of depression it has always been possible to see some things that were solid and upon which you could base hope. But as I look about, I now see nothing to give ground for hope, nothing of man."[30] Similarly, Francis Perkins, US Labor secretary under President Franklin Roosevelt said of the times: "It is hard today to reconstruct the atmosphere of 1933 and to evoke the terror caused by unrelieved poverty and prolonged unemployment."[31] "Looking back on those days, I wonder how we ever lived through them."[32]

The pride of West Branch, Iowa, President Herbert Hoover was responsible for navigating the nation through the initial years of the crisis. He came to office in 1929, as one of the most accomplished and admired leaders in America. His exceptional management of relief efforts in Europe during World War I and eight years of service as US secretary of Commerce during the 1920s made him a household name and a relatively easy choice for president. As historian Arthur Schlesinger Jr. noted: "No one was better placed to anticipate catastrophe," having the "unique opportunity to study the workings and influence the policies of the American business system"[33] for years as secretary of commerce. Hoover's biographer Joan Hoff Wilson echoed this view: "No other twentieth-century American has had his range of interests and breadth of understanding of domestic and foreign economic problems, or has developed such a consistent and comprehensive scientific, organizational approach for dealing with the political economy of the United States."[34]

But Hoover soon confronted a crisis he did not anticipate and that only a relative few understood. He insisted that America was about to turn the corner and good times and prosperity were just a stone's throw away. After all, he inherited an American economy humming in 1929—an economy he helped to build and steer as commerce secretary. Yet his optimistic tone proved to be a liability, as his stance proved more and more out of touch as the economy continued to constrict at an ever-quickening rate. With Black Thursday a mere eight months into his term, Hoover found himself doing everything he could to quell the spread of panic throughout the economy.

At first, he made some positive strides, such as ensuring commitments for public work projects to stimulate employment, which among other things, led the *New York Times* to comment in 1930: "No one in his place could have done more. Very few of his predecessors could have done as much."[35] This brief honeymoon, however, would soon fade as consumer spending and unemployment tracked in opposing directions. After a while, Hoover was widely criticized for just about every program he proposed, never seeming to fully grasp the grave threat facing the nation, and never building confidence in his leadership. All of his strenuous efforts could not outpace the crisis. Popular American entertainer Will Rogers quipped correctly at the time that if someone was to bite into an apple and find a worm, Hoover surely would be blamed.[36]

The crisis also didn't play to Hoover's economic textbook. While he wasn't one for laissez-faire economics and believed that the federal government had a role in stewarding the economy, he further believed that government should not individually act in the marketplace and should do nothing to obstruct the rights of an individual. In other words, he "wanted business, not government, to expand."[37] Moreover, he was a doctrinaire for a balanced budget, believing a clean balance sheet was essential to maintain public confidence. According to this school of thought, if the American people believed Hoover couldn't keep his house in order, how could he expect them too as well? Despite the initial success he enjoyed with a public works stimulus, his strict dogma to a balanced budget didn't allow him to make additional investments, however good it would be for the economy.

Once more, the president didn't do himself any favors by allowing an oversized public caricature of his likeness to develop. Hoover seemed to lack warmth, compassion, or an interest in the lives of individuals. He loathed superficial discourse, and was depicted as out-of-touch, insensitive, and often grim, with a particular penchant for blue-double-breasted suits. This parlayed into a bevy of punch lines representing people's troubles: from Hoover blankets, which were newspapers used to protect from the cold; to Hoover flags, which were empty pockets flipped inside out; to Hoover hogs, which were armadillos ready for eating; and so on.

His skills as an external communicator made it impossible to change this ever-growing narrative or to leverage the bully pulpit to shape public opinion and elevate confidence. Unable to convey sympathy for the unemployed, he once responded when asked about Americans peddling on street corners: "Many people have left their jobs for the more profitable one of selling apples."[38]

Three plus anguishing years of stress and challenge took its toll on Hoover. He wore the heavy burden. His hair turned white and he dropped twenty-five pounds. It should be no surprise that he came to conflate the challenges of the presidency with that of a repairman behind a dike: "No sooner is one leak plugged up than is it necessary to dash over and stop another that has broken out. There is no end to it."[39]

To make matters worse, his landside loss to Franklin Roosevelt in November 1932, ushered in a four-month period of national economic paralysis, as uncertainty mounted over what the new administration would do. The 117 days between Election Day, November 8 and Inauguration Day, March 4, was nothing short of an eternity. With possibly the exception of the 1860 to 1861 transition, and the onset of the Civil War, there had never been a more consequential presidential transition. With the ratification of the Twentieth Amendment in 1933, which moved the presidential inauguration date to January 20, never again would a four-month interregnum pass.

Adding to the drama, Roosevelt sought to distance himself from Hoover during the transition, refusing to act on what he believed were poor proposals. Moreover, in mid-February, an Italian-born US citizen, Giuseppe Zangara, stood in a crowd around FDR's car in Miami, Florida and peppered shots in the direction of the president-elect, yelling out "too many people are starving to death."[40] Although Roosevelt avoided harm, several bystanders were not as fortunate, including Chicago Mayor Anton Cermak, who was mortally wounded. The incident further sent shockwaves through a system just over two weeks from the transfer of presidential power.

On the eve of Inauguration Day 1933, Roosevelt and Hoover met at the White House as part of the long-standing tradition of a president-elect calling on the outgoing president. Hoover used the occasion to make a final plea for joint action to quell the bank crisis. FDR again refused and as he stood up to leave, he said in passing that because the president had much to do, he, Roosevelt, "would understand if the President did not return the call."[41] Hoover looked FDR square in face and said: "Mr. Roosevelt, when you have been in Washington as long as I have been, you will learn that the President of the United States calls on nobody."[42]

The circumstances of the Depression were difficult for most Americans to comprehend. Almost everything in current view seemed gray and bleak. With only a scant number of people even having the dimmest of childhood memories of the Civil War, nothing was more threatening to the survival of the Union. Why were so many good people forced to simply survive? Why couldn't the crisis be resolved? Even the lifeblood of capitalism came into question. So too were the tenets of the American Dream. Revolution was on the menu across America's meager dinner tables, especially in the heartland. Half of all farm mortgage debt was delinquent in 1933,[43] and multigenerational farms foreclosed at a breakneck pace as agricultural income precipitously declined from six billion dollars to nearly two billion. Coupled with international headlines highlighting the rise of fascism, from Adolf Hitler in Germany to Benito Mussolini in Italy, the fate of self-government was at play.

America was a country in crisis. A country on the brink. A country devoid of confidence in itself and the future. A country led by a president who, according to historian Jordan Schwartz, found himself cast in the role as the "defender of faith,"[44] and who bleakly noted to his secretary on his last day in office: "We are at the end of our string . . . there is nothing more we can do."[45] The fate of a nation hung on President-elect Franklin Roosevelt's next steps.

The Makings of Franklin Roosevelt's Confidence

Along the banks of the Hudson River, among farm country just north of Poughkeepsie, New York, the nation's thirty-second president was born the evening of January 30, 1882. The estate, Hyde Park, which shared the provincial town's name, would serve as Franklin Roosevelt's home throughout his life. The 600 acres of property, or the equivalent of one square mile, was adorned with abundant fruits and vegetables from orchards and gardens, scenic fields, a stocked pond for fishing, and woods ideal for exploring and getting lost. Winters brought their own set of experiences, from ice skating, to sledding, to tobogganing down a declivitous slope extending from the estate's southern porch to the riverbank below. Hyde Park was everything to FDR as he would note: "All that is in me goes back to the Hudson."[46]

But this bucolic, even indulgent setting was anything but as FDR came into the world. Across a grueling twenty-five-hour labor, Franklin's twenty-seven-year-old mother Sara struggled to survive. She had to be administered chloroform in an attempt to save her life, as it was assumed baby Franklin would be stillborn. Born blue and unbreathing, the on-site doctor provided mouth-to-mouth resuscitation to the newborn. Although mother and son both lived to tell the tale, the hardship was enough to ensure that Sara would never put herself through another childbirth again.

Tall and regal, with both a strong posture and will, Sara Delano descended from a pedigree established over centuries in France and which arrived in America on the Mayflower in 1621. Traditionally described as overprotective, she indulged her son's every whim, instilling in Franklin a passion for learning and hobbies such as collecting coins, maps, model ships, and stamps. The latter he cultivated throughout his life and called upon a few hours a week during his presidency to help relax and refresh his mind and spirit. Grace Tully would often find FDR "sitting at his desk, a stamp album in front of him, a magnifying glass in hand, Scott's Stamp Catalogue, scissors, and packages of stickers."[47] This "form of recreation gave him a release for short periods," she added, so as to escape "the problems that beset him."[48]

His mother, Sara also instilled in her son the Delano family's love of adventure, from experiences of her own childhood visiting Hong Kong and extensive travels to Europe, to the worldly spirit of Franklin's maternal grandfather, Warren Delano, who made a fortune in trade with China, and was a great influence on FDR. Annual trips abroad became a childhood ritual for Franklin, and by the age of fourteen he had visited Europe eight times, even attending school in Germany in 1891.

On one return trip home when he was three, the ocean liner *Germania* was struck by a huge wave, knocking the captain unconscious. When asked about the experience, Sara Delano said: "I never get frightened."[49] Her grace under fire set an example for her son, and it's hard not to appreciate how important this lesson was to him in assuming the presidency in 1933. FDR's daughter Anna would later note: "Granny [Sara] was a martinet, but she gave father the assurance he needed to prevail over adversity. Seldom has a young child been more constantly attended and incessantly approved by his mother."[50]

To this end, Roosevelt biographer, Jean Edward Smith noted that Sara transmitted to her son "the unshakeable confidence that characterized his presidential leadership."[51] In fact, the man who would later assert during his first presidential inauguration "that the only thing we have to fear is fear itself,"[52] was himself only fearful of one thing—fire—which emanated from witnessing an alcohol lamp fire that tragically took his aunt's life.

Through her son's eyes, Sara Delano saw unlimited potential, and she raised him with the confidence to believe anything was within reach. Her highest ideal was for Franklin "to grow up to be like his father, straight and honorable, just and kind, an upstanding American."[53]

FDR's father, James Roosevelt, or "Popsy" as Franklin endearingly called him, was twice Sara's age when they met, but similarly, came from a prominent Hudson Valley family. The Roosevelt's traced their roots in the new world to the mid-1600s, prospering in the West Indian sugar trade and the Manhattan real estate market. In college, Franklin took a deep dive into the Roosevelt family legacy and found not only a democratic spirit but also a scrappiness: "They have never felt that they were born in a good position they could put their hands in their pockets and succeed.

They have felt, rather, that being born in a good position, there was no excuse for them if they did not do their duty by their community."[54]

Franklin's great-grandfather, Isaac, supported the American Revolution, helped draft the Empire State's first constitution, and served a five-year term as president of the Bank of New York. FDR was fond of telling the story of how Isaac led George Washington's horse in the first inaugural parade.[55] A Gilbert Stuart painting that rests above the fireplace in the library at Hyde Park exemplifies Isaac's confidence and assurance as an eighteenth-century American patrician, qualities that would be passed down through the Roosevelt lineage.

Franklin's fifth cousin, Theodore was the nation's twenty-sixth president and also embraced the family's commitment to service. Especially impactful for a young FDR were TR's visits to their shared alma mater, Groton, an elite private boy's preparatory school in Massachusetts. In an 1897 letter home to his parents, Franklin recalled: "After supper tonight Cousin Theodore gave us a splendid talk on his adventures when he was on the Police Board. He kept the whole room in an uproar for over an hour, by telling us killing stories about policemen and their doings in New York."[56] FDR's familial connection to Teddy Roosevelt helped him attain a leg up with his classmates and demonstrated that the Roosevelt lineage could thrive as men in the arena. He was selected by the Democratic establishment in New York to run for an open New York State Assembly seat largely because of Teddy's national clout and Republican affiliation. Franklin would go on to serve as assistant secretary of the Navy like TR, and marry the sitting president's niece, Eleanor, in 1905, with Teddy standing in for his deceased brother to walk the bride down the aisle.

Franklin's father, James fully embodied the Roosevelt tradition and his impact on FDR was most prodigious. An alum of Union College and Harvard Law School, a vestryman of the local Episcopal church, and an acquaintance of Sam Houston when Texas was becoming a state,[57] he taught Franklin more from nature than books, affirming that fresh air built strong men, the importance of land stewardship, and how to act like a country gentleman. Through all seasons, the two were inseparable outside companions, relishing in hunting and horseback riding, sailing and fishing off Canada's Campobello Island, and iceboating on the Hudson River. From these formative experiences, a perpetual zest for adventure would burn inside Franklin.

In 1888, James provided his son a glimpse into the future, when at age five, Franklin met President Grover Cleveland in the Oval Office. As the story goes, Cleveland patted FDR on the head and said: "I hope, young man, that you will never be president of the United States."⁵⁸ A half a century later, FDR enjoyed regaling that story to children visiting him at the White House.

Franklin knew he was special from an early age, and his parents took every effort to cultivate his self-confidence, uniqueness, and curiosity, while also seeking to insulate him from the harshness of the outside world. A certain naivete emerged from this insulation that would accompany him throughout life: "As when he talked about his own experiences as a gentleman farmer in Dutchess County, New York as evidence of his understanding of the problems of American agriculture."⁵⁹

As an only child in this environment, he learned to enjoy his own company and to take initiative. The center of his universe, he would recall fondly the peacefulness of these times. It was where he cultivated a spirit of hopeful expectation, which would complement his penchant for adaptability.

Physically, Franklin grew slowly into his eventual six-foot, two-inches, 180-pound frame. Broad shouldered, with brown hair, gray-blue eyes, and fair complexion, President Woodrow Wilson once described FDR as "the handsomest young giant I have ever seen."⁶⁰ His mellow and resonant voice blended with a strong hearty laugh. As an adult, he enjoyed a few cocktails in the evening, but not to excess, and would be considered a chain smoker in modern terms.

Franklin's early formal education is best described as arbitrary and informal, rather than structured, and largely included a mix of tutors. He attended a local German school for a brief stint, where his propensity for verbal communication propelled him to quickly learn the German language. At age fourteen, he began attending Groton. From there, he entered Harvard, where his primary order of business was as editor of the *Harvard Crimson*. He then attended law school at Columbia for two years, never graduated, but passed the bar.

As a student, he flourished in science, history, literature, and debate, honing qualities that would carry him throughout life; from mastering the art of reading people and fitting in, which allowed him to later appeal to different constituencies and viewpoints; to recognizing his penchant for learning by hearing other people talk. It was no surprise that later as president, he would prioritize oral briefings to written reports. This allowed him to interject and ask questions, which, as such, according to Roosevelt adviser Sam Rosenman, made it "easy for him to get the gist right away."⁶¹ According to his wife, Eleanor, Franklin had an "amazing ability to skim through any kind of book and get everything out of it."⁶²

He found enjoyment in the works of Kipling, Dickens, and Twain, as well as historical biography, but was collectively no more than a B student. And coupled with serving as the manager rather than player on the Groton baseball team, he neither stood out academically or athletically. He seemed to learn more by doing in the spirit of George Washington, than by engaging in original thinking like a Thomas Jefferson or Abraham Lincoln. To best brief FDR, Francis Perkins said she "learned to prepare material so that it would photograph itself upon his memory . . . preferably one page, of strictly structural outline material."⁶³ Then she would "discuss the matter with him," answer all his questions, and told him "the opposition to the argument."⁶⁴

As a young lawyer at the New York City law firm of Carter, Ledyard, and Milburn, Roosevelt demonstrated neither a passion nor aptitude for the legal profession. His branding as an intellectual lightweight came into question during the 1932 presidential campaign, and especially later across history books when, just four days into his presidency, former associate justice of the US Supreme Court, Oliver Wendall Holmes, famously quipped about FDR: "A second-class intellect, but a first-class temperament."⁶⁵

Franklin was affable, polite, and authentic, and according to Grace Tully: "One of the great souls of history."⁶⁶ Armed with an uncommon emotional intelligence and a unique capacity to radiate warmth, energy, and charm, he always seemed to wear a smile while exemplifying a vigorous self-assurance. British Prime Minister Winston Churchill equated meeting FDR to "opening a bottle of champagne . . . with all his buoyant sparkle, his iridescence."⁶⁷ Conversely, he could be icy cold and cunning as needed, and had the tendency to elicit hate from his critics. President Harry Truman once noted of Roosevelt: "He was the coldest man I ever met. He didn't give a damn personally for me or you or anyone else in the world as far as I could see."⁶⁸

Roosevelt had very few friends or intimates, with only a select crew privy to behind-the-curtain access and his carefully concealed private life. Historian Arthur Schlesinger Jr. wrote of the sphinxlike masquerading of FDR's two sides: "The public face could never be relied on to express the private man."⁶⁹ Similarly, historian James MacGregor Burns described Franklin as a lion and a fox.⁷⁰ Not surprisingly, it was often difficult for those around FDR to know where he stood. His adviser Harold Ickes once told the president: "You are a wonderful person, but you are one of the most difficult men to work with that I have ever known. . . . You won't talk frankly even with people who are loyal to you and of whose loyalty you are fully convinced. You keep your cards close up against your belly. You never put them on the table."[71] Franklin took criticism like Ickes's well, but like a tiger, he was unable to change stripes.

In this case, Roosevelt didn't believe he could put all his cards on the table as president. Therefore, it could be said that one of his personal strengths was an expert ability at being indirect, which was a difficult game to play for his team. As FDR told his Treasury Secretary Henry Morgenthau Jr. "I never let my right hand know what my left hand is doing."[72]

His political philosophy was largely pragmatic in nature, premised in capitalism, but little else. "Take a method and try it," Roosevelt espoused. "If it fails, admit it and try another. But above all, try something."[73] His lack of ideological conviction allowed him to be nimble and often balance differing positions simultaneously, which offered a stark contrast to his predecessor, Herbert Hoover. "To look upon these programs as the result of a unified plan," Raymond Moley noted of the New Deal, is "to believe that the accumulation of stuffed snakes, baseball pictures, school flags, old tennis shoes, carpenter's tools, geometry books, and chemistry sets in a boy's bedroom could have been put there by an interior decorator."[74]

Optimistic by nature, Franklin expected the best of any situation or storm. His 1932 slogan for president, "Happy Days Are Here Again" exemplified his positive spirit. Yet, his hopeful nature and confidence was often tested. As a Harvard freshman, he stood by the bedside of his father as he passed away. Shortly thereafter, he failed to get into the prestigious Harvard campus club, Porcellian, which his cousin Teddy and other Roosevelt family members belonged to, calling it the "greatest disappointment of my life."[75] In 1914, he tried and came up short in winning the Democratic nomination for an open US Senate seat from New York, and also during the Woodrow Wilson administration, his affair with Lucy Mercer, his wife Eleanor's social secretary, came at the forever cost of the intimate side of his marriage and almost his career, as he knew that any divorcee forfeited a future in American politics.

A year after serving as the Democratic vice presidential nominee in 1920, at age thirty-nine, he received the devastating diagnosis of infantile paralysis or polio. The disability caused him to leave the public eye until he reemerged in 1924, at the Democratic National Convention in New York City. There he provided an address nominating New York Governor Al

Smith as the party's presidential nominee. While he would never recover the full use of his legs, he was able to regain some lost mobility, even learning to use his hips to propel his legs forward in a walking motion. His 1924 Convention address, in particular, represented an incredible feat of fortitude. Any fall or even a mere stumble, and his political future would all but be over. Undeterred, he reached the rostrum, delivered his signature FDR smile, and told those "who come from the great cities of the East, and from the plains and hills of the West, from the slopes of the Pacific and from the homes and fields of the southland,"[76] of the "indomitable courage . . . unflagging perseverance"[77] of Al Smith, which easily could have been said of him.

His efforts on that Madison Square Garden stage and in the years ahead were so convincing that most Americans never realized that he could not walk. FDR used the widespread praise coming out of his 1924 speech to buoy his own run for governor of New York in 1928. In between these years, he continued to rehabilitate relentlessly, ever believing that he would one day be able to walk. The buoyant waters in Warm Springs, Georgia, energized him, as they allowed him to walk in the water. He built up his arms and chest to offset the loss of mobility of his legs. "Maybe my legs aren't so good," he noted, "but look at those shoulders! Jack Dempsey would be green with envy."[78]

These tremendous efforts were complemented by the fantastic lengths taken to conceal his paralysis, including during his time as president, with the outlier being a rare occasion when he was photographed sitting in his wheelchair. Eleanor Roosevelt described her husband's disability as a "blessing in disguise,"[79] because for as challenging as the disabling disease was for FDR, his self-belief, grit, and determination helped shape him to be a better man and president, propelling him to the governorship of New York in 1928, reelection two years later, and the White House in 1932. However, an evening reception of governor's at the White House would firmly alter FDR's perception of Hoover. After being told that "the President would arrive shortly," FDR and his fellow governor's stood in a waiting line for a half hour in the East Room before Hoover arrived. Standing erect with the support of "steel braces from hip to ankle,"[80] along with Eleanor beside him, FDR agonized as his wife explained: "He became tired if he stood without support for any length of time."[81] Twice declining a chair, so as not to show weakness or provoke an "adverse political story," FDR endured through the ordeal as Eleanor internally fumed, believing her husband "was being deliberately put through an endurance test."[82]

160 | Meeting the Moment

Despite the range of defeats and setbacks FDR experienced, and as challenging as these episodes were to him personally, physically, and to his dream of being president, he never lost the confidence and swagger he cultivated in his youth at Hyde Park and beyond. It lifted Roosevelt to lift others who were dealt a similar hand, such as his work to set up the National Foundation for Infantile Paralysis, which is now known as the March of Dimes. Even after facing down an assassin weeks prior to his presidential inauguration, there was "not so much as the twitching of a muscle, the mopping of a brow, or even the hint of a false gaiety to indicate that it wasn't any other evening in any other place,"[83] according to Raymond Moley. "Roosevelt was simply himself—easy, confident, poised, to all appearances unmoved."[84] Similarly, as historian William Leuchtenberg noted: "His zest for life and confidence—always his defining characteristics—grew rather than shrank in the face of his trials."[85]

The Roadmap

Inauguration Day 1933 began cold and gray in the nation's capital, with dire overnight news of bank runs and closings draping the nation in fear. Arthur Krock of the *New York Times* described Washington, DC as "a beleaguered capital in wartime."[86] Franklin Roosevelt confronted this tenuous predicament with a short prayer service with his family, friends, staff, and incoming cabinet at St. John's Episcopal Church, located across Lafayette Square from the White House. "A thought to God is the right way to start off my Administration. . . . It will be the means to bring us out of the depths of despair,"[87] FDR noted. As Arthur Schlesinger Jr. highlighted, the crisis "was in the hand of God."[88]

Shortly before 11 a.m. that same March 4, 1933 morning, Roosevelt met President Hoover on the North Portico of the White House, and together proceeded in an open touring car for the short ride down Pennsylvania Avenue to the Capitol. As chilly as it was in Washington, DC that early March morning, there was an even icier scene between the two men in the car. The iconic picture of the smiling and waving Roosevelt provided a stark contrast to the grim-faced Hoover, even as they shared a blanket to ward off the elements. A Harvard classmate of FDR's, watching from the grandstand, said that Franklin seemed "full of cheer and confidence,"[89] and by contrast, Hoover's face was "like a lump of dough before it goes into the oven, puffy and expressionless."[90]

At 1:06 p.m. Franklin Roosevelt, sans coat or hat protecting against the swift-blowing March wind, took the oath of office as president on the East Portico of the US Capitol building. In front of over 100 thousand onlookers, and as the sun attempted to peek through the overcast sky,[91] he broke with his thirty-one predecessors by repeating every phrase of the presidential oath: "I, Franklin Delano Roosevelt, do solemnly swear . . ."[92] It was as if he was putting his personal allegiance and confidence into every word and public action, establishing a clear break for his administration and any others. "This great Nation will endure as it has endured, will revive and will prosper,"[93] Roosevelt began his iconic first Inaugural Address. "So first of all, let me assert my firm belief that the only thing we have to fear is fear itself."[94] He further and candidly asserted to his fellow Americans that he would "speak the truth, the whole truth, frankly and boldly,"[95] noting that "Only a foolish optimist can deny the dark realities of the moment."[96] Balancing self-confidence with a streak of humbleness, he concluded by asking God to "protect each and every one" and to guide him "in the days to come."[97]

Thus, on a day that began with and was anchored in prayer, his speech helped set the right opening tone. He made clear that new leadership was in charge and moved swiftly to get his team in place. Talking to reporters after returning to the White House, Eleanor Roosevelt noted: "The crowds were so tremendous, and you felt that they would do anything—if only someone would tell them what to do."[98]

After the inaugural parade concluded around six o'clock, Roosevelt retired to his second-floor study. Members of his cabinet joined him, and for the first time in history, the collective group "was sworn in at the same time and in the same place and by the same official administering the oaths."[99] Supreme Court Justice Benjamin N. Cardozo did the honors, leaving Roosevelt to smile and call the new precedent a "little family party,"[100] as he handed each cabinet officer their commission.

At two-thirty the following afternoon, Roosevelt formally met with his cabinet where he was informed by Treasury Secretary William H. Woodin that hastily assembled bankers from across the country "had no plan of their own."[101] Unflinching, Roosevelt then, according to Francis Perkins: "outlined, more coherently than I had heard outlined before, just what this banking crisis was and what the legal problems involved were."[102] The group, according to Interior Secretary Harold Ickes, considered whether the president should issue an executive order, "which will be to close every bank in the United States for a bank holiday, . . . stop the exportation of gold, and put into effect other emergency regulations designed to stop the run on the banks and to prevent the hoarding of gold or gold certificates."[103] The president further gleaned from his Attorney General Homer Cummings an obscure 1917 precedent that authorized the president's ability to investigate and regulate the hoarding of currency.

On Monday, March 6, at 1:00 a.m., FDR issued presidential Proclamation 2039, establishing a four-day bank holiday in which "no such banking institution or branch shall pay out, export, earmark, or merit the withdrawal or transfer in any manner or by any divide whatsoever, any gold or silver coin or bullion or currency or take any other action which might facilitate the hoarding thereof."[104] The American people would not have access to banks or banking services, including withdrawing, transferring, or making deposits. Franklin's proclamation, according to historian Arthur Schlesinger Jr., gave the banking crisis "the punctuation of a full stop, as if this were the bottom and hereafter things could only turn upward."[105] The banking holiday was to extend to Thursday, March 9, which allowed for a Special Session of Congress within four days aimed at drafting legislation to reopen banks in an orderly manner. This led Senator Burton K. Wheeler of Montana to predict: "Congress will jump through a hoop to put them through."[106] The banking holiday would eventually stretch to a week, giving the president until March 13 to restore confidence in America's failed banking system.

Facing more questions than answers, Franklin leveraged his network to help develop a plan of action, from inviting prominent bankers to work with his administration on draft legislation, to bringing in the nation's governors to meet with the cabinet at the White House. Regarding the latter, after ten minutes of impromptu remarks, the president was given a standing ovation and a pledge of bipartisan support: "Without regard to the political affiliations we Governors of the States . . . hereby express our confidence and faith in our President and urge the Congress and all the people of our united country to cooperate with him. . . . He is ready to lead if we are ready to follow. He needs the united support of all our people in carrying out his plans."[107]

In this same spirit, holdovers from the Hoover administration were among the expertise the president cultivated. They knew the particulars of the challenge inside and out and their sense of duty made them eager to help. Roosevelt adviser Raymond Moley said of the shared mission: we had "forgotten to be Republicans or Democrats. . . . We were just a bunch of men trying to save the banking system."[108]

It was clear that across these endeavors, FDR was forging confidence through consensus and a spirit of collaboration. For the president, bickering was a dying art form in this orbit. According to FDR biographer, Kenneth Davis, Franklin recognized that there was "something stronger than his own will," and his responsibility was "not to bring in any plan of his own" or to "devise or undertake anything" but to "hear everything, remember everything . . . put everything in its proper place."[109] His all-hands-on-deck approach went into translating volumes of financial data, research, and legalese into saving the banking system in a way that the bankers would support; as opposed to changing the system or nationalizing it, for which there currently were no plans. This collective work aimed at getting draft legislation ready for congressional consumption and toward ensuring the crucial March 13 bank reopenings. The response to these critical outcomes would determine the fate of the banking system, his abecedarian administration, and the nation.

What banks should open? Who makes those decisions? Things were moving so quickly that as Raymond Moley recognized: "Everyone was aware that in the rush serious mistakes might be made. . . . Some banks would be reopened that should have remained closed, and others would be closed that might have weathered the storm."[110] Francis Perkins explained FDR's general style on planning: "Roosevelt's plans . . . were bourgeoning plans; they were next steps. . . . one plan grew out of another. Gradually they fitted together and supplemented one another."[111] He also believed that "nothing in human judgment is final," as "one may courageously take the step that seems right today because it can be modified tomorrow if it does not work well."[112] Inherently, FDR was of the school that he could modify his path until he got it right.

Roosevelt and his team worked around the clock, with the president conferring with advisers well past midnight, night after night. Other than a quick snooze, bite to eat, or shower, the focus of the president and his team was on the development of emergency legislation that needed to be ready by Thursday at lunchtime, as Congress assembled from across the country.

On Wednesday, March 8, shortly after 10 a.m., Roosevelt held his first press conference. Sitting at his desk in the Oval Office, he engaged in a forty minute off-the-cuff, give-and-take discussion with members of the White House press corps. This new practice broke the mold for presidential pressers as they had been traditionally formal in nature, with his most recent predecessors such as Coolidge and Hoover requesting questions from the press in advance. Roosevelt even shook hands with each reporter and relished in this engagement. The *New York Times* reported that "There was little sign of the strain he has undergone—and is still under—since he became President."[113]

Later that day, the president got his hands on the first draft of the banking bill. With his affinity for maps, he especially liked how his Treasury Department team color-coded the banks based on their solvency strength. Later Wednesday, the draft was shared with the majority and minority leaders in both houses of Congress. Roosevelt began meeting with congressional leaders at the White House at nine o'clock in the evening, with discussions extending past 1 a.m., Thursday morning. As the president explained, the plan was grounded in the 1917 Trading with the Enemy Act and amalgamated around a decision to reopen banks in stages based on financial stability, while increasing presidential regulation over gold and foreign exchange and the government's ability to print new money backed by assets in the Federal Reserve system. Several edits later, FDR had the support of congressional leaders, but it was not until 3 a.m. that the bill was teed up for printing. When asked if the bill was finished, the exhausted but clear-headed Treasury Secretary Bill Woodin said: "Yes, it is finished. My name is Bill and I'm finished too."[114]

The president rose early on Thursday to draft a presidential message in longhand to accompany the bill. The *New York Times* reported that as each page was completed: "It was copied on the typewriter and sent immediately to the executive office for stenciling."[115] FDR urged "upon the Congress the clear necessity for immediate action,"[116] giving the executive branch "control over the banks," to protect depositors, to ascertain bank soundness, and to reorganize and reopen banks as needed.[117]

Roosevelt made clear this was just the beginning: "In the short space of five days it is impossible for us to formulate completed measures to prevent the recurrence of the evils of the past. This does not and should not, however, justify any delay in accomplishing this first step."[118] A more "rounded program of national restoration"[119] was on its way. With only minutes to spare, Roosevelt's team met the Thursday deadline, delivering one of just a few copies of the banking bill in existence to Chairman Henry Steagall of the House Banking Committee, who quickly announced: "Here's the bill. . . . Let's pass it."[120] The chairman's enthusiasm for action would likely have been as high even if the bill was written on the back of a napkin.

Just five breakneck days since the inauguration, the Congress convened at noon, "the most momentous gathering of the country's legislators since war was declared in 1917."[121] Great seriousness filled the air. The galleries were crammed full, largely with out-of-towners converging on the nation's capital in hopes of observing the historic gathering. Sitting among the House gallery was Roosevelt's wife, Eleanor, whose hopeful white attire projected a confidence that emanated from the new administration. While most sitting among her seemed to have the gravity of the moment etched on their faces, Eleanor exhibited a sense of calm in the storm as "she knitted almost constantly."[122]

The House rules for H.R. 1491 were clear and simple as framed by House majority leader Joseph Byrns—no amendments would be considered and debate would be limited, restricted to only forty minutes. As the legislation was introduced at 2:55 p.m., minority leader Bertrand Snell urged his Republican colleagues, who ran a three-to-one deficit in representation in the House, to pass the measure: "The House is burning down and the President of the United States says this is the way to put out the fire."[123] Snell also recognized the unprecedented nature of the moment, calling the legislative action "entirely out of the ordinary,"[124] given that the bill was being acted on despite most members not actually having seen a printed version of the draft, yet alone actually having read the text. It was an act of faith by the Congress's rank and file based on what their leadership supported, but also their leaders' investment in the confidence of their president. With shouts of "Vote, Vote" rising from the floor, and less than forty minutes of debate, a voice vote was taken shortly after four o'clock in the afternoon with not a single echo of dissent.

The Senate, on the other hand, benefited by having a full opportunity to see the bill before beginning their debate. As the *New York Times* reported: "Some of the most conservative members of the Senate were at pains to point out, [the new banking measure] has obvious imperfections as well as distasteful features, but it is designed to meet an emergency. No doubt it will be received in that spirit."[125]

The Democrats brought forward a few amendments seeking to enhance regulation, but those were quickly shouted down. Exemplifying the scene, Louisiana US Senator Huey Long brought forward an amendment aiming to permit the president to include state banks within the Federal Reserve System as a means to protect small depositors. As he droned on, Carter Glass, US senator from Virginia became increasingly enraged.

Glass had polished the "phraseology of the bill,"[126] so he was well versed in the technical aspects of the legislation. The former treasury secretary in the Woodrow Wilson Administration "rose from his chair once or twice, his fingers drummed on his desk and he leaned forward and held to the outside edge as if about to hurl himself out of his seat."[127] After a short exchange between the two senators, Long "finally gave up his attack and moved on."[128]

At just before seven thirty, by a vote of seventy-three to seven, with the nays coming from largely rural Democrats, including Huey Long, the measure passed and within the hour the bill was couriered to the White House for the president's signature. In his second-floor study, Roosevelt signed the first bill of his presidency, mere hours after it was introduced. The legislation represented the first of the famous Hundred Day Congress, which ran from March 9 to June 15, and set the benchmark for governmental speed and productivity.

With sincere appreciation for Congress's action, FDR knew, however, the true litmus test would be on Monday morning, March 13, when the banks reopened. The flurry of action by the administration and the Congress was significant, but the fate of the financial system rested in the hearts and minds of the American people. Summing up this sentiment, Raymond Moley noted: "The American people wanted their government to do something, anything, so long as it acted with assurance and vigor."[129] They also wanted to know if this was the bottom and that things could only get better. The bank holiday was one thing, but that far from quelled questions from abounding. Would they feel confident enough to deposit their money and savings? Could they put their faith back into an institution that had failed so many of their neighbors and friends? And if they didn't or couldn't, what would become of the banking system? What would become of the United States?

A lot had transpired over the course of the last week, from state proclamations, to Congressional legislation, to federal regulation that FDR believed should be explained for the benefit of the average citizen.[130] The president understood that the confidence of the people in their government would strengthen, especially if he completely leveled with them right out of the gate. He also understood the success of his nationwide address depended on how clear he could communicate and persuade to the American people that the crisis was over. If he was unconvincing, panicked depositors would continue withdrawing what was left of their savings causing the total collapse of the US financial system. He had three days to deliver his case.

The Fireside Chat

Across the frenetic opening days of his presidency, Franklin Roosevelt was presented a number of important opportunities to fine-tune his messaging about the crisis, from providing an overview to his cabinet and the press, to lobbying legislators on the merits of the banking bill. The shape of his March 12 Fireside Chat first took form in a draft written by Charles Michelson, director of publicity for the Democratic National Committee, who "was told to prepare an address for the President."[131] Michelson told Woodin and others that he needed somebody to keep him "straight on fiscal nomenclature . . . so they assigned a young man to sit up with me while I batted out on the typewriter the first draft of the document."[132] Michelson, who was also reportedly known as "Hoover's Gadfly" or "Nemesis," was responsible for "scores of speeches that had slashed and pummeled the Hoover administration."[133]

Michelson's first draft then quickly morphed into a follow-up draft by Arthur Ballantine, who FDR beat out three decades earlier for editor of the *Harvard Crimson*. Ballantine's effort came at the behest of Raymond Moley, who then shared the amalgamated version with the president. Wasting no time, FDR proceeded to discard what was prepared, and stretching out on the couch in his White House study, "dictated his own speech."[134]

Looking up at the unadorned wall, the president tried to "visualize the individuals he was seeking to help."[135] He could see "a mason at work on a new building, a girl behind a counter, a farmer in his field, all of them saying 'Our money is in the Poughkeepsie bank, and what is this all about?' "[136] The president was additionally inspired, as Louis Howe recalled, by watching a workman break down the inauguration scaffolding outside a White House window. "He was out there the day I started working on my speech about the banking crisis. I decided I'd try to make a speech that the workman could understand. So you see," FDR grinned, "I really made the speech to him."[137] Francis Perkins recalled a similar scene: "He was conscious of their faces and hands, their clothes and homes."[138] "He thought of them sitting on a suburban porch after supper on a summer evening. He thought of them gathered around a dinner table at a family meal. He never thought of them as 'the masses.' "[139] "The intellectual and spiritual climate" around Roosevelt was "that the people mattered."[140]

The president was fully focused on his audience's psychology in helping to construct his radio pitch. And as he dictated from a reclined position on the couch, Grace Tully feverishly scribbled every utterance. Simply, FDR was following a process for him that was tried and true. As Samuel Rosenman pointed out, the president's March 12 address followed his standard routine: "The speeches delivered were his—and his alone—no matter who the collaborators were. They all expressed the personality, the convictions, the spirit, the mood of Roosevelt. . . . It was Roosevelt himself."[141]

As highlighted in the notes which accompanied the speech announcement, FDR was determined to explain the banking crisis in "non-technical language" so that the American people "would be relieved of their anxiety as to whether they would ever see their money again."[142] Thus, he began his March 12 address: "I want to talk for a few minutes with the people of the United States about banking . . . what has been done in the last few days, why it was done, and what the next steps are going to be."[143]

With the vibe of a calming teacher, the president was engaging "as though he were actually sitting on the front porch or parlor with them," nodding his head, with his hands moving "in simple, natural, comfortable gestures,"[144] along with a smile that lit up his face and radiated.[145] He was making clear from the beginning that he was talking "to each person in the nation,"[146] not at them, while providing a roadmap for sixty million "neighbors" desperate for answers.

Proceeding across a conversational 100 plus-words-per-minute pace, he continued by highlighting how the banking system was supposed to work: "When you deposit money in a bank, the bank does not put the money into a safe deposit vault. It invests your money in many different forms of credit—bonds, commercial paper, mortgages and many other kinds of loans . . . to keep the wheels of industry and of agriculture turning around."[147] The cash on hand "in normal times"[148] is enough to cover the needs of depositors.

His slow, deliberate rate of speaking communicated calm, competence, empathy, and confidence. And by translating the legal and banking industry vernacular into understandable terms without patronizing, it was as if only he alone, a man of confidence and mastery of content, could clearly layout the facts of the dire situation. According to Rex Tugwell, a member of a team of advisers known as FDR's "Brain Trust," the president came across as knowing "what had to be done."[149] Will Rogers quipped that FDR's performance "made everyone understand it, even the bankers."[150]

"What, then happened?"[151] Roosevelt asked the question that was top of mind for many Americans. Like a Hollywood script, he carefully proceeded to lay out the plot and the cast of characters. "We had a bad banking situation,"[152] Roosevelt explained, "and some of our bankers had shown themselves either incompetent or dishonest in their handling of the people's funds. They had used the money entrusted to them in speculations and unwise loans."[153] Here again, Roosevelt was calling out the psychology of a few unscrupulous bankers, and, importantly he noted, that their greed mattered. The collapse of the market and shuttering of banks undermined public confidence in the financial system, FDR believed, and created "a rush so great that the soundest banks could not get enough currency to meet the demand."[154]

Something had to be done. Identifying and empathizing with the fear and uncertainty Americans were experiencing, he continued: "It was the government's job to straighten out this situation and do it as quickly as possible."[155]

He then touted the steps taken: the work of the "national Congress"[156] and their bipartisan "devotion to public welfare"[157] to address the challenge; as well as the series of federal regulations that permitted the banks to "continue their functions to take care of the distribution of food and household necessities and the payment of payrolls."[158] He emphasized the importance of the banking holiday as a means "to issue additional currency on good assets and thus the banks which reopen will be able to meet every legitimate call."[159]

Taken together, Roosevelt made clear that without the bold action the federal government was taking, "there would have been more and greater losses had we continued to drift."[160] He further made clear to the American people that he would not allow the "history of the past few years"[161] to be repeated and he did not want and would not have "another epidemic of bank failures."[162]

Therefore, the next day, Monday, March 13, FDR was taking a measured approach "with the opening of banks in the twelve Federal Reserve Bank cities—those banks which on first examination by the treasury have already been found to be all right."[163] The president's staggered rollout would continue on Tuesday, March 14 with the opening of sound banks in an additional "250 cities of the United States,"[164] and on "Wednesday and succeeding days"[165] by banks "in smaller places all through the country."[166] This was necessary, FDR noted, "in order to permit the banks to make applications for necessary loans, to obtain currency needed to meet their requirements and to enable the government to make common sense checkups."[167]

For those Americans with doubts, the president confidently addressed their fears, asserting that the banks would "take care of all needs,"[168] and that it was "safer to keep your money in a reopened bank than under the mattress."[169] He further asserted that any "bank that opens on one of the subsequent days is in exactly the same status as the bank that opens tomorrow."[170] Yet, far from being a "foolish optimist," as he noted in his first inaugural, he made no assurances that every bank would reopen or that people would not lose money.

To all those Americans who were hoarding, a practice he called an "exceedingly unfashionable pastime,"[171] he offered a lifeline and a way back in by calling on them not to give up on their system of government. He asked them to work together, as the "success of our whole great national program depends, of course, upon the cooperation of the public—on its intelligent support and use of a reliable system."[172]

FDR closed the radio address cloaked in a theme of confidence. He expressed appreciation for the "note of confidence from all over the country"[173] and "loyal support,"[174] even if "all our processes may not have seemed clear to them."[175] More than anything, he added in an inspired plea—it was "the confidence of the people"[176] and the essential qualities of "confidence and courage"[177] that would determine the success or failure of his plan. Like George Washington in his Farewell Address, Roosevelt was calling on the type of American who would do the right thing. Those who would return their money to the bank. Those who kept their faith in their government through the storm. And those who would trust in his confidence to solve the crisis.

In recognition that public opinion was the lynchpin, he centered the American people as the chief protagonist in his plot, using the personal pronouns "you" or "yours" twenty-four times. "*You* people must have faith; *you* must not be stampeded by rumors or guesses, Roosevelt continued."[178] He then called on them in the same spirit as his Inaugural Address, to unite with him "in banishing fear."[179]

In making his final plea, Roosevelt said that he had "provided the machinery to restore our financial system,"[180] and it was now "up to you to support and make it work."[181] With a shared confidence between the people and their president, Roosevelt exclaimed: "Together we cannot fail."[182] It was a line that Robert Sherwood noted "was the first real demonstration of Roosevelt's superb ability to use the first person plural and bring the people into the White House with him."[183]

Following the radio broadcast, Roosevelt huddled with advisers in his oval study, including Bill Woodin, Raymond Moley, and Arthur Ballantine. Soon thereafter, Louis Howe and Samuel Rosenman joined. After a breakneck week for the ages, the president and his team had given their all to reassure the country. A final verdict would not emerge until morning, leaving Roosevelt to announce: "I think it's time for beer."[184]

Impact and Legacy

The news emanating across the nation on Monday morning was clear and definitive. The depositors, who only weeks earlier made withdraws in panic, lined up in droves to return their hoarded cash from under their mattresses. Newspapers across the country amplified the positive sentiment: "It was obvious that the people had full confidence in the banks which received licenses to reopen from the Federal Reserve Bank," wrote the *New York Times*.[185] The *Chicago Tribune* simply declared: "City Recovers Confidence."[186] Journalist Walter Lippmann added: "In one week, the nation, which had lost confidence in everything and everybody, has regained confidence in the government and in itself."[187]

The raw data only advanced the storylines; by the end of March, two-thirds of the hoarded cash, nearly $1.2 billion, was infused back into the banks, and after a two-week break, the New York Stock Exchange reopened on Wednesday, March 15, 15 percent higher, the largest single-day increase ever recorded at that time. Also, within a week of FDR's address, three-quarters of the recently closed banks reopened, and although thousands of others would stay closed, the number of banks that were revived far exceeded the expectations of even Roosevelt's team.

In less than fifteen minutes and across 1,792 astonishing powerful and transformative words, FDR fundamentally elevated the nation's confidence and stemmed the immediate banking crisis. Much like Lincoln's Gettysburg Address was a turning point in the Civil War, so too was Roosevelt's Fireside Chat to the Great Depression. Raymond Moley declared the address "as simple and moving as any presidential utterance in the history of this country," and through FDR's "swiftness and boldness," he rallied "the confidence . . . of the public."[188] Roosevelt speechwriter, Robert

Sherwood described the first Fireside Chat as representing a tone shift in presidential discourse;[189] the chat was "itself surprising and immeasurably stimulating;" a departure from an "Address" or an "elaborate apologia, or a stern lecture."[190]

Chair of the Democratic National Committee, Jim Farley, echoed the high praise, noting: "Capitalism had been saved in eight days."[191] Illinois US Senator J. Hamilton Lewis was reported to note: "That popular trust in the administration had resulted in restoring confidence and creating a better situation for a revival of business than has existed since 1929."[192] As one of only a few members to represent two states in the US Congress, Lewis added his own historical context: "I have never seen within my political life such a real transformation in sentiment from discouragement to encouragement, from despair to complete hope and to immediate new trust and new hope."[193] Republicans were also generous. Hoover's Secretary of State Henry L. Stimson, who viewed Roosevelt's inaugural message with suspicion, now shared with the president: "I am delighted with the progress of your first week and send you my heartiest congratulations."[194]

As a result of Franklin's efforts, "A flush of hope swept the nation,"[195] observed Roosevelt biographer, James MacGregor Burns. Exemplifying this feeling were the nearly half-million letters that poured into the White House in the few days after. Mr. and Mrs. F. B. Graham from Dubuque, Iowa, wrote the next day: "The President of the greatest Nation on earth honored every home with a personal visit last night. . . . He came into our living-room in a kindly neighborly way and in simple words explained the great things he had done so that all of us unfamiliar with the technicalities might understand. When his voice died away we realized our 'friend' had gone home again but left us his courage, his faith and absolute confidence."[196]

James A. Green from Cincinnati, Ohio, remarked of FDR: "It almost seemed the other night, sitting in my easy chair in the library, that you were across the room from me. A great many of my friends have said the same thing."[197] Mrs. Louise Hill from Chicago stated that Roosevelt's broadcast over the radio transformed "our little home [into] a church, our radio a pulpit—and you the preacher. Thank you for the courage and faith you have given us."[198] And the *New York Times* summarized the public sentiment with a few quotations: "Created feeling of confidence in me and my family"; "Going direct to the people with the facts has inspired every confidence in the reopening of the banks"; and "A masterpiece in the circumstances and worthy of the historical precedent it established."[199]

In the way President's John Kennedy and Ronald Reagan later mastered television, and President Donald Trump leveraged social media, FDR became the voice of radio, establishing a presidential hold over the major communication platform of the time and forever changing American popular culture. Gone were the days when a public figure would have to orate from a lectern or the back of a train car to reach only as far as their voice would carry. With radio, the world seemed to get smaller, as the medium connected people from Poughkeepsie to Portland around common interests, voices, and shared convictions and facts. A farmer in North Dakota and a banker from New York City were united for the first time in shared, instant communication, breaking down barriers among urban and rural, men and women, old and young, and geographic affinity. Moreover, as an everyday form of communication, a voice on a radio could radiate warmth and intimacy in ways an inherent coldness of a printed newspaper page could not.

FDR benefited tremendously from the rapid proliferation this technology, as radios flowed into Americans homes at just the right time, doubling in ownership to eighteen million from 1928 to 1932. FDR used this period when he was governor of New York to develop his craft, including through his "waffle-iron" campaign in 1930 and as a weapon to solicit public support for policy proposals. Grace Tully recalled then Governor Roosevelt's early frustration with the New York legislature: "I'll take the issue to the people."[200]

Radio helped Roosevelt to resonate across small towns and big cities. Having smoothed out the rough edges in his use of the new medium in Albany, as president, he was more than prepared to leverage the technology to meet the moment. In addition, the countless mail generated from Roosevelt's radio outreach poured into legislative offices, overwhelmingly supporting his proposals. Taking this advocacy directly to the people in New York State and then later to the American people became a key tool in FDR's toolkit. Not to mention, the firsthand intel he received proved invaluable, particularly the thoughts of Americans on key issues. Armed with this insight, FDR could capitalize on this information to lobby legislators and ultimately win reelection.

However, even as he established an intimate relationship with the public through radio, he also understood the limits of too much of a good thing and the adage of always leaving your audience wanting more. He would only deliver four Fireside Chats in 1933, and among his approximately 300 radio addresses over his twelve years as president, he only designated 27 as "Fireside Chats."²⁰¹ Samuel Rosenman credited this to Roosevelt's "acute sense of timing,"²⁰² noting that the president wanted to preserve the rhetorical force and public appeal of the "chats." Roosevelt spaced them so that he would not "talk so frequently as to wear out his welcome in the homes of his listeners, but not so seldom as to lose the potentiality of the radio appeal."²⁰³

On one such occasion, FDR sought to bring America back again from the brink—this time during an international crisis. During the February 23, 1942 Fireside Chat, he offered his view "On the Progress of the War" two months after the Japanese attack on Pearl Harbor, a week after the fall of Singapore, and at a particularly low point for American morale. In invoking the trials of George Washington at Valley Forge, he affirmed that despite many lean days during the War for Independence, America prevailed. He also cited the famous words of Thomas Paine in 1776: "Tyranny, like hell, is not easily conquered, yet we have this consolation with us, that the harder the sacrifice, the more glorious the triumph."²⁰⁴

However, the most revealing moment of this Fireside Chat was his request for Americans to have of a world map beside them as he spoke. And he didn't disappoint, as his voice echoed across America's kitchens and living rooms. "Look at your map,"²⁰⁵ he said, speaking of "strange" and "never heard of–places" that were "now the battleground for civilization."²⁰⁶ In laying out the problem, he explained "what the overall strategy of the war has to be."²⁰⁷ It would be a different type of war—one that called on US forces to meet their enemies in faraway lands, and which served as a reminder that freedom and security depended on "the security of the rights and obligations of liberty and justice everywhere in the world."²⁰⁸ Much like his first Fireside Chat, his confidence again proved crucial in reaching everyday Americans at such a time of need: "Just heard your speech . . . it cheered me up,"²⁰⁹ noted a telegram sent to FDR the day after the broadcast by J. B. Manuel, a grieving parent from Connecticut who lost his son at Pearl Harbor.

Examples like the "map" Fireside Chat or FDR's January 6, 1941 Four Freedom's speech, where he presented a case for American involvement to support Great Britain against the advancing German Army, demonstrate how Franklin's confidence extended into the future.²¹⁰ How he used his confidence to meet challenges head-on, resuscitating America's swagger and her spirit at some of the nation's most perilous moments. As Arthur Schlesinger Jr. noted: "Roosevelt, armored in some inner faith, remained calm and inscrutable, confident that American improvisation could meet the future on its own terms."[211] It was a future where FDR intended to lead a postwar world order and a domestic reorganization, but also where he never adequately allowed for a succession plan.

But without his first Fireside Chat, and FDR's "soaring rhetoric [that] roused imaginations and stirred souls,"[212] none of this was possible. Those tenuous days in March 1933 set the tone for all that would follow, cementing confidence as his distinctive leadership quality and presenting the stark contrast of Roosevelt saving freedom and democracy against the rising tide of fascism across the globe.

In Franklin's voice, people sensed warmth. They sensed confidence and self-assurance. And they sensed an authenticity of the kind that can't be faked or contrived. Charles Michelson remarked that they "were ready to believe FDR could see in the dark."[213] American's believed in him, in his words, and in his ability to make things better. And without ever prior meeting, and by just hearing his voice through the airwaves in their own homes, most shared the sentiment offered by Eleanor Roosevelt of her husband: "I've never known a man who gave one a greater sense of security. I never heard him say there was a problem that he thought it was impossible for human being to solve. . . . I never knew him to face life or any problem that came up with fear."[214]

Yet, despite his consistently high-rank among historians, and his regard among leaders of the twentieth century, FDR's successes did not come without flaws. He largely ignored racial desegregation. He failed to support antilynching legislation for fear of losing Southern congressional New Deal support. He interned Japanese-Americans during World War II. He also initiated a timid response to Hitler's persecution of Jews across Germany and Europe, among other things.

Taken altogether, however, short of George Washington who founded the nation, or Abraham Lincoln who preserved it, no other president has been more impactful on the presidency and American history than FDR. At the end of the day, his presidential legacy is significantly defined by his efforts on the evening of March 12, 1933, where he demonstrated the critical importance of confidence in a leader and in a president, and how this distinguishing quality can be used to serve the greater good as a rising tide to lift all boats. In doing so, he rescued America from the brink.

Chapter 6

Optimism

> My dream is that you will travel the road ahead with liberty's lamp guiding your steps and opportunity's arm steadying your way.
>
> —Ronald Reagan

The United States was founded as an optimistic idea, and by nature, Americans tend to look on the bright side. For nearly a quarter of a millennium, observers have marveled at America's seemingly endless optimism. Alexis de Tocqueville, a French diplomat, noted in the early nineteenth century: "They have all a lively faith in the perfectibility of man; they are of an opinion that the effects of the diffusion of knowledge must necessarily be advantageous, and the consequences of ignorance fatal; they all consider society as a body in a state of improvement, humanity as a changing scene, in which nothing is, or ought to be, permanent; and they admit that what appears to them to be good-to-day may be superseded by something better to-morrow."[1] US presidents have shared this congruous sense of optimism and hope for the future. Bill Clinton, in channeling the words of Christine McVie of the rock band Fleetwood Mac, reminded folks: "Don't stop thinking about tomorrow."[2] George H. W. Bush described America as a nation of community volunteer organizations: "A brilliant diversity spread like stars, like a thousand points of light in a broad and peaceful sky."[3] Dwight Eisenhower defined his leadership with a core belief in: "Optimism—enthusiasm—and the confidence that we can do it."[4] And, in his first Inaugural Address on the eve of the Civil War, Abraham Lincoln tapped into America's optimistic tradition to appeal for unity: "We are not enemies, but friends. We must not be enemies. Though passion may have strained, it must not break our bonds of affection. The mystic chords of memory, stretching from every battlefield and patriot grave to every living heart and hearthstone, all over this broad land, will yet swell the chorus of Union, when again touched as surely they will be, by the better angels of our nature."[5]

At the same time, there are presidents like John Quincy Adams, who self-described as "reserved, cold, austere, and forbidding."[6] Others, like Herbert Hoover and Donald Trump espoused a hollower optimism. In May 1930, six months after the stock market crash of 1929, Hoover told the nation: "I am convinced we have now passed the worst and with continued unity of effort we shall rapidly recover."[7] As we know from the previous chapter, the bottom would take nearly two more years to reach. Similarly, President Donald Trump reported in the spring of 2020 that the COVID-19 pandemic would disappear. Several years would pass before the pandemic lifted, but in Trump's defense, he did optimistically call for a vaccine at "Warp Speed,"[8] which was developed in just ten months, significantly less time than other crucial vaccines, such as measles, which took ten years to develop.[9]

Taken together, the most renowned presidents have proven to be ones who led with a strong sense of optimism. It's a central reason why Thomas Jefferson bested John Adams in 1800; Andrew Jackson defeated John Quincy Adams in 1828; and FDR won over Herbert Hoover in 1932. The challenger in each of these cases offered a greater sense of hope than the incumbent. It is also why Jimmy Carter lost to Ronald Reagan in 1980, a challenger who embodied optimism as a presidential quality more than any other—a quality that would eventually break down walls and transform America's place in the world.

The Scene

On Monday May 18, 1987, Assistant for Communications and Planning Thomas Griscom, Deputy Assistant and Director of Speechwriting Anthony Dolan, and presidential speechwriters, Dana Rohrabacher, Josh Gilder, Clark Judge, and Peter Robinson stepped through the White House Oval Office doorway at 1:46 p.m. The group settled evenly into the facing white couches separated by a coffee table situated near the center of the room. President Ronald Reagan took a seat in the left of dual armchairs positioned in front of the room's fireplace and just below the Charles Wilson Peale painting of George Washington hanging above the mantle. Across from the president, and filling out the southernmost third of the room, was the Resolute Desk, crafted from timbers of the H. M. S. *Resolute*, an abandoned British vessel discovered by an American ship and returned to the United Kingdom. Queen Victoria gifted the desk to President Rutherford B. Hayes in 1880, and, with the exception of Lyndon Johnson, Richard Nixon, and Gerald Ford, it has been used since by every American chief executive.

The Oval Office itself was designed and built through the expansion of the "West Wing" under President William Howard Taft in 1909. Over fourteen presidents, from Taft to Reagan, the physical space of the room changed little except for FDR moving the Oval Office to its present location on the West Wing's southeast corner overlooking the Rose Garden in 1934. However, as is tradition, presidents have enjoyed leaving their mark by way of decorating the space, and Ronald Reagan was no different. His West-inspired decor was found in everything from his choice of earthy hues, western art, and the jar of Jelly Belly's, to the sweeping sunny vibe emanating from the room amplified by two plaques on his desk: "It can be done" and "There's no limit to what a man can do or where he can go if he doesn't mind who gets the credit."[10]

Yet as thunderstorms crossed the outside sky on a hot and humid afternoon in the nation's capital, the group of communicators visiting President Reagan were far from admiring the room's Western adornments. Quite the opposite. Too much was at stake as heads were down and pens were moving at a feverish pace along bright yellow legal pads. The preceding Friday, May 15, the group submitted draft remarks for Reagan's June trip to Venice, Rome, and Berlin. After the president's weekend review, the wordsmiths were receiving crucial "input"[11] for the upcoming G7 Summit in Venice and Reagan's time with the Pope in Rome. Each moment was precious, and the attendees hung on the president's every word, not only because they sought to capture his phraseologies, but also because Reagan, as Treasury Secretary James Baker explained: "Believed that giving speeches was one of the president's most important duties."[12]

Discussion of the all-important Berlin speech was reserved for last. Turning to the president, Tom Griscom asked Reagan for his feedback. The president responded succinctly: "Well, that's a good draft, I like that."[13] Upon hearing this, the speechwriter for this assignment, Peter Robinson, became internally inconsolable. While most would feel good that their boss, yet alone the president of the United States liked their work, Robinson was of a different mind. He hoped to get the president "talking, revealing himself."[14] In these settings it was always his goal to have "a question or two"[15] for the president that he hoped would "intrigue him."[16] Earlier in the meeting, speechwriter Josh Gilder, who drafted the president's remarks for the Vatican asked Reagan: "What role he believed religion might play in the reform of Eastern Europe?"[17] The president responded with a "beautiful little disquisition on the need for religious renewal in the Soviet Union itself," which "exposed an aspect of his thinking" none of those sitting on the couch had seen."[18] It was exactly the type of exchange that Robinson was hoping for.

So, the speechwriter leaned into the moment. "Mr. President," Robinson said. "I learned on the advance trip that your speech will be heard not only in West Berlin but throughout East Germany."[19] This, of course, depended on weather conditions, but it was possible for radios to receive Reagan's speech as far as the Kremlin. Continuing, Robinson asked: "Is there anything you'd like to say to people on the other side of the Berlin Wall?"[20] Sitting back in his chair with his head tilted in thought, Reagan responded: "Well, there's that passage about tearing down the wall. That wall has to come down. That's what I'd like to say to them."[21]

The Time and Place

As our next story begins in 1987, America was immersed in the four-decades-long Cold War, a term captured in a speech at the South Carolina State House in 1947 by Bernard Baruch, a wealthy financier and adviser to presidents from Woodrow Wilson to Harry Truman, to describe the ever-frosting relationship between the United States and the Soviet Union.[22] The term represented a "real war"[23] in every sense of those words, "in which the survival of the free world is at stake."[24] This superpower struggle defined the global landscape over the second half of the twentieth century.

Prior to the start of the Cold War, the United States and Soviet Union were engaged with Great Britain as part of a World War II Grand Alliance. Their leadership was defined by the "Big Three"—US President Franklin Roosevelt, British Prime Minister Winston Churchill, and Soviet Union leader Joseph Stalin. Their important collaboration and overall cordial relationship included the Yalta Conference in February 1945, where they met in anticipation of Nazi Germany's defeat, and agreed to meet again to determine the postwar borders in Europe. Yet by the time these global powers reconvened at Potsdam in July 1945, the world had changed. Germany was defeated, FDR died, and Churchill lost a general election. A "New Big Three" emerged as Stalin was joined by US President Harry Truman and British Prime Minister Clement Atlee.

A consequence of Potsdam was a divided Europe, split into zones of military occupation. It was also where Truman informed Stalin, who he described in his diary at the time as "honest, but smart as hell,"[25] that the United States had successfully detonated the world's first atomic bomb and planned to "drop the most powerful explosive ever made on the Japanese."[26] The Soviet leader responded with a smile, and while appreciating the briefing, noted: "He didn't know what [Truman] was talking about—the Atomic Bomb!"[27] Contrary to Truman's armchair personality assessment of the Soviet leader, Stalin wasn't being honest. He was fully briefed about the bomb through his own intelligence channels. However, fulfilling his Potsdam pledge weeks later, Truman made the decision to demonstrate the devastating power of the weaponry at Hiroshima and Nagasaki, swiftly bringing an end to the Pacific Theater of the war. It was a victory after three and a half years and at a cost of over 400 thousand Americans from among a staggering sixty million lives lost worldwide.

After Potsdam, the "Big Three" would never convene again to collaboratively discuss postwar reconstruction. The sense of common cause and cooperation that defined the Grand Alliance during the war soon gave way to an era of division, mistrust, and suspicion. Much was a reprise of the ideological divisions that tied to the Russian Revolution of 1917, when the Soviet Union became the world's first Communist state dedicated to the overthrow of capitalism. In sharp contrast to the US and Great Britain's fervent commitment to freedom, human rights, democracy, and open markets, Stalin ruled through a dictatorship, utilizing secret police, prison camps, and terror to maintain order.

Already concerned over the Soviet domination of Eastern Europe, the two North Atlantic allied nations became increasingly convinced that Stalin was committed to expanding Soviet control over wider swaths of the globe, including Western Europe. At a joint session of Congress in March 1947, President Truman announced that the US was giving aid to Greece and Turkey as part of a broader strategy to contain Communism worldwide. His chief advocate for the policy of containment, George Kennan, further elaborated in the pages of *Foreign Affairs* in July 1947: "The main element of any United States policy toward the Soviet Union must be that of a long-term, patient but firm and vigilant containment of Russian expansive tendencies."[28] Known as the Truman Doctrine, the strategy aimed at supporting "free peoples who are resisting attempted subjugation by armed minorities or by outside pressures."[29] It was put to the test quickly on the Korean Peninsula: "If we let Korea down," Truman expressed to his advisers on June 25, 1950, after learning of North Korea's invasion of South Korea, "The Soviet[s] will keep right on going and swallow up one [place] after another."[30]

A decade later, Truman's school of thought laid the groundwork for America's incursion into the Vietnam War. Putting an artist's touch on Truman's plain-spoken vernacular, President John Kennedy elegantly conveyed in his 1961 Inaugural Address: "Let every nation know, whether it wishes us well or ill, that we shall pay any price, bear any burden, meet any hardship, support any friend, oppose any foe to assure the survival and the success of liberty."[31] The Truman Doctrine would also undergird US efforts to overthrow a left-wing government in Guatemala in 1954, support an unsuccessful invasion of Cuba in 1961, and invade the Dominican Republic and Grenada in 1965 and 1983, respectively.

World War II left terrible destruction across Europe and beyond. In 1947, the United States proposed the Marshall Plan, a massive financial aid initiative named for US Secretary of State George C. Marshall, which not only aimed to rebuild Europe and "the confidence of the European people in the economic future of their own countries and of Europe as a whole,"[32] but to draw Europeans away from Communism and Soviet expansionism and toward US commerce. In announcing the plan during a commencement address at Harvard University on June 5, 1947, Secretary of State Marshall noted: "The United States should do whatever it is able to do to assist in the return of normal economic health in the world, without which there can be no political stability and no assured peace."[33]

As part of Marshall's plan, the Soviet Union was offered aid to support Eastern Europe, but turned it down, instead employing Communist systems across Bulgaria, Czechoslovakia, Hungary, Poland, Romania, and eastern parts of Germany. The Soviets sought to safeguard against any renewed threat from Germany by seeking to spread communism worldwide on a largely ideological basing. Winston Churchill described this Soviet sphere of influence as the "Iron Curtain" in a March 1946 speech at Westminster College in Fulton, Missouri, which "has extended across the [European] Continent . . . From Stettin in the Baltic to Trieste in the Adriatic."[34]

The impact of the Iron Curtain over the succeeding four decades was devastating to the personal and political freedom, and health and life expectancy of Eastern Europeans. Undeterred, Soviet leadership continued to champion communism over capitalism as encapsulated in the 1956 remarks by Soviet Premier Nikita Khrushchev: "Whether you like it or not, history is on our side. We will bury you."[35]

At the center of this struggle between "free peoples" and "subjugation"[36] by the Communists, as President Truman described it, was the former German capital, Berlin, where the Soviet and Allied armies met after destroying Adolf Hitler's German war machine. The city laid deep inside the Soviet occupation zone, and was divided under quadripartite control, with the US, British, French, and Soviet forces each overseeing distinct sectors of the city. The initial plan was for Germany to run under a Joint Allied Control Council, as sovereign authority passed to the victorious Grand Alliance. But a common consensus over the nation's future proved intractable, particularly as destruction brought on by the war was staggering with an estimated one in four homes across Germany left inhabitable, increasing to 50 percent in many cities.

By March 1948, the US, Britain, and France planned to set up a democratic German government in the zones they occupied, and by June 1948, they introduced new currency, the deutsche mark. Enflamed by these actions, the Soviet Union responded by withdrawing from the Council and cutting off food, electricity, gas, and other supplies from the West, as well as road, rail, and water links to the Western occupation zones in Berlin. The US and Britain countered with an airlift over the better part of a year, which supplied the over two million residents of West Berlin with some two million tons of aid to mitigate the harsh winter.

Although the Soviet Union eventually reversed course and lifted the misguided blockade in the spring of 1949, the die was cast. The confrontation over Berlin cemented the Cold War division of Europe and accelerated the political integration of the Western zones. The Federal Republic of Germany, or West Germany was formally established in September 1949 as a democratic government, and two weeks later, the Soviet's turned their occupation zone into the Communist-ruled German Democratic Republic.

In defense of Western Europe, the United States agreed to the North Atlantic Treaty Organization alliance, which West Germany would join in 1955. The Soviets responded with the Warsaw Pact, an organization of Eastern European nations. At the same time, an arms race with the Soviet Union accelerated after the Soviets exploded their first atomic warhead in 1949, and the US tested the world's first hydrogen bomb on Elugelab Island in the Pacific Ocean in 1952, which left a crater more than a mile wide in diameter and was 450 times more destructive than the atomic bombs used during World War II. Also developed were long-range intercontinental missiles capable of carrying nuclear warheads, as well as early warning systems capable of detecting nuclear strikes or to prompt counterstrikes. While the United States maintained a distinct superiority in nuclear weapons over the Soviet Union into the early 1960s, the theory of nuclear deterrence emerged, as neither side could launch a full-scale war without itself suffering immense destruction. Still, the world remained under a precarious cloud of nuclear annihilation.

All the while, a space race emerged with the Soviet Union launching its first satellite into orbit in October 1957, and the first man into space in April 1961. Soon thereafter, in June 1961, President Kennedy declared in a message to a Joint Session of Congress: "I believe that this nation should commit itself to achieving the goal, before this decade is out, of landing a man on the Moon and returning him safely to the Earth."[37] The pledge was kept in July 1969, when Apollo 11 commander Neil Armstrong stepped foot on the moon.

As the space race picked up steam, so too did an era of espionage and intelligence gathering, secret and double agents, and the development of a permanent surveillance state. Exemplifying this climate among the two superpowers, in May 1960, a US spy plane was shot down by a Soviet missile during a high-flying reconnaissance flight. US pilot Gary Powers survived the ordeal but was made an example of on Soviet television to demonstrate that these types of flights existed. Two years later, Powers returned home after a spy swap with the Soviets that included Rudolf Abel, a KGB spy previously arrested by the United States.

The domestic political front was far from removed from fears of communist subversion, which were epitomized by Wisconsin US Senator Joseph McCarthy, who claimed there was an infiltration by Soviet spies and sympathizers in the federal government and across American society. In particular, McCarthy's swift rise was the result of a Lincoln Day speech to the Women's Republican Club of Wheeling, West Virginia, where he claimed: "While I cannot take the time to name all the men and women in the State Department who have been named as members of the Communist Party and members of a spy ring, I have here in my hand a list of 205."[38] A special Senate subcommittee investigated McCarthy's allegations and rejected them "as a fraud and a hoax,"[39] but in the context of the growing Cold War and the Korean conflict, as well as the perjury conviction of Alger Hiss, ample conjecture abounded to help perpetuate his charges. McCarthy would notoriously advance similar attacks during a June 1954 Army-McCarthy hearing, where lawyer Joseph Welch, in defending a colleague against an attack from McCarthy noted: "Until this moment, Senator, I think I never really gauged your cruelty or your recklessness. . . . Let us not assassinate this lad further, senator. You have done enough. Have you no sense of decency?"[40]

While Berlin remained a divided city in the early 1960s, it was also the only place in which people could move across the "Iron Curtain" separating Eastern and Western Europe. Each month, thirty thousand East Germans were navigating through this passageway to bear witness to the prosperity and freedom of West Germany, while leaving behind the hardships of the Communist state-controlled economy in the East. In 1961, Soviet leader Nikita Khrushchev threatened war if Western troops did not withdraw from West Berlin in six months, to which President John Kennedy responded by committing to fight and defend West Berlin, putting the threat of nuclear war on the table. Instead of war, however, and despite East German Premier Walter Ubricht's claim on June 15, 1961 that "Nobody intends to put up a wall,"[41] Khrushchev instructed the East German government to build an insurmountable wall between East and West Berlin.

Construction began on August 17, 1961, with little pushback from the West, as they largely accepted the Wall as a more palatable solution to a dangerous situation, helping to bring stability to the continent. Yet for Berliners, the division of their city was a tribulation as family and friends were literally separated building by building, and block by block. It was not uncommon for someone to climb a street lamp to show off a newborn baby to friends and relatives on the other side of the wall. It was equally not uncommon for East German guards to shoot at those attempting to escape from East to West Berlin. While experts debate the number of people who died at the Berlin Wall, according to a 2017 German study, 262 people perished, with most victims "shot by East German guards, drowned trying to swim to the West, or set off anti-personnel mines."[42] It is also believed that upward of five thousand people were captured attempting a similar daring escape.[43]

Reinforced by concrete and barbed wire, the over 100-mile Wall, came to symbolize the potent difference between East and West and the Cold War more extensively. Over time, the Western side became a graffiti-lined tribute to free speech, whereas the buildings closest to the Wall on the Eastern side were cleared to allow room for guards to observe and shoot those who dared to escape.

President John Kennedy highlighted the difference between East and West in a June 1963 speech in West Berlin, five months before his assassination: "There are many people in the world who really don't understand . . . what is the great issue between the free world and the Communist world. Let them come to Berlin. There are some who say that communism is the wave of the future. Let them come to Berlin. . . . All free men, wherever they may live, are citizens of Berlin, and therefore, as a freeman, I take pride in the words: Ich bin ein Berliner."[44]

Kennedy's words came in the aftermath of thirteen days in October 1962, when the Cuban Missile Crisis brought the world as close to nuclear war as it had ever come. A year earlier, the United States backed the unsuccessful invasion of Cuba by exiles opposed to the revolutionary government established by Fidel Castro. To prevent a similar attempt, Castro called on Soviet leader Nikita Khrushchev to provide support to defend Cuba. Khrushchev took the opportunity to shift the nuclear chess pieces by installing nuclear weapons in Cuba to offset those stationed by the US on the Soviet border in Turkey. The US caught wind of the Soviet's action through U-2 spy plane photography, kicking off a robust debate among America's foreign policy establishment as to a response.

Speaking to the nation on October 22, 1962, President Kennedy informed the American people of the "Soviet military buildup on the island of Cuba," and called for "Chairman Khrushchev to halt and eliminate this clandestine, reckless, and provocative threat to world peace and stable relations."[45] He also called, from among a number of measures, "a strict quarantine"[46] and naval blockade of Soviet offensive military equipment to Cuba. This included thirty Soviet ships that came to a sudden stop on October 24, 1962, to which Secretary of State Dean Rusk noted to National Security Advisor McGeorge Bundy: "We're eyeball to eyeball . . . and I think the other fellow just blinked."[47] Cooler heads prevailed, and the Soviet's agreed to withdraw their missiles from Cuba in exchange for an American pledge to not invade Cuba and withdraw its missiles from Turkey. Ultimately, the crisis demonstrated that neither of the two superpowers were ready to initiate a nuclear strike for fear of retaliation.

Around the same time, President Kennedy took action to increase the number of military advisers, CIA agents, and Special Forces in South Vietnam. This uptick, which rested on the shoulders of Truman's decision to move away from FDR's anticolonialism position to support the French, and President Eisenhower's efforts to prop up the Diem regime, led President Lyndon Johnson to transform Vietnam into a Cold War battle and one of the longest and most divisive wars in American history. Despite announcing, "We are not about to send American boys 9 or 10,000 miles away from home to do what Asian boys ought to be doing for themselves,"[48] in a speech at Akron University in October 1964, Johnson won reelection the following month and proceeded to ramp up troop levels and bombing campaigns. In addressing the nation on US war aims in Vietnam, on April 7, 1965, Johnson affirmed his commitment: "We will not be defeated. We will not grow tired. We will not withdraw either openly or under the cloak of a meaningless agreement."[49]

Antiwar protests quickly spread across the globe, and the significant toll and poor trajectory of the war, including chants outside the White House of "Hey, hey, LBJ, how many kids did you kill today?" led Johnson not to seek reelection in 1968. It would not be until 1973 that America completed its withdraw from Vietnam, after a cost of almost a trillion dollars in contemporary terms, and the lives of fifty-eight thousand Americans.[50]

With the election of President Richard Nixon and on through Jimmy Carter, the US pursued a policy of détente, defined as an effort to ease strained relations, including to agreeably halt the nuclear arms race. The Strategic Arms Limitation Talks (SALT) led to an agreement in 1972. SALT II took another seven years to negotiate but ultimately was never ratified by Congress. Also, in 1972, President Nixon became the first US president to visit China, conveying a toast on the occasion: "To the hope of our children that peace and harmony can be the legacy of our generation to theirs."[51]

All the while, the two superpowers continued to back opposite sides in conflicts around the world. In 1973, for example, Soviet-armed Egypt and Syria fought US-armed Israel. In 1979, the Soviet's sent large-scale military forces across its southern border into Afghanistan to defend the communist regime threatened by Afghan mujahidin guerrilla fighters. The invasion was denounced by Western leaders as a blatant act of aggression, ending a period of détente between the US and the Soviet Union. The Soviet act "changed most dramatically" President Jimmy Carter's "opinion of the Russians," as it was "only now dawning upon the world the magnitude of the action that the Soviets undertook in invading Afghanistan."[52] Russia's action followed a pattern of efforts to crush uprisings in East Germany in 1953, Hungary in 1956, and Czechoslovakia in 1968 to preserve communist rule.

Taking office in 1981, President Ronald Reagan was strongly anti-communist, highlighted by his introductory press conference where he boldly questioned Soviet legitimacy, affirming how they reserved unto themselves "the right to commit any crime, to lie, to cheat."[53] In a March 1983 speech to the National Association of Evangelicals, Reagan further denounced the Soviet Union as the "evil empire."[54] He took direct aim at the 1968 Brezhnev Doctrine, which noted that the establishment of a communist regime was irreversible, by increasing aid to anti-Soviet groups in Afghanistan and to opponents of Marxist regimes from Africa and Asia, to Central America.

Reagan came to the presidency believing the United States had grown weak militarily, losing the respect it once carried in global affairs. He therefore sought to significantly expand and diversify America's military and nuclear arsenal in order to elevate US predominance and help bring the Soviets to the bargaining table. One particular tool in his tool shed was the proposed space-based "Star Wars" antiballistic defense system which, aimed to protect the US from missile attacks. As Reagan asked a nationwide television audience on March 23, 1983: "What if free people could live secure in the knowledge that their security did not rest upon the threat of instant U.S. retaliation to deter a Soviet attack, that we could intercept and destroy strategic ballistic missiles before they reached our own soil or that of our allies?"[55]

Reagan's posture of tough words backed with action, along with an aggressive tone adopted by Western leaders, made the Soviet Union fearful of a surprise nuclear strike. The Soviets responded by amassing the largest army in the world, a globe-trotting navy, and an arsenal of thousands of nuclear weapons. During Reagan's first term, US-Soviet relations hit a low point unseen since the Cuban Missile Crisis.

In 1985, however, an abrupt change in direction followed the emergence of Mikhail Gorbachev as Soviet leader. Clear-eyed about the serious problems that pervaded the Soviet bloc, Gorbachev had a strong grounding in how the economies of Communist-ruled states, including the Soviet Union, had been underperforming for decades. He saw how the Soviet Union was slipping dramatically behind the West in technological development, and he accepted his reform mandate of "glasnost," or openness, and "perestroika," or restructuring, in an attempt to liberalize the Soviet political and economic system as an attempt to save it.

When the United States and Soviet Union met in Geneva in November 1985, it was the first attempted summit in six years. The iconic image from the gathering was the seventy-four-year-old Reagan, wearing only his dark blue suit, greeting the younger, fifty-four-year-old Gorbachev, adorned in an overcoat and oversized fur hat. Although no treaty was signed, the two-day meeting allowed both leaders the opportunity to engage and openly discuss next steps. The follow-up summit in Reykjavik in October 1986 also ended without a deal, yet there was deep interest on both sides to significantly reduce strategic weapons, including Gorbachev's proposal to abolish all nuclear weapons. The deal fell through, however, after Gorbachev linked his substantial concessions to a demand that the Star Wars program be limited to a laboratory. Reagan refused and walked out, explaining to his adviser's moments prior: "If we agree to Gorbachev's conditions, won't we be doing so simply in order to leave here with an agreement? Well, we will not agree to that!"[56] Upon hearing Reagan's stance, "An agitated Gorbachev snapped his book shut and stormed out of the room,"[57] according to Reagan's chief negotiator for strategic arms, Edward Rowny.

In the days following the Reykjavik summit, both the American and Soviet sides issued blame, chilling the progressive conversations and bilateral relations. On the home front, Reagan endured the Democratic Party taking control of both houses of Congress during the 1986 off-year elections, as well as a steep decline in his approval ratings, the result of the Iran-Contra scandal, which involved the illegal sale of arms to Iran with the proceeds going to fund the Contras, a right-wing rebel group in Nicaragua. With only eighteen months left in his second term, he officially was a lame-duck president, as maneuvering to become the nation's forty-first president had already begun.

Given the political winds of the day, along with the lack of tangible progress at the negotiating tables in Geneva and Reykjavik: "Few experts in either country believed the Cold War was about the end,"[58] as author Romesh Ratnesar pointed out. As Reagan later explained: "In the spring of 1987 we were still facing a lot of uncertainty regarding the Soviets: Gorbachev had announced his new programs of perestroika and glasnost and it was evident something was up in the Soviet Union, but we still didn't know what it was."[59] German Chancellor Helmut Kohl further noted: The cold war was not yet over, the medium-range missiles were still in position, and the Soviet Union had not yet agreed to real disarmament."[60] It was in this context that the eyes of the world looked to Berlin, and the city's 750th anniversary in the spring of 1987. It was here that the earth shifted with four words at "Ground Zero" of the Cold War.

The Roadmap

At 11:42 a.m. on Friday, June 12, 1987, President Ronald Reagan touched down aboard Air Force One at Tempelhof Central Airport in West Berlin, Germany. Not just any airfield, this historic strip served as the center of the Berlin Airlift in the late 1940s, where American and Western cargo planes landed every three-and-a-half minutes brimming with life-sustaining supplies for the two and a half million West Berliners in need. Four decades removed, a similar sense of optimism imbued the grounds with Reagan's arrival at such a crucial juncture in the Cold War. The president was visiting Berlin for four and a half hours on the last day of a ten-day, 10,135-mile European journey. While the majority of the trip was spent in Venice, Italy, for the G7 Summit, Reagan slipped away to Rome for the good part of a day to meet for nearly an hour with the Pope at the Vatican. His continuing itinerary called for a visit to Bonn later Friday afternoon before being wheels up to Washington by early evening.

Descending Air Force One on a Pan Am stair truck, the president, joined by First Lady Nancy Reagan, waved enthusiastically to the welcoming crowd. The cool, overcast, and breezy day matched "The Grey City's" reputation, and accordingly, many West Berliners opted to wear long sleeves even in June. Reagan was dressed in a dark suit with a white dress shirt, matching handkerchief, and a multicolored tie highlighted with red running the top quarter to the knot, while a small diagonal white stripe separated the distinct tints of navy and teal, which filled out the lowermost portions. The president's look complemented the first lady's white shirt and dark-top and -bottom ensemble.

As the Reagans reached the red-carpet-lined tarmac, they were greeted by US Ambassador to West Germany Richard Burt and his wife Gahl, "as well as a considerable group"[61] of West German officials. After a short receiving ceremony, which included the "Nat. Anthem & review of troops—American,"[62] as Reagan noted in his diary, the president jumped into his expanded four-door, clear-windowed, black presidential limousine for a twenty-seven-minute ride to Bellevue Palace, the stately circa 1786 residence of German President Richard von Weizsäcker. Reagan was joined on the ride by West Berlin Mayor Eberhard Diepgen, who was responsible for the president's visit, formally inviting him to speak at the celebration of Berlin's 750th anniversary, scheduled for after three o'clock, later that afternoon upon the entourage's return to the airport. It was where Reagan would notably quip: "It's an honor to join you today at this 750th birthday party for the city of Berlin. . . . It's not that often I get to go to a birthday party for something that's older than I am."[63]

Upon arrival at "Schloss Bellevue" at about half-past noon, Reagan and Mayor Diepgen joined President Weizsäcker to pose for brief press photos and then spent "a pleasant half hour or so indoors."[64] Shortly after one o'clock, the entourage departed for a short ride to the historic Reichstag government building, where they were joined by German Chancellor Helmut Kohl and his wife Hannelore. Entering the building under the dedication "Dem Deutschen Volke" or "To the German People" etched into the upper face of the building, Reagan proceeded to take in an "exhibit of the Marshal plan & Germanys rebuilding,"[65] a reminder for him of "how America spent billions after World War II helping rebuild the economies of Europe, including those of two of our former enemies."[66] Reagan pondered to himself: "What other nation on earth would have done that?"[67] The president then "met several elderly ladies who had been part of the female force that cleaned bricks from the rubble & played a role in Berlin's rebuilding,"[68] reminding him again of the deep gulf between the American and Communist systems.

As the tour moved along, White House reporter Sam Donaldson yelled out: "Mr. President, some of these demonstrators think [Soviet Leader Mikhail] Gorbachev is more a man of peace than you are?"[69] With a sly smile the president responded: "They just have to learn, don't they."[70] Quickly following up, Donaldson asked: "You upset by the demonstrations, sir?"[71] To which Reagan responded equally swift: "I haven't seen any."[72] Donaldson was referring to the twenty-four thousand demonstrators who took to West Berlin's streets the previous day to protest American policies, including "hooded hooligans,"[73] anarchists, and vandals who burned cars and smashed store front windows.[74] Sixty-seven officers were injured in the rampage, an inauspicious preview to Reagan's visit.[75]

The tour continued out on to a Reichstag observation platform, where the entourage of guests and reporters filled in behind the president. Standing behind makeshift bulletproof Plexiglas overlooking the Spree River and the Berlin Wall into East Berlin, Reagan "could see the graffiti and prodemocracy slogans scrawled on liberty's side of the wall"[76] and, across from it, a government building in East Berlin where he was told there was long-distance monitoring apparatus that "could eavesdrop"[77] on his conversations. One West German official warned him: "Watch what you say."[78] As an inspired Reagan sounded off about what he thought of a government that "penned in its people like farm animals,"[79] East German soldiers were busy photographing him from afar.[80] While he could not recall in his memoir exactly what he said in that moment, he thought that he "may have used a little profanity"[81] in expressing his opinion of Communism, hoping he "would be heard."[82] In no uncertain terms the Berlin Wall represented for Reagan "as stark a symbol as anyone could ever expect to see of the contrast between two different political systems;" on one side, people held captive by a failed and corrupt totalitarian government, on the other, freedom, enterprise, prosperity.[83]

Chancellor Kohl and Mayor Diepgen directed Reagan's attention out into the distance to the gun-toting guard towers and barbed-wire fencing that divided the East from the West. According to Reagan's Deputy Chief of Staff Ken Duberstein, the president was "overtaken with emotion as he confronted the crosses painted on the wall where people had died trying to escape to freedom."[84] The president turned to Duberstein and Chancellor Kohl and conveyed with simplicity: "This is the only wall built to keep people in, not keep people out."[85] It's not hard to imagine that in this moment Reagan's mind drifted back to his initial trips to West Berlin, first, as a private citizen in 1978, where he was visiting to "gain fresh insight into then-current major international problems and opportunities,"[86] and second, as president four years later in 1982.

As part of his first visit, he spent some time in a centralized department store described "as a K-Mart but with almost no inventory."[87] Upon leaving the store, Reagan witnessed "Two East German Volkspolizisten,"[88] People's Police, stop an ordinary citizen carrying shopping bags." One guard forced the man to drop to his knees and raise his hands, while the other guard poked him in the stomach with his machine gun and used the barrel of a gun to "probe the contents of the shopping bags."[89]

Reagan's future National Security Advisor Richard Allen witnessed the episode and the to-be president's angered reaction. And, while powerful, it was Reagan's subsequent reaction to the Berlin Wall that was even more impactful. From the penthouse offices of the Axel Springer publishing house, "which stood right on the border between the two parts of the city,"[90] Reagan viewed the spot where eighteen-year-old Peter Fechter was shot in 1962.

Trying to escape through the thick barbed wire before the concrete block wall was built, Fechter was left to die for nearly an hour by the Grenzpolizei, or border police, hauntingly calling out for his mother as he took his last breaths. Moved deeply by the story, Reagan "just gritted his teeth"[91] and stared at the wall intently with "his body stiffened, hands tightly clenched, and his jaw set."[92] Turning ever so slowly, without losing eye contact with the concrete barrier, he said: "We've got to find a way to knock this thing down!"[93] The future president also, more broadly: "Came away with a vivid impression of a city that is more than a place on the map—a city that is a testament to what is both inspiring and most troubling about the time we live in."[94]

In 1982, Reagan returned to Berlin as president. After a speech at the Charlottenburg Palace where he affirmed: "Our commitment to Berlin is a lasting one,"[95] Reagan toured the Berlin Wall by car, including a stop at Checkpoint Charlie,[96] where he approached the white line that separated the US and Soviet zones. When White House reporter Sam Donaldson cautioned Reagan: "Don't step over the line," Reagan playfully dangled his foot over it but came short of putting it down. As he returned to his car, Donaldson followed up asking Reagan what he thought of the wall. "It's as ugly as the idea behind it," the president replied. As Reagan ducked his head into the presidential limousine, Donaldson yelled out again to the president: "Will Berlin ever be one city again?" "Yes," Reagan said, as he disappeared into the backseat of the vehicle.[97]

Five years later, nearly to the day, and with the entire world watching, the gravity of the moment was again etched on the president's face. As Reagan recalled: "Standing so near the Berlin Wall, seeing it in substance as well as for what it symbolized, I felt an anger well up in me."[98] He clenched his wife Nancy's hand with raw emotion as they exited the Reichstag. Everything he experienced over the previous forty minutes, and across his nearly fourscore years of life, congealed as he took the short ride to the fringes of the Brandenburg Gate. In just minutes he would channel that emotion and a lifetime of experiences into words that would change the arc of American history and the world.

The Makings of Ronald Reagan's Optimism

Situated fifty plus miles east of Davenport, Iowa, 125 miles west of Chicago, is the small village of Tampico, Illinois. In 1911, it was home to over 800 residents[99] and included "a short paved main street, a railroad station, two or three churches, and a couple of stores."[100] In the early morning hours of February 6 of that year, the town was enveloped by nearly a foot of snow and drifts that made the landscape impassible.[101] At 111 Main Street, in a five-room, second-floor apartment flat above a general store,

Nelle Wilson Reagan, after a difficult delivery, gave birth to a strapping ten-pound baby boy named Ronald at 4:16 a.m. "According to family legend,"[102] after running up a long flight of stairs to see his newborn son for the first time, twenty-nine-year-old John Edward "Jack" Reagan said: "He looks like a fat little Dutchman. But who knows, he might grow up to be president some day."[103] This air of possibility would follow the newborn throughout his life.

Ronald Wilson or "Dutch" as would he ask to be called, was the Reagans' second child, following two-year-old John Neil Reagan, or "Moon," who was none too excited about the prospect of a younger brother. Fortified in Irish blood, this newest Reagan brood owed their American ancestry to Michael Reagan (born O'Regan), their paternal grandfather who arrived in America before the Civil War by way of the Emerald Isle's County Tipperary and "England during the potato famine."[104] Their father, Jack, similarly embodied the restlessness of his own father and forebearers, as well as the spirit of the nineteenth-century frontier. His profession as a shoe salesman along with his dream of owning a shoe store, made him perpetually "ready to pull up stakes and move on in search of a better life for himself and his family."[105] As Ronald recalled, "We moved to wherever my father's ambition took him,"[106] which led the small family of four to traipse across Illinois, from Tampico and Chicago, to Galesburg and Monmouth, and back to Tampico and then to Dixon all before Ronald turned nine.

Championing his Hibernian roots, Jack Reagan, according to his youngest son, was "endowed with the gift of blarney and the charm of a leprechaun,"[107] and for his money, there was no one that "could tell a story"[108] better. An orphan raised by his aunt, Jack was a stylish and well-built, five-feet, ten-and-a-half-inch tall, dark, and handsome Irish American with a penchant for dreaming and drinking. He taught Ronald the value of hard work and ambition, the art of storytelling, and his passionate belief in individual destiny and equality regardless of skin color or religion. To this end, there was "no more grievous sin"[109] in the Reagan household "than a racial slur or other evidence of religious or racial intolerance."[110] This sentiment emanated largely from the discrimination Jack experienced growing up in an era where "some stores had signs at their door saying, NO DOGS OR IRISHMEN ALLOWED."[111] Ronald experienced his own prejudices and subsequent scuffles as an Irish Catholic, which was a distinction viewed by some with a jaundiced eye.

Importantly, at a rather formative moment, it was Jack's encouragement of his youngest son to pursue his dream that helped land Ronald his breakthrough job as a sportscaster at station WOC in Davenport, Iowa. But Jack's drinking, while sporadic, was a liability, and at any random moment he could slip into a speakeasy, "jump off the wagon,"[112] and not see his family for days. Ronald's first real insight into his father's condition occurred "one cold, blustery, winter's night,"[113] when he found Jack lying face-up, arms stretched in the snow near the front door of their rented home. A series of heart attacks led to his father's passing in 1941 at the age of fifty-seven.

Whereas Jack Reagan was more of a cynic and "tended to suspect the worst of people,"[114] Ronald's Scots-English mother, Nelle Wilson: "Always expected to find the best in people and often did."[115] Ingrained with optimism "that ran as deep as the common cold,"[116] she "had a gift for making you believe that you could change the world,"[117] according to Maureen Reagan, Ronald's daughter.

Nelle's "first love"[118] was performing and she actively coaxed both of her sons to follow her on to the small stage. It was there that Ronald's life changed forever, after "people laughed and applauded"[119] his debut. When it came to her husband, Nelle routinely channeled her optimistic spirit to remind her boys how good Jack was to them when he was not drinking. She introduced Ronald to *That Printer of Udell*: "A wonderful book,"[120] as he recalled, that told of the son of a drunken father whose excellent speaking ability guided his path to become a preacher. He viewed the main character, Harold Bell Wright, as "a role model,"[121] and the story had such an impact on him that he decided to join his mother's church, the Disciples of Christ.

Dutch Reagan revered his mother and her impact on him stretched far and wide, ranging from his love of performing, to his belief in the power of prayer. But of all things, it was the sunny optimism he inherited from her that defined his life, including the belief that everything would work out alright because it was part of God's plan.

Another important influence on young Ronald Reagan was the town preacher in Dixon, Rev. Ben Cleaver. He mentored him, helped him get into college, and taught him how to drive. He also happened to be the father of his girlfriend, Margaret, who like his mother, was "short, pretty, auburn haired, and intelligent."[122]

Although neither Jack or Nelle Reagan had extensive formal schooling beyond the elementary grades, they possessed "a natural and intuitive intelligence,"[123] according to their youngest son. It seems fitting that by age five, Ronald had taught himself to read. One day, his father saw him on the living room floor with a newspaper and asked: "What are you doing?" To which, Ronald replied, "Reading the paper."[124] So, Jack asked him to read him something, and he did, and then proceeded to invite all the neighbors over to "hear his five-year-old son read."[125] Trying to make sense of his feat years later, Ronald believed he learned to read "through a kind of osmosis,"[126] as his mother always read him a bedtime story, following "each line on the page with her finger."[127]

Recognizing early on that he had a "pretty good memory,"[128] Ronald took steps to further his path as an "avid reader."[129] With his "own card for the Dixon Illinois Public Library,"[130] he remarked that he "was probably as regular a patron as the library ever had."[131] He was hooked after finding a fictional hero he liked, and "would consume everything"[132] he could about them, from *King Arthur and the Knights of the Round Table*, to *The Count of Monte Cristo*. Ever the dreamer, he likewise read books about college life that led him to envision himself on a college campus, "wearing a college jersey, even as the star on the football team."[133] His "childhood dream"[134] was to become like one of those guys in those books. And he would, noting later that "his reading left an abiding belief in the triumph of good over evil."[135]

Despite his prodigious mind, Ronald's grades progressively worsened as he got older, so much that by his college days, he was pleased with squeezing out a passing grade so he could "remain eligible for football, swimming, track and other school activities."[136] Historian Robert Dallek concluded: Reagan's "purpose of college was not to gain an academic education; it was a vehicle for personal advancement."[137]

Of all the places Ronald lived, it was Dixon, a tranquil dairy town, just under thirty miles northeast of Tampico, where he "really found"[138] himself. "All of us have a place we go back to," he noted. "Dixon is that place for me."[139] Ronald called the bustling town of ten thousand "a small universe" where "almost everyone knew each other . . . and if things were going wrong" for your neighbor, you prayed for them, "and knew they'd pray for you if things went wrong for you."[140] It was where he established roots, made friends, and "learned standards and values"[141] that would guide him through life—things like, "hard work was an essential part of life;"[142] America was a place that "offered unlimited opportunity;"[143] and the personal motto found under his picture in the high school yearbook: "Life is just one great sweet song, so start the music,"[144] which was an excerpt taken from a poem he had written, titled "Life," a nod to youthful optimism.

It was in Dixon that he became self-aware of his family's impoverishment, often sustained by the delicacy of "oatmeal meat,"[145] an amalgamation of oatmeal and hamburger. Yet, exhibiting his glass half-full mind-set early on, Ronald thought it was "the most wonderful thing"[146] he'd ever tasted, not knowing, initially, that it was a dish "born of poverty."[147]

Dixon was situated on the Rock River, which was often called the "Hudson of the West,"[148] an outdoor playground, not unlike FDR's experience, where Dutch ice-skated in winter, and swam, canoed, and fished in summer. At age eleven, it was where he was hauled off to the police station for firing an illegal firework across the river on the eve of the Fourth of July. For seven summers, beginning after his sophomore year in high school, Ronald served as a lifeguard at Lowell Park on the river. Calling it "one of the best jobs"[149] he ever had, he logged in ten- to twelve-hour days, seven days a week, beginning at fifteen dollars a day, and later increasing to twenty dollars. With a knack for the job, he saved seventy-seven lives from rip currents and choppy waters, which was "One of the proudest statistics"[150] of his life. He kept track of these saves by carving a notch into a log near the edge of the river. As his legend grew, it was not uncommon for Reagan to appear on the front page of the local paper for his escapades. During slow times, he taught children to swim, and increasingly took the manager's horse out for a ride, which developed into a lifelong passion.

It was along the banks of the Rock River that he cultivated his talent for "drawing cartoons and caricatures,"[151] while also continuing to nourish a career "as the Great Naturalist,"[152] "exploring the local wilderness," and reading everything he could about "birds and wildlife of the Rock River Valley."[153] His mother gave him a book, *Northern Lights*, which was "based on the lives of the great white wolves of the north."[154] He read it like a textbook, over and over in the tradition of Theodore Roosevelt, imagining himself "with the wolves of the wild." This followed his time in Galesburg, the same town in which Abraham Lincoln debated Stephen A. Douglas, where he got lost for hours among birds' eggs and butterflies enclosed in glass cases left behind in the attic of the family's rented house. It was in this aura of creativity and adventure that he fondly described his childhood in Dixon "as sweet and idyllic as it could be, as close as I could imagine for a young boy to the world created by Mark Twain in *The Adventures of Tom Sawyer*."[155]

Personally, Ronald Reagan was comfortable in his own skin. He radiated warmth and friendliness and possessed a "trademark wink and nod."[156] He was adept at using humor to defuse situations and owned a great laugh for the punch line and at himself. He had a penchant for making people feel good, as his Attorney General Edwin Meese III explained: Reagan "was almost always upbeat, optimistic, enjoyable to be around."[157]

Dutch stood tall, walked with purpose, rarely raised his voice, and was genuinely interested in people and their feelings. His vice president, and former US president, George H. W. Bush said of him: "Ronald Reagan was one of the most decent men I have had the privilege to know. He would no sooner fly to the moon than walk past a waiter or a doorman without saying 'Hello!' "[158] Nancy Reagan, Ronald's second wife remarked: "They broke the mold when they made Ronnie . . . he was the eternal optimist."[159] And it was his optimism that, according to scholar Hugh Heclo, "appealed to his opponents as well as his followers,"[160] and "was quintessentially American,"[161] according to historian Stephen Knott.

If he had a personality blemish, it was his guardedness, which emanated from frequent uprootings as a child. Reagan self-described as being "a little slow in making really close friends."[162] His own son, Ron, said his father was someone who held back "10 percent"[163] of himself, which "remains a considerable mystery."[164] Later trauma, including his divorce from actress Jane Wyman, which he viewed as the worst failing of his life, only strengthened his emotional distance. His biographer Edmund Morris echoed this sentiment: "I wish I had a dollar for each of the friends and family members who complained to me that Dutch never let them 'get anywhere near.' "[165] Similarly, another biographer, Lou Cannon argued that despite being "one of the most successful of men, and outwardly one of the happiest . . . Reagan remained a mystery, even to those who knew him the best."[166] And Nancy Reagan, who knew him better than anyone, noted intimately in her memoirs: "There's a wall around him. He lets me come closer than anyone else, but there are times when even I feel that barrier."[167]

Small for his age, it took Ronald Reagan time to physically grow into his eventual six-feet, one-inch frame, which was complemented by piercing blue eyes, wavy brown hair, and a warm, soothing voice. At five foot three, 108 pounds, Ronald didn't make the high school football team as a freshman. Undeterred, he spent the following summer building up his muscles at thirty-five cents an hour "working with a pick and shovel to help build and remodel houses in and around Dixon."[168] His sophomore year, he made the team and was elected captain of a new football division of players under 135 pounds. By his junior year, he shot up to five-feet, ten-and-a-half-inches and weighed over 160 pounds. He played right guard for the varsity team from then and on through his senior season. In doing so, he realized the "noblest and most glamorous goal"[169] in his life to date: "Filling one of those purple and white jerseys"[170] of the high school football team displayed on mannequins each summer in a Dixon storefront.

In his early teens, he found out he was nearsighted after trying on his mother's glasses that she had left in the backseat of the car, as the family went for a Sunday drive through the green countryside bordering Dixon. Until that moment he assumed everyone saw the world blurry. With doctor-prescribed glasses he became a new person, both in the classroom and on the athletic field. He understood why he felt compelled to sit near the blackboard in class and why he was so poor in catching fly balls in baseball. Now, he was first in line to participate in sports and other activities, from being a drum major in the band, to participating on the swim and football teams.

Graduating from Dixon High School in 1928, Reagan was determined to attend college with his girlfriend, despite financial limitations and the fact that only 7 percent of high school grads of the day received a postsecondary education. Fueled by a "pretty girl and a love for football,"[171] he talked his way into a "Needy Student Scholarship"[172] at Eureka College, a Disciples of Christ school located just over 100 miles southeast of Dixon. He pledged the Tau Kappa Epsilon fraternity and earned enough money washing dishes and serving tables to pay for his meals. The intimate nature of the college allowed Ronald to meet other students and engage in extracurricular activities that he may not have been privy to at a larger university: "I think I would have fallen back in the crowd and never discovered things about myself that I did at Eureka,"[173] Reagan noted.

Acting was at the top of those extracurricular activities, as it was growing up. His high school English teacher, B. J. Frazer, encouraged him to perform in class by reading essays, and soon he was participating in the plays Frazier directed. By his senior year in high school, he was "so addicted to student theatrical production"[174] that he couldn't be kept out of them. Frazer also helped Ronald expand his empathy by showing him how to put himself in another person's shoes to understand a character's motivation. Similarly, at Eureka, he credited a new English professor, Ellen Marie Johnson, for encouraging him, and he went on to appear in more than a dozen college plays. One of particular importance was a prestigious one-act competition at Northwestern University, where afterward, the head of the Wildcats speech department and the sponsor of the contest, told him he should think about making acting his career. According to Reagan, it was "the day the acting bug"[175] really bit him. As historian Garry

Wills pointed out, it also didn't hurt that he had a "movie-star look long before he was a movie star."[176]

On the stage and off, Reagan demonstrated a propensity to lead. Although historian James MacGregor Burns argued that the "real Reagan" was a "committed" leader "who stuck to his beliefs,"[177] it was Dutch's infectious optimistic spirit that drew people to him and defined his leadership essence throughout his life. Tying these strands, historian Michael Beschloss noted that it was his strong beliefs and optimism that "moved him to do things which others might have flinched."[178]

In high school he captained the JV football team, the varsity swim team, and was elected president of the student body. In his freshman year of college, he led a student protest of an administration proposal to cut faculty and programming. While not intending to lead the strike, he gave a rousing speech at the student rally, where he felt his "words reach out and grab"[179] the audience, and after a week, the advocacy led Eureka's president to resign and things returned to normal. Reagan further served as president of the Boosters Club, two years in the student senate, and as Eureka's student body president in his senior year. Asked years later if he could recall from his college years any inkling of running for president, Reagan noted: "Well, actually, the thought first struck me on graduation day when the president handed me my diploma and asked: 'Are you better off today than you were four years ago?'"[180]

Graduating with a bachelors of arts degree in 1932, with majors in economics and social science, he was certainly better off than the young man who advocated for a needy scholarship to enter the freshman class. Upon a return to the college in the run-up to the 1980 presidential election, Reagan reflected: "If I had to do it all over again, I'd come right back here and start where I had before. . . . Everything good that has happened to me—everything—started here on this campus in those four years that still are so much part of my life."[181]

That "everything good" included landing a sports announcing job in 1932, despite better-qualified applicants and in the middle of pervasive Depression-era unemployment. It included following the Chicago Cubs to spring training on Catalina Island and fortuitously parlaying a successful radio career into a casual Hollywood screen test and movie contract. And it included movie stardom and the hit television shows, *General Electric: Theater* and *Death Valley Days*, as well as the role of political surrogate for Barry Goldwater, which kick-started a political career and two-terms as governor of California and as president of the United States.

Reagan's was a life that spanned the twentieth century, from a small-Midwestern town, to the Golden Age of Hollywood, to the White House, and back to California. "Everything good,"[182] along with every storm and season was navigated by Ronald Reagan as the "congenital optimist."[183] We see it in how he was able to "cope with the dark spells caused by Jack Reagan's drinking,"[184] and the domestic and financial instability of his youth. We see it in his love for "oatmeal meat," in his uplifting high school yearbook personal motto, and in his dreams to suit up for the high school football team, go to college, and be in the movies.

We see it during World War II, and despite his eyesight keeping him from combat operations, the "main quality"[185] he exhibited was optimism, according to screenwriter Edward Anhalt, who was assigned with Reagan to the First Motion Picture Unit of the Army Air Corps based in Los Angeles. We see it in the way he was prone to think there was a solution—usually a simple one—to any problem" and how he believed that "good intentions led to good results," according to political scientist John Sloan.[186]

We see it in the run-up to the 1980 presidential election as "a voice of optimism and national destiny,"[187] as Reagan biographer Richard Reeves described, and in the words of Reagan's director of communications, David Gergen: "Within weeks of taking office, Americans said—as they had about FDR—we have a leader in the White House again. He restored hope . . . and made us smile once more."[188] "Consciously and eagerly . . . stamp[ing] this upbeat attitude into the minds of the American people,"[189] as noted by historian James T. Patterson, Reagan in his own words noted: "We had to recapture our dreams, our pride in ourselves and our country, and regain that unique sense of destiny and optimism that has always made America different from any other country in the world."[190]

We see it in the response to his assassination attempt in 1981, when moments before surgery, he removed his oxygen mask to joke: "Please tell me you're all Republicans," or when first seeing his wife at the hospital: "Honey, I forgot to duck,"[191] a reference to boxer Jack Dempsey's famous one-liner. It was also from out of the assassination attempt that he believed God "saved him for some higher purpose," the fall of the Iron Curtain,[192] and according to David Gergen, that he was for "a great many, especially working people . . . the president who had taken a bullet and smiled."[193]

We see it in how Reagan transformed America's mood "from pessimism to optimism,"[194] as historian H. R. Brands noted, and in the president's "optimistic futurism"[195] and the belief that America as a nation is forever young, which he explained through an anecdote about James Allen who noted: "Many thinking people believe America has seen its best days." However, as Reagan optimistically quipped, this was a sentiment Allen expressed in his diary on July 26, 1775![196]

We see it imbued in Reagan's 1984 State of the Union Address: "There is renewed energy and optimism throughout the land. America is back, standing tall,"[197] which was likewise exemplified in "Morning in America . . . one of the most effective campaign spots ever broadcast."[198] Channeling this sentiment, Reagan biographer, Bob Spitz noted of the fortieth president: "His gospel of optimism restored the country's spirit."[199]

We see it in his ability to project the feeling that "everything is going to be all right," his most distinctive quality as president according to his biographer Lou Cannon.[200] This was exemplified in remarks to the nation after the Space Shuttle Challenger disaster in 1986, when Reagan mourned the loss of seven astronauts who "slipped the surly bonds of earth" to "touch the face of God," but also reminded Americans that "our hopes and our journeys continue."[201]

We see it on the small plaque found on his desk in the Oval Office that read: "It CAN be done," a reminder to all that anything is possible, and how he remained cheerful and optimistic as president, unlike peers who came to view the presidency as a "splendid misery,"[202] including Thomas Jefferson who noted two days before James Madison succeeded him as president: "Never did a prisoner, released from his chains, feel such relief as I shall on shaking off the shackles of power."[203]

We see it in his November 5, 1994 letter announcing he had Alzheimer's disease: "When the Lord calls me home, whenever that may be, I will leave with the greatest love for this country of ours and eternal optimism for its future,"[204] and in the words of his longtime postpresidential aide, Peggy Grande, who when informed about his condition, "was overwhelmed by the goodness, the graciousness, and the faith of a man who was being tested and in his time of trial was not crumbling, but rather was rising up with strength and . . . optimism in the depths of life's darkest place."[205]

We see it in his death in 2004, and how etched at his burial site at the Ronald Reagan Library in Simi Valley, California, are the optimistic words by which he chose to be remembered: "I know in my heart that man is good, that what is right will always eventually triumph, and there is purpose and worth to each and every life."[206]

And we see it in the signature moment of his presidency, one that demonstrated the infectiousness of his "naturally sunny"[207] optimism, and the underlying essence of his life and leadership. In a speech heard around the globe and across the ages, Ronald Reagan's words planted a seed that would transform the world and America's place in it, while cementing his own place in the annals of history.

The Berlin Wall Speech

In April 1987, Anthony Dolan, the head of White House speechwriting and author of Reagan's 1983 "Evil Empire"[208] address, assigned the Berlin speech to Peter Robinson, who, up until that point, didn't have a signature sound bite or moment under his belt. Although armed with this potentially plum assignment, Robinson received scarce instructions on how to formulate the remarks, only garnering that the president would be "speaking at the Berlin Wall" to a "likely . . . audience of about ten-thousand."[209] Rightly concluding that Reagan "probably ought to talk about foreign policy,"[210] Robinson, to get "the pulse of the city,"[211] joined a presidential advance team of Secret Service agents, logistical experts, and press officials visiting Berlin in April.

His first stop was the Brandenburg Gate, the proposed site of the president's speech. The iconic, neoclassical gate was built in the late eighteenth century, and stood eighty-five feet in the air and thirty-six-feet deep with two rows of six Doric columns. Once the very center of the city, after World War II, the towering gate fell into the Soviet sector of the city, and after the Berlin Wall started going up in 1961, it became inaccessible to locals and visitors. By 1987, the nearly 200-year-old gate represented the most prominent sight along the wall that divided the city, a symbol of Cold War division into East and West. It also represented the kind of powerful visual that Reagan prized. It was here the president, as historian H. W. Brands noted, could remind "the world of the moral difference between the United States and the Soviet Union,"[212] and as historian John Lewis Gaddis noted, it was a site that played to Reagan's sense for the "dramatic."[213]

Standing at the site himself, Robinson felt the "weight of history."[214] He understood the venue was "unlike any other setting"[215] in which Reagan had ever spoken, and he understood his draft needed to "be equal to the setting," which he feared was a challenge. West German authorities also pushed US officials on this location, as they sought a "less provocative background"[216] for the president than the gate. They were concerned that

204 | Meeting the Moment

Reagan's "tough rhetoric"[217] paired with the "symbolism of the towering gate flying the black, red, and yellow flag of West Germany, would upset the tentative efforts by East and West Germany to move toward increased contacts."[218] It was American persistence in the location that caused West Berlin officials to relent on the site for the speech,[219] yet they were successful in pressing to hold the crowd to 20,000 "though the Americans wanted 40,000."[220]

While in Berlin, Robinson met with "the ranking U.S. State Department Official in Berlin," John Kornblum, who, in offering advice on what to say, proceeded to provide "several pages of notes of what the President should not say," according to Robinson. Things like: "No chest thumping. No Soviet-bashing. And no inflammatory statements about the Berlin Wall."[221] Kornblum went even as far to say that "West Berliners . . . had long ago gotten used to the structure that encircled them."[222] The rare positive suggestions included efforts to obtain more air routes into West Berlin and to amplify American support to turn West Berlin into an international conference center.[223]

Undeterred, Robinson later attended a private dinner party thrown for him in a residential suburb of Berlin by Dieter and Ingeborg Elz. Dieter was a former World Bank alum in Washington, who shared common friends with Robinson. The eclectic assembled group included over a dozen people from all walks of life: medicine to academia, homemakers to students. After some chitchat about the weather and German wine, Robinson threw out to the group: "By the way, the top State Department official here in Berlin told me that you've all gotten used to the Wall."[224] "Is this true?"[225] Robinson followed up. "Have you gotten used to the wall?"[226]

Absolute crickets: an awkward silence engulfed the room. Finally, one man raised his arm, pointed to the East and shared: "My sister lives just a few kilometers in that direction, and I haven't seen her in more than twenty years. How do you think we feel about the Wall?"[227] Another man followed: "I walk to work each day, I follow the same route, I pass directly under a guard tower, and a young man with a rifle over his shoulder peers down at me with binoculars. We speak the same language, we share the same history, but one of us is an animal and the other is a zookeeper, and I have never been able to decide which was which."[228] One by one the guests took turns talking about the wall. Hearing all the stories, the hostess for the evening became angry, pounding her clenched fist into the palm of her opposing hand: "If this man Gorbachev is serious with this talk, this glasnost, this perestroika, he can prove it by coming here and getting rid of this wall."[229]

There it was—the moment when the Berlin speech crystallized into form. Back at the Eisenhower Executive Office Building in Washington, DC, Robinson told Anthony Dolan about his idea to make getting rid of the wall the center of the speech. Pushing back in his chair from his desk, Dolan exclaimed: "Fantastic, wonderful, great, perfect . . . and other inadequate exclamations."[230] More broadly for Dolan, the Berlin event was the "quintessential chance—in front of Communism's most evocative monument—to enunciate the anti-Soviet counterstrategy that Reagan had been putting in place since his first weeks in office."[231] Similarly, speechwriter Dana Rohrabacher saw the speech as "what we had all been working for. It was going to be the speech of the Cold War."[232] To initially sell the idea, Dolan and Robinson proceeded to Tom Griscom's office in the West Wing. "The two of you thought you'd have to work real hard to keep me from saying 'no,'"[233] Griscom recalled. "But when you told me about the trip, particularly this point of learning from some Germans just how much they hated the wall, I thought to myself, You know, calling for the wall to be torn down—it might just work."[234]

The positive reinforcement from his supervisors didn't stop Robinson from struggling early with the phrasing, even offering the line in German in an opening draft: "Herr Gorbachev, machen Sie theses Tor auf."[235] Dolan quickly stepped in to set him straight: "Peter, when your client is the President of the United States, give him his big lines in English." So, "Mr. Gorbachev, tear down this wall."[236]

It was this draft language that Reagan approved in the decisive twenty-one-minute Oval Office meeting on May 18, and which Dolan would ecstatically celebrate immediately thereafter. Slamming the door to his office behind Peter Robinson, he shouted: "Can you believe it? He said what you were thinking. He said it himself."[237] Clearly, as far as the head of speechwriting was concerned, the line was Reagan's now. Yet, despite Reagan's blessing and Dolan's exuberance, over the next three weeks the draft was put through the interagency wringer, as a bitter dispute played out in memoranda, phone calls, and endless meetings. Both the State Department and the National Security Council tried to strike the "tear down this wall" phrasing, using language like "clumsy," "naïve" and "needlessly provocative."[238] Even Reagan's Chief of Staff Howard Baker said the phasing sounded "unpresidential,"[239] and that ultimately, "words were not going to bring the wall tumbling down."[240]

At the National Security Council, a longtime senior staffer Peter Rodman "protested the speech" in memoranda, and Deputy National Security Council Advisor Colin Powell called out Robinson in Tom Griscom's West Wing office to "recite all the arguments against the speech." Going "nose to nose"[241] with Powell in an "equally forceful manner,"[242] Robinson recited "all the arguments in favor of the speech."[243]

In follow-up to the exchange Rodman wrote Powell on June 2 in frustration: "We tried every tactic," he noted. "We offered general guidance, and general suggestions in the margins; we offered detailed rewrites. Neither tactic worked."[244] Overall, the National Security Council's position was that the phrase was "too provocative," that it would "embarrass German Chancellor Helmut Kohl."[245] One of their edits to an early draft included a large X over the phrase calling for the wall to be torn down.[246] Another draft contained the feedback: "Since [Gorbachev] will have just been there [Berlin], this device seems silly even as edited."[247] Yet another draft included the word "Drop" on the fringes of a page next to "Mr. Gorbachev, open this gate."[248]

At Foggy Bottom, the assistant secretary of State for Eastern European Affairs, Rozanne Ridgeway, "challenged the speech by telephone;"[249] the ranking diplomat in Berlin, John Kornbaum provided an alternative draft; and Secretary of State George Schultz twice attempted to squash the line. On one of those occasions, Tom Griscom was called on by Schultz and Chief of Staff Howard Baker a few days before the team traveled to Europe. The secretary of State said: "I really think that line about tearing down the wall is going to be an affront to Mr. Gorbachev."[250] Rebutting Schultz, Griscom noted: "The President has commented on this particular line and he's comfortable with it. And I can promise you that this line will reverberate."[251] After Baker learned the language was "Reagan's words . . . he said leave it in."[252] However, as Griscom later recalled, Schultz was "clearly not happy"[253] with the outcome. To the surprise of very few, he made a second run at the phase shortly thereafter in Venice, this time calling on Deputy Chief of Staff Ken Duberstein to reaffirm his stance that the "line was too rough on Gorbachev."[254] This was the popular view of many, as historian Michael Beschloss pointed out: "Most of [Reagan's] diplomats feared a seemingly hopeless demand would only enflame the Soviet leader."[255] With Schultz, Baker, and Powell leading the foreign policy establishment in advocating against the phrasing, there was also an undercurrent of support among many in this school of thought who wanted to hear something more benign and low profile, especially with Congress investigating the Iran-Contra affair.

With no end in sight to the in-fighting, Duberstein took the matter back to President Reagan to review the central passage on June 5. In a garden at the Villa Condulmer in Veneto, Italy, the president, after looking at the language, said slyly: "Now, Ken, I'm the President, aren't I?" To which, Duberstein responded, "Yes, Mr. President, we're clear about that much." Quickly following up, Reagan asked: "So if I say that line stays in, it stays in?" "Yes, sir, it is your decision,"[256] Duberstein confirmed. And with a "wonderful, knowing smile on his face,"[257] Reagan said: "Well then, it stays in."[258]

That still didn't stop the State Department from trying to strike the phase until the bitter end. Anthony Dolan recalled: "With a fervor and relentlessness I hadn't seen over the prior seven years even during disputes about 'the ash-heap of history' or 'evil empire,' they kept up the pressure until the morning Reagan spoke the line."[259] At a senior staff meeting at the Cipriani Hotel in Venice the morning of the speech, Dolan turned to Tom Griscom and said: "Is that what I think it is?"[260] It was a cable National Security Council Advisor Frank Carlucci was "nudging at us across the table."[261] Shaking his head with a smile, Griscom confirmed the "last-minute plea"[262] from the State Department to drop the key phrase.

No fewer than seven alternative drafts emerged during the process, including the State Department's eleventh-hour effort. In each and every draft, the call to get rid of the wall was withheld, despite these advocates and agencies having no objection to the destruction of the wall. The objections were attune to a warm bath, best summed up by the phasing offered in Kornbaum's draft from US Mission Berlin: "One day, this ugly wall will disappear."[263] Importantly, this was the same draft the National Security Council championed, while also echoing the "strong request" of Berlin Mayor Diepgen and Chancellor Kohl "that there be no harsh polemics against the Soviet Union."[264] It was as if Reagan's foreign policy apparatus was okay with the president espousing that the wall should come down, but that he could only use language so un-Reaganesque as to be unconvincing.

As Reagan's limousine pulled up to the Brandenburg Gate to give his speech, the president reaffirmed his plan to stick with the line. Slapping Ken Duberstein on the knee, he said: "The boys at State are going to kill me for this, but it's the right thing to do."[265]

In preparation for Reagan's address workers stood up a bulletproof Plexiglas wall behind the stage to shield the president from any attempt to his life from East Germany, only 100 hundred yards behind him. The screen was large enough to provide a stunning backdrop to the Brandenburg Gate and the eight-foot high, graffiti-lined Berlin Wall, "including the freshly painted" and "boldly stroked"[266] words: "Welcome Ronald Reagan"[267] directly behind the speakers' platform, which covered an "anti-Reagan slogan"[268] that had been painted during protests the previous day. One could also see the electrified fencing, armed sentries, border stands, and an inherent grayness that pervaded the German Democratic Republic.

The dais in front of the screen was fronted with West Germany's tricolor palate and equal horizontal bands of black, red, and gold. Chairs were set up on the dais for dignitaries, as the stage was also lined with American and West German flags, except for the portion of the screen just behind the nondescript speaker's podium, which looked out onto picturesque Tiergarten Park. The "symbolic setting"[269] was also just blocks from the former site of Adolf Hitler's underground command bunker, where the Nazi leader took his life just before Soviet troops surged into Berlin in April 1945.

The event was protected by particularly tight security measures following a night of demonstrations where sixty-seven police officers were injured. Barricades were put up to keep protesters at least a mile away from the podium, as the area was set to be guarded by approximately ten thousand police officers.[270] Not to be outdone, "Soviet guards"[271] also prepared to watch "the proceedings through cameras, binoculars, and video equipment,"[272] while East German guards stood atop the eighteenth-century Brandenburg Gate "peering down at the crowd"[273] with a "view of the president through [the] bulletproof window behind him."[274]

Shortly after two o'clock, Ronald Reagan stepped forward and was met with a great ovation, as thousands of those gathered on the "Strasse des 17 Juni"[275] proudly waved small American and West German flags high in the air. The outpouring of applause and support for the president from the approximately twenty thousand spectators, including "a large contingent of U.S. military personnel, and many Americans"[276] led those on the dais to rise up out of their seats as well. A great energy abounded as the president's voice echoed out into the afternoon air: "Thank you very much. Chancellor Kohl, Governing Mayor Diepgen, ladies and gentleman,"²⁷⁷ Reagan began. "Twenty-four years ago, President John F. Kennedy visited Berlin speaking to the people of this city and the world at the city hall. Well, since then two other presidents have come, each in his turn, to Berlin. And today I, myself, make my second visit to your city. We come to Berlin, we American Presidents, because it's our duty to speak, in this place, of freedom."²⁷⁸ And "like so many Presidents" before him, Reagan noted from a popular old song: "Ich Hab Noch Einen Koffer in Berlin" (I Still Have a Suitcase in Berlin), which drew a laugh and applause after his "slight mispronunciation."²⁷⁹

Reagan was referring to President Kennedy's June 26, 1963 speech at the Rudolph Wilde Platz in Berlin, where he famously noted: "Two thousand years ago the proudest boast was civis Romanus sum. Today, in the world of freedom, the proudest boast is Ich bin ein Berliner [I am a Berliner]."²⁸⁰ In doing so Reagan was giving a nod to Kennedy's prose and historical benchmark, before elevating the stakes with his own signature moment on the international stage.

In addition to Kennedy, the president also referenced two additional predecessors, Richard Nixon and Jimmy Carter. Nixon traveled to West Berlin a month into his presidency on February 27, 1969, telling those assembled upon his arrival at Tempelhof Airport: "Berlin is known as a four-power city. But there is a fifth power in Berlin. That fifth power is the determination of the free people of Berlin to remain free and the determination of free people everywhere to stand by those who desire to remain free."²⁸¹ At a wreath-laying ceremony at the Airlift Memorial in West Berlin on July 15, 1978, Jimmy Carter, in paying tribute to the "78 Americans, Britons, and Germans who lost their lives in the Airlift,"²⁸² echoed a familiar Kennedy and Reagan sentiment about the city on the hill. "The Bible says a city that is set on a hill cannot be hidden,"²⁸³ Carter began. "As a city of human freedom, human hope, and human rights, Berlin is a light to the whole world; a city on a hill—it cannot be hidden; the eyes of all people are upon you. Was immer sei, Berlin bleibt frei [No matter what happens, Berlin will stay free]."²⁸⁴

Reagan understood his speech had a wide audience across the world; domestic politically in the face of Iran-Contra at home, and abroad, from allies focused on how he would engage Moscow to those living behind the Iron Curtain, including Soviet leader Mikhail Gorbachev, singularly, as a number of Reagan's passages were personally addressed to him. After recognizing those listening across Western Europe and North America, Reagan extended his "warmest greetings and the good will of the American people"²⁸⁵ to those listening throughout Eastern Europe. He was still "furious," however, after peering through binoculars as he first mounted the speaker platform and saw "East Berliners trying to hear him being pushed away by police."²⁸⁶ Approximately 500 East Berliners gathered to listen on Unter den Linden, a main thoroughfare, but police lines kept them "several hundred yards from the Wall,"²⁸⁷ near a border checkpoint where his words were unintelligible because of "poor amplification."²⁸⁸ Reagan thus decided he would speak louder to be heard over the wall that divided them.

Speaking to both sides of the divide, he stressed his "firm" and "unalterable belief" that there is only one Berlin ("Es gibt nu rein Berlin") despite the "vast system of barriers," the "barbed wire, concrete, dog runs, and guard towers" that divided Germany and the "entire continent of Europe." At the heart of that was the Berlin Wall, which as Lou Cannon reported for the *Washington Post*: "There was nothing conciliatory . . . about Reagan's description of the Berlin Wall."²⁸⁹ Most clearly, as Reagan continued, it was the Wall that "Imprinted this brutal division of a continent upon the mind of the world."²⁹⁰ And standing that day in front of the Brandenburg Gate, Reagan noted: "Every man is a German . . . Every man is a Berliner, forced to look upon a scar."²⁹¹ For Reagan, as long as the gate remained closed and the wall was "permitted to stand,"²⁹² the future of Berlin as a city was not just a German question "but the question of freedom for all mankind."²⁹³

Reagan's trademark optimism shined as he discussed finding in the city "a message of hope even in the shadow of this wall, a message of triumph."²⁹⁴ This is not unfamiliar to his optimistic view of America. And even as he spoke of the devastation the city suffered as they emerged from air raid shelters in the spring of 1945, he countered with the Marshall Plan, and particularly the "Wirtschaftswunder" or economic miracle that helped West Berlin and Western Europe rebuild and recover, doubling the standard of living from 1950 to 1960. Similarly, whereas four decades prior in Berlin "there was rubble," by 1987 Berliners "rebuilt a city" that ranked as "one of the greatest on Earth,"²⁹⁵ according to Reagan. And whereas Soviet Premier Nikita Khrushchev predicted: "We will bury you,"²⁹⁶ the "free world"²⁹⁷ responded with "a level of prosperity and well-being unprecedented in human history."²⁹⁸ Why did this economic miracle happen? For Reagan, the contrast came down to "one great and inescapable conclusion: Freedom leads to prosperity . . . Freedom is the victor."²⁹⁹ It was no surprise to him then that instead of burying the West, the Soviet Union was dangerously teetering on the edge of collapse.

That's not to say the Soviet Union was not taking important, but limited steps in this direction. Gorbachev's hopeful overtures of reform and openness included action steps like releasing political prisoners, lessening state control over business, and allowing select foreign news outlets to broadcast without being jammed.

Reagan then asked his audience: "Are these the beginnings of profound changes in the Soviet state? Or are they token gestures intended to raise false hopes in the West, or to strengthen the Soviet system without changing it?"[300] It hard not to sense Reagan's optimism for better relations with the East as he answered this rhetorical question by welcoming the Soviet Union's "change and openness."[301] However, for Reagan there was "one sign"[302] the Soviets could make "that would be unmistakable, that would advance dramatically the cause of freedom and peace."[303]

Approaching the punch line of the speech, Reagan's raw emotion translated out through his voice: "General Secretary Gorbachev, if you seek peace, if you seek prosperity for the Soviet Union and Eastern Europe, if you seek liberalization: Come here to this gate!"[304] Then with absolute firmness he stated: "Mr. Gorbachev, open this gate!"[305] which prompted twenty seconds of uninterrupted applause. Reagan attempted to continue, "Mr. Gorbachev . . ." but the applause continued fully for another five seconds. As that ovation began to fade, Reagan firmed up his voice again, as the crowd seemed to hold its breath in anticipation. In that moment, he felt an "anger well up"[306] in him again, which was "reflected"[307] as his next words rang out: "Mr. Gorbachev, tear down this wall!"[308]

The crowd erupted at the Brandenburg Gate for another fifteen seconds and for much longer in countless silenced spaces across the world. As journalist Brett Baier noted: "Reagan liked to think that there were many silent cheers emanating from the hopeful hearts of those on the other side of the wall."[309] Reagan's biographer Bob Spitz added: "It was the line they'd been waiting for, a line that gave voice to the captivity of their city from the mouth of the President of the United States."[310]

After the long applause subsided, Reagan affirmed America's support to confront the pain of division, as well as a commitment to resist Soviet expansion. It was here that he was defending his administration's Cold War policy, including to credit his firm stance with the Soviets to get them back to the negotiating table, allowing the potentially to eliminate, "for the first time," an "entire class of nuclear weapons from the face of the Earth."[311] In pursuing these arms reductions, Reagan made clear his commitment to deter Soviet aggression "at any level at which it might occur,"[312] including through his "Star Wars" Strategic Defense Initiative. Ultimately, he was reassuring West German and European allies that his goal was to "increase the safety of Europe and all the world,"[313] which narrowed down to the same "crucial fact"[314] he initially shared with Gorbachev in Geneva two years earlier: "East and West do not mistrust each other because we are armed; we are armed because we mistrust each other."[315]

Reagan then warned the Soviet Union that they faced a choice—in an age of "redoubled economic growth, of information and innovation"[316] the Soviets needed to make fundamental changes or become obsolete. Again, channeling his sense of optimism, Reagan expressed that this opportunity "represents a moment of hope."[317] After telling Gorbachev to tear down the wall only a moment earlier, he was now saying that the West stood "ready to cooperate with the East to promote true openness to break down barriers that separate people, to create a safer, freer world."[318]

For Reagan, there was "no better place" than Berlin, "the meeting place of East and West, to make a start."[319] He again called out "Mr. Gorbachev" to invite him to work together to "bring the Eastern and Western parts of the city closer together . . . To open Berlin still further to all Europe."[320] To this end, he called for several initiatives. First, he called for the day when West Berlin can "become one of the chief aviation hubs in all central Europe."[321] Second, with the support of the French and British, Reagan intended to bring international meetings to Berlin, such as serving as a site for United Nations meetings or global conferences focused on front-page issues from human rights to arms control. Third, Reagan called for "summer youth exchanges, cultural events and other programs for young Berliners from the East"[322] as a way to "establish hope for the future" through the enlightenment of young minds. He also hoped that East Berlin would sponsor visits from "young people of the Western sectors."[323] Last, Reagan pitched an idea "close to his heart,"[324] for Germany to host an Olympic Games "here in Berlin, East and West."[325]

The president closed his speech by affirming Berliner's love for their city, which was "both profound and abiding."[326] He then pivoted to the central contrast between East and West. Moments earlier Reagan was at the Reichstag, "the embodiment of German unity,"[327] where he noticed "words crudely spray-painted upon a wall," perhaps as he noted, by a young Berliner: "This wall will fall. Beliefs become reality."[328] Reagan agreed wholeheartedly with the sentiment, telling the audience: "Yes, across Europe, this wall will fall. For it cannot withstand faith; it cannot withstand truth. The wall cannot withstand freedom."[329] With an "impromptu remark,"[330]

Reagan made his final point, calling out the protesters who had opposed his visit the day prior, wondering if "they have ever asked themselves that if they should have the kind of government they apparently seek, no one would ever be able to do what they're doing again."[331]

Impact and Legacy

With his final words: "Thank you, and God Bless you all,"[332] a loud celebratory cheer and fervent American and West German flag waving swept the crowd. Those on the dais rose from their seats again with a complementary verve as the band began to play.

Reagan's signature phrase: "Mr. Gorbachev, tear down this wall,"[333] was replayed on televisions around the world and filled newspaper headlines across the United States, from the *Philadelphia Inquirer*'s "Reagan to Soviets: Raze Berlin Wall,"[334] to the *Chicago Tribune*'s "Reagan: Only one Berlin,"[335] to the *Los Angeles Times*'s "Tear Down Berlin Wall, Reagan Asks."[336] The *Washington Post* covered the speech on their front page over two days, running journalists Helen Thomas's June 12 article: "Reagan to Call for Berlin Wall's End,"[337] and Lou Cannon's June 13 article: "Reagan Challenges Soviets To Dismantle Berlin Wall."[338]

Overall, the initial feedback was largely positive and even encompassed Secretary of State George Shultz, who noted to Tom Griscom after the speech: "You were right."[339] However, a dose of skepticism also peppered the coverage including the *Philadelphia Inquirer*, which argued that the speech "did not present any kind of coherent Western strategy to hasten the day when the wall might indeed come down, nor did it help ease tensions between the two Germanies.[340] Among the president's inner circle, National Security Advisor Frank Carlucci thought to himself: "It's a great speech, but it [the wall coming down] will never happen."[341]

And historians John Lewis Gaddis, Richard Reeves, and Edmund Morris each added respectfully: "For once, a Reagan performance fell flat,"[342] the "speech itself was not very important,"[343] and "the occasion too staged, the crowd too small and well-primed to make for genuine drama."[344] In particular, Reeves's justification relied on the premise that the *New York Times* covered the speech on page three of their June 13, 1987 edition. However, excerpts of the speech ran on the front page of the same edition.

Considering Reagan's tone, the response from Moscow was surprisingly restrained, although Eastern bloc outlets echoed wide criticisms. The

Soviet news agency, Telegraph Agency of the Soviet Union (TASS), noted that "Reagan delivered an openly provocative, warmongering speech, in the spirit of the times of the Cold War."[345] An official for the East German news agency Allgemeiner Deutscher Nachrichtendienst (ADN) commented that the address would "not diminish the wall but make it higher,"[346] and the Soviet newspaper *Pravda* mocked Reagan's appeal to tear down the wall as "crocodile tears,"[347] because Reagan "seemed to have mistaken the Berlin Wall for the Wailing Wall in Jerusalem."[348]

Beyond the initial media coverage, however, one would be hard pressed to find a noteworthy initial result from Reagan's pronouncement. Back in DC, speechwriter Peter Robinson was made aware that US intelligence services had picked up "unusual cable traffic between Moscow and East Germany," which conveyed that the Soviets wanted the East Germans to make the Berlin Wall "less offensive to the West," such as opening more checkpoints or easing travel restrictions "for those who wanted to see relatives."[349] But nothing more.

This likely would have meant little to Reagan in the moment, as he saw the landscape differently. What Reagan saw was a future to a post-Soviet world, and as a son of the rural Midwest, his signature line about the wall is best likened to a farmer planting a seed in the spring of 1987. Twenty-nine months later, on November 9, 1989, it harvested into the fall of the Berlin Wall to the people of Berlin who fulfilled Reagan's call to make the city one again. German Chancellor Helmut Kohl called it a "message of hope . . . Reagan meant what he said, and he was right. . . . Today we know that the final phase of the East-West conflict began in 1987."[350]

When asked about it by journalist Sam Donaldson after the wall opened after massive opposition demonstrations, Reagan replied: "I have to tell you, I'm an eternal optimist. . . . I believed with all of my heart, it was in the future."[351] In the *New York Times* Reagan was described as a "modern-day Joshua at the battle of Jericho," living to see "the Berlin Wall come tumbling down."[352]

In another thirteen months Reagan watched the Soviet Union dissolve. In his *Memoirs*, he later reiterated what he said in his Berlin speech: "The Soviet Union faced a choice. Either it made fundamental changes or it became obsolete. Gorbachev saw the handwriting on the Wall and opted for change."[353] It was an outcome that was at best remote only two years earlier, as "few in Washington and even fewer in Moscow expected that."[354] As such, Reagan could be credited for winning the Cold War as former

British Prime Minister Margaret Thatcher famously quipped, "Without firing a shot,"[355] and as Reagan's first Secretary of State Alexander Haig added, without storming "the trenches."[356] Rather, the enemy suddenly rose up and left, and the Soviet Union was no more."[357] President George H. W. Bush called this development in his 1992 State of the Union address: "The biggest thing that has happened in the world in my life, in our lives,"[358] and Ronald Reagan called it his "greatest accomplishment,"[359] along with giving America "back its optimism,"[360] according to Nancy Reagan.

And the Berlin speech was a catalyst. Richard Allen called the speech "The Great Accelerator of the end of the Cold War, as the people of East Germany in tearing down the wall had been encouraged by the words of the Leader of the Free World."[361] Romesh Ratnesar termed the remarks: "Indispensable to that achievement."[362] This became the consensus view for most of Reagan's acolytes, from Chief of Staff Howard Baker who noted that the president's address "set in motion the tearing down of that concrete barrier,"[363] to First Lady Nancy Reagan who remarked that her husband believed the Berlin Wall fell because "the people made it happen, and he was happy to have helped them in any way possible."[364] Reporter Mike Wallace added: "The Berlin Wall surely began to fall during Reagan's presidency."[365]

But it was historian Garry Wills who may have summed up Reagan's role best when writing about the former president in 1996: "Part of Reagan's legacy is what we do not see now. We see no Berlin Wall. He said, 'Tear down this wall,' and it was done. We see no Iron Curtain. In fact, we see no Soviet Union. He called it an Evil Empire, and it evaporated overnight."[366] Similarly, political scientist Charles Dunn noted that soon after Reagan's challenge: "The Berlin Wall toppled, and the Communists tumbled from power in the Soviet Union and its satellite states in Central and Eastern Europe."[367] These geopolitical developments led Ted Kennedy to note of his rival: "Reagan will be honored as the president who won the Cold War."[368]

On the other hand, some view the fall of the wall differently. In particular, journalists Peter Baker and Susan Glasser downplayed Reagan's role, as they concluded that no American leader "did anything tangible to make it happen."[369] Historian John Lewis Gaddis offered the thesis that Reagan "had been pushing up against an open door,"[370] and a *New York Times* op-ed by Ted Widmer on the twenty-fifth anniversary of the speech argued that the wall fell "not because Mr. Gorbachev tore it down, but because he did nothing at all."[371] But even across these naysayers, one would be hard pressed not to admit that it was "more than coincidence" that the fall began on Reagan's watch."[372]

In a speech covering 2,693 words over twenty-six minutes that contained thoughts Reagan felt "strongly about,"[373] the president, by his own estimation, was interrupted with applause twenty-eight times,[374] or a pace better than one per minute or every hundred words—of which, there was no thought that he felt more strongly about than the simple, optimistic, clear, and committed four-word sound bite: "Tear down this wall."[375] The four words captured the essence of Reagan's optimistic leadership and stand as the most important moment of his presidency.

They represent the culmination of four decades of his speaking out against Communism, and the "high-water mark"[376] for patriotic presidential discourse, according to historian Douglas Brinkley. They represent, as Richard Allen explained, the "basic reinstatement of what Reagan uttered spontaneously in November 1978, nine years earlier"[377] at the wall, which was part of a vernacular described by Secretary of State George Schultz as Reagan's "vocabulary of opportunity"[378] to imagine a better future.

They represent Reagan's sense of optimism that was "not a trivial or peripheral quality,"[379] as Lou Cannon noted, but rather an "essential ingredient of an approach to life"[380] that carried Reagan from the rural Midwest to Hollywood and to the Oval Office and represented his "most distinctive quality as president."[381] They represent Reagan's sound judgment to overrule the naysayers, as well as his faith sprinkled with realism, including a belief that it was only a matter of time before Soviet communism collapsed, which is an outcome that without Reagan would not of happened, "or certainly not as soon as it did,"[382] according to political scientist Jeffrey Chidester.

They represent his conviction that you could sit down with someone and "through a personal exchange take the measure of the man,"[383] which is exactly what Reagan did with Gorbachev during their initial November 1985 meeting in Geneva that initially was scheduled for twenty minutes but lasted seventy-five. From there, both "innate"[384] optimists established a "remarkable relationship,"[385] which historian Melvyn Leffler described as built on "a sense of optimism, an appreciation of human agency, and a sense of destiny."[386] And they represent a defining moment in American history as "One would have to look back to Franklin Roosevelt's reaction to Pearl Harbor or John F. Kennedy's Berlin speech, or even Lincoln's

Gettysburg Address," according to American novelist Winston Groom, "to find anything comparable by an American president."[387]

What might be most extraordinary about the entire episode is that the four most important words of the Cold War and among the most important in American history were almost left unsaid. It was only because of Reagan's sense of optimism about America's future in the world that they echoed out across Tiergarten Park and continue to inspire us today. It's the same optimism that guided his life and is found in his favorite story about a man with two sons—one a "pessimist beyond recall," and the other an "optimist beyond reason."[388] Very concerned about his children, the father talked to a child psychiatrist who told him: "I think we can fix that,"[389] and offered a suggestion. "We'll get a room and we'll fill it with the most wonderful toys any boy ever had . . . And we'll put the pessimist in and when he finds out they're for him, he'll get over being a pessimist."[390] The father followed up: "What will you do about the optimist?"[391] "Well," the child psychiatrist said: "I have a friend who's got a racing stable and they clean out the stalls every morning. . . . And I can get quite an amount of that substance. We'll put that in another room, and when the optimist who's seen his brother get all those toys is then shown into that room and that's there, he'll get over being an optimist."[392] So, as the scenario played out over several minutes as was prescribed, the door to the pessimistic child opened and he was sitting and crying "as if his heart would break."[393] The child said: "I know somebody's going to come in and take these away from me."[394] They then visited the other room where the optimistic child was getting along as "happy as a clam . . . throwing the manure over his shoulders as fast as he could."[395] The child was asked, "What are you doing?" And he replied, "There's got to be a pony in here somewhere."[396]

That latter child was Ronald Reagan. That's how he lived his life—a life that began with humble beginnings in Tampico, Illinois, where outside his birthplace there is a plaque etched with his own optimistic words: "Whatever else history may say about me when I'm gone, I hope it will record that I appealed to your best hopes, not your worst fears; to your confidence rather than your doubts. My dream is that you will travel the road ahead with liberty's lamp guiding your steps and opportunity's arm steadying your way."[397] That was also Reagan's great hope for his four transformational words that changed the world.

Epilogue

In an era of increased polarization, where faith in the American presidency as an institution has slipped to less than a quarter of the citizenry,[1] the stories in this book serve not only as a reminder of the transformational impact of presidential leadership, but also how it can be found at the intersection of a president's defining leadership quality and their action to meet the moment and advance America.

In chapter 1, it is found in Washington's judgment in becoming the first leader in two millenniums to relinquish power, while also leaving for posterity a Farewell Address offering a composite picture of his judgment, including lessons learned, warnings, and inspiration for generations of Americans. In chapter 2, it is found in the ingenuity of Thomas Jefferson and his charge letter to Robert Livingston, US minister to France; a watershed moment in America's territorial crisis with France that would eventually yield the Louisiana Purchase, Jefferson's "greatest accomplishment," which forever changed the physical landscape of the United States.[2] In chapter 3, it is found in the dedication of Abraham Lincoln through his 272-word Gettysburg Address, which represented not only a great turning point in the national crisis, but the great convergence of national purpose during the Civil War and the difficult fight ahead. In chapter 4, it is found in Theodore Roosevelt's courage in taking on the most existential issue of his time—the conservation of natural resources and bringing those important efforts to the mainstream of American discourse. In chapter 5, it is found in the confidence of Franklin Roosevelt, who in the depth of the Great Depression and banking crisis helped to restore America's confidence with 1,792 words echoed through the nation's radio airwaves during his first Fireside Chat. In chapter 6, it is found in Ronald Reagan's optimism in challenging Soviet Premier Mikhail Gorbachev to "tear down" the Berlin

Wall, casting the die in motion for the wall to fall twenty-nine months later. And it can be found across American presidential history at varying forms and impact like how Barack Obama embodied empathy along with "Amazing Grace" to provide a moving eulogy for the Honorable Rev. Clementa Pinckney in the aftermath of the June 2015 shootings at Mother Emanual Church in Charleston, South Carolina.[3] Or how George H. W. Bush exemplified fidelity, including in faithfulness to honor his Gulf War charge: "Seven months ago, America and the world drew a line in the sand. We declared that the aggression against Kuwait would not stand. And tonight, America and the world have kept their word."[4] Or how Harry S. Truman epitomized decisiveness in assuming the presidency after the death of Franklin Roosevelt, making clear to his cabinet in their first meeting that he would be president in his "own right" and that he "would assume full responsibility for such decisions as had to be made . . . and that all final policy decisions"[5] would be his.

In the end, there is an inherent danger in writing about American presidents as the decades and centuries pass. These bellwethers become more remote, more difficult to place or to know. This book has aimed right at the heart of that danger, to bring to life the leadership essence of six presidents, honed during a lifetime of lived experience and revealed at the intersection of their defining leadership quality and action in times of trial. The fact that these six leaders navigated this intersection so well is why scholars routinely place them at the top of presidential rankings. In no small order, Washington demonstrated to posterity that no one has the right to the US presidency. Jefferson made America a continental nation, and Lincoln kept it whole. Theodore Roosevelt ensured its natural wonder. And Franklin Delano Roosevelt and Reagan gave hope to the world.

Taken together, these six leaders' stories inform us that there is no set formula for leadership, as there are many qualities that comprise it, depending on the leader and the circumstances. Dedication and ingenuity work on some occasions. Confidence and courage on others. Judgment is needed across the board, and an optimistic spirit can move a nation. And they also inform us that the type of leadership they exemplify is not exclusive to 1600 Pennsylvania Avenue, but rather it's a school of thought that can be applied to any leader, at any level, to meet their moment.

We are heirs to this leadership legacy—one that includes six of America's most consequential documents: Washington's Farewell Address; Jefferson's Louisiana Purchase charge; Lincoln's Gettysburg Address; Theodore Roosevelt's First Annual Address; FDR's first Fireside Chat; and

Reagan's Berlin Wall speech. It is left to us to lean into the spirit of these documents and the qualities that defined them to ensure that the American experiment remains strong for what George Washington described as the "unborn millions," and to advance the "Shining City upon a Hill" in the words and essence of Ronald Reagan.

Notes

Introduction

1. As Mark Twain noted: "Courage is resistance to fear, mastery of fear—not absence of fear"; Mark Twain, *Pudd'nhead Wilson* (Hartford, CT: American Publishing Co.), 1894, 155. The quality of confidence differs from courage in that it is a feeling of trust in one's abilities, qualities, and judgment. Confidence is often the consequence of the courage to act.

2. Michael Beschloss, *Presidential Courage: Brave Leaders and How They Changed America, 1789-1789* (New York: Simon & Schuster, 2007); this book provides an important historical focus on courage as a defining characteristic of presidential leadership. Of note, he profiles Abraham Lincoln's courage in issuing the Emancipation Proclamation as well as Theodore Roosevelt's courage in taking on powerful financial interests.

3. Theodore Roosevelt, "First Annual Message," December 3, 1901; https://www.presidency.ucsb.edu/documents/first-annual-message-16.

4. Ronald Reagan, "Remarks on East-West Relations at the Brandenburg Gate in West Berlin," June 12, 1987; https://www.presidency.ucsb.edu/documents/remarks-east-west-relations-the-brandenburg-gate-west-berlin.

5. Richard E. Neustadt, *Presidential Power: The Politics of Leadership* (New York: Free Press, 1960), 10.

6. Richard J. Ellis and Michael Nelson, ed., *Debating the Presidency: Conflicting Perspective on the American Executive*, 5th ed. (Thousand Oaks, CA: Sage, 2021), 144. Similarly, Edwards adds in his book, *On Deaf Ears: The Limits of the Bully Pulpit*: "Although sometimes they are able to maintain public support for themselves and their polices, presidents typically do not succeed in their efforts to change public opinion;" George C. Edwards III, *On Deaf Ears: The Limits of the Bully Pulpit* (New Haven, CT: Yale University Press, 2003), 241.

7. Highlighting the importance of presidential character is Robert Wilson's edited text, *Character Above All: Ten Presidents from FDR to George Bush*, which brings together biographers and journalists such as Doris Kearns Goodwin and

Peggy Noonan to profile presidents from FDR to George H. W. Bush with a focus on the broader aspects of each president's character; Robert A. Wilson, ed. *Character Above All: Ten Presidents from FDR to George Bush* (New York: Simon & Schuster), 1995. In addition, Paul Quirk points out in Richard J. Ellis's and Michael Nelson's edited work, *Debating the Presidency: Conflicting Perspective on the American Executive*: "American presidential history is replete with examples in which character and leadership qualities have been of decisive importance in accounting for presidential success and failure;" Ellis and Nelson, ed., *Debating the Presidency*, 109.

    8. David, Gergen *Eyewitness to Power: The Essence of Leadership—Nixon to Clinton* (New York: Simon & Schuster), 2000, 200.

    9. Michael Genovese, *Presidential Leadership in an Age of Change* (New Brunswick, NJ: Transaction 2016), 72.

    10. Fred I. Greenstein, *The Presidential Difference: Leadership Style from FDR to Barack Obama*, 3rd ed. (Princeton: Princeton University Press, 2009), 22–25.

    11. Thomas E. Cronin and Michael A. Genovese, *The Paradoxes of the American Presidency*, 2nd ed. (Oxford, UK: Oxford University Press, 2004), 115–122.

    12. Marc Landy and Sidney M. Milkis, *Presidential Greatness* (Lawrence: University of Kansas Press, 2000), 198.

    13. Charles O. Jones, *The Presidency in a Separated System* (Washington, DC: Brookings, 2005), 1.

    14. Fred Greenstein's criteria/formula in *The Presidential Difference* is the most comprehensive in the scholarship and important to understanding presidential leadership. This book differs in assessing the criteria for leadership at the intersection of a president's definitive personal quality and their action to transform their times and America's trajectory.

    15. Cronin and Genovese, *The Paradoxes of the American Presidency*, 25; importantly, they also highlight that there is a "fine line between boldness and recklessness, between strong self-confidence and what the Greeks called "hubris," between dogged determination and pigheaded stubbornness" (9).

    16. Fred I. Greenstein, *Inventing the Job of President: Leadership Style from George Washington to Andrew Jackson* (Princeton, NJ: Princeton University Press, 2009), 1. For views of strong presidential power see William C. Howell's and Terry M. Moe's *Relic: How Our Constitution Undermines Effective Government—And Why We Need a More Powerful Presidency*. Howell and Moe argue for updating the US Constitution to ensure a strong presidency because the document was originally designed over two centuries ago for an agrarian society and written by men suspicious of strong executive power. In addition, Arthur Schlesinger Jr., in *The Imperial Presidency*, which was written during the age of the Vietnam War and Watergate, highlights the growth of presidential power during World War II and into the Cold War. He notes: "The postwar Presidents, through Eisenhower

and Kennedy markedly less than Truman, Johnson and Nixon, almost came to see sharing of power with Congress in foreign policy as a derogation of the Presidency. Congress, in increasing self-abasement, almost came to love its impotence;" Arthur M. Schlesinger Jr., *The Imperial Presidency* (New York: Houghton Mifflin, 1973), 206. While affirming the rise of presidential power in the twentieth century, especially a president's war-making capabilities, none of the stories profiled in this book overstep reasonable limits of power, thereby thwarting American democracy and crossing over into an "imperial presidency."

17. William Safire, *Lend Me Your Ears: Great Speeches in History* (New York: W. W. Norton, 1997), 860.

Chapter 1

1. Euripides, translated by Edward P. Coleridge, *The Plays of Euripides* (London: George Bell and Sons, 1906), 345.

2. The Federalist No. 57, February 19, 1788; https://founders.archives.gov/documents/Hamilton/01-04-02-0206.

3. John Kennedy, "The City upon a Hill Speech," January 9, 1961; https://www.jfklibrary.org/learn/about-jfk/historic-speeches/the-city-upon-a-hill-speech.

4. Jimmy Carter, "Address to the Nation on Energy and National Goals: "The Malaise Speech," July 15, 1979; https://www.presidency.ucsb.edu/documents/address-the-nation-energy-and-national-goals-the-malaise-speech.

5. Joseph Ellis, *Founding Brother: The Revolutionary Generation* (New York: Vintage, 2003), 50.

6. Alexander Hamilton, *The Federalist Papers: No 70*, March 18, 1788; https://avalon.law.yale.edu/18th_century/fed70.asp.

7. George Washington to David Stuart, July 1, 1787; https://founders.archives.gov/documents/Washington/04-05-02-0225.

8. George Washington to David Stuart.

9. James Madison, Convention Debates, July 17, 1787; https://avalon.law.yale.edu/18th_century/debates_717.asp.

10. Convention Debates, September 4, 1787; https://avalon.law.yale.edu/18th_century/debates_904.asp.

11. Article II, US Constitution.

12. George Washington to Marquis de Lafayette, February 7, 1788; https://founders.archives.gov/documents/Washington/04-06-02-0079.

13. Gouverneur Morris to George Washington, December 6, 1788; https://founders.archives.gov/documents/Washington/05-01-02-0123.

14. Benjamin Franklin to Jean-Baptiste Le Roy, November 13, 1789; https://constitutioncenter.org/blog/benjamin-franklins-last-great-quote-and-the-constitution.

15. George Washington to Catharine Sawbridge Macaulay Graham, January 9, 1790; https://founders.archives.gov/documents/Washington/05-04-02-0363.

16. George Washington to John Augustine Washington, June 15, 1783; https://founders.archives.gov/documents/Washington/99-01-02-11462.

17. George Washington to Boston Selectmen, July 28, 1795; https://founders.archives.gov/documents/Washington/05-18-02-0305.

18. David C. Claypoole, "Certification of David C. Claypoole, *Memoirs of Historical Society of Pennsylvania, Volume 1*, February 22, 1826; Paltsits, Victor Hugo ed., *Washington's Farewell Address* (New York: New York Public Library, 1935), 290–91.

19. Claypoole, "Certification of David C. Claypoole."

20. Claypoole, "Certification of David C. Claypoole."

21. Claypoole, "Certification of David C. Claypoole."

22. Henry Lee, *Funeral Oration on the Death of General Washington* (Boston: Printed for Joseph Nancrede and Manning & Loring), 1800; Congress asked Henry Lee to deliver the national funeral oration.

23. Claypoole, "Certification of David C. Claypoole"; Paltsits, *Washington's Farewell Address*, 290–91.

24. Paltsits, *Washington's Farewell Address*, 290–91.

25. Paltsits, *Washington's Farewell Address*, 290–91.

26. Paltsits, *Washington's Farewell Address*, 290–91.

27. Paltsits, *Washington's Farewell Address*, 290–91.

28. George Washington, "Diary Entry," September 19, 1796.

29. Washington George and Jared Sparks, ed., *The Writings of George Washington, Being His Correspondence, Addresses, Messages and Other Papers Official and Private, Volume 2* (Boston: Russell, Odiorne, and Metcalf, 1834), 506.

30. George Washington to Lafayette, December 8, 1784; https://founders.archives.gov/documents/Washington/04-02-02-0140.

31. Ellis, *Founding Brother*, 124.

32. Douglas Southhal Freeman, *George Washington, A Biography: Patriot and President* (New York: Augustus, 1975), 195.

33. John Frost, *Pictorial Life of George Washington: Embracing a Complete History of the Seven Years' War, the Revolutionary War, the Formation of the Federal Constitution, and the Administration of Washington* (Philadelphia: Thomas, Cowperthwait, 1848), 18.

34. Frost, 18.

35. Garry Wills, *Cincinnatus: George Washington and the Enlightenment* (New York: Doubleday, 1984), 68.

36. Gordon Wood, *Revolutionary Characters* (New York: Penguin Press, 2006), 33.

37. Gordon Wood, 33.

38. W. F. Bynum, and Roy Porter, ed., *Oxford Dictionary of Scientific Quotations* (Oxford, UK: Oxford University Press, 2005), 21: 9.

39. Whereas this book argues that the essence of Washington's leadership was his judgment, another book, *Strategic Instincts: The Adaptive Advantages of Cognitive Biases in International Politics*, Dominic D. P. Johnson argues that it was his overconfidence. Johnson notes: "Washington in particular would not have made the decision to fight and keep fighting, if it had not been for this remarkable level of confidence-arguably overconfidence . . . Where others saw disaster, he believed he could win" (86).

40. John Jay to George Washington, May 10, 1779; https://founders.archives.gov/documents/Washington/03-20-02-0367.

41. Calvin Coolidge, "Address Regarding Washington's Birthday," February 22, 1927; https://millercenter.org/the-presidency/presidential-speeches/february-22-1927-address-regarding-washingtons-birthday.

42. John Adams to Sylvanus Bourne, August 30, 1789; https://founders.archives.gov/documents/Adams/99-02-02-0737.

43. Thomas Jefferson to Walter Jones, January 2, 1814; http://tjrs.monticello.org/letter/2153.

44. John Marshall, *The Life of George Washington* (Philadelphia, PA: James Crissy, 1838), 377.

45. John E. Ferling, *The First of Men: A Life of George Washington* (London: Oxford University Press, 2010), 261.

46. "Report of a Committee of Arrangements for the Public Audience," December 22, 1783, *The Papers of Thomas Jefferson*, 6: 410n1.

47. George Washington to United States Congress, December 23, 1783; https://founders.archives.gov/documents/Washington/99-01-02-12223.

48. George Washington to United States Congress.

49. George Washington to United States Congress.

50. Editorial Note: George Washington's Resignation as Commander-In-Chief; https://founders.archives.gov/documents/Jefferson/01-06-02-0319-0001.

51. United States Congress to George Washington, December 23, 1783; https://founders.archives.gov/documents/Washington/99-01-02-12224.

52. Nannie McCormick Coleman, *The Constitution and Its Framers* (Chicago, IL: Progress Company, 1910), 293.

53. "Extract of a Letter from a Gentleman in Annapolis," *New Jersey Gazette*, 6 January 1784, 3.

54. John E. Ferling, *Almost a Miracle: The American Victory in the War of Independence* (New York: Oxford University Press, 2009), 556.

55. Ferling, *Almost a Miracle*, 556.

56. George Washington, Address to New York Legislature, June 26, 1775; https://founders.archives.gov/documents/Washington/03-01-02-0019.

57. George Washington to the State, June 8, 1783; Wills, *Cincinnatus*, 13.
58. James Thomas Flexner, *Washington and the New Nation: 1783–1793* (New York: Little, Brown, 1970), 220.
59. Thomas Fleming, *The Perils of Peace* (New York: Collins, 2007), 321.
60. H. A. Washington, ed., *Writings of Thomas Jefferson, Vol. III* (New York: H. W. Derby, 1861), 30.
61. Paltsits, *Washington's Farewell Address*, 9–10.
62. George Washington to James Madison, February 19, 1792; https://founders.archives.gov/documents/Washington/05-10-02-0260.
63. Madison's Conversations with Washington, May 5–25, 1792; https://founders.archives.gov/documents/Washington/05-10-02-0222.
64. Madison's Conversations with Washington.
65. Madison's Conversations with Washington.
66. Madison's Conversations with Washington.
67. Madison's Conversations with Washington.
68. Madison's Conversations with Washington.
69. Madison's Conversations with Washington.
70. Madison's Conversations with Washington.
71. Madison's Conversations with Washington.
72. Madison's Conversations with Washington.
73. Madison's Conversations with Washington.
74. Madison's Conversations with Washington.
75. Madison's Conversations with Washington.
76. Madison's Conversations with Washington.
77. Madison's Conversations with Washington.
78. Madison's Conversations with Washington.
79. Madison's Conversations with Washington.
80. Madison's Conversations with Washington.
81. Madison's Conversations with Washington.
82. Madison's Conversations with Washington.
83. Madison's Conversations with Washington.
84. Madison's Draft of the Farewell Address, June 20, 1792; https://founders.archives.gov/documents/Washington/05-10-02-0318-0002.
85. Madison's Draft of Farewell Address.
86. Thomas Jefferson to George Washington, May 23, 1792; https://founders.archives.gov/documents/Jefferson/01-23-02-0491.
87. Thomas Jefferson to George Washington.
88. Alexander Hamilton to George Washington, July 30–August 3, 1792; https://founders.archives.gov/documents/Hamilton/01-12-02-0109.
89. Wills, *Cincinnatus*, 23.
90. Tobias Lear to George Washington, July 21, 1792; https://founders.archives.gov/documents/Washington/05-10-02-0388.

91. Tobias Lear to George Washington, August 5, 1792; https://founders.archives.gov/documents/Washington/05-10-02-0415.

92. Edmund Randolph to George Washington, August 5, 1792; https://founders.archives.gov/documents/Washington/05-10-02-0417.

93. Thomas Jefferson's Conversation with Washington, October 1, 1792; https://founders.archives.gov/documents/Washington/05-11-02-0095.

94. Elizabeth Willing Powel to George Washington, November 17, 1792; https://founders.archives.gov/documents/Washington/05-11-02-0225.

95. Elizabeth Willing Powel.

96. Elizabeth Willing Powel.

97. Elizabeth Willing Powel.

98. Henry Lee to George Washington, January 20, 1793; https://founders.archives.gov/documents/Washington/05-12-02-0012.

99. Shortly after winning a landslide reelection in 1936, President Franklin D. Roosevelt proposed a "court-packing" plan, whereby a justice would be added to the US Supreme Court for every justice currently serving who was over age seventy and had ten years of service. The move brought instant backlash and failed. But this episode is important to note in the line between FDR's defining confidence and how that quality can bleed into hubris or even arrogance. Beginning with Joseph Alsop and Turner Catledge's 1938 work, *The 168 Days*, the scholarly consensus is that Roosevelt's court-packing action was an act of arrogance. Noteworthy, is Laura Kalman's book, *FDR's Gambit: The Court Packing Fight and the Rise of Legal Liberalism*. Kalman challenges this conventional wisdom by explaining that Roosevelt's actions demonstrated the "same shrewdness that enabled him to win a massive 1936 re-election victory despite the best efforts of an antagonistic press and angry elites"; Laura Kalman, *FDR's Gambit: The Court Packing Fight and the Rise of Legal Liberalism* (New York: Oxford Academic, 2022), Preface.

100. *New York Journal*, December 7, 1793; *National Gazette*, March 2, 1793.

101. George Washington to Edmund Pendleton, January 22, 1795; https://founders.archives.gov/documents/Washington/05-17-02-0282.

102. Mary V. Thompson, *Statements Regarding the Physical Appearance*, 47; https://www.mountvernon.org/george-washington/the-first-president/the-farewell-address/.

103. Thomas Jefferson to James Madison, March 27, 1796; https://founders.archives.gov/documents/Madison/01-16-02-0185.

104. Timothy Pickering, *Review of the Correspondence between the Hon. John Adams and the late William Cunningham, ESQ Beginning in 1803, and Ending in 1812* (Salem, MA: Cushing and Appleton, 1824), 72.

105. Ellis, *Founding Brother*, 138.

106. John Ferling, *The Ascent of George Washington: The Hidden Political Genius of an American Icon* (New York: Bloomsbury Press, 2009), 345.

107. Thomas Jefferson to Philip Mazzei, April 24, 1796; https://founders.archives.gov/documents/Jefferson/01-29-02-0054-0002.

108. Ellis, *His Excellency*, 233.

109. John Jay to George Washington, 18 April 1796; https://founders.archives.gov/documents/Washington/05-20-02-0048.

110. George Washington to John Jay, May 8, 1796; https://founders.archives.gov/documents/Washington/05-20-02-0085.

111. Alexander Hamilton to George Washington, May 10, 1796; https://founders.archives.gov/documents/Hamilton/01-20-02-0105-0002.

112. George Washington to Alexander Hamilton, May 15, 1796; https://founders.archives.gov/documents/Hamilton/01-20-02-0106.

113. George Washington to Alexander Hamilton, August 25, 1796; https://founders.archives.gov/documents/Hamilton/01-20-02-0197.

114. George Washington to Alexander Hamilton, May 15, 1796.

115. George Washington to Alexander Hamilton.

116. Alexander Hamilton to George Washington, July 30, 1796; https://founders.archives.gov/documents/Hamilton/01-20-02-0181-0001.

117. Alexander Hamilton to George Washington, August 10, 1796; https://founders.archives.gov/documents/Hamilton/01-20-02-0191-0001.

118. George Washington to Alexander Hamilton, August 25, 1796.

119. Alexander Hamilton to George Washington, September 5, 1796; https://founders.archives.gov/documents/Hamilton/01-20-02-0204.

120. Alexander Hamilton to George Washington, July 5, 1796; https://founders.archives.gov/documents/Hamilton/01-20-02-0157.

121. Introductory Note: To George Washington, May 10, 1796; https://founders.archives.gov/documents/Hamilton/01-20-02-0105-0001.

122. Richard Brookhiser, *George Washington on Leadership* (New York: Basic Books, 2009), 73.

123. Brookhiser, *George Washington on Leadership*.

124. George Washington, "The Address of General Washington to the People of the United States," *David Claypoole's American Daily Advertiser*, Philadelphia, September 16, 1796.

125. Washington, "Address of General Washington."

126. Washington, "Address of General Washington."

127. Washington, "Address of General Washington."

128. Washington, "Address of General Washington."

129. Washington, "Address of General Washington."

130. Washington, "Address of General Washington."

131. Washington, "Address of General Washington."

132. Washington, "Address of General Washington."

133. Washington, "Address of General Washington."

134. Washington, "Address of General Washington."

135. Washington, "Address of General Washington."
136. Washington, "Address of General Washington."
137. Washington, "Address of General Washington."
138. Washington, "Address of General Washington."
139. Washington, "Address of General Washington."
140. Washington, "Address of General Washington."
141. Washington, "Address of General Washington."
142. Washington, "Address of General Washington."
143. Washington, "Address of General Washington."
144. Washington, "Address of General Washington."
145. Washington, "Address of General Washington."
146. Washington, "Address of General Washington."
147. Washington, "Address of General Washington."
148. Washington, "Address of General Washington."
149. Ellis, *His Excellency*, 271.
150. Ellis, *His Excellency*, 271.
151. Ellis, *His Excellency*, 271.
152. Ellis, *His Excellency*, 271.
153. Ellis, *His Excellency*, 271.
154. Ellis, *His Excellency*, 271.
155. Ellis, *His Excellency*, 271.
156. Ellis, *His Excellency*, 271.
157. Ellis, *His Excellency*, 271.
158. George Washington to Charles Carroll, May 1, 1796; https://founders.archives.gov/documents/Washington/05-20-02-0073.
159. Washington, "Address of General Washington."
160. Washington, "Address of General Washington."
161. Washington, "Address of General Washington."
162. Washington, "Address of General Washington."
163. Washington, "Address of General Washington."
164. Washington, "Address of General Washington."
165. Washington, "Address of General Washington."
166. Washington, "Address of General Washington."
167. Washington, "Address of General Washington."
168. Washington, "Address of General Washington."
169. Washington, "Address of General Washington."
170. Washington, "Address of General Washington."
171. Washington, "Address of General Washington."
172. Washington, "Address of General Washington."
173. Washington, "Address of General Washington."
174. Washington, "Address of General Washington."
175. Washington, "Address of General Washington."

176. Washington, "Address of General Washington."
177. Washington, "Address of General Washington."
178. Ellis, *His Excellency*, 40.
179. Washington, "The Address of General Washington To The People of The United States," *David Claypoole's American Daily Advertiser*, Philadelphia, September 16, 1796.
180. Washington, "Address of General Washington."
181. Washington, "Address of General Washington."
182. Washington, "Address of General Washington."
183. Washington, "Address of General Washington."
184. Paltsits, *Washington's Farewell Address*, 56.
185. James McHenry to George Washington, September 25, 1796; https://founders.archives.gov/documents/Washington/05-20-02-0319.
186. Paltsits, *Washington's Farewell Address*, 60.
187. Paltsits, *Washington's Farewell Address*, 60.
188. Ferling, *Ascent of George Washington*, 344.
189. Douglas Southall Freeman, *Washington* (New York: Scribner, 2011).
190. Stanley M. Elkins and Eric L. McKitrick, *The Age of Federalism: The Early American Republic 1788–1800* (New York: Oxford University Press, 1993), 489.
191. Washington was convinced America was ill-prepared to confront Great Britain for at least twenty years, and therefore believed that the best path forward was to buy time.
192. Thomas Jefferson, "First Inaugural Address," March 4, 1801; https://avalon.law.yale.edu/19th_century/jefinau1.asp.
193. Washington, "Address of General Washington."
194. Coleman, *Constitution and Its Framers*, 293.
195. Andrew Jackson, "Farewell Address," March 4, 1837; https://www.presidency.ucsb.edu/documents/farewell-address-0.
196. Jackson, "Farewell Address."
197. 198. Washington, "Address of General Washington."
199. Ethan M. Fishman, William D. Pederson, and Mark J. Rozell, *George Washington: Foundation of Presidential Leadership and Character* (New York: Praeger, 2001), 87.
200. Dwight Eisenhower, "Farewell Radio and Television Address to the American People, January 17, 1961; https://www.presidency.ucsb.edu/documents/farewell-radio-and-television-address-the-american-people.
201. Ronald Reagan, "Farewell Address to the Nation," January 11, 1989; https://www.presidency.ucsb.edu/documents/farewell-address-the-nation.
202. Reagan, "Farewell Address to the Nation."
203. Barack Obama, "Farewell Address to the Nation from Chicago, Illinois, January 10, 2017; https://www.presidency.ucsb.edu/documents/farewell-address-the-nation-from-chicago-illinois.

204. Obama, "Farewell Address to the Nation."
205. Abraham Lincoln, *Collected Works of Abraham Lincoln, Volume 5* (New Brunswick, NJ: Rutgers University Press), 1953, 136.
206. Lincoln, *Collected Works of Abraham Lincoln*, 136.
207. https://www.senate.gov/artandhistory/history/minute/Washingtons_Farewell_Address.htm.
208. https://www.senate.gov/artandhistory/history/resources/pdf/Humphrey-Page.pdf.
209. https://www.rollcall.com/2021/02/23/washingtons-farewell-gets-personal-for-retiring-sen-portman/.
210. https://rollcall.com/2022/02/28/retiring-sen-leahy-reflects-on-fragile-democracy-as-he-reads-washingtons-farewell/.
211. https://www.allmusicals.com/lyrics/hamilton/onelasttime.htm.
212. *New York Times*, March 4, 1909, 8; Ron Chernow, *Washington: A Life* (New York: Penguin, 2010), xx, 32.
213. Thomas Jefferson to Vermont Legislature, December 10, 1807; https://teachingamericanhistory.org/document/letter-to-the-legislature-of-vermont/.
214. Jefferson to Vermont Legislature.
215. Jefferson to Vermont Legislature.
216. Chernow, *Washington*, xix.

Chapter 2

1. Memo from President John Kennedy to Vice President Lyndon Johnson, 2 April 1961; https://history.nasa.gov/Apollomon/apollo1.pdf.
2. Memo from President John Kennedy.
3. Memo from President John Kennedy.
4. John Kennedy, "Special Message to the Congress on Urgent National Needs," May 25, 1961; https://www.presidency.ucsb.edu/documents/special-message-the-congress-urgent-national-needs.
5. John Kennedy, "Remarks at the NASA Manned Spacecraft Center in Houston," September 12, 1962; https://www.presidency.ucsb.edu/documents/remarks-the-nasa-manned-spacecraft-center-houston.
6. John Noble Wilford, "Neil Armstrong, First Man on the Moon, Dies at 82," *New York Times*, August 25, 2012.
7. Kennedy, "Remarks at the NASA Manned Spacecraft."
8. Jerald Mast, *Climate Change Politics and Policies in America: Historical and Modern Documents in Context* (Santa Barbara, CA: ABC-CLIO, 2018), 435.
9. Barack Obama, *Public Papers of the President of the United States, Barack Obama, 2009, Book II* (Washington, DC: Office of the Federal Register, National Archives and Records Administration), 1212.

10. Donald Trump, "Remarks by President Trump at the Operation Warp Speed Vaccine Summit," December 8, 2020; https://trumpwhitehouse.archives.gov/briefings-statements/remarks-president-trump-operation-warp-speed-vaccine-summit/.

11. Trump, "Remarks by President Trump."

12. Franklin Roosevelt, "Press Conference," December 17, 1940; https://www.presidency.ucsb.edu/documents/press-conference-3.

13. Lou Cannon, *President Reagan: The Role of a Lifetime* (New York: Public Affairs, 2008), 408.

14. https://www.whitehouse.gov/about-the-white-house/presidents/herbert-hoover/.

15. https://www.battlefields.org/learn/primary-sources/lincoln-great-emancipator.

16. https://www.battlefields.org/learn/articles/bleeding-kansas.

17. Calvin Coolidge, "Address to the American Society of Newspaper Editors, Washington, DC," January 17, 1925; https://www.presidency.ucsb.edu/documents/address-the-american-society-newspaper-editors-washington-dc.

18. William Shakespeare, *Sonnet 98: From you have I been absent in the spring*.

19. Franklin Roosevelt, *The Public Papers and Addresses of Franklin D. Roosevelt, Volume 10*, ed. Samuel Irving Rosenman (United States: Macmillan, 1941), 139.

20. Abigail Adams to Mary Cranch, November 21, 1800; https://founders.archives.gov/documents/Adams/04-14-02-0204.

21. Thomas Jefferson to St. George Tucker, June 3, 1801; https://founders.archives.gov/documents/Jefferson/01-34-02-0205.

22. Fawn McKay Brodie, *Thomas Jefferson: An Intimate History* (New York: W. W. Norton, 1974), 365.

23. Jon Meacham, *Thomas Jefferson: The Art of Power* (New York: Random House, 2012), 363.

24. Thomas Jefferson to Thomas Mann Randolph, November 16, 1801; https://founders.archives.gov/documents/Jefferson/01-35-02-0517.

25. John Kennedy, *Public Papers of the Presidents: John F. Kennedy, 1962* (Washington, DC: Office of the Federal Register, National Archives and Records Administration), 347.

26. Thomas Jefferson to Robert Livingston, April 18, 1802; https://founders.archives.gov/documents/Jefferson/01-37-02-0220.

27. Henry Adams, *History of the United States of American during the Administrations of Thomas Jefferson* (New York: Library of American Edition, 1986), 109.

28. Thomas Jefferson to Samuel Adams, March 29, 1801; https://founders.archives.gov/documents/Jefferson/01-33-02-0421.

29. Frank Parker Stockbridge, *History of the Louisiana Purchase Exposition* (Saint Louis, MO: Universal Exposition, 1905), 38.

30. Andrew Cunningham McLaughlin, "The Confederation and the Constitution, 1783–1789." *The American Nation: A History, Volume 10*, ed. Albert Bushnell Hart (New York: Harper & Brothers, 1905), 99.

31. Thomas Jefferson to Robert Livingston, April 18, 1802.

32. Thomas Jefferson to Robert Livingston, April 18, 1802.

33. Thomas Jefferson to Thomas Cooper, 29 November 1802; https://founders.archives.gov/documents/Jefferson/01-39-02-0070.

34. Walter Nugent, *Habits of Empire: A History of American Exceptionalism* (New York: Knopf, 2008), 57.

35. Robert Livingston to James Madison, March 14, 1802; https://founders.archives.gov/documents/Madison/02-03-02-0029.

36. Dumas Malone, *Jefferson: The Virginian, Volume One* (Boston: Little, Brown, 1948), 4.

37. Thomas Jefferson to Thomas Cooper, September 10, 1814; https://founders.archives.gov/documents/Jefferson/03-07-02-0471.

38. Thomas Jefferson to Thomas Mann Randolph, Jr., August 27, 1786; https://founders.archives.gov/documents/Jefferson/01-10-02-0226.

39. Malone, *Jefferson the Virginian*, 56–67; *Memoirs of Thomas Jefferson Randolph*, Edgehill Randolph Papers, University of Virginia.

40. Adams, *History*, 277.

41. Merrill D. Peterson, *Thomas Jefferson and the New Nation: A Biography* (New York: Hill and Wang, 1986), viii.

42. Dumas Malone, *Jefferson and His Time: The Sage of Monticello, Vol. 6* (Charlottesville: University of Virginia Press, 1981), 169–70.

43. John Adams, *Diary and Autobiography of John Adams*, ed. L. H. Butterfield (Cambridge, MA: Harvard University Press, 1961), 3: 335.

44. John Quincy Adams and Charles Francis Adams, ed., *Memoirs of John Quincy Adams, Comprising Portions of his Diary from 1795 to 1848* (Philadelphia: J. B. Lippincott, 1874), 317.

45. Elkins and McKitrick, *The Age of Federalism*, 197.

46. Gordon S. Wood, *Friends Divided: John Adams and Thomas Jefferson* (New York: Penguin Books, 2017), 10.

47. Thomas Jefferson to Thomas Jefferson Smith, February 21, 1825; https://founders.archives.gov/documents/Jefferson/98-01-02-4987.

48. Thomas Jefferson to Martha Jefferson, May 5, 1787; https://founders.archives.gov/documents/Jefferson/01-11-02-0327.

49. Thomas Jefferson, *The Writings of Thomas Jefferson, Volume 1*, ed. H. A. Washington (Cambridge, UK: Cambridge University Press, 2011), 2.

50. Thomas Jefferson to Giovanni Fabbroni, June 8, 1778; https://founders.archives.gov/documents/Jefferson/01-02-02-0066.

51. Thomas Jefferson to Benjamin Henry Latrobe, October 10, 1809; https://founders.archives.gov/documents/Jefferson/03-01-02-0468.

52. https://www.wm.edu/about/history/historiccampus/wrenbuilding/.

53. Thomas Jefferson to John Taylor, December 29, 1794; https://founders.archives.gov/documents/Jefferson/01-28-02-0172.

54. Thomas Jefferson to James Monroe, November 14, 1801; https://founders.archives.gov/documents/Jefferson/01-35-02-0506.

55. Thomas Jefferson to the American Philosophical Society, January 28, 1797; https://founders.archives.gov/documents/Jefferson/01-29-02-0218.

56. Meacham, *Art of Power*, xx.

57. James Parton, *Life of Thomas Jefferson* (Boston, MA: James R. Osgood, 1874), 165.

58. Wood, *Friends Divided*, 10.

59. Thomas Jefferson to John Minor, August 30, 1814, including Thomas Jefferson to Bernard Moore, [ca. 1773?]; https://founders.archives.gov/documents/Jefferson/03-07-02-0455.

60. Thomas Jefferson, "Summary View of the Rights of British America," 1774; https://avalon.law.yale.edu/18th_century/jeffsumm.asp.

61. Thomas Jefferson to Henry Lee, May 8, 1825; https://founders.archives.gov/documents/Jefferson/98-01-02-5212.

62. Thomas Jefferson, *The Papers of Thomas Jefferson, Vol. 1, 1760–1776*, ed. Julian P. Boyd (Princeton, NJ: Princeton University Press, 1950), 429–33.

63. "Thomas Jefferson: Design for Tombstone and Inscription, before 4 July 1826, 4 July 1826"; https://founders.archives.gov/documents/Jefferson/98-01-02-6185.

64. "Thomas Jefferson: Design for Tombstone."

65. Thomas Jefferson to Robert Livingston, April 18, 1802.

66. Thomas Jefferson to Robert Livingston, April 18, 1802.

67. Thomas Jefferson to Robert Livingston, April 18, 1802.

68. Thomas Jefferson to Robert Livingston, April 18, 1802.

69. Thomas Jefferson to Robert Livingston, April 18, 1802.

70. Thomas Jefferson to Robert Livingston, April 18, 1802.

71. Draft of Letter to John Jay, Explaining His Instructions, [17 October] 1780; https://founders.archives.gov/documents/Madison/01-02-02-0080.

72. Thomas Jefferson to Robert Livingston, April 18, 1802.

73. Thomas Jefferson to Robert Livingston, April 18, 1802.

74. Thomas Jefferson to Robert Livingston, April 18, 1802.

75. Thomas Jefferson to Robert Livingston, April 18, 1802.

76. Harry Truman, "Address at the National War College," December 19, 1952; https://www.presidency.ucsb.edu/documents/address-the-national-war-college.

77. Thomas Jefferson to Robert Livingston, April 18, 1802.

78. Thomas Jefferson to Robert Livingston, April 18, 1802.

79. Pierre Samuel Du Pont de Nemours to Thomas Jefferson, April 24, 1802; https://founders.archives.gov/documents/Jefferson/01-37-02-0254,

80. Thomas Jefferson to Pierre Samuel Du Pont de Nemours, April 24, 1802; https://founders.archives.gov/documents/Jefferson/01-37-02-0263.

81. Thomas Jefferson to Pierre Samuel Du Pont de Nemours, April 24, 1802.
82. Robert Livingston to James Madison, July 30, 1802; https://founders.archives.gov/documents/Madison/02-03-02-0552.
83. Robert Livingston to James Madison, July 30, 1802.
84. Robert Livingston to James Madison, August 10, 1802; https://founders.archives.gov/documents/Madison/02-03-02-0594.
85. Robert Livingston to James Madison, September 1, 1802; https://founders.archives.gov/documents/Madison/02-03-02-0673.
86. Robert Livingston to James Madison, September 1, 1802.
87. Thomas Jefferson to Albert Gallatin, August 20, 1802; https://founders.archives.gov/documents/Jefferson/01-38-02-0233.
88. Thomas Jefferson to Albert Gallatin, August 20, 1802.
89. Robert Livingston to James Madison, January 24, 1803; https://founders.archives.gov/documents/Madison/02-04-02-0324.
90. Robert Livingston to James Madison, January 24, 1803.
91. Robert Livingston to James Madison, January 24, 1803.
92. Robert Livingston to James Madison, August 16, 1802; https://founders.archives.gov/documents/Madison/02-03-02-0623.
93. Thomas Jefferson to James Madison; September 13, 1802; https://founders.archives.gov/documents/Jefferson/01-38-02-0346.
94. Samuel Du Pont De Nemours to Thomas Jefferson, October 4, 1802; https://founders.archives.gov/documents/Jefferson/01-38-02-0399.
95. Robert Livingston to Thomas Jefferson, October 28, 1802; https://founders.archives.gov/documents/Jefferson/01-38-02-0528.
96. Robert Livingston to James Madison, November 2, 1802; https://founders.archives.gov/documents/Madison/02-04-02-0078.
97. Thomas Jefferson to Robert Livingston, October 10, 1802; https://founders.archives.gov/documents/Jefferson/01-38-02-0435.
98. Thomas Jefferson to Robert Livingston, October 10, 1802.
99. Robert Livingston to James Madison, November 10, 1802; https://founders.archives.gov/documents/Madison/02-04-02-0110.
100. Robert Livingston to James Madison, January 24, 1803.
101. Robert Livingston to James Madison, January 24, 1803.
102. Robert Livingston to James Madison, November 11, 1802; https://founders.archives.gov/documents/Madison/02-04-02-0114.
103. Robert Livingston to James Madison, January 24, 1803.
104. Thomas Jefferson to Robert Livingston, April 18, 1802.
105. Thomas Jefferson to Robert Livingston, February 3, 1803; https://founders.archives.gov/documents/Jefferson/01-39-02-0382.
106. Robert Johnson to James Madison, December 5, 1802; https://founders.archives.gov/documents/Madison/02-04-02-0186.
107. James Madison to Robert Livingston, December 17, 1802; https://founders.archives.gov/documents/Madison/02-04-02-0217.

108. James Madison to Robert Livingston, December 17, 1802.
109. Thomas Jefferson to James Monroe, January 10, 1803; https://founders.archives.gov/documents/Jefferson/01-39-02-0262.
110. Commission for James Monroe and Robert R. Livingston, January 12, 1803; https://founders.archives.gov/documents/Jefferson/01-39-02-0274.
111. Thomas Jefferson to James Monroe, January 13, 1803; https://founders.archives.gov/documents/Jefferson/01-39-02-0283.
112. Thomas Jefferson to James Monroe, January 13, 1803.
113. Thomas Jefferson to James Monroe, January 13, 1803.
114. James Madison to Robert Livingston, January 18, 1803; https://founders.archives.gov/documents/Madison/02-04-02-0304.
115. James Madison to Robert Livingston, January 18, 1803.
116. James Madison to Robert Livingston, February 23, 1803; https://founders.archives.gov/documents/Madison/02-04-02-0421.
117. James Madison to Robert Livingston, January 18, 1803.
118. Robert Livingston to James Madison, March 3, 1803; https://founders.archives.gov/documents/Madison/02-04-02-0454.
119. Robert Livingston to James Madison, March 18, 1803; https://founders.archives.gov/documents/Madison/02-04-02-0515.
120. Robert Livingston to James Madison, March 18, 1803.
121. Robert Livingston to James Madison, March 3, 1803.
122. Robert Livingston to James Madison, April 11, 1803; https://founders.archives.gov/documents/Madison/02-04-02-0606.
123. Robert Livingston to James Madison, March 3, 1803.
124. Robert Livingston to James Madison, March 11, 1803; https://founders.archives.gov/documents/Madison/02-04-02-0484.
125. Robert Livingston to James Madison, March 11, 1803.
126. Robert Livingston to James Madison, March 18, 1803; https://founders.archives.gov/documents/Madison/02-04-02-0515.
127. Robert Livingston to James Madison, March 3, 1803.
128. Thomas Jefferson to Robert Livingston, February 3, 1803.
129. James Monroe to Thomas Jefferson, March 7, 1803; https://founders.archives.gov/documents/Jefferson/01-40-02-0025.
130. James Monroe to Thomas Jefferson, March 7, 1803.
131. "I. Recipient's Copy," March 12, 1803; https://founders.archives.gov/documents/Jefferson/01-40-02-0037-0002.
132. Robert Livingston to James Madison, February 18, 1803; https://founders.archives.gov/documents/Madison/02-04-02-0405.
133. Robert Livingston to James Madison, February 18, 1803.
134. Robert Livingston to James Madison, March 11, 1803.
135. Robert Livingston to James Madison, February 18, 1803.
136. Robert Livingston to James Madison, March 11, 1803.
137. Robert Livingston to James Madison, February 18, 1803.

138. Robert Livingston to James Madison, February 18, 1803.
139. Robert Livingston to James Madison, February 18, 1803.
140. Robert Livingston to James Madison, February 18, 1803.
141. Robert Livingston to James Madison, February 18, 1803.
142. "I. Recipient's Copy."
143. Robert Livingston to James Madison, March 11, 1803.
144. Robert Livingston to James Madison, March 11, 1803.
145. Robert Livingston to James Madison, February 18, 1803.
146. Robert Livingston to James Madison, February 18, 1803.
147. Robert Livingston to James Madison, 18 March 1803.
148. Robert Livingston to James Madison, February 18, 1803.
149. Robert Livingston to James Madison, March 3, 1803.
150. Robert Livingston to James Madison, February 18, 1803.
151. Robert Livingston to James Madison, February 18, 1803.
152. "I. Recipient's Copy."
153. "I. Recipient's Copy."
154. Robert Livingston to James Madison, February 18, 1803.
155. Robert Livingston to James Madison, March 11, 1803.
156. "I. Recipient's Copy."
157. "I. Recipient's Copy."
158. Thomas Jefferson to James Madison, March 19, 1803; https://founders.archives.gov/documents/Madison/02-04-02-0518.
159. Irving Brandt, *James Madison: Secretary of State, 1800–1909, Volume 4* (Indianapolis, IN: Bobbs-Merrill, 1941), 64.
160. Thomas Jefferson to Robert Livingston, April 18, 1802.
161. Fred L. Israel, *Major Presidential Decisions* (New York: Chelsea House, 1980), 29–30.
162. Francis Barbe Marbois, *History of Louisiana: Particularly of the Cession of that Colony to the United States of America: with an Introductory Essay on the Constitution and Government of the United States, Volume 1* (Philadelphia, PA: Carey & Lea, 1830), 264.
163. Nathaniel Pitt Langford, "The Louisiana Purchase and Preceding Spanish Intrigues for Dismemberment of the Union," *Minnesota Historical Society,* St. Paul, MN (1901), 482.
164. Langford, "Louisiana Purchase," 485.
165. Robert Livingston to James Madison, April 13, 1803; https://founders.archives.gov/documents/Madison/02-04-02-0615.
166. Marbois, *History of Louisiana*, 264.
167. Robert Livingston to James Madison, May 12, 1803; https://founders.archives.gov/documents/Madison/02-04-02-0703.
168. Langford, "Louisiana Purchase," 483.
169. Henry Adams, *History of the United States: From the Discovery of the Continent, Volume 2* (New York: Charles C. Little and James Brown, 1940), 27.

170. Robert Livingston to James Madison, April 11, 1803; https://founders.archives.gov/documents/Madison/02-04-02-0606.

171. Robert Livingston to James Madison, April 11, 1803.

172. Robert Livingston to James Madison, April 11, 1803.

173. Robert Livingston and James Monroe to James Madison, May 13, 1803; https://founders.archives.gov/documents/Madison/02-04-02-0711.

174. Robert Livingston to James Madison, April 11, 1803; https://founders.archives.gov/documents/Madison/02-04-02-0606.

175. Robert Livingston to James Madison, April 11, 1803.

176. Robert Livingston to James Madison, April 11, 1803.

177. Robert Livingston to James Madison, April 11, 1803.

178. Robert Livingston to James Madison, April 11, 1803.

179. Robert Livingston to James Madison, April 13, 1803.

180. Robert Livingston to James Madison, May 12, 1803; https://founders.archives.gov/documents/Madison/02-04-02-0703.

181. Joseph J. Ellis, *American Creation: Triumphs and Tragedies at the Founding of the Republic* (New York: Vintage Books, 2007), 221.

182. Robert Livingston to James Madison, April 13, 1803.

183. Robert Livingston to James Madison, April 13, 1803.

184. Robert Livingston to James Madison, April 13, 1803.

185. Robert Livingston to James Madison, April 13, 1803.

186. Robert Livingston to James Madison, April 13, 1803.

187. Robert Livingston to James Madison, April 13, 1803.

188. Robert Livingston to James Madison, April 13, 1803.

189. Robert Livingston to James Madison, April 13, 1803.

190. Robert Livingston to James Madison, April 13, 1803.

191. Robert Livingston to James Madison, April 13, 1803.

192. Robert Livingston to James Madison, April 13, 1803.

193. Robert Livingston to James Madison, April 13, 1803.

194. Robert Livingston to James Madison, April 13, 1803.

195. Robert Livingston to James Madison, April 13, 1803.

196. Robert Livingston to James Madison, April 13, 1803.

197. Robert Livingston to James Madison, April 13, 1803.

198. Robert Livingston to James Madison, April 13, 1803.

199. Robert Livingston to James Madison, April 13, 1803.

200. Robert Livingston to Thomas Jefferson, April 14, 1803; https://founders.archives.gov/documents/Jefferson/01-40-02-0146.

201. Robert Livingston to Thomas Jefferson, April 14, 1803.

202. Robert Livingston to James Madison, April 17, 1803; https://founders.archives.gov/documents/Madison/02-04-02-0631.

203. James Monroe to James Madison, April 15, 1803; https://founders.archives.gov/documents/Madison/02-04-02-0625.

204. Robert Livingston to James Madison, April 17, 1803.
205. Robert Livingston to James Madison, April 17, 1803.
206. Robert Livingston to James Madison, April 17, 1803.
207. Robert Livingston to James Madison, April 17, 1803.
208. Robert Livingston to James Madison, April 17, 1803.
209. Robert Livingston to James Madison, April 17, 1803.
210. Robert Livingston to James Madison, April 17, 1803.
211. Langford, "Louisiana Purchase," 484.
212. Robert Livingston to James Madison, May 12, 1803.
213. Robert Livingston and James Monroe to James Madison, May 13, 1803.
214. Robert Livingston to James Madison, April 17, 1803.
215. James Monroe to James Madison, May 14, 1803; https://founders.archives.gov/documents/Madison/02-04-02-0717.
216. James Monroe to James Madison, May 14, 1803.
217. James Monroe to James Madison, May 18, 1803; https://founders.archives.gov/documents/Madison/02-05-02-0012.
218. James Monroe to James Madison, May 18, 1803.
219. James Madison to James Monroe, June 25, 1803; https://founders.archives.gov/documents/Madison/02-05-02-0142.
220. Robert Livingston to Thomas Jefferson, May 26, 1803; https://founders.archives.gov/documents/Jefferson/01-40-02-0328.
221. James Monroe to James Madison, May 23, 1803; https://founders.archives.gov/documents/Madison/02-05-02-0028.
222. Thomas Jefferson to Thomas Mann Randolph, July 5, 1803; https://founders.archives.gov/documents/Jefferson/01-40-02-0505.
223. Thomas Jefferson to Thomas Mann Randolph, July 5, 1803.
224. James Madison to Robert Livingston, July 29, 1803; https://founders.archives.gov/documents/Madison/02-05-02-0270.
225. James Madison to Robert Livingston, July 29, 1803.
226. Thomas Jefferson to John Breckinridge, August 12, 1803; https://founders.archives.gov/documents/Jefferson/01-41-02-0139.
227. Despite variable grammatical errors, the referenced quotation is intentionally maintained in its original form.
228. *National Intelligencer*, July 4, 1803.
229. "The Purchase of Louisiana," *New York Evening Post*, July 5, 1803.
230. "To James Madison and Family," *The Papers of Thomas Jefferson*, 40: 667.
231. Thomas Jefferson to Thomas Mann Randolph, July 5, 1803.
232. Horatio Gates to Thomas Jefferson, July 7, 1803; https://founders.archives.gov/documents/Jefferson/01-40-02-0515.
233. Thomas Jefferson to James Madison, July 17, 1803; https://founders.archives.gov/documents/Madison/02-05-02-0229.

242 | Notes to Chapter 3

234. Thomas Jefferson to Meriwether Lewis, July 4, 1803; https://founders.archives.gov/documents/Jefferson/01-40-02-0500.

235. Thomas Jefferson to Albert Gallatin, August 23, 1803; https://founders.archives.gov/documents/Jefferson/01-41-02-0190.

236. Thomas Jefferson to Wilson Cary Nicholas, September 7, 1803; https://founders.archives.gov/documents/Jefferson/01-41-02-0255.

237. Thomas Jefferson, "Third Annual Message to Congress," October 17, 1803; https://avalon.law.yale.edu/19th_century/jeffmes3.asp.

238. In *The Imperial Presidency* Schlesinger defends Jefferson's action to present the Louisiana Purchase as a treaty on national security grounds: "Congress set up the clamor for Louisiana, conformed the envoys who negotiated the purchase, appropriated the funds for the purchase, ratified the treaty consummating the purchase and passed statures authorizing the President to receive the purchase and to establish government and law in the newly acquired territories" (23–24). Other scholars, like Stephen Skowronek in *The Politics Presidents Make* (79) and Marc Landy and Sidney Milkis in *Presidential Greatness* (77–78) see Jefferson's actions more in the line with him abandoning a strict-constructionist view of the U.S. Constitution in the face of crisis and opportunity.

239. Thomas Jefferson, "Inaugural Address," March 4, 1805; https://www.presidency.ucsb.edu/documents/inaugural-address-20.

240. Thomas Jefferson to John B. Colvin, September 20, 1810; https://founders.archives.gov/documents/Jefferson/03-03-02-0060.

241. Thomas Jefferson to Pierre Samuel Du Pont de Nemours, April 25, 1802.

242. Carl Becker, "What Is Still Living in the Political Philosophy of Thomas Jefferson." *American Historical Review* 48, no. 4 (July 1943): 701.

243. Stephen Ambrose, *Undaunted Courage: Meriwether Lewis, Thomas Jefferson, and the Opening of the American West* (New York: Simon & Schuster, 1996), Introduction.

244. Andrew Jackson to Thomas Jefferson, August 7, 1803; https://founders.archives.gov/documents/Jefferson/01-41-02-0117.

245. Thomas Jefferson to the Rev. Charles Clay, January 27, 1790; https://founders.archives.gov/documents/Jefferson/01-16-02-0074.

246. Thomas Jefferson to Edward Dowse, April 19, 1803; https://founders.archives.gov/documents/Jefferson/01-40-02-0168.

247. Becker, "What Is Still Living," 706.

Chapter 3

1. Morton Luce, ed., *The Works of William Shakespeare: Twelfth Night or What You Will* (London: Methuen, 1906), 154.

2. https://www.reaganfoundation.org/education/virtual-learning-hub/the-great-communicator/.

3. Philip Sheldon Foner, ed. *The Complete Writing of Thomas Paine, Volume 1* (New York, NY: The Citadel Press, 1945), 49.

4. James Thomas Flexner, *Washington: The Indispensable Man* (Boston, MA: Little, Brown), 1974.

5. Editorial Note: Death of Franklin; https://founders.archives.gov/documents/Jefferson/01-19-02-0005-0001.

6. John Quincy Adams and Allan Nevins, eds., *The Diary of John Quincy Adams, 1794–1845: American Political, Social and Intellectual Life from Washington to Polk* (London: Longmans, Green, 1928), 51.

7. Franklin Roosevelt, "Inaugural Address," March 4, 1933; https://www.presidency.ucsb.edu/documents/inaugural-address-8.

8. Gerald Ford, "Statement and Responses to Questions from Members of the House Judiciary Committee Concerning the Pardon of Richard Nixon," October 17, 1974; https://www.presidency.ucsb.edu/documents/statement-and-responses-questions-from-members-the-house-judiciary-committee-concerning.

9. Hans Louis Trefousse, *Andrew Johnson. A Biography* (New York: W. W. Norton), 236.

10. Sean Conant, *The Gettysburg Address: Perspectives on Lincoln's Greatest Speech* (London: Oxford University Press, 2015), 151.

11. "The Gettysburgh Celebration," *New York Times*, November 21, 1863.

12. Allen Thorndike Rice, ed., *Reminiscences of Abraham Lincoln by Distinguished Men of His Time* (New York: Haskel House, 1971), 511.

13. Rice, ed., *Reminiscences of Abraham Lincoln*, 511.

14. Lincoln, *Collected Works, Volume 7*, 17.

15. Kenneth Milton Stampp, *The Peculiar Institution: Slavery in the Ante-Bellum South* (New York: Knopf, 1961).

16. Donald, *Lincoln*, 14.

17. Charles Carleton Coffin, *Abraham Lincoln (Life of Lincoln)* (New York: Harper and Brothers, 1893), 330.

18. Lincoln, *Collected Works, Volume 6*, 29.

19. Benjamin B. French Diary, February 18, 1863, in Donald B. Cole and John J. McDonough, eds., *Witness to the Young Republic: A Yankee's Journal, 1828–1870* (Hanover, NH: University of New England, 1989), 417.

20. Scott Bowden and Bill Ward, *Last Chance for Victory: Robert E. Lee and the Gettysburg Campaign* (Cambridge, MA: De Capo, 2001), 280.

21. David S. Reynolds, *Abe: Abraham Lincoln in His Times* (New York: Penguin, 2020), 850.

22. "The President to the Country," *New York Times*, July 6, 1863.

23. French, *Witness to the Young Republic*, 424–25.

24. Michael Burlingame, *Abraham Lincoln: A Life, Volume 2* (Baltimore, MD: Johns Hopkins University Press, 2013), 511.

25. Adams Sentinel, "Our Apology," July 7, 1863; https://www.penncivilwar.com/post/a-terrible-and-yet-glorious-reality.

26. Sentinel, "Our Apology."
27. William J. Jackson, *New Jerseyans in the Civil War: For Union and Liberty* (New Brunswick, NJ: Rutgers University Press, 2000), 142.
28. David Wills to Abraham Lincoln, Robert Todd Lincoln Papers, Manuscript Division Library of Congress, November 2, 1863.
29. Lincoln, *Collected Works, Volume 7*, 16.
30. David Herbert Donald, *Lincoln* (New York: Simon & Schuster, 1996), 463.
31. Lincoln, *Collected Works, Volume 7*, 24.
32. *New York Tribune*, November 20, 1863, 1.
33. Lincoln, *Collected Works, Volume 7*, 16.
34. Lincoln, *Collected Works, Volume 7*, 16.
35. "The Gettysburg Cemetery—Serenade to the President—His Speech," *New York Daily Tribune*, November 20, 1863, 1.
36. Thaddeus Stevens was a U.S. House member from Pennsylvania, Radical Republican, and fierce opponent of slavery and discrimination against African Americans.
37. Conant, *The Gettysburg Address*, 153.
38. George W. Bush, "Remarks at the Performance of "Lincoln Seen and Heard." February 11, 2005; https://www.presidency.ucsb.edu/documents/remarks-the-performance-lincoln-seen-and-heard.
39. Ward Hill Lamon, *Recollections of Abraham Lincoln, 1847–1865*, Dorothy Lamon, ed. (Chicago: A. C. McClurg, 1895), 171.
40. Lamon, *Recollections of Abraham Lincoln*, 171.
41. Garry Wills, *Lincoln at Gettysburg: The Words that Remade America* (New York: Simon & Schuster, 2006), 40.
42. Abraham Lincoln, "Address to the People of Sangamon County," March 9, 1832.
43. Donald, *Lincoln*, 27.
44. Michael Burlingame, *Abraham Lincoln: A Life, Volume 1* (Baltimore, MD: Johns Hopkins University Press, 2013), 648; Thomas Gray wrote the poem "Elegy Written in a Country Churchyard" in 1750.
45. William Lyon Phelps, ed., *Selections from the Poetry and Prose of Thomas Gray* (Boston: Ginn, 1894).
46. William Henry Herndon, *Herndon's Lincoln: The True Story of a Great Life: The History and Personal Recollections of Abraham Lincoln, Volume 1* (London: Forgotten Books, 2015), 4.
47. William Henry Herndon and Jesse William Weik, *Abraham Lincoln: The True Story of a Great Life, Volume 1* (New York: D. Appleton, 1892), 10.
48. Herndon and Weik, *Abraham Lincoln*, 3.
49. Walt Whitman and Emory Holloway, ed., *The Uncollected Poetry and Prose of Walt Whitman: With Various Early Manuscripts, Volume 1* (New York:

Doubleday, Page, 1921), 23; Whitman's "War-Time Letter" was sent to Nathaniel Bloom and John F. S. Gray on March 19, 1863.

50. William D. Pederson, ed. et al, *Lincoln's Ensuring Legacy: Perspective from Great Thinkers, Great Leaders, and the American Experiment* (New York: Rowman & Littlefield, 2010), 94.

51. William Baringer, *Lincoln's Rise to Power* (New York: Scholarly Press, 1971), 50.

52. *Philadelphia Inquirer*, February 20, 1861.

53. Helen Nicolay, *Personal Traits of Abraham Lincoln* (New York: Century, 1912), 254.

54. Abraham Lincoln, *Collected Works of Abraham Lincoln, Volume 5* (New Brunswick, NJ: Rutgers University Press, 1953), 346.

55. Doris Kearns Goodwin, *Team of Rivals: The Political Genius of Abraham Lincoln* (New York: Simon & Schuster, 2005).

56. Lincoln, *Collected Works, Volume 3*, 27.

57. Lincoln, Abraham, "Brief Autobiography," June 15, 1858.

58. Lincoln, *Collected Works, Volume 4*, 62.

59. Donald, *Lincoln*, 32.

60. Donald, *Lincoln*, 32.

61. Richard Brookhiser, *Founders' Son: A Life of Abraham Lincoln* (New York: Basic Books, 2014), 5.

62. Lincoln, *Collected Works, Volume 4*, 236.

63. John F. Kennedy, "City Upon a Hill Speech," January 9, 1961; https://www.jfklibrary.org/archives/other-resources/john-f-kennedy-speeches/massachusetts-general-court-19610109.

64. Lincoln, *Collected Works, Volume 1*, 510.

65. Henry Ketcham, *The Life of Abraham Lincoln* (New York: A. L. Burt, 1901), 44.

66. Noted on the Abraham Lincoln Bicentennial Foundation website: http://www.lincolnbicentennial.org/resources/abraham-lincolns-life/lincoln-in-illinois/new-salem.

67. Henry Louis Gates Jr. and Donald Yacovone, *Lincoln on Race and Slavery* (Princeton, NJ: Princeton University Press, 2011), LXIII.

68. Lincoln, *Collected Works, Volume 2*, 461.

69. Lincoln, *Collected Works, Volume 4*, 271.

70. Dwight Eisenhower, *Public Papers of the President, Dwight D. Eisenhower: 1954: Containing the Public Messages, Speeches, and Statements of the President, January 1 to December 31, 1954* (Washington, DC: Office of the Federal Register, National Archives and Records Service, General Services Administration, 1960), 416.

71. Lincoln, *Collected Works, Volume 2*, 126.

72. Lincoln, *Collected Works, Volume 6*, 29.

73. Mark K. Updegrove, *Baptism by Fire: Eight Presidents Who Took Office in Times of Crisis* (New York: Thomas Dunne Books, 2008), 110.
74. French, *Witness to the Young Republic*, 434.
75. French, *Witness to the Young Republic*, 434.
76. *Adams Sentinel*, November 24, 1863.
77. French, *Witness to the Young Republic*, 435.
78. French, *Witness to the Young Republic*, 435.
79. *New York Daily Tribune*, November 20, 1863, 1.
80. "The Celebration at Gettysburg," the *Press* (Philadelphia, PA), November 21,1863, 2.
81. "The Gettysburgh Celebration, *New York Times*, November 21, 1863.
82. "The Celebration at Gettysburg," the *Press* (Philadelphia, PA), November 21, 1863, 2.
83. French, *Witness to the Young Republic*, 435.
84. "The Celebration at Gettysburg," the *Press* (Philadelphia, PA), November 21, 1863, 2.
85. *New York Daily Tribune*, November 20, 1863, 2.
86. Donald, *Lincoln*, 464.
87. *Philadelphia Daily Age*, November 21, 1863; Michael Burlingame, *Abraham Lincoln: A Life, Volume 2* (Baltimore, MD, Johns Hopkins University Press, 2013), 573.
88. French, *Witness to the Young Republic*, 435.
89. Gabor Boritt, *The Gettysburg Gospel: The Lincoln Speech That Nobody Knows* (New York: Simon & Schuster, 2008), 112.
90. Rufus Rockwell Wilson, *Intimate Memories of Lincoln* (Elmira, NY: Primavera Press, 1945), 478.
91. Daniel Kilham Dodge, *Abraham Lincoln: Master of Words* (New York: D. Appleton, 1924), 100.
92. Jefferson, Thomas, *The Declaration of Independence*. Washington, DC: Library of Congress, July 4, 1776, para. 2, sentence 1.
93. Lincoln, *Collected Works, Volume 6*, 319.
94. Lincoln, *Collected Works, Volume 6*, 319.
95. Lincoln, *Collected Works, Volume 7*, 17.
96. Lincoln, *Collected Works, Volume 6*, 319.
97. Lincoln, *Collected Works, Volume 6*, 320.
98. Lincoln, *Collected Works, Volume 2*, 276.
99. Brookhiser, *Founders' Son*, 7.
100. Ronald Reagan, *Public Papers of the Ronald Reagan: 1983* (Washington DC: Office of the Federal Register, National Archives and Records Service, General Services Administration, 1984–85), 1112.
101. *Cincinnati Daily Commercial*, November 23, 1863.
102. *Cincinnati Daily Commercial*; Burlingame, *Abraham Lincoln, Volume 2*, 572–73.

103. Abraham Lincoln, "Address to the New Jersey State Senate," February 21, 1861.

104. Abraham Lincoln, "Address to New Jersey State Senate."

105. Abraham Lincoln, "July 4th Message to Congress," July 4, 1861; https://millercenter.org/the-presidency/presidential-speeches/july-4-1861-july-4th-message-congress.

106. Wills, *Lincoln at Gettysburg*, 129. Lincoln, *Collected Works, Volume 2*, 129.

107. Theodore Parker, *The Collected Works of Theodore Parker: Discourses of Slavery, Vol. 5* (London: Trubner, 1863), 105.

108. Lincoln, *Collected Works, Volume 7*, 23.

109. Lamon, *Recollections of Abraham Lincoln*, 178.

110. Wilson, *Intimate Memories of Lincoln*, 479.

111. Lamon, *Recollections of Abraham Lincoln*, 171.

112. Wilson, *Intimate Memories of Lincoln*, 479.

113. French, *Witness to the Young Republic*, 435–36.

114. Ronald C. White, *Abraham Lincoln: A Biography* (New York: Random House, 2010), 609; https://rmc.library.cornell.edu/gettysburg/ideas_more/reactions_p1.htm#chicago_tribune.

115. White, *Abraham Lincoln*, 609. https://rmc.library.cornell.edu/gettysburg/ideas_more/reactions_p1.htm#chicago_tribune.

116. "The Celebration at Gettysburg," the *Press* (Philadelphia, PA), November 21, 1863, 2.

117. https://rmc.library.cornell.edu/gettysburg/ideas_more/reactions_p1.htm#chicago_tribune.

118. https://rmc.library.cornell.edu/gettysburg/ideas_more/reactions_p2.htm#harrisburg_patriot.

119. Louis Austin Warren, *Lincoln's Gettysburg Declaration: "A New Birth of Freedom."* Lincoln National Life Foundation, 1964, 144.

120. Lincoln, *Collected Works, Volume 7*, 25.

121. Joseph H. Barrett, *Abraham Lincoln and His Presidency, Volume 2* (New York: D. Appleton, 1924), 208.

122. Lincoln, *Collected Works, Volume 7*, 24.

123. French, *Witness to the Young Republic*, 436.

124. "The Celebration at Gettysburg," the *Press* (Philadelphia, PA), November 21, 1863, 2.

125. "The Celebration at Gettysburg," 2.

126. "The Celebration at Gettysburg," 2.

127. William Eleroy Curtis, *The True Abraham Lincoln* (Philadelphia, PA: J. B. Lippincott, 1905), 87.

128. Herb Boyd, *Martin Luther, Jr.* (New York: Baronet Books, 2006), 225.

129. Jared Peatman, *The Long Shadow of Lincoln's Gettysburg Address* (Carbondale, IL: Southern Illinois University Press, 2013), 78.

130. Jeffrey Tulis, *The Rhetorical Presidency* (Princeton, NJ: Princeton University Press, 1987), 19. In this important and widely cited and debated book, Tulis argues that the twentieth-century practice of popular leadership represented a "basic change in the understanding of the place of the presidency in the political order" (13). He inferences that presidents should lessen their reliance on popular pleas, as a comparison to nineteenth-century peers that did not give policy speeches. In contrast to Tulis, not only do the stories profiled in this book highlight how popular pleas of presidents across every century of American existence have moved the nation, but they also include Lincoln's Gettysburg Address, which represents one of numerous examples of "the rhetorical presidency" in the nineteenth century. In fact, as great as Theodore Roosevelt's efforts were to gain passage of the Hepburn Act of 1906, a landmark railroad regulation bill, Lincoln's advocacy at Gettysburg lays a stronger claim than TR to the term "the father of the rhetorical presidency" (19).

131. "President Obama's Reading List," *New York Times*, January 18, 2017; interview with NYT's Michiko Kakutani, January 16, 2017.

132. Eisenhower, *Public Papers of the President, 1954*, 415.

133. Lyndon Johnson, *Public Papers of the President, Containing the Public Messages, Speeches, and Statements of the President, Volume 1* (Washington, DC: U.S. Government Printing Office, 1965), 176.

134. Johnson, *Public Papers of the President*, 176.

135. Johnson, *Public Papers of the President*, 176–77.

136. Gramm, *Lincoln's Elegy at Gettysburg*, 130.

137. James Hilty, "Lincoln and Public Memory," 2009.

138. Charles Sumner to Lt M. Morrill, *The Selected Letters of Charles Sumner*, ed. Beverly W. Palmer (Boston, MA: Northeastern University Press, 1990), 2: 306.

139. Abraham Lincoln, "Eulogy on Henry Clay," July 16, 1852.

Chapter 4

1. Carol Lea Mueller, *The Quotable John Wayne: The Grit and Wisdom of an American Icon* (New York: Taylor Trade, 2007), 25.

2. John Locke, *The Works of John Locke, Vol. III* (London: Burt et al., 1751), 49.

3. Lillian Herlands Hornstein, Leon Edel, and Horst Frenz, *The Reader's Companion to the World*, 2nd ed. (New York: New American Library, 2002), 509; Leighton Parks highlighted the dynamic between courage and recklessness in a tribute to Theodore Roosevelt at St. Bartholomew's Church in New York City on January 12, 1919. He noted that TR's opponents said Roosevelt had a "recklessness of speech" (6). Rather, for Parks, those who heard Roosevelt knew what he thought and what he would do; Leighton Parks, *Theodore Roosevelt: A Tribute* (New York: Washburn, 1919).

4. https://www.merriam-webster.com/dictionary/courage.

5. Barack Obama, Remarks on Presenting Posthumously the Congressional Medal of Honor to Staff Sergeant Robert J. Miller, October 6, 2010; https://www.presidency.ucsb.edu/documents/remarks-presenting-posthumously-the-congressional-medal-honor-staff-sergeant-robert-j.

6. "28 January 1791," *Journal of the Senate of the United States of America, 1789–1793. A Century of Lawmaking for a New Nation, U.S. Congressional documents and Debates, 1774–1875.*

7. *Gazette of the United States*, September 25, 1794.

8. Andrew Jackson, "Proclamation 43: Regarding the Nullifying Laws of South Carolina," December 10, 1832; https://www.presidency.ucsb.edu/documents/proclamation-43-regarding-the-nullifying-laws-south-carolina.

9. Andrew Jackson to Lewis Cass, December 17, 1832; https://www.loc.gov/resource/maj.01082_0244_0245/?sp=1&st=text.

10. Fred I. Greenstein with Dale Anderson, *Presidents and the Dissolution of the Union: Leadership Style from Polk to Lincoln* (Princeton, NJ: Princeton University Press, 2013), 91.

11. https://www.usatoday.com/story/news/politics/2022/07/26/biden-criticizes-trump-jan-6-lacked-courage-act/10151187002/.

12. John Kennedy, *Profiles in Courage* (New York: Harper Perennial, 2006), 225 (Kindle edition).

13. U.S. Constitution, Article II, Section 3, Clause 1.

14. James K. Polk, "Fourth Annual Message," December 5, 1848; https://www.presidency.ucsb.edu/documents/fourth-annual-message-6.

15. Abraham Lincoln, "Second Annual Message," December 1, 1862; https://www.presidency.ucsb.edu/documents/second-annual-message-9.

16. Franklin D. Roosevelt, "Annual Message to Congress on the State of the Union," January 6, 1941; https://www.presidency.ucsb.edu/documents/annual-message-congress-the-state-the-union.

17. Gerald R. Ford, "Address before a Joint Session of Congress Reporting on the State of the Union," January 15, 1975; https://www.presidency.ucsb.edu/documents/address-before-joint-session-the-congress-reporting-the-state-the-union-1.

18. William J. Clinton, "Address before a Joint Session of the Congress on the State of the Union," January 23, 1996; https://www.presidency.ucsb.edu/documents/address-before-joint-session-the-congress-the-state-the-union-10.

19. George W. Bush, "Address before a Joint Session of the Congress on the State of the Union," January 29, 2002; https://www.presidency.ucsb.edu/documents/address-before-joint-session-the-congress-the-state-the-union-22.

20. "Heard the Message: Congress Attentive to the Words of the President," *Evening Star*, Washington, DC, December 3, 1901.

21. "Heard the Message."

22. "Heard the Message."

23. "Heard the Message."
24. Abigail Adams to Mary Cranch, November 21, 1800; https://founders.archives.gov/documents/Adams/04-14-02-0204.
25. George Washington to Thomas Jefferson, March 4, 1792; https://founders.archives.gov/documents/Washington/05-10-02-0012.
26. Henry R. Luce, "The American Century," *Life*, February 17, 1941, 61–65.
27. "Heard the Message: Congress Attentive to the Words of the President," *Evening Star*, Washington, DC, December 3, 1901.
28. "Heard the Message."
29. Edmund Morris, *Theodore Rex* (New York: Random House, 2001), 27.
30. Morris, *Theodore Rex*.
31. Morris, *Theodore Rex*.
32. "Congress Listens to President's Message," *New York Times*, December 4, 1901, 1.
33. "Major O. L. Pruden Dead," *New York Times*, April 20, 1902, 7.
34. "Major O. L. Pruden Dead."
35. "Heard the Message: Congress Attentive to the Words of the President," *Evening Star*, Washington, DC, December 3, 1901; "Senators Deeply Interested," *Washington Times*, December 4, 1901.
36. "Congress Listens to President's Message," *New York Times*, December 4, 1901, 1.
37. "Heard the Message: Congress Attentive to the Words of the President," *Evening Star*, Washington, DC, December 3, 1901.
38. "Heard the Message."
39. "The Message to Congress," *Washington Times*, December 4, 1901.
40. "Senators Deeply Interested," *Washington Times*, December 4, 1901.
41. 42. Theodore Roosevelt, "First Annual Message," December 3, 1901; https://www.presidency.ucsb.edu/documents/first-annual-message-16.
43. https://www.britannica.com/biography/Leon-Czolgosz.
44. https://www.census.gov/history/www/through_the_decades/fast_facts/1900_fast_facts.html; https://www.census.gov/history/www/through_the_decades/fast_facts/1800_fast_facts.html.
45. Katharine Lee Bates, "America the Beautiful," 1895.
46. Frederick J. Turner, "The Significance of the Frontier in American History," (1893); https://www.historians.org/about-aha-and-membership/aha-history-and-archives/historical-archives/the-significance-of-the-frontier-in-american-history-(1893).
47. Lloyd Irland, "Maine Forests: A Century of Change, 1900–2000 . . . and Elements of Policy Change for a New Century," *Maine Policy Review* 9, no. 1, (Winter 2000), 66; https://digitalcommons.library.umaine.edu/cgi/viewcontent.cgi?article=1288&context=mpr.

48. https://www.mnhs.org/foresthistory/learn/timeline.
49. Douglas Brinkley, *The Wilderness Warrior: Theodore Roosevelt and the Crusade for America* (New York: Harper Collins, 2009), 9.
50. Brinkley, *Wilderness Warrior: Theodore Roosevelt*, 10.
51. Brinkley, *Wilderness Warrior: Theodore Roosevelt*, 10.
52. George P. Marsh, *Man and Nature; on Physical Geography as Modified by Human Action* (London: Sampson, Low, Son and Marston), 1864.
53. "Guarding the Adirondacks," *New York Times*, July 5, 1942, section E, 8.
54. Henry David Thoreau, "Walking," *Atlantic* (June 1862); https://www.theatlantic.com/magazine/archive/1862/06/walking/304674/.
55. William Ellsworth Smythe, *The Conquest of Arid America* (New York: Harper & Brothers, 1900).
56. John Muir, "Features of the Proposed Yosemite National Park," *Century Magazine* XL, no. 5 (September 1890); https://vault.sierraclub.org/john_muir_exhibit/writings/features_of_the_proposed_yosemite_national_park.
57. https://vault.sierraclub.org/john_muir_exhibit/about/.
58. Gifford Pinchot, *The Fight for Conservation* (New York: Doubleday, Page, 1910), 48.
59. Brinkley, *The Wilderness Warrior*, 76.
60. Mary C. Rabbitt, *The United States Geological Survey: 1879–1989* (Washington, DC: United States Government Printing Office, 1989), Introduction.
61. Benjamin Harrison, *Public Papers and Addresses of Benjamin Harrison, Twenty-Third President of the United States, March 4, 1889 to March 4, 1893* (Washington, DC: Government Printing Office, 1893), 257.
62. B. Fernow, *Appendix to Report on Forestry Investigations*, U.S. Department of Agriculture, December 1, 1898, 202.
63. Benjamin Harrison, *Proclamation 310: Clarifying the Boundaries of a Public Forest Reservation in Wyoming*, September 10, 1891; https://www.presidency.ucsb.edu/documents/proclamation-310-clarifying-the-boundaries-public-forest-reservation-wyoming.
64. 50th Congress, 2d Session, U.S. House of Representatives, *Bulletin of the United States Fish Commission for 1887*, vol. VII (Washington, DC: Government Printing Office, 1889), 47.
65. "The Executive Documents of the House of Representatives," *United States Congressional Serial Set, Volume 3307* (Washington, DC: Government Printing Office, 1895), 660.
66. Theodore Roosevelt, *An Autobiography of Theodore Roosevelt* (New York: Charles Scribner's Sons, 1913), 9.
67. Roosevelt, *Autobiography of Theodore Roosevelt*, 9.
68. Roosevelt, *Autobiography of Theodore Roosevelt*, 5.
69. Edmund Morris, *The Rise of Theodore Roosevelt* (New York: Random House, 1979), XI.

70. Roosevelt, *Autobiography*, 13.
71. Roosevelt, *Autobiography*, 13.
72. Roosevelt, *Autobiography*, 27.
73. Roosevelt, *Autobiography*, 27.
74. Roosevelt, *Autobiography*, 27.
75. Roosevelt, *Autobiography*, 27.
76. Morris, *Rise of Theodore Roosevelt*, 17.
77. Roosevelt, *Autobiography*, 13.
78. Roosevelt, *Autobiography*, 13.
79. Morris, *Rise of Theodore Roosevelt*, 34.
80. Morris, *Rise of Theodore Roosevelt*, 34.
81. Roosevelt, *Autobiography*, 6.
82. Roosevelt, *Autobiography*, 7.
83. Roosevelt, *Autobiography*, 7.
84. Roosevelt, *Autobiography*, 7.
85. Roosevelt, *Autobiography*, 318.
86. Roosevelt, Theodore, *African Game Trails: An Account of the African Wanderings of an American Hunter-Naturalist*, vol. 1 (New York: Charles Scribner Sons, 1910), ix.
87. Roosevelt, *Autobiography*, 322.
88. Roosevelt, *Autobiography*, 23.
89. Roosevelt, *Autobiography*, 23.
90. Roosevelt, *Autobiography*, 23.
91. Roosevelt, *Autobiography*, 24.
92. Paul Russell Cutright, *Theodore Roosevelt: The Naturalist* (New York: Harper & Brothers, 1956), Preface. xiii.
93. Roosevelt, *Autobiography*, 7.
94. Roosevelt, *Autobiography*, 9.
95. Roosevelt, *Autobiography*, 9.
96. Roosevelt, *Autobiography*, 9.
97. Roosevelt, *Autobiography*, 7.
98. Roosevelt, *Autobiography*, 8.
99. Roosevelt, *Autobiography*, 10.
100. Doris Kearns Goodwin, *Leadership in Turbulent Times* (New York: Simon & Schuster, 2018), 27.
101. Goodwin, *Leadership in Turbulent Times*, 27.
102. Goodwin, *Leadership in Turbulent Times*, 27.
103. Roosevelt, *Autobiography*, 52.
104. Roosevelt, *Autobiography*, 52.
105. Roosevelt, *Autobiography*, 52.
106. Roosevelt, *Autobiography*, 52.

107. Roosevelt, *Autobiography*, 52.
108. Roosevelt, *Autobiography*, 52.
109. Roosevelt, *Autobiography*, 52.
110. Roosevelt, *Autobiography*, 52.
111. Roosevelt, *Autobiography*, 52.
112. Roosevelt, *Autobiography*, 53.
113. Roosevelt, *Autobiography*, 27.
114. Roosevelt, *Autobiography*, 28.
115. Roosevelt, *Autobiography*, 30.
116. Roosevelt, *Autobiography*, 236.
117. Roosevelt, *Autobiography*, 28.
118. Mike Donovan, *The Roosevelt That I Know* (New York: B. W. Dodge, 1909), 9.
119. Roosevelt, *Autobiography*, 45.
120. Roosevelt, *Autobiography*, 45.
121. J. J. Jusserand, *What Me Befell* (London: Constable, 1933), 330.
122. Carol Felsenthal, *Princess Alice: The Life and Times of Alice Roosevelt Longworth* (New York: St. Martin's, 2003), 105.
123. Clara Barrus, *The Life and Letters of John Burroughs* (New York: Houghton Mifflin, 1925), 364.
124. Morris, *Theodore Rex*, 81.
125. Morris, *The Rise of Theodore Roosevelt*, xxx.
126. Roosevelt, *Autobiography*, 22.
127. Doris Kearns Goodwin, *Leadership in Turbulent Times* (New York: Simon & Schuster, 2018), 30.
128. Goodwin, *Leadership in Turbulent Times*, 30.
129. Roosevelt, *Autobiography*, 1.
130. Roosevelt, *Autobiography*, 4.
131. Roosevelt, *Autobiography*, 7.
132. Roosevelt, *Autobiography*, 4.
133. Roosevelt, *Autobiography*, 11.
134. Roosevelt, *Autobiography*, 11.
135. Roosevelt, *Autobiography*, 11.
136. Morris, *The Rise of Theodore Roosevelt*, 6.
137. Morris, *The Rise of Theodore Roosevelt*, 6.
138. Roosevelt, *Autobiography*, 11.
139. Roosevelt, *Autobiography*, 14.
140. Theodore Roosevelt, *Letters from Theodore Roosevelt to Anna Roosevelt Cowles, 1870-1918* (New York: Charles Scribner's Sons, 1924), 261.
141. Roosevelt, *Letters*, 14.
142. Roosevelt, *Letters*, 15.

143. Edward P. Kohn, *A Most Glorious Rise: The Diaries of Theodore Roosevelt, 1877–1886* (Albany: State University of New York Press, 2015), 146.

144. Theodore Roosevelt, *Theodore Roosevelt Papers: Series 8: Personal Diaries, 1878–1884; Vol. 7, 1884*, Feb. 14–Dec. 17, 1884. Manuscript/Mixed Material; https://www.loc.gov/item/mss382990724/.

145. Goodwin, *Leadership in Turbulent Times*, 127.

146. https://www.nps.gov/places/maltese-cross-cabin.htm.

147. Robert Lawrence Wilson and Gregory Curtin Wilson, *Theodore Roosevelt, Outdoorsman* (Madison: University of Wisconsin–Madison, 1971), 53.

148. Franklin and Theodore Roosevelt were fifth cousins.

149. Theodore Roosevelt, *The Works of Theodore Roosevelt*, National Edition, Volume X (New York: Charles Scribner's, 1926), 342.

150. Theodore Roosevelt, *What Roosevelt Says (from the Congressional Record)* (United States, 1904), 25.

151. Gary DeMoss Ursiny and Mark Ybaben, *The Top Performer's Guide to Attitude: Essential Skills That Put You on Top* (Naperville, IL: Sourcebooks, 2008), 54.

152. L. Frank Baum, *The Wonderful Wizard of Oz* (New York: Sterling, 2005), 110.

153. Morris, *Rise of Theodore Roosevelt*, 681.

154. "A Saddening Glimpse at a Closet of Hearts," *Life* 17 (September 1971), 70.

155. George Monteiro, "Hemingway's Notion of "Grace," *Studies in American Fiction* (Johns Hopkins University Press, vol. 18, no. 1 (Spring 1990), 111–12.

156. Roosevelt, *Autobiography*, 62.

157. Theodore Roosevelt, "Address at Milwaukee, Wisconsin," October 14, 1912.

158. Steve Jobs, "Commencement Address," Stanford University, June 12, 2005.

159. Roosevelt, *Autobiography*, 168.

160. Roosevelt, *Autobiography*, 170.

161. Roosevelt, *The Works of Theodore Roosevelt*, vol. 20, 239.

162. Marcus Tullius Cicero, *Cicero's Tusculan Disputations* (New York: Harper & Brothers, 1894), 97.

163. Theodore Roosevelt, *Public Papers of Theodore Roosevelt, Governor 1899–1900* (Albany, NY: Brandow Printing, 1899), 296.

164. Roosevelt, "First Annual Message," December 3, 1901.

165. George Washington, "First Annual Address to Congress," January 8, 1790; https://www.presidency.ucsb.edu/documents/first-annual-address-congress-0.

166. Abraham Lincoln, "First Annual Message," December 3, 1861; https://www.presidency.ucsb.edu/documents/first-annual-message-9.

167. "The Message to Congress," *Washington Times*, December 4, 1901.

168. "Message to Congress."

169. "Message to Congress."
170. "Message to Congress."
171. Roosevelt, "First Annual Message," December 3, 1901.
172. "Message Shows Hands of Master," *Chicago Daily Tribune*, December 4, 1901, 1.
173. "Message Shows Hands."
174. "Message Shows Hands."
175. "Message Shows Hands."
176. "Message Shows Hands."
177. "Message Shows Hands."
178. "Message Shows Hands."
179. "Message Shows Hands."
180. "Message Shows Hands."
181. "Message Shows Hands."
182. "Message Shows Hands."
183. "Message Shows Hands."
184. "Message Shows Hands."
185. "The Message to Congress," *Washington Times*, December 4, 1901.
186. Roosevelt, "First Annual Message," December 3, 1901.
187. Roosevelt, "First Annual Message."
188. "Heard the Message: Congress Attentive to the Words of the President," *Evening Star*, Washington, DC, December 3, 1901.
189. "Senators Deeply Interested," *Washington Times*, December 4, 1901.
190. "Senators Deeply Interested."
191. "Senators Deeply Interested."
192. Roosevelt, "First Annual Message," December 3, 1901.
193. https://www.senate.gov/senators/FeaturedBios/Featured_Bio_Aldrich.htm.
194. "John C. Spooner Dies in City Home," *New York Times*, June 11, 1919.
195. "Congress Listens to President's Message," *New York Times*, December 4, 1901.
196. *Washington Post*, December 4, 1901, 6.
197. *Washington Post*.
198. Roosevelt, "First Annual Message."
199. Roosevelt, "First Annual Message."
200. Roosevelt, "First Annual Message."
201. Roosevelt, "First Annual Message."
202. Roosevelt, "First Annual Message."
203. Roosevelt, "First Annual Message."
204. "Senators Deeply Interested," *Washington Times*, December 4, 1901.
205. "Senators Deeply Interested."
206. "Senators Deeply Interested."

207. "Message Shows Hands of Master," 1.
208. "Message Shows Hands of Master."
209. "Message Shows Hands of Master."
210. Roosevelt, "First Annual Message," December 3, 1901.
211. Roosevelt, "First Annual Message."
212. Roosevelt, "First Annual Message."
213. Roosevelt, "First Annual Message."
214. Roosevelt, "First Annual Message."
215. *Evening Star*, Washington, DC, December 3, 1901.
216. Roosevelt, "First Annual Message."
217. Roosevelt, "First Annual Message."
218. Roosevelt, "First Annual Message."
219. Roosevelt, "First Annual Message."
220. Roosevelt, "First Annual Message."
221. Roosevelt, "First Annual Message."
222. Roosevelt, "First Annual Message."
223. Roosevelt, "First Annual Message."
224. Roosevelt, "First Annual Message."
225. Roosevelt, "First Annual Message."
226. Roosevelt, "First Annual Message."
227. Roosevelt, "First Annual Message."
228. Roosevelt, "First Annual Message."
229. Roosevelt, "First Annual Message."
230. Roosevelt, "First Annual Message."
231. Roosevelt, "First Annual Message."
232. Roosevelt, "First Annual Message."
233. Roosevelt, "First Annual Message."
234. Roosevelt, "First Annual Message."
235. Roosevelt, "First Annual Message."
236. Roosevelt, "First Annual Message."
237. "The Roosevelt Administration," *New York Times*, March 4, 1909, 8.
238. Roosevelt, "First Annual Message.
239. Roosevelt, *Autobiography*, 62.
240. Roosevelt, *Autobiography*, 411.
241. Roosevelt, "First Annual Message."
242. Roosevelt, "First Annual Message."
243. Cutright, *Theodore Roosevelt*, 164–65.
244. Roosevelt, "First Annual Message."
245. Roosevelt, "First Annual Message."
246. Roosevelt, "First Annual Message."
247. Roosevelt, "First Annual Message."
248. Roosevelt, "First Annual Message."
249. Roosevelt, "First Annual Message."

250. Roosevelt, "First Annual Message."
251. Roosevelt, "First Annual Message."
252. Roosevelt, "First Annual Message."
253. Roosevelt, "First Annual Message."
254. Roosevelt, "First Annual Message."
255. Roosevelt, "First Annual Message."
256. Roosevelt, *Autobiography*, 400.
257. Roosevelt, "First Annual Message."
258. Roosevelt, "First Annual Message."
259. Roosevelt, "First Annual Message."
260. "Washington Comment on the Message," *New York Times*, December 4, 1901, 1.
261. Roosevelt, "First Annual Message," December 3, 1901.
262. Roosevelt, "First Annual Message."
263. Roosevelt, "First Annual Message."
264. Roosevelt, "First Annual Message."
265. Roosevelt, "First Annual Message."
266. Roosevelt, "First Annual Message."
267. Roosevelt, "First Annual Message."
268. Roosevelt, "First Annual Message."
269. Roosevelt, "First Annual Message."
270. Roosevelt, "First Annual Message."
271. Roosevelt, "First Annual Message."
272. Roosevelt, "First Annual Message."
273. Roosevelt, "First Annual Message."
274. Roosevelt, "First Annual Message."
275. Roosevelt, "First Annual Message."
276. Roosevelt, "First Annual Message."
277. Roosevelt, "First Annual Message."
278. "Senators Deeply Interested," *Washington Times*, December 4, 1901.
279. "The President's Message: An Able Document," *Minneapolis Tribune*, December 4, 1901.
280. *Washington Post*, December 4, 1901, 1.
281. "Message Shows Hands of Master," 1.
282. "Message Shows Hands of Master," 12.
283. *Washington Post*, December 4, 1901, 1.
284. "President Roosevelt's First Message," *Washington Post*, December 4, 1901, 6.
285. "President Roosevelt's First Message," 6.
286. "Message Shows Hands of Master," 12.
287. "Message Shows Hands of Master," 12.
288. "Message Shows Hands of Master," 12.
289. "Message Shows Hands of Master," 12.

290. "Message Shows Hands of Master," 12.

291. "The Message Praised," *New York Times*, December 4, 1901, 2; "Message Shows Hands of Master," 12.

292. *New York Times*, December 4, 1901, 1.

293. *Chicago Daily Tribune*, December 4, 1901, 12.

294. *The Times of India* (Mumbai), December 4, 1901, 5.

295. *New York Times*, December 5, 1901, 3.

296. *Chicago Daily Tribune*, December 4, 1901, 12.

297. "Message Shows Hands of Master," 12.

298. http://law2.umkc.edu/faculty/projects/ftrials/shipp/lynchingyear.html; six weeks earlier, Roosevelt received an outpouring of condemnation from Southern white politicians and press on the heels of his historic October 16, 1901 White House dinner with Booker T. Washington, for being the first president to entertain a man of color.

299. "Statesmen at White House," *Washington Post*, December 4, 1901, 4.

300. Morris, *Theodore Rex*, 77.

301. Theodore Roosevelt, "Remarks at Grand Canyon, Arizona," May 6, 1903; https://www.presidency.ucsb.edu/documents/remarks-grand-canyon-arizona.

302. Roosevelt, "Remarks at Grand Canyon."

303. https://www.census.gov/data/tables/time-series/dec/popchange-data-text.html.

304. Roosevelt, *Autobiography*, 413.

305. Roosevelt, *Autobiography*, 416.

306. Roosevelt, *Autobiography*, 420.

307. Brinkley, *The Wilderness Warrior*, 19.

308. Doris Kearns Goodwin, *The Bully Pulpit: Theodore Roosevelt, William Howard Taft, and the Golden Age of Journalism* (New York: Simon & Schuster, 2013), 351.

309. Theodore Roosevelt, *Outdoor Pastimes of an American Hunter* (New York: Charles Scribner's, 1905), 317.

310. "The Roosevelt Administration," *New York Times*, March 4, 1909, 8.

311. "The Roosevelt Administration," 8.

312. "The Roosevelt Administration," 8.

313. https://www.nps.gov/thrb/learn/historyculture/trandthenpsystem.htm.

314. Theodore Roosevelt, "The Strenuous Life," Chicago, Illinois, April 10, 1899.

Chapter 5

1. https://prologue.blogs.archives.gov/2019/09/12/john-hancock-and-his-signature/.

2. https://finance.yahoo.com/news/obama-says-confidence-probably-prerequisite-163600167.html.

3. George W. Bush, *Decision Points* (New York: Random House, 2010), 126.

4. https://abcnews.go.com/US/September_11/florida-students-witnessed-moment-bush-learned-911-terror/story?id=14474518.

5. Bush, *Decision Points*, 127.

6. Bush, *Decision Points*, 127.

7. George W. Bush, "Remarks by the President after Two Planes Crashed into World Trade Center," September 11, 2001; https://georgewbush-whitehouse.archives.gov/news/releases/2001/09/20010911.html.

8. Bush, *Decision Points*, 128.

9. George W. Bush, "Address to the Nation on the Terrorist Attacks," Washington, DC, September 11, 2001; https://www.presidency.ucsb.edu/documents/address-the-nation-the-terrorist-attacks.

10. https://georgewbush-whitehouse.archives.gov/911/response/01.html.

11. Bush, *Decision Points*, 151.

12. Bush, *Decision Points*, 151.

13. *Roget's Thesaurus of Words for Intellectuals* (New York: Simon & Schuster, 2011), 174.

14. Jimmy Carter, "Address to the Nation on Energy and National Goals: 'The Malaise Speech,'" July 15, 1979; https://www.presidency.ucsb.edu/documents/address-the-nation-energy-and-national-goals-the-malaise-speech.

15. Alfred Rollins, *Roosevelt and Howe* (New York: Knopf, 1962), 383.

16. Blanche Wiesen Cook, *Eleanor Roosevelt, Volume 2: The Defining Years, 1933–1938* (New York: Penguin Books, 2000), 33.

17. https://archive.nytimes.com/www.nytimes.com/books/first/d/doyle-oval.html.

18. Franklin D. Roosevelt, "The Great Communicator," the Master Speech Files, 1898, 1910–1945, Series 2: "You have nothing to fear but fear itself": FDR and the New Deal file no. 616-1; March 12, 1933; Fireside Chat #1—The Banking Crisis.

19. Roosevelt, "The Great Communicator."

20. Grace Tully, *My Boss* (Chicago: The People's Book Club, 1949), 92.

21. Tully, *My Boss*, 92.

22. Tully, *My Boss*, 92.

23. Tully, *My Boss*, 93.

24. https://www.whitehousehistory.org/the-fireside-chats-roosevelts-radio-talks.

25. https://www.c-span.org/video/?298210-1/president-franklin-roosevelts-fireside-chat.

26. Calvin Coolidge, "Remarks to the American Society of Newspaper Editors in Washington D.C.," January 17, 1925; https://www.presidency.ucsb.edu/documents/address-the-american-society-newspaper-editors-washington-dc.

27. Ben Bernanke, "On Milton Friedman's Ninetieth Birthday," Remarks by Governor Ben S. Bernanke at the Conference to Honor Milton Friedman, University of Chicago, Chicago, IL, November 8, 2002.

28. Cohen, Adam, *Nothing to Fear: FDR's Inner Circle and the Hundred Days That Created Modern America* (New York: Penguin Press, 2009), 15.

29. In Ben Bernanke's Nobel Prize Lecture: "Banking, Credit and Economic Fluctuations" given on December 9, 2022, he noted a 1933 survey looking at twenty-two cities showed the mortgage delinquency rates ranging from 21 to 62 percent of homeowners were behind on their payments.

30. William C. Spragens, *Popular Images of American Presidents* (New York: Greenwood, 1988), 340.

31. Francis Perkins, *The Roosevelt I Knew* (New York: Viking, 1946), 174.

32. Perkins, *The Roosevelt I Knew*, 203.

33. Arthur M. Schlesinger, *Crisis of the Old Order, 1919–1933* (New York: Houghton Mifflin, 1957), 161.

34. Joan Hoff Wilson, *Forgotten Progressive* (New York: Harper Collins, 1975), 274.

35. David Kennedy, *Freedom from Fear: The American People in Depression and War, 1929–1945* (Oxford, UK: Oxford University Press, 2004), 51.

36. Richard Norton Smith and Timothy Walch, "The Ordeal of Herbert Hoover, Part 2," *Prologue Magazine* 36, no. 2 (Summer 2004); https://www.archives.gov/publications/prologue/2004/summer/hoover.

37. Jordan Schwartz, *The Interregnum of Despair* (Urbana: University of Illinois Press, 1970), 116.

38. Robert A. Caro, *The Path to Power: The Years of Lyndon Johnson* (New York: Vintage, 1990), 246.

39. Richard Norton Smith and Timothy Walch, "The Ordeal of Herbert Hoover, Part 2," *Prologue Magazine* 36, no. 2 (Summer 2004); https://www.archives.gov/publications/prologue/2004/summer/hoover-2.html.

40. James MacGregor Burns, *Roosevelt: The Lion and the Fox*, vol. 1 (New York: Harcourt, Brace, 1956), 147.

41. Burns, *Roosevelt*, 162.

42. Burns, *Roosevelt*, 162.

43. Ben Bernanke, "Banking, Credit, and Economic Fluctuations," Nobel Prize Lecture, December 9, 2022.

44. Schwartz, *The Interregnum of Despair*, 110.

45. Eric Goldman, *Rendezvous with Destiny: A History of Modern American Reform* (Chicago: Ivan R. Dee, 2001), 323.

46. Joseph P. Lash, *Eleanor and Franklin: The Story of Their Relationship* (New York: W. W. Norton, 1971), 116.

47. Tully, *My Boss*, 7.

48. Tully, *My Boss*, 7.

49. Jonathan Alter, *The Defining Moment: FDR's Hundred Days and the Triumph of Hope* (New York: Simon & Schuster, 2007), 17.

50. Bernard Asbell, *The F.D.R. Memoirs* (New York: Doubleday, 1973), 24.

51. Smith, *FDR*, 25.

52. Franklin D. Roosevelt, "Inaugural Address," Washington DC, March 4, 1933; https://www.presidency.ucsb.edu/documents/inaugural-address-8.

53. Geoffrey C. Ward and Ken Burns, *The Roosevelts: An Intimate History* (New York: Knopf Doubleday, 2014), 53.

54. Dallek, *Franklin D. Roosevelt*, 30.

55. Tully, *My Boss*, 12.

56. Franklin Roosevelt to his Parents, June 4, 1897.

57. Tully, *My Boss*, 12.

58. Kenneth Davis, *Beckoning of Destiny, 1882–1928: A History* (New York: Putnam, 1972), 62–63, 220–21.

59. Alan Brinkley, "Hoover and Roosevelt: Two Approaches to Leadership," *Profiles in Leadership: Historians on the Elusive Quality of Greatness*, Walter Isaacson, ed. (New York: W. W. Norton, 2010), 451.

60. Jan Pottker, *Sara and Eleanor: The Story of Sara Delano Roosevelt and Her Daughter-in-Law, Eleanor Roosevelt* (New York: St. Martin's, 2005), 156.

61. A. J. Wann, *The President as Chief Administrator: A Study of Franklin D. Roosevelt* (New York: Public Affairs Press, 1968), 34.

62. Cook, *Eleanor Roosevelt*, vol. 2, 29.

63. Perkins, *The Roosevelt I Knew*, 161.

64. Perkins, *The Roosevelt I Knew*, 161.

65. Geoffrey C. Ward, *A First Class Temperament: The Emergence of Franklin Roosevelt, 1905–1928* (New York: Vintage, 2014), xv.

66. Tully, *My Boss*, 2.

67. Jon Meacham, *Franklin and Winston: An Intimate Portrait of an Epic Friendship* (New York: Random House, 2003), xii.

68. Robert H. Ferrell, *Choosing Truman: The Democratic Convention of 1944* (Columbia: University of Missouri Press, 2013), 97.

69. Schlesinger, *Crisis of the Old Order*, 331.

70. James MacGregor Burns, *Roosevelt: The Lion and the Fox* (New York: Harcourt, Brace, 1956).

71. Fred I. Greenstein, *The Presidential Difference: Leadership Style from Roosevelt to Clinton* (New York: The Free Press, 2000), 18; Schlesinger, *Coming of the New Deal*, 538.

72. Smith, *FDR*, xi.

73. Donald A. Ritchie, *Electing FDR: The New Deal Campaign of 1932* (Lawrence: University of Kansas Press, 2007), 87.

74. William E. Leuchtenburg, *The FDR Years: On Roosevelt and His Legacy* (New York: Columbia University Press, 1995), 3–4.

75. Dallek, *Franklin D. Roosevelt*, 31.

76. Franklin D. Roosevelt—"The Great Communicator; The Master Speech Files, 1898, 1910–1945, Series 1: Franklin D. Roosevelt's Political Ascension, file no. 248, June 26, 1924, Speech Nominating Smith, 4; http://www.fdrlibrary.marist.edu/_resources/images/msf/msf00252.

77. Franklin D. Roosevelt—"The Great Communicator; The Master Speech Files, 1898, 1910–1945, Series 1: Franklin D. Roosevelt's Political Ascension, file No. 248, June 26, n1924, Speech Nominating Smith, 13; http://www.fdrlibrary.marist.edu/_resources/images/msf/msf00252.

78. Miriam Greenblatt, *Franklin D. Roosevelt: 32nd President of the United States* (New York: Garrett Educational, 1989), 35.

79. Russell Freedman, *Eleanor Roosevelt: A Life of Discovery* (New York: Turtleback, 1997), 74.

80. Schwartz, *The Interregnum of Despair*, 108.

81. Eleanor Roosevelt, *The Autobiography of Eleanor Roosevelt* (New York: Harper, 1961), 156.

82. Roosevelt, *Autobiography of Eleanor Roosevelt* 156.

83. Raymond Moley, *After Seven Years* (United States: Da Capo, 1972), 147.

84. Moley, *After Seven Years*, 147.

85. William E. Leuchtenburg, "Franklin D. Roosevelt: Life before the Presidency"; https://millercenter.org/president/fdroosevelt/life-before-the-presidency.

86. https://www.nytimes.com/2006/05/07/books/chapters/0507-1st-alter.html.

87. Jean Edward Smith, *FDR* (New York: Random House, 2008), 300.

88. Schlesinger, *Crisis of the Old Order*, 485.

89. Robert Dallek, *Franklin D. Roosevelt: A Political Life* (New York: Penguin Publishing, 2017), 136.

90. Dallek, *Franklin D. Roosevelt*, 136.

91. David A. Norris, "Four Terms with Franklin," *History Magazine* (October/November 2012), 16.

92. https://www.archives.gov/files/social-media/transcripts/transcript-president-roosevelt-inaugurated-39046.pdf.

93. Franklin D. Roosevelt, "Inaugural Address," Washington, DC, 4 March 1933; https://www.presidency.ucsb.edu/documents/inaugural-address-8.

94. Roosevelt, "Inaugural Address."

95. Roosevelt, "Inaugural Address."

96. Roosevelt, "Inaugural Address."

97. Roosevelt, "Inaugural Address."

98. Burns, *Roosevelt: The Lion and the Fox*, 165.

99. *New York Times*, March 5, 1933.

100. Arthur M. Schlesinger Jr., *The Coming of the New Deal* (Boston, MA: Houghton Mifflin, 1958), 2.

101. Schlesinger, *Coming of the New Deal*, 4.
102. Perkins, *The Roosevelt I Knew*, 75.
103. Harold Ickes, *The Secret Diary of Harold L. Ickes: The First Thousand Days, 1933–1936* (New York: Simon and Schuster, 1953), 3.
104. https://www.presidency.ucsb.edu/documents/proclamation-2039-bank-holiday-march-6-9-1933-inclusive.
105. Schlesinger, *The Coming of the New Deal*, 6.
106. Conrad Wirth, *Parks, Politics, and the People* (Norman:: University of Oklahoma Press, 1980), 69.
107. Pledge of Support to the President by the Governors' Conference, March 6, 1933; https://www.presidency.ucsb.edu/documents/pledge-support-from-governors-conference.
108. Schlesinger, *The Coming of the New Deal*, 5–6.
109. Kenneth Sydney Davis, *FDR, The New Deal Years, 1933–1937: A History* (New York: Random House, 1995), 38–39.
110. Raymond Moley, *The First New Deal* (New York: Harcourt, Brace & World, 1966), 191.
111. Perkins, *The Roosevelt I Knew*, 163.
112. Perkins, *The Roosevelt I Knew*, 164.
113. *New York Times*, March 9, 1933.
114. Schlesinger, *The Coming of the New Deal*, 7.
115. *New York Times*, March 10, 1933.
116. Franklin D. Roosevelt, Message to Congress on Resumption of Banking, March 9, 1933;
https://www.presidency.ucsb.edu/documents/message-congress-resumption-banking.
117. Roosevelt, Message to Congress.
118. Roosevelt, Message to Congress.
119. Roosevelt, Message to Congress.
120. Cohen, *Nothing to Fear*, 79.
121. *New York Times*, March 10, 1933.
122. *New York Times*, March 10, 1933.
123. George C. Edwards, *The Strategic President: Persuasion and Opportunity in Presidential Leadership* (Princeton, NJ: Princeton University Press, 2012), 112; *New York Times*, March 10, 1933.
124. Cohen, *Nothing to Fear*, 79.
125. *New York Times*, March 10, 1933.
126. *New York Times*, March 10, 1933.
127. *New York Times*, March 10, 1933.
128. *New York Times*, March 10, 1933.
129. Moley, *The First New Deal*, 339.
130. Moley, *The First New Deal*, 339.

264 | Notes to Chapter 5

131. Charles Michelson, *The Ghost Talks* (New York: G. P. Putnam's, 1944), 56.
132. Michelson, *The Ghost Talks*, 56.
133. Burns, *Roosevelt: The Lion and the Fox*, 140; Michelson, *The Ghost Talks*, 34.
134. Michelson, *The Ghost Talks*, 56.
135. Schlesinger, *The Coming of the New Deal*, 12.
136. Schlesinger, *The Coming of the New Deal*, 12.
137. Lela Stiles Cleveland, *The Man Behind Roosevelt: The Story of Louis McHenry Howe* (New York: World Publishing, 1954), 245.
138. Perkins, *The Roosevelt I Knew*, 72.
139. Perkins, *The Roosevelt I Knew*, 71–72.
140. Perkins, *The Roosevelt I Knew*, 173.
141. Samuel Rosenman, *Working with Roosevelt* (New York: Harper, 1952), 11–12.
142. Franklin D Roosevelt, "The Year of Crisis," *Public Papers of the President of the United States, Volume 2, 1933*, 60.
143. Franklin Roosevelt, "Fireside Chat on Banking," March 12, 1933; https://www.presidency.ucsb.edu/documents/fireside-chat-banking.
144. Perkins, *The Roosevelt I Knew*, 72.
145. Perkins, *The Roosevelt I Knew*, 72.
146. Rosenman, *Working with Roosevelt*, 92.
147. Roosevelt, "Fireside Chat," March 12, 1933.
148. Roosevelt, "Fireside Chat," March 12, 1933.
149. Rexford Guy Tugwell, *The Democratic Roosevelt: A Biography of Franklin D. Roosevelt* (New York: Doubleday, 1957), 273.
150. Alter, *The Defining Moment*, 269.
151. Roosevelt, "Fireside Chat," March 12, 1933.
152. Roosevelt, "Fireside Chat," March 12, 1933.
153. Roosevelt, "Fireside Chat," March 12, 1933.
154. Roosevelt, "Fireside Chat," March 12, 1933.
155. Roosevelt, "Fireside Chat," March 12, 1933.
156. Roosevelt, "Fireside Chat," March 12, 1933.
157. Roosevelt, "Fireside Chat," March 12, 1933.
158. Roosevelt, "Fireside Chat," March 12, 1933.
159. Roosevelt, "Fireside Chat," March 12, 1933.
160. Roosevelt, "Fireside Chat," March 12, 1933.
161. Roosevelt, "Fireside Chat," March 12, 1933.
162. Roosevelt, "Fireside Chat," March 12, 1933.
163. Roosevelt, "Fireside Chat," March 12, 1933.
164. Roosevelt, "Fireside Chat," March 12, 1933.
165. Roosevelt, "Fireside Chat," March 12, 1933.
166. Roosevelt, "Fireside Chat," March 12, 1933.

167. Roosevelt, "Fireside Chat," March 12, 1933.
168. Roosevelt, "Fireside Chat," March 12, 1933.
169. Roosevelt, "Fireside Chat," March 12, 1933.
170. Roosevelt, "Fireside Chat," March 12, 1933.
171. Roosevelt, "Fireside Chat," March 12, 1933.
172. Roosevelt, "Fireside Chat," March 12, 1933.
173. Roosevelt, "Fireside Chat," March 12, 1933.
174. Roosevelt, "Fireside Chat," March 12, 1933.
175. Roosevelt, "Fireside Chat," March 12, 1933.
176. Roosevelt, "Fireside Chat," March 12, 1933.
177. Roosevelt, "Fireside Chat," March 12, 1933.
178. Roosevelt, "Fireside Chat," March 12, 1933.
179. Roosevelt, "Fireside Chat," March 12, 1933.
180. Roosevelt, "Fireside Chat," March 12, 1933.
181. Roosevelt, "Fireside Chat," March 12, 1933.
182. Roosevelt, "Fireside Chat," March 12, 1933.
183. Robert E. Sherwood, *Roosevelt and Hopkins: An Intimate History* (New York: Harper, 1948), 42.
184. Alter, *The Defining Moment*, 271.
185. *New York Times*, March 14, 1933.
186. *Chicago Tribune*, March 14, 1933.
187. Schlesinger, *The Coming of the New Deal*, 13.
188. Moley, *After Seven Years*, 155.
189. Sherwood, *Roosevelt and* Hopkins, 42–43.
190. Sherwood, *Roosevelt and* Hopkins, 42–43.
191. Sherwood, *Roosevelt and* Hopkins, 155.
192. *New York Times*, March 14, 1933.
193. *New York Times*, March 14, 1933.
194. Schlesinger, *The Coming of the New Deal*, 13.
195. Burns, *Roosevelt: The Lion and the Fox*, 68.
196. Lawrence L. Levine and Cornelia R. Levine, *The People and the President: America's Conversation with FDR* (Boston, MA: Beacon Press, 2002), 36.
197. Levine and Levine, *People and the President*, 43–44.
198. Levine and Levine, *People and the President*, 37.
199. *New York Times*, March 14, 1933.
200. Tully, *My Boss*, 88.
201. Amos Kiewe, *FDR's First Fireside Chat: Public Confidence and the Banking Crisis* (College Station: Texas A&M University Press, 2007), 20.
202. Samuel Irving Rosenman and Dorothy Reuben Rosenman, *Presidential Style: Some Giants and a Pygmy in the White House* (United States: Harper & Row, 1976), 335.
203. Rosenman and Rosenman, *Presidential Style*, 335.

204. Franklin Roosevelt, "Fireside Chat," February 23, 1942; https://www.presidency.ucsb.edu/documents/fireside-chat-6.

205. Franklin Roosevelt, "Fireside Chat," February 23, 1942.

206. http://www.fdrlibrary.marist.edu/daybyday/resource/february-1942-3/.

207. http://www.fdrlibrary.marist.edu/daybyday/resource/february-1942-3/.

208. Franklin Roosevelt, "Fireside Chat," February 23, 1942; https://www.presidency.ucsb.edu/documents/fireside-chat-6.

209. http://www.fdrlibrary.marist.edu/daybyday/resource/february-1942-3/.

210. Of note, George C. Edwards III, in *On Deaf Ears*, downplays the significance of Roosevelt's ability to move the public during his first Fireside Chat and his "map" Fireside Chat. Edwards argues: "People were not opposed to looking at maps or participating in aiding the war effort. Nor did they offer much resistance to banking. . . . Roosevelt was moving people in the direction they already wanted to go" (99).

211. Schlesinger, *Crisis of the Old Order*, 485.

212. Greenstein, *The Presidential Difference*, 22.

213. Alter, *The Defining Moment*, 270.

214. Cook, *Eleanor Roosevelt*, vol. 2, 29.

Chapter 6

1. Alexis de Tocqueville, *Democracy in America*, vol. 1 (London: Longman, Green, Longman, and Roberts, 1862), 470.

2. https://www.youtube.com/watch?v=QV9JJmSCiI8.

3. https://www.youtube.com/watch?v=QV9JJmSCiI8.

4. Dwight Eisenhower, "Remarks in Indianapolis at the Columbia Republican Club," October 15, 1954; https://www.presidency.ucsb.edu/documents/remarks-indianapolis-the-columbia-republican-club.

5. Abraham Lincoln, "Inaugural Address," March 4, 1861; https://www.presidency.ucsb.edu/documents/inaugural-address-34.

6. John Quincy Adams, "Diary Entry," June 4, 1819; https://www.masshist.org/publications/jqadiaries/index.php/document/jqadiaries-v31-1819-06-04-p122.

7. Herbert Hoover, "Address to the Chamber of Commerce of the United States," May 1, 1930; https://www.presidency.ucsb.edu/documents/address-the-chamber-commerce-the-united-states.

8. https://trumpwhitehouse.archives.gov/briefings-statements/remarks-president-trump-operation-warp-speed-vaccine-summit/.

9. https://www.mckinsey.com/featured-insights/coronavirus-leading-through-the-crisis/charting-the-path-to-the-next-normal/mind-over-matter-how-the-world-developed-covid-19-vaccines-in-record-time.

10. https://www.reaganfoundation.org/library-museum/permanent-exhibitions/oval-office/.
11. https://www.reaganfoundation.org/ronald-reagan/white-house-diaries/diary-entry-05181987/.
12. Romesh Ratnesar, *A City, A President, and the Speech that Ended the Cold War* (New York: Simon & Schuster, 2009), 2.
13. Peter Robinson, "A Turn of Phrase," *New Criterion* 32, no. 5 (January 2014).
14. Peter Robinson, Peter, *How Ronald Reagan Changed My Life* (New York: HarperCollins, 2003), 100.
15. Robinson, *How Ronald Reagan Changed*, 100.
16. Robinson, *How Ronald Reagan Changed*, 100.
17. Peter Robinson, "Mr. Gorbachev, Open This Gate. Mr. Gorbachev, Tear Down This Wall!" *American History* 38, no. 4 (October 2003).
18. Robinson, "Mr. Gorbachev."
19. Peter Robinson, "Tear Down This Wall: How Top Advisors Opposed Reagan's Challenge to Gorbachev—But Lost," *Prologue Magazine* 39, no. 2 (Summer 2007).
20. Robinson, "Tear Down This Wall."
21. Robinson, "Tear Down This Wall."
22. Andrew Glass, "Bernard Baruch Coins Term 'Cold War,' April 16, 1947," *Politico*, April 16, 2010.
23. National Security Council #68: United States Objectives and Programs for National Security, April 7, 1950; https://irp.fas.org/offdocs/nsc-hst/nsc-68.htm.
24. National Security Council #68.
25. Harry Truman, "Diary Entry," July 17, 1945.
26. https://www.trumanlibrary.gov/photograph-records/63-1456-46a.
27. https://www.trumanlibrary.gov/photograph-records/63-1456-46a.
28. George Kennan, "The Sources of Soviet Conduct," *Foreign Affairs*, July 1, 1947; https://www.foreignaffairs.com/articles/russian-federation/1947-07-01/sources-soviet-conduct.
29. Harry Truman, "Special Message to the Congress on Greece and Turkey: The Truman Doctrine," March 12, 1947; https://www.presidency.ucsb.edu/documents/special-message-the-congress-greece-and-turkey-the-truman-doctrine.
30. Melvyn P. Leffler, *A Preponderance of Power: National Security, the Truman Administration, and the Cold War* (Stanford, MA: Stanford University Press, 1992), 366.
31. John Kennedy, "Inaugural Address," January 20, 1961; https://www.presidency.ucsb.edu/documents/inaugural-address-2.
32. George C. Marshall, "Marshall Plan Speech," June 5, 1947; https://www.oecd.org/general/themarshallplanspeechatharvarduniversity5june1947.htm.

33. Marshall, "Marshall Plan Speech."

34. Winston Churchill, "Iron Curtain Speech," March 5, 1946; https://www.nationalarchives.gov.uk/education/resources/cold-war-on-file/iron-curtain-speech/.

35. Antony Jay, ed. *Lend Me Your Ears: Oxford Dictionary of Political Quotations*, 4th ed. (Oxford, UK: Oxford University Press, 2010), 170; Khrushchev made the statement on November 18, 1956.

36. Harry Truman, "Special Message to the Congress on Greece and Turkey: The Truman Doctrine," March 12, 1947; https://www.presidency.ucsb.edu/documents/special-message-the-congress-greece-and-turkey-the-truman-doctrine.

37. John Kennedy, "Special Message to the Congress on Urgent National Needs," May 25, 1961; https://www.presidency.ucsb.edu/documents/special-message-the-congress-urgent-national-needs.

38. Joseph McCarthy, "Speech to the Women's Republican Club of Wheeling, West Virginia," February 9, 1950.

39. https://www.senate.gov/senators/FeaturedBios/Featured_Bio_McCarthy.htm.

40. https://www.senate.gov/about/powers-procedures//investigations/mccarthy-hearings/have-you-no-sense-of-decency.htm.

41. "New Conference Remarks by Chairman Ulbricht Spelling Out the Consequences of Creating a "Free City" of West Berlin, June 15, 1961," *Documents on Germany, 1944–1970, Committee on Foreign Relations, United States Senate* (Washington: US Government Printing Office, 1971), 531.

42. "East German Border Claimed 327 Lives, Says Berlin Study," *BBC*, June 8, 2017; https://www.bbc.com/news/world-europe-40200305.

43. Ratnesar, *A City, A President, and the Speech*, 5.

44. John Kennedy, "Remarks in the Rudolph Wilde Platz, Berlin," June 26, 1963; https://www.presidency.ucsb.edu/documents/remarks-the-rudolph-wilde-platz-berlin.

45. John Kennedy, "Radio and Television Report to the American People on the Soviet Arms Buildup in Cuba," October 22, 1962; https://www.presidency.ucsb.edu/documents/radio-and-television-report-the-american-people-the-soviet-arms-buildup-cuba.

46. Kennedy, "Radio and Television Report."

47. *New York Times*, December 22, 1994; https://www.nytimes.com/1994/12/22/obituaries/dean-rusk-secretary-of-state-in-vietnam-war-is-dead-at-85.html.

48. Lyndon Johnson, "Remarks in Memorial Hall, Akron University," October 21, 1964; https://www.presidency.ucsb.edu/documents/remarks-memorial-hall-akron-university.

49. Lyndon Johnson, "Address at Johns Hopkins University: 'Peace without Conquest,'" April 7, 1965; https://www.presidency.ucsb.edu/documents/address-johns-hopkins-university-peace-without-conquest.

50. 51. Richard Nixon, February 25, 1972; https://china.usc.edu/richard-nixon-and-zhou-enlai-toasts-banquet-honoring-premier-february-25-1972.

52. Jimmy Carter, "ABC News Interview," December 31, 1979; https://www.cfr.org/blog/history-cold-war-40-quotes.

53. Reagan Ronald, "The President's News Conference," January 29, 1981; https://www.presidency.ucsb.edu/documents/the-presidents-news-conference-992.

54. Ronald Reagan, "Remarks at the Annual Convention of the National Association of Evangelicals in Orlando, Florida," March 8, 1983; https://www.presidency.ucsb.edu/documents/remarks-the-annual-convention-the-national-association-evangelicals-orlando-florida.

55. Ronald Reagan, "Address to the Nation on Defense and National Security," March 23, 1983; https://www.presidency.ucsb.edu/documents/address-the-nation-defense-and-national-security.

56. Gilbert A. Robinson, Gilbert A., "Richard Perle," *Reagan Remembered* (New York: Beaufort Books, 2015).

57. Gilbert A. Robinson, "Edward Rowny," *Reagan Remembered* (New York: Beaufort Books, 2015).

58. Ratnesar, *A City, A President, and the Speech*, 4.

59. Ronald Reagan, *Ronald Reagan: An American Life* (New York: Simon & Schuster, 1990), 683.

60. Peter Hannaford, "Helmut Kohl," *Recollections of Reagan: A Portrait of Ronald Reagan* (New York: William Morrow, 1997), 83.

61. Ronald Reagan, "White House Diary," June 12, 1987; https://www.reaganfoundation.org/ronald-reagan/white-house-diaries/diary-entry-06121987/.

62. Reagan, "White House Diary."

63. Ronald Reagan, "Remarks on the 750th Anniversary of the Founding of Berlin," June 12, 1987; https://www.presidency.ucsb.edu/documents/remarks-the-750th-anniversary-the-founding-berlin.

64. Ronald Reagan, "White House Diary," June 12, 1987; https://www.reaganfoundation.org/ronald-reagan/white-house-diaries/diary-entry-06121987/.

65. Reagan, "White House Diary."

66. Reagan, *An American Life*, 680.

67. Reagan, *An American Life*, 680.

68. Reagan, "White House Diary"; https://www.reaganfoundation.org/ronald-reagan/white-house-diaries/diary-entry-06121987/.

69. "President Reagan's Trip to West Berlin on June 12, 1987," Reagan Library; https://www.youtube.com/watch?v=VJbrRfAdIu0.

70. "President Reagan's Trip to West Berlin."

71. "President Reagan's Trip to West Berlin."

72. "President Reagan's Trip to West Berlin."

73. "Hooded Anarchists Battle Police in Berlin on Eve of Reagan Visit," *Sun Sentinel*, Fort Lauderdale, June 12, 1987, 14A.

74. "24,000 Demonstrators in Berlin against Reagan's Visit Today," *New York Times*, June 12, 1987, A1.

75. "'Tear Down This Wall' Soviets Rip Reagan's Challenge," *Sun Sentinel*, Fort Lauderdale, June 13, 1987, 1A.
76. Reagan, *An American Life*, 680.
77. Reagan, *An American Life*, 680.
78. Reagan, *An American Life*, 680.
79. Reagan, *An American Life*, 681.
80. *Washington Post*, 13 June 1987, A1.
81. Reagan, *An American Life*, 681.
82. Reagan, *An American Life*, 681.
83. Reagan, *An American Life*, 680.
84. Gilbert A. Robinson, "Kenneth M. Duberstein," *Reagan Remembered* (New York: Beaufort Books, 2015).
85. Robinson, "Kenneth M. Duberstein."
86. Gilbert A. Robinson, "Richard V. Allen," *Reagan Remembered* (New York: Beaufort Books, 2015).
87. John H. Fund, "Ronald Reagan's Berlin," *American Spectator* 43, no. 10 (December 2009).
88. Gilbert A. Robinson, "Richard V. Allen," *Reagan Remembered* (New York: Beaufort Books, 2015).
89. Robinson, "Richard V. Allen."
90. Robinson, "Richard V. Allen."
91. Ratnesar, *A City, A President*, and the Speech, 5.
92. Robinson, "Richard V. Allen."
93. Robinson, "Richard V. Allen."
94. Ronald Reagan, "Remarks to the People of Berlin," June 11, 1982; https://www.presidency.ucsb.edu/documents/remarks-the-people-berlin.
95. Reagan, "Remarks to the People of Berlin."
96. "President Reagan at Checkpoint Charlie in West Berlin on June 11, 1982," Reagan Library; https://www.youtube.com/watch?v=vr-4QaBabDw.
97. "President Reagan at Checkpoint."
98. Reagan, *An American Life*, 683.
99. https://www.census.gov/history/pdf/tampico-il-1910.pdf.
100. Reagan, *An American Life*, 23.
101. Anne Edwards, *Early Reagan: The Rise to Power* (Lanham, MD: Taylor Trade, 1987), 34.
102. Reagan, *An American Life*, 21.
103. Reagan, *An American Life*, 21.
104. Reagan, *An American Life*, 21.
105. Reagan, *An American Life*, 22.
106. Reagan, *An American Life*, 23.
107. Reagan, *An American Life*, 21.
108. Reagan, *An American Life*, 21.

109. Reagan, *An American Life*, 30.
110. Reagan, *An American Life*, 30.
111. Reagan, *An American Life*, 30.
112. Reagan, *An American Life*, 33.
113. Reagan, *An American Life*, 33.
114. Reagan, *An American Life*, 22.
115. Reagan, *An American Life*, 22.
116. Reagan, *An American Life*, 21.
117. Beschloss, *Presidential Courage*, 285.
118. Reagan, *An American Life*, 35.
119. Reagan, *An American Life*, 35.
120. Reagan, *An American Life*, 32.
121. Kiron K. Skinner, Annelise Anderson, and Martin Anderson, eds. *Reagan: A Life in Letters* (New York: Free Press, 2003), 6.
122. Reagan, *An American Life*, 40.
123. Reagan, *An American Life*, 23.
124. Reagan, *An American Life*, 25.
125. Reagan, *An American Life*, 25.
126. Reagan, *An American Life*, 25.
127. Reagan, *An American Life*, 25.
128. Reagan, *An American Life*, 25.
129. *Reagan: A Life in Letters*, 6.
130. Reagan, *An American Life*, 6.
131. Reagan, *An American Life*, 7.
132. Reagan, *An American Life*, 31.
133. Reagan, *An American Life*, 32.
134. Reagan, *An American Life*, 32.
135. Lou Cannon, *Governor Reagan: His Rise to Power* (New York: Public Affairs, 2003), 19.
136. Reagan, *An American Life*, 53.
137. Robert Dallek, *Ronald Reagan: The Politics of Symbolism* (Cambridge, MA: Harvard University Press, 1999), 5.
138. Reagan, *An American Life*, 26.
139. *Reagan: A Life in Letters*, 1.
140. Reagan, *An American Life*, 27.
141. Reagan, *An American Life*, 27.
142. Reagan, *An American Life*, 27.
143. Reagan, *An American Life*, 27.
144. Lou Cannon, *His Rise to Power*, 30.
145. Reagan, *An American Life*, 28.
146. Reagan, *An American Life*, 29.
147. Reagan, *An American Life*, 29.

148. Reagan, *An American Life*, 29.
149. Reagan, *An American Life*, 40.
150. Reagan, *An American Life*, 40.
151. Reagan, *An American Life*, 31.
152. Reagan, *An American Life*, 31.
153. Reagan, *An American Life*, 31.
154. Reagan, *An American Life*, 31.
155. Reagan, *An American Life*, 29.
156. Ron Reagan, *My Father at 100* (London: Penguin, 2011), 7.
157. Edwin Meese III, *Reagan: The Inside Story* (New York: Regnery, 1992), 63–64 of 546, chapter 2 (Kindle edition).
158. Gilbert A. Robinson, "George H. W. Bush," *Reagan Remembered* (New York: Beaufort Books, 2015).
159. Nancy Reagan, "The Eternal Optimist: Ronald Wilson Reagan (1911–2004)," *Time Magazine*, June 14, 2004.
160. Hugh Heclo, "The Mixed Legacies of Ronald Reagan," *The Enduring Reagan*, ed. Charles W. Dunn (Lexington: University Press of Kentucky, 2009), 17–39.
161. Stephen Knott, "Mr. Reagan Goes to Washington." *The Enduring Reagan*, ed. Charles W. Dunn (Lexington: University of Kentucky Press, 2009), 88.
162. Reagan, *An American Life*, 31.
163. Reagan, *My Father at 100*, 7.
164. Reagan, *My Father at 100*, 7.
165. Edmund Morris, *Dutch: A Memoir of Ronald Reagan* (New York: Random House, 1999), 11.
166. Lou Cannon, *President Reagan: The Role of a Lifetime* (New York: Public Affairs, 1991), 19.
167. Nancy Reagan, with William Novak, *My Turn: The Memoirs of Nancy Reagan* (New York: Random House, 1989), 106.
168. Reagan, *An American Life*, 39.
169. Reagan, *An American Life*, 34.
170. Reagan, *An American Life*, 34.
171. Reagan, *An American Life*, 45.
172. Reagan, *An American Life*, 45.
173. Reagan, *An American Life*, 46.
174. Reagan, *An American Life*, 41.
175. Reagan, *An American Life*, 58.
176. Garry Wills, *Reagan's America: Innocents at Home* (New York: Doubleday, 1987), 29.
177. *Washington Post*, October 24, 1999, B07.
178. Beschloss, *Presidential Courage*, 323.

179. Reagan, *An American Life*, 48.
180. Ronald Reagan, "Remarks at Eureka College," February 6, 1984; https://www.presidency.ucsb.edu/documents/remarks-eureka-college-eureka-illinois.
181. *Reagan: A Life in Letters*, 1; Cannon, *His Rise to Power*, 34.
182. *Reagan: A Life in Letters*, 1.
183. Garry Wills, "It's His Party," *New York Times*, August 11, 1996, SM30.
184. Cannon, *The Role of a Lifetime*, 226.
185. Cannon, *The Role of a Lifetime*, 226.
186. Eric J. Schmertz, Natalie Datlof, and Alexej Ugrinsky, ed., *Ronald Reagan's America*, vol. 2 (Westport, CT: Greenwood Press, 1997), 535.
187. Richard Reeves, *President Reagan: The Triumph of Imagination* (New York: Simon & Schuster, 2005), xvi.
188. Gilbert A. Robinson, "David R. Gergen," *Reagan Remembered* (New York: Beaufort Books, 2015).
189. W. Elliot Brownlee and Hugh Davis Graham, eds., *The Reagan Presidency: Pragmatic Conservatism and It's Legacies* (Lawrence: University Press of Kansas, 2000), 357.
190. Reagan, *An American Life*, 219.
191. https://time.com/3752477/reagan-assassination-reaction/.
192. Gilbert A. Robinson, "Aram Bakshian, Jr.," *Reagan Remembered* (New York: Beaufort Books, 2015).
193. Gergen, *Eyewitness to Power*, 176.
194. H. W. Brands, *Reagan: The Life* (New York: Anchor Books, 2015), 487.
195. *New York Times*, August 11, 1996, SM30.
196. Ronald Reagan, "Speech at 1992 Republican National Convention," August 17, 1992.
197. Ronald Reagan, "Address before a Joint Session of the Congress on the State of the Union. January 25, 1984; https://www.presidency.ucsb.edu/documents/address-before-joint-session-the-congress-the-state-the-union-4.
198. *New York Times*, May 8, 2016, BU.5.
199. Bob Spitz, *Reagan: An American Journey* (New York: Penguin Books, 2018), 760.
200. Cannon, *The Role of a Lifetime*, 226.
201. Ronald Reagan, "Address to the Nation on the Explosion of the Space Shuttle Challenger," January 28, 1986; https://www.presidency.ucsb.edu/documents/address-the-nation-the-explosion-the-space-shuttle-challenger.
202. Cannon, *The Role of a Lifetime*, 19.
203. Thomas Jefferson to Pierre Samuel Du Pont De Nemours, March 2, 1809; https://founders.archives.gov/documents/Jefferson/99-01-02-9936.
204. https://www.reaganlibrary.gov/reagans/ronald-reagan/reagans-letter-announcing-his-alzheimers-diagnosis.

205. Peggy Grande, *The President Will See You Now: A Memoir: My Stories and Lessons from Ronald Reagan's Final Years* (New York: Hachette Books, 2017), chapter 17, 227–28 (Kindle edition).
206. https://www.reaganfoundation.org/library-museum/permanent-exhibitions/memorial/.
207. Reagan, *My Father at 100*, 7.
208. Ronald Reagan, "Remarks at the Annual Convention of the National Association of Evangelicals in Orlando, Florida," March 8, 1983; https://www.presidency.ucsb.edu/documents/remarks-the-annual-convention-the-national-association-evangelicals-orlando-florida.
209. Robinson, *How Ronald Reagan*, 95.
210. Robinson, *How Ronald Reagan*, 95.
211. *National Public Radio's Weekend Edition*, July 11, 1999.
212. Brands, *The Life*, 2015, chapter 104, 1113–14 (Kindle edition).
213. John Lewis Gaddis, *The Cold War: A New History* (New York: Penguin, 2005), 235.
214. Robinson, "A Turn of Phrase," January 2014.
215. Robinson, "A Turn of Phrase."
216. Robert C. Rowland and John M. Jones, "Reagan at the Brandenburg Gate: Moral Clarity Tempered by Pragmatism," *Rhetoric & Public Affairs* 9, no. 1 (Spring 2006).
217. Rowland and Jones, "Reagan at the Brandenburg Gate.
218. Rowland and Jones, "Reagan at the Brandenburg Gate.
219. *Philadelphia Inquirer*, June 13, 1987, A.1.
220. "Tear Down Berlin Wall, Reagan Asks: Challenge Issued to Soviet Leader in Divided City," *Los Angeles Times*, June 13, 1987, 1.
221. Robinson, *How Ronald Reagan*, 96.
222. Robinson, *How Ronald Reagan*, 96.
223. Robinson, *How Ronald Reagan*, 96.
224. Robinson, "A Turn of Phrase."
225. Robinson, *How Ronald Reagan*, 97.
226. Robinson, *How Ronald Reagan*, 97.
227. Robinson, "A Turn of Phrase."
228. Robinson, "A Turn of Phrase."
229. Robinson, "A Turn of Phrase."
230. Gilbert A. Robinson, "Anthony R. Dolan," *Reagan Remembered* (New York: Beaufort Books, 2015).
231. Robinson, "Anthony R. Dolan."
232. Ratnesar, *A City, A President, and the Speech*, 6.
233. Robinson, *How Ronald Reagan*, 98.
234. Robinson, *How Ronald Reagan*, 98.
235. Robinson, "A Turn of Phrase."

236. Robinson, "A Turn of Phrase."
237. Robinson, "Anthony R. Dolan."
238. Robinson, "Mr. Gorbachev, Open This Gate," October 2003.
239. *Fox on the Record*, June 6, 2002, Lexis-Nexis.
240. Reeves, *The Triumph of Imagination*, 400.
241. Jennifer Hickey, "A Speech Heard 'Round the World," *Insight on the News*, November 29, 1999, 14.
242. Robinson, "Tear Down This Wall," Summer 2007.
243. Robinson, "Tear Down This Wall."
244. Peter W. Rodman to Colin L. Powell, "Today's Meeting with Griscom: Berlin Speech, June 2, 1987; NSC#8704216.
245. Hickey, "A Speech Heard," 14.
246. Peter Robinson, "Draft of Presidential Address: Brandenburg Gate, May 21, 1987, Speechwriting, WHO OF, Research Office Records, Ronald Reagan Library.
247. Peter Robinson, "Draft of Presidential Address: Brandenburg Gate, May 29, 1987, ID #501963, WHORM: Subject File, Ronald Reagan Library, 5.
248. Peter Robinson, "Draft of Presidential Address: Brandenburg Gate, June 1, 1987, ID #501964, WHORM: Subject File, Ronald Reagan Library, 5.
249. Robinson, "Mr. Gorbachev, Open This Gate," October 2003.
250. Robinson, "Mr. Gorbachev, Open This Gate."
251. Robinson, "Mr. Gorbachev, Open This Gate."
252. Brands, *The Life*, 2015, chapter 104, 1113–14 of 1462 (Kindle edition).
253. Robinson, "Mr. Gorbachev, Open This Gate."
254. Robinson, "Tear Down This Wall."
255. Beschloss, *Presidential Courage*, 315.
256. Robinson, "A Turn of Phrase."
257. Robinson, "Mr. Gorbachev, Open This Gate."
258. Robinson, "A Turn of Phrase."
259. Robinson, "Anthony R. Dolan."
260. Robinson, "Anthony R. Dolan,"
261. Robinson, "Anthony R. Dolan."
262. Robinson, "Anthony R. Dolan."
263. Robinson, "Mr. Gorbachev, Open This Gate."
264. Memo from William Henkel to General Colin Powell, May 28, 1987; NSC #8704162.
265. Robinson, *How Ronald Reagan*, 103.
266. *Boston Globe*, June 13, 1987, 1.
267. *Philadelphia Inquirer*, June 13, 1987, A1.
268. *Philadelphia Inquirer*, June 13, 1987, A1.
269. *Chicago Tribune*, June 13, 1987, 1.
270. *Los Angeles Times*, June 13, 1987, 1.
271. *Chicago Tribune*, June 13, 1987, 1.

272. *Chicago Tribune*, June 13, 1987, 1.
273. *Philadelphia Inquirer*, June 13, 1987, A1.
274. *Boston Globe*, June 13, 1987, 1.
275. June Seventeenth Street commemorated a 1953 anti-Soviet uprising in East Berlin; *Los Angeles Times*, June 13, 1987, 1.
276. *Philadelphia Inquirer*, June 13, 1987, A1.
277. Ronald Reagan, "Remarks on East-West Relations at the Brandenburg Gate in West Berlin," June 12, 1987; https://www.presidency.ucsb.edu/documents/remarks-east-west-relations-the-brandenburg-gate-west-berlin.
278. Reagan, "Remarks on East-West Relations."
279. *Philadelphia Inquirer*, June 13, 1987, A1; *New York Times*, June 13, 1987, 1:3.
280. John Kennedy, "Remarks in the Rudolf Wilde Platz, Berlin," June 26, 1963; https://www.presidency.ucsb.edu/documents/remarks-the-rudolph-wilde-platz-berlin.
281. Richard Nixon, "Remarks on Arrival at Tempelhof Airport in West Berlin," February 27, 1969; https://www.presidency.ucsb.edu/documents/remarks-arrival-tempelhof-airport-west-berlin.
282. Jimmy Carter, "Berlin, Federal Republic of Germany Remarks at a Wreathlaying Ceremony at the Airlift Memorial," July 15, 1978; https://www.presidency.ucsb.edu/documents/berlin-federal-republic-germany-remarks-wreath-laying-ceremony-the-airlift-memorial.
283. Carter, "Berlin, Federal Republic."
284. Carter, "Berlin, Federal Republic."
285. Ronald Reagan, "Remarks on East-West Relations at the Brandenburg Gate in West Berlin," June 12, 1987.
286. Beschloss, *Presidential Courage*, 315; Cannon, *The Role of a Lifetime*, 774.
287. *Washington Post*, June 13, 1987, A1.
288. *Los Angeles Times*, June 13, 1987, 1.
289. *Washington Post*, June 13, 1987, A1.
290. Ronald Reagan, "Remarks on East-West Relations at the Brandenburg Gate in West Berlin," June 12, 1987.
291. Reagan, "Remarks on East-West Relations."
292. Reagan, "Remarks on East-West Relations."
293. Reagan, "Remarks on East-West Relations."
294. Reagan, "Remarks on East-West Relations."
295. Reagan, "Remarks on East-West Relations."
296. Reagan, "Remarks on East-West Relations."
297. Reagan, "Remarks on East-West Relations."
298. Reagan, "Remarks on East-West Relations."
299. Reagan, "Remarks on East-West Relations."
300. Reagan, "Remarks on East-West Relations."

301. Reagan, "Remarks on East-West Relations."
302. Reagan, "Remarks on East-West Relations."
303. Reagan, "Remarks on East-West Relations."
304. Reagan, "Remarks on East-West Relations."
305. Reagan, "Remarks on East-West Relations."
306. Reagan, *An American Life*, 683.
307. Reagan, *An American Life*, 683.
308. Ronald Reagan, "Remarks on East-West Relations at the Brandenburg Gate in West Berlin," June 12, 1987.
309. Bret Baier, with Catherine Whitney, *Three Days in Moscow: Ronald Reagan and the Fall of the Soviet Empire* (New York: HarperCollins, 2018), 242 (Kindle Edition).
310. Bob Spitz, *Reagan: An American Journey* (New York: Penguin Random House, 2018), 1,155 (Kindle Edition).
311. Ronald Reagan, "Remarks on East-West Relations."
312. Reagan, "Remarks on East-West Relations."
313. Reagan, "Remarks on East-West Relations."
314. Reagan, "Remarks on East-West Relations."
315. Reagan, "Remarks on East-West Relations."
316. Reagan, "Remarks on East-West Relations."
317. Reagan, "Remarks on East-West Relations."
318. Reagan, "Remarks on East-West Relations."
319. Reagan, "Remarks on East-West Relations."
320. Reagan, "Remarks on East-West Relations."
321. Reagan, "Remarks on East-West Relations."
322. Reagan, "Remarks on East-West Relations."
323. Reagan, "Remarks on East-West Relations."
324. Reagan, "Remarks on East-West Relations."
325. Reagan, "Remarks on East-West Relations."
326. Reagan, "Remarks on East-West Relations."
327. Reagan, "Remarks on East-West Relations."
328. Reagan, "Remarks on East-West Relations."
329. Reagan, "Remarks on East-West Relations."
330. *Los Angeles Times*, June 13, 1987, 1.
331. Ronald, "Remarks on East-West Relations."
332. Reagan, "Remarks on East-West Relations."
333. Reagan, "Remarks on East-West Relations."
334. *Philadelphia Inquirer*, June 13, 1987, A1.
335. *Chicago Tribune*, June 13, 1987, 1.
336. *Los Angeles Times*, June 13, 1987, 1.
337. *Washington Post*, June 12, 1987, 1.
338. *Washington Post*, June 13, 1987, 1.

339. Peter Robinson, *Wall Street Journal (Online)*, June 8, 2012.
340. Philadelphia Inquirer, June 14, 1987, E:6.
341. Fund, "Ronald Reagan's Berlin," December 2009.
342. Gaddis, *The Cold War*, 235.
343. Reeves, *The Triumph of Imagination*, 2005, 401 (Kindle edition).
344. Morris, *Dutch*, 624.
345. *Chicago Tribune*, June 13, 1987, 1.
346. *Los Angeles Times*, June 13, 1987, 1.
347. *Newsday*, June 14, 1987, 13.
348. *Los Angeles Times*, June 14, 1987, 5.
349. Peter Robinson, *Wall Street Journal (Online)*, June 8, 2012.
350. "Helmut Kohl," *Recollections of Reagan*, 83–84.
351. Fund, "Ronald Reagan's Berlin."
352. *New York Times*, June 6, 2004, 1:1.
353. Reagan, *An American Life*, 708.
354. Wills, *Reagan's America*, Introduction, 2017 edition.
355. James C. Humes, *The Reagan Persuasion: Charm, Inspire, and Deliver* (Naperville, IL: Sourcebooks, 2010), 1.
356. Wills, *Reagan's America*, Introduction, 2017 ed.
357. Wills, *Reagan's America*, Introduction.
358. George H. W. Bush, "Address before a Joint Session of the Congress on the State of the Union," January 28, 1992; https://www.presidency.ucsb.edu/documents/address-before-joint-session-the-congress-the-state-the-union-0.
359. Nancy Reagan, "The Eternal Optimist," June 14, 2004.
360. Nancy Reagan, "The Eternal Optimist."
361. Gilbert A. Robinson, "Richard V. Allen."
362. Ratnesar, *A City, A President, and the Speech*, 10.
363. *Ronald Reagan: 100 Years*.
364. Peter Robinson, *Wall Street Journal (Online)*, June 8, 2012.
365. Schmertz, Datlof, and Ugrinsky, eds., *Ronald Reagan's America*, 9.
366. Garry Wills, "It's His Party."
367. Dunn, *The Enduring Reagan*, 5.
368. Dunn, *The Enduring Reagan*, 97.
369. Peter Baker and Susan Glasser, *The Man Who Ran Washington: The Life and Times of James A. Baker III* (New York: Anchor Books, 2020), 360.
370. Gaddis, *The Cold War*, 236.
371. *New York Times*, June 12, 2012, A.25.
372. Wills, "It's His Party."
373. Reagan, *An American Life*, 681.
374. https://www.reaganfoundation.org/ronald-reagan/white-house-diaries/diary-entry-06121987/.

375. Reagan, "Remarks on East-West Relations at the Brandenburg Gate in West Berlin," June 12, 1987.
376. *Weekend Edition*, July 11, 1999.
377. Robinson, "Richard V. Allen," *Reagan Remembered*.
378. George P. Shultz, *Memorial Services in the Congress of the United States and Tributes in Eulogy of Ronald Reagan Late a President of the United States* (Washington: US Government Printing Office, 2005), 3.
379. Cannon, *The Role of a Lifetime*, 26.
380. Cannon, *The Role of a Lifetime*, 11.
381. Cannon, *The Role of a Lifetime*, 11.
382. Jeffrey L. Chidester and Paul Kengor, eds., *Reagan's Legacy in a World Transformed* (Cambridge, MA: Harvard University Press, 2015), 53.
383. *A Life in Letters*, George Shultz Introduction.
384. William Taubman, *Gorbachev: His Life and Times* (New York: W. W. Norton, 2017).
385. Melvyn P. Leffler, *For the Soul of Mankind: The United States, The Soviet Union, and The Cold War* (New York: Hill and Wang, 2007), 422.
386. Leffler, *For the Soul of Mankind*, 422.
387. Winston Groom, *Ronald Reagan: Our 40th President* (Washington, DC: Regenery, 2012), 187–88 (Kindle edition).
388. Ronald Reagan, "Remarks to the Reagan Administration Executive Forum," January 20, 1982; https://www.presidency.ucsb.edu/documents/remarks-the-reagan-administration-executive-forum-1.
389. Reagan, "Remarks to the Reagan Administration."
390. Reagan, "Remarks to the Reagan Administration."
391. Reagan, "Remarks to the Reagan Administration."
392. Reagan, "Remarks to the Reagan Administration."
393. Reagan, "Remarks to the Reagan Administration."
394. Reagan, "Remarks to the Reagan Administration."
395. Reagan, "Remarks to the Reagan Administration."
396. Reagan, "Remarks to the Reagan Administration."
397. https://www.reaganlegacyfoundation.org/letter-michael-reagan/.

Epilogue

1. https://nypost.com/2022/07/05/fewer-than-1-in-4-americans-still-confident-in-presidency-poll/.
2. Landy and Milkis, *Presidential Greatness*, 70.
3. Barack Obama, "Eulogy at the Funeral Service for Pastor Clementa C. Pinckney of the Emanual African Methodist Episcopal Church in Charleston, South

Carolina, June 26, 2015; https://www.presidency.ucsb.edu/documents/eulogy-the-funeral-service-for-pastor-clementa-c-pinckney-the-emanuel-african-methodist.

4. George H. W. Bush, "Address to the Nation on the Suspension of Allied Offensive Combat Operations in the Persian Gulf, February 27, 1991; https://www.presidency.ucsb.edu/documents/address-the-nation-the-suspension-allied-offensive-combat-operations-the-persian-gulf.

5. Harry S. Truman, *The Memoirs of Harry S. Truman: A Reader's Edition* (Columbia: University of Missouri Press, 2019), 109.

Bibliography

Books Consulted

Adams, Henry, *History of the United States: From the Discovery of the Continent, Volume 2*. New York: Charles C. Little and James Brown, 1940.

———, *History of the United States of American during the Administrations of Thomas Jefferson*. New York: Library of American Edition, 1986.

Adams, John, *Diary and Autobiography of John Adams*, ed. L. H. Butterfield. Cambridge, MA: Harvard University Press, 1961.

Adams, John Quincy, and Charles Francis Adams, ed., *Memoirs of John Quincy Adams, Comprising Portions of his Diary from 1795 to 1848*. Philadelphia, PA: J. B. Lippincott, 1874.

Adams, John Quincy, and Allan Nevins, eds., *The Diary of John Quincy Adams, 1794–1845: American Political, Social and Intellectual Life from Washington to Polk*. London: Longmans, Green and Company, 1928.

Alter, Jonathan, *The Defining Moment: FDR's Hundred Days and the Triumph of Hope*. New York: Simon & Schuster, 2007.

Alsop, Joseph, and Turner Catledge, *The 168 Days*. New York: Doubleday and Doran, 1938.

Ambrose, Stephen, *Undaunted Courage: Meriwether Lewis, Thomas Jefferson, and the Opening of the American West*. New York: Simon & Schuster, 1996.

Asbell, Bernard, *The F.D.R. Memoirs*. New York: Doubleday, 1973.

Baier, Bret with Catherine Whitney, *Three Days in Moscow: Ronald Reagan and the Fall of the Soviet Empire*. New York: HarperCollins, 2018.

Baker, Peter, and Susan Glasser, *The Man Who Ran Washington: The Life and Times of James A. Baker III*. New York: Anchor Books, 2020.

Barber, James, *The Presidential Character: Predicting Performance in the White House*. New York: Prentice Hall, 1972.

Baringer, William, *Lincoln's Rise to Power*. New York: Scholarly Press, 1971.

Barrett, Joseph H., *Abraham Lincoln and His Presidency, Volume 2*. New York: D. Appleton, 1924.

Barrus, Clara, *The Life and Letters of John Burroughs*. New York: Houghton Mifflin, 1925.

Baum, L. Frank, *The Wonderful Wizard of Oz*. New York: Sterling, 2005.

Beschloss, Michael, *Presidential Courage: Brave Leaders and How They Changed America, 1789–1989*. New York: Simon & Schuster, 2008.

Boritt, Gabor, *The Gettysburg Gospel: The Lincoln Speech That Nobody Knows*. New York: Simon & Schuster, 2008.

Bowden, Scott, and Bill Ward, *Last Chance for Victory: Robert E. Lee and the Gettysburg Campaign*. Cambridge, MA: De Capo Press, 2001.

Boyd, Herb, *Martin Luther, Jr.* New York: Baronet Books, 2006.

Brands, H. W., *Reagan: The Life*. New York: Anchor Books, 2015.

Brandt, Irving, *James Madison: Secretary of State, 1800–1909, Volume 4*. Indianapolis, IN: Bobbs-Merrill, 1941.

Brinkley, Douglas, *The Wilderness Warrior: Theodore Roosevelt and the Crusade for America*. New York: Harper Collins, 2009.

Brodie, Fawn McKay, *Thomas Jefferson: An Intimate History*. New York: W. W. Norton, 1974.

Brookhiser, Richard, *George Washington on Leadership*. New York: Basic Books, 2009.

———, *Founders' Son: A Life of Abraham Lincoln*. New York: Basic Books, 2014.

Bulletin of the United States Fish Commission for 1887, vol. VII. Washington, DC: Government Printing Office, 1889.

Brownlee, W. Elliot, and Hugh Davis Graham, eds., *The Reagan Presidency: Pragmatic Conservatism and It's Legacies*. Lawrence: University Press of Kansas, 2000.

Burlingame, Michael, *Abraham Lincoln: A Life, Volume 1*. Baltimore, MD: Johns Hopkins University Press, 2013.

———, *Abraham Lincoln: A Life, Volume 2*. Baltimore, MD: Johns Hopkins University Press, 2013.

Burns, James MacGregor, *Roosevelt: The Lion and the Fox, Volume 1*. New York: Harcourt, Brace, 1956.

Bush, George W., *Decision Points*. New York: Random House, 2010.

Bynum, W. F., and Roy Porter, ed., *Oxford Dictionary of Scientific Quotations*. Oxford, UK: Oxford University Press, 2005.

Cannon, Lou, *President Reagan: The Role of a Lifetime*. New York: Public Affairs, 1991.

———, *Governor Reagan: His Rise to Power*. New York: Public Affairs, 2003.

———, *President Reagan: The Role of a Lifetime*. New York: Public Affairs, 2008.

Caro, Robert A., *The Path to Power: The Years of Lyndon Johnson*. New York: Vintage Books, 1990.

Chernow, Ron, *Washington: A Life*. New York: Penguin, 2010.

Chidester, Jeffrey L., and Paul Kengor, eds., *Reagan's Legacy in a World Transformed*. Cambridge, MA: Harvard University Press, 2015.

Cicero, Marcus Tullius, *Cicero's Tusculan Disputations*. New York: Harper & Brothers, 1894.

Claypoole, David C., "Certification of David C. Claypoole, *Memoirs of Historical Society of Pennsylvania* 1 (February 22, 1826).

Cleveland, Lela Stiles, *The Man behind Roosevelt: The Story of Louis McHenry Howe*. New York: World Publishing, 1954.

Cohen, Adam, *Nothing to Fear: FDR's Inner Circle and the Hundred Days That Created Modern America*. New York: Penguin Press, 2009.

Coffin, Charles Carleton, *Abraham Lincoln (Life of Lincoln)*. New York: Harper and Brothers, 1893.

Cole, Donald B., and John J. McDonough, eds., *Witness to the Young Republic: A Yankee's Journal, 1828–1870*, "Benjamin B. French Diary, 18 February 1863." Hanover, NH: University of New England, 1989.

Coleman, Nannie McCormick, *The Constitution and Its Framers*. Chicago, IL: Progress, 1910.

Coleridge, Edward P., *The Plays of Euripides*. London: George Bell, 1906.

Cook, Blanche Wiesen, *Eleanor Roosevelt, Volume 2: The Defining Years, 1933–1938*. New York: Penguin Books, 2000.

Conant, Sean, *The Gettysburg Address: Perspectives on Lincoln's Greatest Speech*. London: Oxford University Press, 2015.

Cronin, Thomas E., and Michael A. Genovese, *The Paradoxes of the American Presidency*, 2nd ed. Oxford, UK: Oxford University Press, 2004.

Curtis, William Eleroy, *The True Abraham Lincoln*. Philadelphia, PA: J. B. Lippincott, 1905.

Cutright, Paul Russell, *Theodore Roosevelt: The Naturalist*. New York: Harper & Brothers, 1956.

Dallek, Robert, *Ronald Reagan: The Politics of Symbolism*. Cambridge, MA: Harvard University Press, 1999.

———, *Franklin D. Roosevelt: A Political Life*. New York: Penguin, 2017.

Davis, Kenneth, *Beckoning of Destiny, 1882–1928: A History*. New York: Putnam, 1972.

Davis, Kenneth Sydney, *FDR, The New Deal Years, 1933–1937: A History*. New York: Random House, 1995.

De Tocqueville, Alexis, *Democracy in America, Volume 1*. London: Longman, Green, Longman, and Roberts, 1862.

Dodge, Daniel Kilham, *Abraham Lincoln: Master of Words*. New York: D. Appleton, 1924.

Donald, David Herbert, *Lincoln*. New York: Simon & Schuster, 1996.

Donovan, Mike, *The Roosevelt That I Know*. New York: B. W. Dodge, 1909.

Dunn, Charles W., ed., *The Enduring Reagan*. Lexington: University of Kentucky Press, 2009.
Edwards, Anne, *Early Reagan: The Rise to Power*. Lanham, MD: Taylor Trade, 1987.
Edwards III, George C., *On Deaf Ears: The Limits of the Bully Pulpit*. New Haven, CT: Yale University Press, 2003.
———, George C., *The Strategic President: Persuasion and Opportunity in Presidential Leadership*. Princeton, NJ: Princeton University Press, 2012.
Eisenhower, Dwight, *Public Papers of the President, Dwight D. Eisenhower: 1954: Containing the Public Messages, Speeches, and Statements of the President, January 1 to December 31, 1954*. Washington, DC: Office of the Federal Register, National Archives and Records Service, General Services Administration, 1960.
Elkins, Stanley M., and Eric L. McKitrick, *The Age of Federalism: The Early American Republic 1788–1800*. New York: Oxford University Press, 1993.
Ellis, Joseph, *Founding Brother: The Revolutionary Generation*. New York, Vintage, 2003.
———, *His Excellency: George Washington*. New York: Alfred A. Knopf, 2004.
———, *American Creation: Triumphs and Tragedies at the Founding of the Republic*. New York: Vintage, 2007.
Ellis, Richard J., and Michael Nelson, eds., *Debating the Presidency: Conflicting Perspective on the American Executive*, 5th ed. Thousand Oaks, CA: Sage, 2021.
Felsenthal, Carol, *Princess Alice: The Life and Times of Alice Roosevelt Longworth*. New York: St. Martin's, 2003.
Ferling, John E., *Almost a Miracle: The American Victory in the War of Independence*. New York: Oxford University Press, 2009.
———, *The Ascent of George Washington: The Hidden Political Genius of an American Icon*. New York: Bloomsbury Press, 2009.
———, *The First of Men: A Life of George Washington*. London: Oxford University Press, 2010.
Fernow, B., *Appendix to Report on Forestry Investigations*, US Department of Agriculture, December 1, 1898.
Ferrell, Robert H., *Choosing Truman: The Democratic Convention of 1944*. Columbia: University of Missouri Press, 2013.
Fishman, Ethan M, William D. Pederson, Mark J. Rozell, *George Washington: Foundation of Presidential Leadership and Character*. New York: Praeger, 2001.
Fleming, Thomas, *The Perils of Peace*. New York, Collins, 2007.
———, *Washington and the New Nation: 1783–1793*. New York: Little, Brown, 1970.
———, *Washington: The Indispensable Man*. Boston: Little, Brown, 1974.
Foner, Philip Sheldon, ed., *The Complete Writing of Thomas Paine, Volume 1*. CreateSpace, 2014.
Freedman, Russell, *Eleanor Roosevelt: A Life of Discovery*. New York: Turtleback, 1997.

Freeman, Douglas Southall, *George Washington, A Biography: Patriot and President*. New York: Augustus, 1975.
———, *Washington*. New York: Touchstone, 2011.
Frost, John, *Pictorial Life of George Washington: Embracing a Complete History of the Seven Years' War, the Revolutionary War, the Formation of the Federal Constitution, and the Administration of Washington*. Philadelphia, PA: Thomas, Cowperthwait, 1848.
Gaddis, John Lewis, *The Cold War: A New History*. New York: Penguin, 2005.
Gates, Henry Louis, Jr., and Donald Yacovone, *Lincoln on Race and Slavery*. Princeton, NJ: Princeton University Press, 2011.
Genovese, Michael, *Presidential Leadership in an Age of Change*. New Brunswick, NJ: Transaction, 2016.
Gergen, David, *Eyewitness to Power: The Essence of Leadership: Nixon to Clinton*. New York: Simon & Schuster, 2000.
Goldman, Eric, *Rendezvous with Destiny: A History of Modern American Reform*. Chicago: Ivan R. Dee, 2001.
Goodwin, Doris Kearns, *Team of Rivals: The Political Genius of Abraham Lincoln*. New York: Simon & Schuster, 2005.
———, *The Bully Pulpit: Theodore Roosevelt, William Howard Taft, and the Golden Age of Journalism*. New York: Simon & Schuster, 2013.
———, *Leadership in Turbulent Times*. New York: Simon & Schuster, 2018.
Grande, Peggy, *The President Will See You Now: A Memoir: My Stories and Lessons from Ronald Reagan's Final Years*. New York: Hachette Books, 2017.
Greenblatt, Miriam, *Franklin D. Roosevelt: 32nd President of the United States*. New York: Garrett Educational, 1989.
Greenstein, Fred I., *Inventing the Job of President: Leadership Style from George Washington to Andrew Jackson*. Princeton, NJ: Princeton University Press, 2009.
———, ed., *Leadership in the Modern Presidency*. Cambridge, MA, Harvard University Press, 1988.
———, *The Presidential Difference: Leadership Style from Roosevelt to Clinton*, 3rd ed. New York: Free Press, (2000) 2009.
Greenstein, Fred I., with Dale Anderson, *Presidents and the Dissolution of the Union: Leadership Style from Polk to Lincoln*. Princeton, NJ: Princeton University Press, 2013.
Groom, Winston, *Ronald Reagan: Our 40th President*. Washington, DC: Regenery, 2012.
Hannaford, Peter, *Recollections of Reagan: A Portrait of Ronald Reagan*. New York: William Morrow, 1997.
Harrison, Benjamin, *Public Papers and Addresses of Benjamin Harrison, Twenty-Third President of the United States, March 4, 1889 to March 4, 1893*. Washington, DC: Government Printing Office, 1893.

Herndon, William Henry, *Herndon's Lincoln: The True Story of a Great Life: The History and Personal Recollections of Abraham Lincoln, Volume 1*. London: Forgotten Books, 2015.
Herndon, William Henry, and Jesse William Weik, *Abraham Lincoln: The True Story of a Great Life, Volume 1*. New York: D. Appleton, 1892.
Hornstein, Lillian Herlands, Leon Edel, and Horst Frenz: *The Reader's Companion to the World*, 2nd ed. New York: New American Library, 2002.
Howell, William G., and Terry M. Moe, *Relic: How Our Constitution Undermines Effective Government—And Why We Need a More Powerful Presidency*. New York: Basic Books, 2016.
Humes, James C., *The Reagan Persuasion: Charm, Inspire, and Deliver*. Naperville, IL: Sourcebooks, 2010.
Ickes, Harold, *The Secret Diary of Harold L. Ickes: The First Thousand Days, 1933–1936*. New York: Simon and Schuster, 1953.
Israel, Fred L., *Major Presidential Decisions*. New York: Chelsea House, 1980.
Jackson, William J., *New Jerseyans in the Civil War: For Union and Liberty*. New Brunswick, NJ: Rutgers University Press, 2000.
Jay, Antony, ed., *Lend me Your Ears: Oxford Dictionary of Political Quotations*, 4th ed. Oxford, UK: Oxford University Press, 2010.
Jefferson, Thomas, *The Papers of Thomas Jefferson, Vol. 1, 1760–1776*, ed. Julian P. Boyd. Princeton, NJ: Princeton University Press, 1950.
———, *The Writings of Thomas Jefferson, Volume 1*, ed. H. A. Washington. Cambridge, UK: Cambridge University Press, 2011.
Johnson, Dominic D. P., *Strategic Instincts: The Adaptive Advantages of Cognitive Biases in International Politics*. Princeton, NJ: Princeton University Press, 2020.
Johnson, Lyndon, *Public Papers of the President, Containing the Public Messages, Speeches, and Statements of the President, Volume 1*. Washington, DC: US Government Printing Office, 1965.
Jones, Charles O., *The Presidency in a Separated System*. Washington, DC: Brookings, 2005.
Journal of the Senate of the United States of America, 1789–1793: A Century of Lawmaking for a New Nation, U.S. Congressional Documents and Debates, 1774–1875.
Jusserand, J. J., *What Me Befell*. London: Constable, 1933.
Kalman, Laura, *FDR's Gambit: The Court Packing Fight and the Rise of Legal Liberalism*. New York: Oxford Academic, 2022.
Kellerman, Barbara, *The Political Presidency: Practice of Leadership*. Ann Arbor: University of Michigan Press, 1984.
Kennedy, David, *Freedom from Fear: The American People in Depression and War, 1929–1945*. Oxford, UK: Oxford University Press, 2004.
Kennedy, John, *Profiles in Courage*. New York: Harper Perennial, 2006.

———, *Public Papers of the Presidents: John F. Kennedy, 1962*. Washington, DC: Office of the Federal Register, National Archives and Records Administration.
Ketcham, Henry, *The Life of Abraham Lincoln*. New York: A. L. Burt, 1901.
Kiewe, Amos, *FDR's First Fireside Chat: Public Confidence and the Banking Crisis*. College Station: Texas A&M University Press, 2007.
Kohn, Edward P., *A Most Glorious Rise: The Diaries of Theodore Roosevelt, 1877–1886*. Albany: State University of New York Press, 2015.
Landy, Marc, and Sidney M. Milkis, *Presidential Greatness*. Lawrence: University of Kansas Press, 2000.
Lamon, Ward Hill, *Recollections of Abraham Lincoln, 1847–1865*, Dorothy Lamon, ed. Chicago, IL: A. C. McClurg, 1895.
Lash, Joseph P., *Eleanor and Franklin: The Story of Their Relationship*. New York: W. W. Norton, 1971.
Lee, Henry, *Funeral Oration on the Death of General Washington*. Boston, MA: Joseph Nancrede and Manning & Loring, 1800.
Levine, Lawrence W., and Cornelia R. Levine, *The People and the President: America's Conversation with FDR*. Boston, MA: Beacon Press, 2002.
Leuchtenburg, William E., *The FDR Years: On Roosevelt and His Legacy*. New York: Columbia University Press, 1995.
Leffler, Melvyn P., *A Preponderance of Power: National Security, the Truman Administration, and the Cold War*. Stanford, CA: Stanford University Press, 1992.
———, *For the Soul of Mankind: The United States, The Soviet Union, and The Cold War*. New York: Hill and Wang, 2007.
Lincoln, Abraham, *Collected Works of Abraham Lincoln, Volume 5*. New Brunswick, NJ: Rutgers University Press, 1953.
———, *Collected Works of Abraham Lincoln, Volume 7*. New Brunswick, NJ: Rutgers University Press, 1953.
Locke, John, *The Works of John Locke*, Vol. III. London: Burt, 1751.
Luce, Morton, ed., *The Works of William Shakespeare: Twelfth Night or What You Will*. London: Methuen, 1906.
Malone, Dumas, *Jefferson: The Virginian, Volume One*. Boston, MA: Little, Brown, 1948.
Marbois, Francis Barbe, *History of Louisiana: Particularly of the Cession of that Colony to the United States of America: With an Introductory Essay on the Constitution and Government of the United States, Volume 1*. Philadelphia, PA: Carey & Lea, 1830.
Marsh, George, P., *Man and Nature; on Physical Geography as Modified by Human Action*. London: Sampson, Low, Son and Marston, 1864.
Marshall, John, *The Life of George Washington*. Philadelphia, PA: James Crissy, 1838.
Mast, Jerald, *Climate Change Politics and Policies in America: Historical and Modern Documents in Context*. Santa Barbara, CA: ABC-CLIO, 2018.

McLaughlin, Andrew Cunningham, "The Confederation and the Constitution, 1783–1789." *The American Nation: A History, Volume 10*, ed. Albert Bushnell Hart. New York: Harper, 1905.
Meacham, Jon, *Franklin and Winston: An Intimate Portrait of an Epic Friendship*. New York: Random House, 2003.
———, *Thomas Jefferson: The Art of Power*. New York: Random House, 2012.
Meese, Edwin, III, *Reagan: The Inside Story*. New York: Regnery, 1992.
Memoirs of Thomas Jefferson Randolph, Edgehill Randolph Papers, University of Virginia.
Michelson, Charles, *The Ghost Talks*. New York: G. P. Putnam, 1944.
Moley, Raymond, *The First New Deal*. New York: Harcourt, Brace & World, 1966.
———, *After Seven Years*. Boston, MA: Da Capo Press, 1972.
———, *The Rise of Theodore Roosevelt*. New York: Random House, 1979.
———, *Dutch: A Memoir of Ronald Reagan*. New York: Random House, 1999.
———, *Theodore Rex*. New York: Random House, 2001.
Mueller, Carol Lea, *The Quotable John Wayne: The Grit and Wisdom of an American Icon*. New York: Taylor Trade, 2007.
Muir, William Ker, Jr., *The Bully Pulpit: The Presidential Leadership of Ronald Reagan*. San Francisco, CA: ICS Press, 1992.
Neustadt, Richard E., *Presidential Power: The Politics of Leadership*. New York: Free Press, 1960.
Nicolay, Helen, *Personal Traits of Abraham Lincoln*. New York: Century, 1912.
Nugent, Walter, *Habits of Empire: A History of American Exceptionalism*. New York: Knopf, 2008.
Obama, Barack, *Public Papers of the President of the United States, Barack Obama, 2009, Book II*. Washington, DC: Office of the Federal Register, National Archives and Records Administration.
Paltsits, Victor Hugo, ed., *Washington's Farewell Address*. New York: New York Public Library, 1935.
Parker, Theodore, *The Collected Works of Theodore Parker: Discourses of Slavery*, vol. 5. London: Trubner, 1863.
Parks, Leighton, *Theodore Roosevelt, A Tribute*. New York: Washburn, 1919.
Parton, James, *Life of Thomas Jefferson*. Boston, MA: James R. Osgood, 1874.
Peatman, Jared, *The Long Shadow of Lincoln's Gettysburg Address*. Carbondale: Southern Illinois University Press 2013.
Pederson, William D., Frank J. Williams, and Robert P. Watson, eds., *Lincoln's Ensuring Legacy: Perspective from Great Thinkers, Great Leaders, and the American Experiment*. New York: Rowman & Littlefield, 2010.
Perkins, Francis, *The Roosevelt I Knew*. New York: Viking Press, 1946.
Peterson, Merrill D., *Thomas Jefferson and the New Nation: A Biography*. New York: Hill and Wang, 1986.

Phelps, William Lyon, ed., *Selections from the Poetry and Prose of Thomas Gray.* Boston, MA: Ginn, 1894.
Pickering, Timothy, *Review of the Correspondence Between the Hon. John Adams and the Late William Cunningham, ESQ Beginning in 1803, and Ending in 1812.* Salem, MA: Cushing and Appleton, 1824.
Pinchot, Gifford, *The Fight for Conservation.* New York: Doubleday, Page, 1910.
Pottker, Jan, *Sara and Eleanor: The Story of Sara Delano Roosevelt and Her Daughter-in-Law, Eleanor Roosevelt.* New York: St. Martin's, 2005.
Rabbitt, Mary C., *The United States Geological Survey: 1879-1989.* Washington, DC: United States Government Printing Office, 1989.
Ratnesar, Romesh, *A City, A President, and the Speech that Ended the Cold War.* New York: Simon & Schuster, 2009.
Reagan, Ronald, *Public Papers of the Ronald Reagan: 1983.* Washington, DC: Office of the Federal Register, National Archives and Records Service, General Services Administration, 1984-85.
Reagan, Nancy, with William Novak, *My Turn: The Memoirs of Nancy Reagan.* New York: Random House, 1989.
Reagan, Ron, *My Father at 100.* London: Penguin, 2011.
Reagan, Ronald, *Ronald Reagan: An American Life.* New York: Simon & Schuster, 1990.
Reeves, Richard, *President Reagan: The Triumph of Imagination.* New York: Simon & Schuster, 2005.
Reynolds, David S., *Abe: Abraham Lincoln in His Times.* New York: Penguin, 2020.
Rice, Allen Thorndike, ed., *Reminiscences of Abraham Lincoln by Distinguished Men of His Time.* New York: Haskel House, 1971.
Ritchie, Donald A., *Electing FDR: The New Deal Campaign of 1932.* Lawrence: University of Kansas Press, 2007.
Robinson, Gilbert A., *Reagan Remembered.* New York: Beaufort Books, 2015.
Robinson, Peter, *How Ronald Reagan Changed My Life.* New York: HarperCollins, 2003.
Roget's Thesaurus of Words for Intellectuals. New York: Simon & Schuster, 2011.
Rollins, Alfred, *Roosevelt and Howe.* New York: Knopf, 1962.
Roosevelt, Eleanor, *The Autobiography of Eleanor Roosevelt.* New York: Harper, 1961.
Roosevelt, Franklin D., "The Year of Crisis," *Public Papers of the President of the United States, Volume 2, 1933.*
Roosevelt, Franklin, *The Public Papers and Addresses of Franklin D. Roosevelt, Volume 10,* ed. Samuel Irving Rosenman. New York: Macmillan, 1941.
———, *Theodore Roosevelt Papers: Series 8: Personal Diaries, 1878-1884; Vol. 7, 1884.*
———, *Public Papers of Theodore Roosevelt, Governor 1899-1900.* Albany, NY: Brandow, 1899.

———, *What Roosevelt Says (from the Congressional Record)*. United States, 1904.
———, *Outdoor Pastimes of an American Hunter*. New York: Charles Scribner's, 1905.
———, *African Game Trails: An Account of the African Wanderings of an American Hunter-Naturalist, Volume 1*. New York: Charles Scribner's, 1910.
———, *An Autobiography of Theodore Roosevelt*. New York: Charles Scribner's, 1913.
———, *Letters from Theodore Roosevelt to Anna Roosevelt Cowles, 1870–1918*. New York: Charles Scribner's, 1924.
———, *The Works of Theodore Roosevelt, National Edition, Volume X*. New York: Charles Scribner's, 1926.
Rosenman, Samuel, *Working with Roosevelt*. New York: Harper, 1952.
Rosenman, Samuel Irving, and Dorothy Reuben Rosenman, *Presidential Style: Some Giants and a Pygmy in the White House*. New York: Harper & Row, 1976.
Rossiter, Clinton, *The American Presidency*. New York: New American Library, 1962.
Safire, William, *Lend Me Your Ears: Great Speeches in History*. New York: W. W. Norton, 1997.
Schlesinger, Arthur M., Jr. *Crisis of the Old Order, 1919–1933*. New York: Houghton Mifflin, 1957.
———, *The Coming of the New Deal*. Boston, MA: Houghton Mifflin, 1958.
———, *The Imperial Presidency*. New York: Houghton Mifflin, 1973.
The Selected Letters of Charles Sumner, ed. Beverly W. Palmer. Boston, MA: Northeastern University Press, 1990.
Schmertz, Eric J, Natalie Datlof, and Alexej Ugrinsky, eds., *Ronald Reagan's America, Volume 1*. Westport, CT, Greenwood Press, 1997.
———, eds., *Ronald Reagan's America, Volume 2*. Westport, CT, Greenwood Press, 1997.
Schwartz, Jordan, *The Interregnum of Despair*. Urbana: University of Illinois Press, 1970.
Sherwood Robert E., *Roosevelt and Hopkins: An Intimate History*. New York: Harper, 1948.
Skinner, Kiron K., Annelise Anderson, and Martin Anderson, eds. *Reagan: A Life in Letters*. New York: Free Press, 2003.
Skowronek, Stephen, *The Politics Presidents Make: Leadership from John Adams to Bill Clinton*. New York: Belnap Press, 1997.
Smith, Jean Edward, *FDR*. New York: Random House, 2008.
Smythe, William Ellsworth, *The Conquest of Arid America*. New York: Harper & Brothers, 1900.
Spitz, Bob, *Reagan: An American Journey*. New York: Penguin Books, 2018.
Spragens, William C., *Popular Images of American Presidents*. New York: Greenwood, 1988.
Stampp, Kenneth Milton, *The Peculiar Institution: Slavery in the Ante-Bellum South*. New York: Knopf, 1961.

Stockbridge, Frank Parker, *History of the Louisiana Purchase Exposition*. Saint Louis, MO: Universal Exposition, 1905.
Taubman, William, *Gorbachev: His Life and Times*. New York: W. W. Norton, 2017.
Trefousse, Hans Louis, *Andrew Johnson. A Biography*. New York: W. W. Norton, 1989.
Truman, Harry S., *The Memoirs of Harry S. Truman: A Reader's Edition*. Columbia: University of Missouri Press, 2019.
Tugwell, Rexford Guy, *The Democratic Roosevelt: A Biography of Franklin D. Roosevelt*. New York: Doubleday, 1957.
Tulis, Jeffrey, *The Rhetorical Presidency*. Princeton, NJ: Princeton University Press, 1987.
Tully, Grace, *My Boss*. Chicago: People's Book Club, 1949.
Twain, Mark, *Pudd'nhead Wilson*. Hartford, CT: American Publishing, 1894.
United States Congressional Serial Set, Volume 3307. Washington, DC: Government Printing Office, 1895.
Updegrove, Mark K., *Baptism by Fire: Eight Presidents Who Took Office in Times of Crisis*. New York: Thomas Dunne Books, 2008.
Ursiny, Gary DeMoss, and Mark Ybaben, *The Top Performer's Guide to Attitude: Essential Skills That Put You on Top*. Naperville, IL: Sourcebooks, 2008.
Wann, A. J., *The President as Chief Administrator: A Study of Franklin D. Roosevelt*. New York: Public Affairs Press, 1968.
Ward, Geoffrey C., and Ken Burns, *The Roosevelts: An Intimate History*. New York: Knopf Doubleday, 2014.
Ward, Geoffrey C., *A First Class Temperament: The Emergence of Franklin Roosevelt, 1905–1928*. New York: Vintage, 2014.
Washington, George, and Jared Sparks, eds., *The Writings of George Washington, Being His Correspondence, Addresses, Messages and Other Papers Official and Private, Volume 2*. Boston, MA: Russell, Odiorne, and Metcalf, 1834.
Washington, H. A., ed., *Writings of Thomas Jefferson, Vol III*. New York: H. W. Derby, 1861.
White, Ronald C., *Abraham Lincoln: A Biography*. New York: Random House, 2010.
Whitman, Walt, and Emory Holloway, ed., *The Uncollected Poetry and Prose of Walt Whitman: With Various Early Manuscripts. Volume 1*. New York: Doubleday, Page, 1921.
Wills, Garry, *Cincinnatus: George Washington and the Enlightenment*. New York: Doubleday, 1984.
———, *Reagan's America: Innocents at Home*. New York: Doubleday, 1987.
———, *Certain Trumpets: The Call of Leaders*. New York: Simon & Schuster, 1994.
———, *Lincoln at Gettysburg: The Words that Remade America*. New York. Simon & Schuster, 2006.
Wilson, Joan Hoff, *Forgotten Progressive*. New York: Harper Collins, 1975.
Wilson, Robert A., ed. *Character above All: Ten Presidents from FDR to George Bush*. New York: Simon & Schuster, 1995.

Wilson, Robert Lawrence, and Gregory Curtin Wilson, *Theodore Roosevelt, Outdoorsman*. Madison: University of Wisconsin–Madison, 1971.
Wilson, Rufus Rockwell, *Intimate Memories of Lincoln*. Elmira, NY: Primavera Press, 1945.
Wirth, Conrad, *Parks, Politics, and the People*. Norman: University of Oklahoma Press, 1980.
Wood Gordon, *Revolutionary Characters*. New York: Penguin, 2006.
Wood, Gordon S., *Friends Divided: John Adams and Thomas Jefferson*. New York: Penguin, 2017.

Articles and Essays

"A Saddening Glimpse at a Closet of Hearts," *Life* (September 17, 1971).
Becker, Carl, "What Is Still Living in the Political Philosophy of Thomas Jefferson," *American Historical Review* 48, no. 4 (July 1943).
Bernanke, Ben, "On Milton Friedman's Ninetieth Birthday," Remarks by Governor Ben S. Bernanke at the Conference to Honor Milton Friedman, University of Chicago, Chicago, IL, November 8, 2002.
———, "Banking, Credit, and Economic Fluctuations," Nobel Prize Lecture, December 9, 2022.
Brinkley, Alan, "Hoover and Roosevelt: Two Approaches to Leadership," in *Profiles in Leadership: Historians on the Elusive Quality of Greatness*, edited by Walter Isaacson (New York: W. W. Norton, 2010).
Fund, John H., "Ronald Reagan's Berlin," *American Spectator* 43, no. 10 (December 2009).
Heclo, Hugh, "The Mixed Legacies of Ronald Reagan," in *The Enduring Reagan*, edited by Charles W. Dunn (Lexington: University Press of Kentucky, 2009).
Hickey, Jennifer, "A Speech Heard 'Round the World," *Insight on the News*, November 29, 1999.
Irland, Lloyd, "Maine Forests: A Century of Change, 1900–2000 . . . and Elements of Policy Change for a New Century," *Maine Policy Review* 9, no. 1 (Winter 2000).
Jobs, Steve, "Commencement Address," Stanford University, June 12, 2005.
Kennan, George, "The Sources of Soviet Conduct," *Foreign Affairs*, July 1, 1947.
Langford, Nathaniel Pitt, "The Louisiana Purchase and Preceding Spanish Intrigues for Dismemberment of the Union," *Minnesota Historical Society*, St. Paul, MN, 1901.
Luce, Henry R., "The American Century," *Life*, February 17, 1941.
Monteiro, George, "Hemingway's Notion of "Grace," *Studies in American Fiction* 18, no. 1 (Spring 1990).
Muir, John, "Features of the Proposed Yosemite National Park," *Century Magazine* XL, no. 5 (September 1890).

Norris, David A., "Four Terms with Franklin," *History Magazine* (October/November 2012).
Reagan, Nancy, "The Eternal Optimist: Ronald Wilson Reagan (1911–2004)." *Time Magazine*, June 14, 2004.
Robinson, Peter, "Mr. Gorbachev, Open This Gate. Mr. Gorbachev, Tear Down This Wall!" *American History* 38, no. 4 (October 2003).
———, "Tear Down This Wall: How Top Advisors Opposed Reagan's Challenge to Gorbachev—but Lost," *Prologue Magazine* 39, no. 2 (Summer 2007).
———, "A Turn of Phrase," *New Criterion* 32, no. 5 (January 2014).
Roosevelt, Theodore, "The Manly Virtues and Practical Politics," *The Forum, Vol. XVII, March–August* (New York: Forum, 1894).
Rowland, Robert C., and John M. Jones, "Reagan at the Brandenburg Gate: Moral Clarity Tempered by Pragmatism." *Rhetoric & Public Affairs* 9, no. 1 (Spring 2006).
Smith, Richard Norton, and Timothy Walch, "The Ordeal of Herbert Hoover, Part 2," *Prologue Magazine* 36, no. 2 (Summer 2004).
Thoreau, Henry David, "Walking," *The Atlantic* (June 1862).
Turner, Frederick, J., "The Significance of the Frontier in American History," *Annual Report of the American Historical Association* (1893).

Web Pages

https://avalon.law.yale.edu
https://www.battlefields.org
https://founders.archives.gov
https://www.jfklibrary.org
https://millercenter.org/the-presidency
http://tjrs.monticello.org/
https://mountvernon.org
https://history.nasa.gov
https://www.presidency.ucsb.edu
https://www.reaganfoundation.org
https://www.senate.gov/artandhistory/history
https://teachingamericanhistory.org
https://www.whitehouse.gov

Magazines, Journals, and Newspapers

Adams Sentinel
American Historical Review
American Journal of Political Science

American Political Science Review
The Atlantic
Boston Globe
Chicago Daily Tribune
Chicago Tribune
Cincinnati Daily Commercial
David Claypoole's American Daily Advertiser
Diplomatic History
Evening Star
Foreign Affairs
Gazette of the United States
Harrisburg Patriot
Journal of American History
Journal of Southern History
Los Angeles Times
Minneapolis Tribune
Minnesota Historical Society
National Gazette
National Intelligencer
National Public Radio's Weekend Edition
New Jersey Gazette
Newsday
New York Evening Post
New York Journal
New York Post
New York Times
New York Daily Tribune
New York Tribune
Philadelphia Daily Age
Philadelphia Inquirer
Political Science Quarterly
Politico
Presidential Studies Quarterly
The Press (Philadelphia, PA)
Rollcall
Sun Sentinel
Times of India
USA Today
Wall Street Journal
Washington Post
Washington Times
Weekend Edition
YouTube

Index

9/11, 143–45

Abigail Adams, 19, 47, 115
Adams, John, 21; annual messages of, 113; belief in America, 82; challenges with the French as president, 49; classical education of, 16; as "Colossus of Independence," 82; election as president and, 50; election loss in 1800, 178; final words of, 79; "monarchical principles" of, 21; recollection of protests at President's House, 26; and Santo Domingo policy, 67; support for independence of, 101; Thomas Jefferson's reserved nature, view on, 53; Treaty of Mortefontaine and, 82; Washington's decision making process, view on, 16; Washington's education, view on, 15
Adams, John Quincy: cold nature of, 178; commitment to service of, 82; and creation of roads and canals, 45; defeat in 1828 of, 178; and federal government enlargement, 32; Jefferson's storytelling, view on, 54; role in Louisiana Purchase of, 78
Aldrich, Nelson, 133

Allison, William, 133
American Independence, 25, 58, 72; British recognition of, 17; declaring of, 8; FDR evoking, 174; and foreign intrigue, 33; George Washington and, 16; learning lessons from, 62; shared bonds and, 32; Thomas Jefferson and the case for, 56; unity and, 31
Apollo 11, 44, 184
Atlee, Clement, 181

Ballantine, Arthur, 167, 171
Baker, Howard, 205, 206, 215
Baker, James, 178
Barbé-Marbois, François de: engagement with Robert Livingston, 69–72; and Napoleon's decision to cede Louisiana Territory, 68
Biden, Joseph R.; on Donald Trump's response to January 6, 2021, 113
Bonaparte, Joseph, 61, 64–65, 66
Bonaparte, Napoleon, 18; assurances for America's treaties with Spain, 61; cardinal rule for negotiating with, 59; cedes Louisiana Territory; 68–69, 70, 71–72, 75–78; defiance of, 62; drawing room gathering in Paris and, 66; everything went through, 60, 64; geopolitical

296 | Index

Bonaparte, Napoleon *(continued)*
thought of, 68; immovability and, 62, 65; launches expeditionary force, 67; Livingston chose not to meet with, 65; negotiated the Treaty of San Ildefonso, 51; realism of, 68; Treaty of Mortefontaine and, 82; vision for Louisiana Territory and, 52; wavering on Louisiana deal, 66

Boone and Crockett Club, 120, 129; 135

Brandenburg Gate; presidential advance trip and, 203; Reagan's speech at, 3, 193, 207, 208, 211

Bryan, William Jennings; on the Gettysburg Address, 107

Buchanan, James; failed to prevent Southern secession, 8, 46, 82, 113, 145

Bulloch, Martha "Mittie" (Theodore Roosevelt's mother), 127; death of, 128; influence on Theodore Roosevelt, Jr., 127–28

Burns, John L., 107

Burroughs, John, 126

Bush, George H. W. Bush: championed legislation for the disabled, 5; experience of, 4; State of the Union speech (1992) and, 215; thousand points of light and, 177

Bush, George W.: Abraham Lincoln's writing process, view on, 91; "axis of evil" and, 114; financial crisis of 2007 to 2008 and, 25; President's Emergency Plan for AIDS Relief (PEPFAR) program and, 46; response to 9/11, 143–45; Ronald Reagan, view on, 198

Card, Andrew, 143–44
Cardozo, Benjamin N., 161

Carlucci, Frank, 207, 213

Carter, Jimmy: character of, 4; Camp David Accords and, 47; challenges of, 47; crisis of confidence and, 8, 145; détente policy of, 187; loss to Ronald Reagan in 1980, 178; Russians; view of, 187; travelled to Berlin, 209

Churchill, Winston, 157, 180, 181, 182

Civil War: Gettysburg as bloodiest battle of, 2; Gettysburg Address as turning point for, 3, 171, 219; lack of unity and, 31; Louisiana Purchase's impact on, 78; slavery and, 46

Claypoole, David C., 12–13

Cleaver, Ben, 195

Cleveland, Grover; protection of wildlife, 121

Clinton, Bill, 8; "era of big government is over" and, 114; impeachment and, 8, 25; and growth of the internet, 46; intelligence of, 15; interpersonal skills of, 4; Lewinsky scandal and, 25; optimism of, 177; posthumously awarded Medal of Honor to Theodore Roosevelt, 130

Cold War, 3, 81, 184, 189, 190, 214; Berlin Wall as symbol of, 185, 203; impact of Berlin on, 183; key speech of, 205, 215, 217; Reagan administration's policy on, 211; Reagan winning of, 214, 215; tensions and, 44; termed, 180; Vietnam and, 187

Compromise of 1790, 8, 48
Compromise of 1820, 84
Conservation movement, 119–22
Coolidge, Calvin, 145, 148; George Washington, view on, 16;

governance legacy and, 47; Great Depression, view on, 149; press engagement and, 163

Constitutional Convention of 1787, 9, 17, 51; delegates to, 9; Committee on Postponed Matters and, 9

Cummings, Homer, 162

Declaration of Independence: Charles Carroll as last living signer, 33; committee assigned to draft, 67; as connecting Thomas Jefferson and John Adams, 79; and Gettysburg Address, 101–104; as historic document, 12, 17, 40, 79; John Hancock's signature on, 143; reenergize principles of, 96; as a secret, 116; Thomas Jefferson and, 2, 56, 76; the Union's purpose and, 100

Diepgen, Eberhard, 190, 191, 192, 207, 208

Donaldson, Sam, 191, 193, 214

Douglas, Stephen A.; debates with Abraham Lincoln and, 94, 97, 197

Duberstein, Ken, 192, 206, 207

Du Pont de Nemours, Samuel, 59–60, 61, 76, 77

Eisenhower, Dwight, 38, 45; Agricultural Trade Development and Assistance Act and, 46; Farewell Address and, 38, 108; on leadership, 177; Little Rock, Arkansas and, 112; national highway system and, 45; optimism of, 178; residence in Gettysburg, 108; and Vietnam, 186

Electoral College; establishment of, 9; in 1789, 10; in 1793, 24–25

Everett, Edward, 90, 103, 106; greets Lincoln at Gettysburg, 90; note to Lincoln post-Gettysburg, 106; reaction to his Gettysburg remarks, 100; remarks at cemetery dedication, 99–100; seated at the cemetery dedication, 99

Fillmore, Millard: backed 1850 Compromise, 46; fell short in preventing Civil War, 145

Fireside Chats; "map" chat, 174

Ford, Gerald; and pardon of Richard Nixon, 82; Resolute Desk and, 179; State of the Union Address (1975) and, 114

Founding Fathers, 78; and breaking with Jefferson, 105; fear of monarchy and, 10; gathered in Philadelphia, 8; importance of judgment to, 7; Lincoln going beyond, 104; Lincoln's reverence for, 95; recognized Washington's talents, 10

Franklin, Benjamin, 10, 54, 55

French, Benjamin Brown, 98, 105

Garfield, James, 46, 115, 132

Gettysburg (PA), 2; during Civil War battle, 87; impact on the town, 88–89

Gettysburg Address, 2, 92, 217, 220; as Civil War turning point, 3, 171, 219; discussion of, 98–104; legacy of, 40, 107–108; reaction to, 105–106

Gilder, Josh, 178, 180

Gitt, George; as witness to Gettysburg Address, 100, 105

Gorbachev Mikhail; and concern with upsetting, 206, 207; Geneva and, 212, 216; and glasnost, 188, 189, 211; impact of Berlin Wall speech and, 214; as man of peace, 191; and

Gorbachev Mikhail *(continued)* "tear down this wall," 3, 205, 211, 212, 213, 219; and Reykjavik, 189

Grant, Ulysses S.; establishing Yellowstone National Park and, 121; protection of Pribilof Islands and, 120–21; and victory at Vicksburg, 95

Great Crash of 1929, 149

Great Depression, 81; and background of, 148–53; Calvin Coolidge's preceding leadership and, 47; FDR response to, 3, 219; fireside chat as a turning point for, 171; Herbert Hoover's failure to overcome, 8, 145; as a leading crisis, 82, 148

Grinnell, George Bird, 120

Griscom, Thomas: and Berlin Wall speech, 178, 179, 205, 213; confronted opposition to "tear down this wall," 206, 207

Hamilton, 39

Hamilton, Alexander 11, 21, 30, 56, 127; aspirations of, 21; and battles with Thomas Jefferson, 55; Compromise of 1790 and, 8; as favored by George Washington, 12; coordinated meeting with David C. Claypoole, 12; and Louisiana Purchase, 74; and support for strong executive, 9; lobbied George Washington against retiring, 23: Whiskey Rebellion and, 111; work on Farewell Address and, 27–29

Hanna, Mark, 132

Hanks, Nancy (Abraham Lincoln's mother), 93

Harding, Warren, 145

Harrison, Benjamin: established Sequoia, Yosemite and General Grant National Parks, 121; protection of salmon fisheries in Alaska and, 121

Hayes, Rutherford B.: founded U.S. Geological Survey, 121; and Resolute Desk, 179

Henderson, David, 115, 116

Herndon, William, 93

Hoover, Herbert, 8; and contrast with FDR, 160; FDR distances from, 152. 159; hollow optimism of, 178; as "The Great Humanitarian," 46; lack of nimbleness of, 158; missing the mark in crisis and, 47, 145, 151; press engagement of, 163; as well-equipped for Great Depression, 145, 150–51

Hough, Franklin B., 119

Howe, Lewis: and dinner with FDR prior to first Fireside Chat, 146

Hyde Park, 153, 155, 160

Independence Hall, 9, 12

Industrialization: and the beginning of the twentieth century, 117–19, and the lead up to the Civil War, 84–85

Iran-Contra, 189, 207, 209

Iron Curtain, 182, 185, 202, 209, 215

Jackson, Andrew; and farewell address, 37; and Indian Removal Act of 1830, 113; Louisiana crisis and, 78; presidential election of 1828 and, 178; and Tariff of 1828, 112

January 6, 2021, 40, 113, 146

Jay, John, 16, 29; and consultation on Farewell Address, 28; and lobbying Washington for third term, 27; as Minister of Madrid, 58; "monarchial principles" of, 21; as Secretary of Foreign Affairs, 50;

and travel to London for treaty, 25–26
Jay Treaty, 11; 25; and pro-British leaning, 59; ratification of, 27; reaction to, 26
Jefferson, Peter (Thomas Jefferson's father), 52
Jefferson, Thomas, 18, 19, 41, 49, 84; 115, 123; and agrarian vision of America, 92; appointing Monroe and, 62–63; architectural prowess of, 54–55; and becoming vice president, 50; birth of, 52; breaking tradition of Annual Address to Congress and, 113; and calm after first inauguration, 50; and Compromise of 1790, 8, 48; and constitutional amendment, 75; death of, 79; decision making of, 53, 94; and Declaration of Independence, 101, 104; discipline of, 54; and downside to Louisiana Purchase, 78; DuPont backchannel and, 59; education of, 54; election of 1800 and, 50, 178; entangling alliances termed by, 37; epitaph of, 57; and France, 34; greatest accomplishment of, 219; impact of nature on, 52; impact of two-term precedent on, 40; threat posed by France and, 57–59; ingenuity of, 2, 47, 56–57, 76, 219; as inventor, 55; Jane Randolph and, 53; leadership of French crisis and, 59, 61, 62, 63, 64, 66, 76–78; Lincoln's break from, 105; Louisiana Purchase charge and, 49, 220; machinations of, 27; and making America a continental nation, 220; as member of the cabinet, 11; meeting with Pichon and, 67; and negotiating with France, 59; and office as president, 48–49; office attire of, 48; and opposition to Jay Treaty, 26, 27; original thinking of, 157; and penchant for entertaining, 48; Peter Jefferson and, 52; personality of, 53; physical attributes of, 53; presidential power, view of, 9; President's House, view of, 48; questioning of Livingston's strategy, 60, 66; reaction to Jay Treaty and, 26–27; reaction to Treaty of San Ildefonso and, 51; realpolitik of, 59; relief to end presidency and, 202; as renaissance man, 55–56; as scientist, 55; slavery and, 52; storytelling of, 54; Summary View of the Rights of British America and, 2, 56; temperament of, 53; Virginia Stature for Religious Freedom and, 2, 56, 57; Washington's communication skills, view of, 15; Washington's prudence, view of, 16; and Washington serving a second presidential term, 23, 24, 30
Johnson, Andrew: and efforts to thwart Reconstruction, 82; on Washington's Farewell Address, 39; lack of ingenuity of, 47
Johnson, Lyndon, 179; on Abraham Lincoln, 108; Great Society and, 45; political skills of, 4; space race and, 44; Vietnam and, 187
Johnson, Robert Underwood, 120
Judge, Clark, 178

Kansas-Nebraska Act of 1854: signed by Franklin Pierce, 46; and Lincoln's speech about, 101; passage of, 97
Kennan George, 181
Kennedy, John: Berlin and, 185, 186, 209, 216; charm of, 15; courage and, 113; Cuban Missile Crisis and,

Kennedy, John *(continued)*
186; dedication and, 96; City upon a Hill speech and, 7; inaugural address of (1961), 182; moon charge of, 44, 45, 184; Nobel Peace Prize remarks of, 49; judgment and, 7; television and, 173; Vietnam and, 186; vision of, 4
Kennedy, Ted, 215
Khrushchev, Nikita, 183, 185, 186, 210
King, Jr., Martin Luther: and "I Have a Dream" speech, 107
Kohl, Helmut, 189, 206, 207; reaction to Berlin Wall speech and, 214; as recognized in Berlin Wall speech, 208; and tour of Reichstag with Reagan, 191–92
Kornbaum, John, 204, 206, 207

Lafayette, Marquis de, 10
Lamon, Ward Hill: and greeting of Lincoln in Gettysburg, 90; and preview of Gettysburg Address, 91–92; and introduction of Lincoln for cemetery dedication, 100; Lincoln's reaction to Gettysburg Address and, 105
Lear, Tobias, 12, 24
Leclerc, Charles, 67–68
Lee, Robert E., 86–88, 98
Lewis, J. Hamilton, 172
Lewis, Meriwether, 48; Lewis and Clark expedition and, 74–75, 77
Lincoln, Abraham, 81, 83, 115, 175, 220; and arrival at Gettysburg, 83, 89; assassination of, 25, 132; birth of, 92; cemetery dedication and, 99, 100; Civil War stakes and, 114; and confidence of the people, 145; conservation and, 120; dedication of, 2. 96–97, 104, 108–109; education of, 95–96, 157; and election in 1860; 85; debate against Stephen Douglas and, 197; decision making and, 94; drafting the Gettysburg Address and, 91–92, 98, 103; Emancipation Proclamation and, 46, 86; expanded American manufacturing and, 84; and fear of losing border states, 86; and first inaugural address, 177; and first message to Congress, 131, 139–40; and foresight for future generations, 142; Gettysburg Address and, 2, 3, 100; health of Tad Lincoln and, 90; humble beginnings of, 92, 93; influence of Declaration of Independence on, 101, 103, 104; invitation to Gettysburg and, 89; as inventor, 46; optimism of, 178; personality of, 94, 95; physical characteristics of, 94; physical wear of, 86; post-address in Gettysburg and, 106–107; procession to cemetery dedication and, 99; proclamation honoring George Washington's birthday and, 38; and reaction to Gettysburg Address, 105, 106; remarks at Gettysburg town square by, 90–91; 101; and Southern traction in Civil War, 86; storytelling gift of, 123; tour of Gettysburg battlefield and, 98; travel to Gettysburg by, 2, 83, 90, 92; and upset with Meade after Gettysburg, 88; White House remarks of (July 7, 1863), 101; at Wills House, 91; Willy Lincoln's death and, 90; and youth as candidate, 130
Lincoln, Abraham (Abraham Lincoln's grandfather), 93
Lincoln, Mary (Abraham Lincoln's wife), 90

Lincoln, Thomas (Abraham Lincoln's father) 93
Livingston, Robert: and charge letter from Jefferson, 2, 49, 57, 76, 219; and diplomacy with France, 52, 58, 59, 60–62, 63–67, 68–73, 74, 75, 76, 77, 78; and drawing room with Napoleon, 66; and overtures to Joseph Bonaparte, 64; and response to Monroe's appointment, 63
Lodge, Henry Cabot; and reaction during annual address reading, 132; on Theodore Roosevelt's spirit, 126
Long, Huey, 165, 166
Louisiana Territory: history of, 50–51; New Orleans and, 57; importance of Mississippi River and, 50, 51, 58, 61, 62, 63, 65; Spanish interest in, 51; threat of war with France over, 58
L'Ouverture, Toussaint, 67
Luce, Henry, 115

Madison, James, 202; and burning of Washington DC, 25; and Compromise of 1790, 8; and drafting of Farewell Address (1792), 20–23, 31; and drafting of Farewell Address (1792), 27, 28, 29, 30, 35; and lobbying Washington to remain president, 21–22; and Louisiana Purchase, 52, 58–63, 66—68, 70–74, 78; Monroe's appointment and, 64; and opposition to Jay Treaty, 26
Marsh, George Perkins, 119
Marshall, George C., 182
Marshall, John, 17
Mason, George, 9
Meade, George, 86–88, 99
Mercer, Lucy: and affair with FDR, 158
McCarthy, Joseph, 184–85

McClellan, George B., 97
McKinley, William: assassination of, 25, 115, 117, 122, 136; established Mount Rainer National Park, 121; tribute in 1901 annual address to Congress of, 131, 134, 135
Michelson, Charles, 167, 175
Mifflin, Thomas, 17, 18
Moley, Raymond, 158, 160, 162, 163, 166, 167, 171
Monroe, James, 68, 78; and arrival dinner in France, 69; diplomacy of, 71, 72–75; Monroe Doctrine and, 46, 135; offered presidential envoy, 62–64; Washington's Crossing and, 17; and weather delay to France, 64
Mount Vernon, 13, 15, 16, 22, 27, 32
Muir, John, 120, 136

Newell, Frederick Hayes, 136
Nixon, Richard, 8, 179; Berlin and, 209; China and, 46; détente policy of, 187; intelligence of, 15; resignation of, 25; opening of China and, 46, 187; pardon of, 82; strategic insight of, 4; Watergate and, 8, 113

Obama, Barack, 45; charm of, 15; commencement speech of, 44–45; empathy of, 220; farewell address of 38; Gettysburg Address and, 108; importance of confidence and, 143; intellect of, 15

Perkins, Francis, 150, 157, 161, 163, 167
Philadelphia (PA): as birthplace of the United States, 8; and Jefferson drafting the Declaration of Independence, 56; and President's House, 12, 16, 20, 26

Pierce, Franklin: signed Kansas-Nebraska Act, 46; fell short in preventing Civil War, 145
Pinchot, Gifford: appointed chief of Division of Forestry, 120; and support of 1901 annual address to Congress, 136
Platt, Orville, 132–33
Polk, James: expanded America to Pacific Ocean, 45; western migration and, 114
Powel, Elizabeth, 24
Powell, Colin, 206
Powers, Gary, 184
Presidential election of 1933, 152; consequential transition and, 152
Presidential terms: debate over, 9; second terms as, 25
President's House (Philadelphia, PA), 12, 16, 26
President's House (Washington, DC), 48, 67
Pruden, Octavius, L.: hand delivers Theodore Roosevelt's annual address to Congress, 116

Randolph, Jane (Thomas Jefferson's mother), 53
Reagan, John "Jack" (Ronald Reagan's father): and birth of Ronald Reagan, 194; and impact on Ronald Reagan, 194–95, 201
Reagan, John Neil "Moon" (Ronald Reagan's brother), 194
Reagan, Michael (Ronald Reagan's grandfather), 194
Reagan, Nancy (Ronald Reagan's second wife): arrival in Berlin (1987), 190; on Ronald Reagan's mystery, 198; on Ronald Reagan's optimism, 198, 215; and touring the Reichtag, 194; on why the Berlin Wall fell, 215
Reagan, Nelle Wilson (Ronald Reagan's mother): and birth of Ronald Reagan, 194; and impact on Ronald Reagan, 195
Reagan, Ronald: acting and, 199–200; and Alzheimer's Disease, 202; as anti-communist, 188; and appreciation for Gettysburg Address, 108; assassination attempt and, 201; and attire in Berlin, 190; as avid reader, 196; and Berlin Wall, 3, 191–92; and Berlin Wall Speech, 2, 203–13; and Berlin visit (1982), 193; and Berlin visit (1978), 192; and Berlin visit (1987), 3, 190–92; birth of, 194; charisma of, 4; communication skills, 15; decency of, 198; and Dixon, 196; education of, 196; Eureka College and, 199, 200; evil empire remark and, 188, 203, 207, 215; eyesight of, 199; Farewell Address of, 38; and football, 198–99, 200; at Geneva, 188–89; guardedness of, 198; impact of father on, 194–95, 201; impact of mother on, 195; Iran-Contra and, 189; as lifeguard, 197; as leader, 83, 188, 201, 202; as naturalist, 197; and oatmeal meat; 197; optimism of, 3, 177, 198, 201–203; oratory skills of, 15; Oval Office and, 179; personality of, 197; physique of, 198; and presidential election (1980), 178; reaction to Berlin Wall speech of, 213–17; at Reykjavik, 189; and "shining city on a hill," 38; and Space Shuttle disaster, 202; as sportscaster, 195, 200; as student body president,

200; and "tear down this wall" line, 180, 207, 211; and television, 173; and White House meeting with speechwriters, 178; World War II service and, 201
Residence Act of 1790, 8, 48
Reynolds, John F., 87, 98
Rice, Cecil Spring, 126
Rice, Condoleezza, 144
Robinson, Peter: advance trip to Berlin and, 203–205; challenged by administration officials about Berlin Wall speech, 206–207; as speechwriter for Berlin Wall speech, 203, 205; Oval Office meeting with Reagan and, 178–80; and uptick in cable traffic after the Berlin Wall speech, 214
Rogers, Will, 151, 169
Rohrabacher, Dana, 178, 205
Roosevelt, Alice (Theodore Roosevelt's first wife): death of, 128
Roosevelt, Cornelius (Theodore Roosevelt's grandfather), 122
Roosevelt, Edith Kermit Carow (Theodore Roosevelt's second wife): and family with Theodore Roosevelt, 129
Roosevelt, Eleanor (FDR's wife): on FDR's ability to pick things up quickly, 157; on FDR's confidence, 175; on FDR's polio disease, 159; inauguration day (1933), view of, 161; as married to FDR, 129, 155; impact of FDR's affair with Lucy Mercer on, 158; and projecting optimism, 165
Roosevelt, Franklin: and appreciation for Gettysburg Address, 108; and attire for fireside chat, 147; banking crisis and, 2; birth of, 154; confidence of, 3, 154, 156, 175; education of, 156–57; initial actions as president and, 161–67; first Fireside Chat and, 2, 167–71; first Inaugural Address of, 82; flaws of, 175; foundation for United Nations and Bretton Woods institutions and, 45; and Grover Cleveland White House visit, 155–56; and Herbert Hoover, 152, 160; impact of Theodore Roosevelt on, 155; inauguration of (1933), 160–61; ingenuity of Lend-Lease program and, 45; as lawyer, 157; and lost fireside chat remarks, 147; month of April, view on, 47; oath of office and (1933), 161; Oliver Wendall Holmes quip about, 157; optimism of, 158; oratory skills of, 15; personality of, 157; physical attributes of, 156; polio and 158–60; political philosophy of, 158; reaction to first Fireside Chat of, 171–72; sphinxlike nature of, 157–58; Supreme Court packing and, 25; third term of, 40; use of radio and, 3, 173–74; warmth of, 175; World War II aims and, 114
Roosevelt, Isaac (FDR's great-grandfather), 155
Roosevelt, James (FDR's father): and influence on FDR, 154–56
Roosevelt, Sara (FDR's mother): and FDR's challenging birth, 153; and influence on FDR, 153–54
Roosevelt, Jr., Theodore: assistant secretary of the Navy and, 129; birth of, 122; boxing and, 126; Bullock family history and, 127–28; bully pulpit of, 135; as center of attention, 126; conservation of

Roosevelt, Jr., Theodore *(continued)* natural resources and, 3; courage of, 3, 111, 113, 125 siblings of, 128–29; 126, 129, 142, 219; education of, 123–25; energy of, 122; ensured America's natural wonder and, 220; family history of, 127; First Annual Address to Congress and, 2, 115, 116–17, 131–38, 220; as founder of Boone and Crockett Club, 120; "funeral oration" of William McKinley and, 131–32; Harvard and, 124, 126, 127; impact of conservation by, 140–42; and loss in New York City Mayor race, 129; love for reading of, 123; natural world passion of, 124, 197; New York City Police Commissioner and, 129; physical transformation of, 125–26, 129; reaction to annual address of, 138–40; Rough Riders and, 129, 140; siblings of, 124, 128–29; and sickly boy, 123; storytelling gift of, 123; and Valentine's Day (1884), 128; youthful spirit of, 126

Roosevelt, Sr., Theodore (Theodore Roosevelt's father): death of 127; and influence on Theodore Roosevelt, Jr., 124–25; and townhouse in New York City, 122

Rose, Henry M., 117, 131

Rosenman, Sam: on FDR's quick mind, 156; on FDR's sense of timing, 174; on the first Fireside Chat as solely FDR's, 168; and joining FDR after first Fireside Chat, 171

Rove, Karl, 143

Sargent, Charles Sprague, 120

Schultz, George, 206, 216

Seward, William Henry: and meeting with Lincoln, 98; and Alaska purchase, 121; as seated during cemetery dedication, 99; and tour of Gettysburg battlefield, 98

Shakespeare, William; and dedication, 81; Abraham Lincoln's penchant for, 94; on month of April, 47

Smythe, William E., 120

Snell, Bertrand, 165

Spooner, John Coil, 133

Stalin, Joseph, 180, 181

State of the Union: George H. W. Bush (1992) and, 215; overview of, 113–14, Ronald Reagan (1984) and, 202

Talleyrand-Perigord, Charles Maurice de, 60, 68, 69

Tariff of 1828, 112

Taylor, Zachary, 145

Thoreau, Henry David, 119, 120

Tocqueville, Alexis de, 177

Treaty of Mortefontaine, 82

Truman Doctrine, 182

Truman, Harry, 180; "buck stops here" and, 59; containment and, 181; decisiveness of, 220; on FDR, 157; and integrating armed forces, 112; and Joseph Stalin, 181; and Marshall Plan 46, 82; "New big three," as part of, 181; and supporting the French in Vietnam, 186; and Truman Doctrine, 182; Washington's Farewell Address and, 37

Trump, Donald: and America First, 37; bravado of, 146; confidence of, 146; COVID-19 vaccine and, 45; impeachment and, 8; January 6 and, 83, 113; optimism of, 178; social media and, 173

Tugwell, Rex, 168–69
Tully, Grace: and note taking for fireside chat remarks, 168; on FDR's personality, 157; and FDR's reaction to lost remarks for fireside chat, 147; on FDR's stamp hobby, 154; on FDR's use of radio, 173

United States Capitol Building: history of, 115; January 6, 2021 and, 40, 83, 113; and scene of Theodore Roosevelt's first annual address, 115
United States Constitution: Benjamin Franklin on, 10; first eleven amendments of, 11, 56; as first of its kind, 8–9; Gettysburg Address and, 105; as historic document, 12, 76; and importance to George Washington, 11; as ratified, 10, 28, 127; and "State of the Union," 113; and Thomas Jefferson and the constitutional amendment, 75–76, 77; treaties and, 11; twenty-second amendment and, 40

Vermont, 11, 36, 39, 40

Waddle Jr., William H, 120
Wade, Virginia "Ginnie," 88
War of 1812, 11, 34, 37, 107, 112, 115, 144
Washington, Augustine (George Washington's father), 14
Washington, George, 10, 11, 49; and ability to make the right call, 16; birth of, 14; cherry tree story and, 15; communication skills of, 15; on constitutional convention's success, 10; countenance of, 15; decision making of, 9, 16–17, 24; duplicity of Madison and 20, 21; education of, 15, 16; electoral college in 1789 and, 10; electoral college of 1793 and, 24–25; exhaustion after first term and, 20; Father of the Country and, 12, 13; and Farewell Address (1796) 2, 13; and Farewell Address draft (1792), 20–25; and Farewell Address draft (1796), 27–29; and Farewell Address (1796), 2, 29–41; as general, 16; importance of Constitution to, 11; as indispensable man, 81; and Jay Treaty, 25–27; and judgment 8, 9–12, 14, 16, 24, 29–35, 40–41; and oath of office, 67; personality of, 15; physical description of, 14; and retirement as general, 17–18, 19, 23; and retirement considered as president (1792) 20–25; and retirement as President (1796), 12–13, 25–27; and rise of two-party system, 11, 21; presidential achievements of, 11–12; as product of Virginia, 14; and publication of Farewell Address, 23; and scheming troop plot, 19; and setting precedents, 10, 11, 12; siblings of, 14–15; and slavery, 16; "talents and virtues' of, 10; U.S. Constitution and, 11; Valley Forge and, 81; Washington's Crossing and, 17
Washington, Martha (George Washington's wife), 13, 16
Washington, Mary Ball (George Washington's mother), 14
Washington's Crossing, 17, 95
Whiskey Rebellion, 11, 12, 111
White House Oval Office: and George W. Bush after 9/11, 144; and FDR's meeting with Grover Cleveland, 155; and FDR's meeting with

White House Oval Office *(continued)*
    the press corps, 163; optimism
    carried Reagan to, 216; overview
    of, 179; and Reagan meeting with
    speechwriters, 178, 205; small
    plaque on Reagan's desk and, 202
White House Yellow Oval Room:
    as FDR's personal study, 146–47;
    history of, 146–47
Wills, David: and greeting Lincoln
    in Gettysburg, 90; and Lincoln
    finishing the Gettysburg Address,
    91; and Lincoln lodging at his
    home, 90, 91, 98, 99, 106
Wilson, Woodrow: and in-person
    address to Congress, 114; and
    League of Nations, 25, 45; and
    physical description of FDR,
    156; and power of president, 5;
    segregationist policies of, 83; stroke
    of, 25
Winthrop, John, 5, 38
Woodin, William, 161, 165, 167
World War I: Herbert Hoover and,
    150; policy of neutrality followed
    until, 11
World War II: aims and, 114; atomic
    bombs and, 184; destruction of,
    182; eve of American involvement
    in, 45; grand alliance and, 180;
    international system that followed,
    45; and isolationists, 37; Japanese
    internment and, 175; Marshall Plan
    and, 191
Wyman, Jane (Ronald Reagan's first
    wife), 198

www.ingramcontent.com/pod-product-compliance
Lightning Source LLC
Chambersburg PA
CBHW030808090425
24824CB00002B/181